Roots Schmoots

Roots Schmoots
JOURNEYS AMONG JEWS

Howard Jacobson

THE OVERLOOK PRESS
WOODSTOCK • NEW YORK

First paperback published in 1995 by
The Overlook Press
Lewis Hollow Road
Woodstock, New York 12498

Library of Congress Cataloging-in-Publication Data

Jacobson, Howard
Roots schmoots / Howard Jacobson.
p. cm.
1. Jews-Identity. 2. Jacobson, Howard-Journeys
I. Title.
DS143.J323 1994
910.4'089924-dc20   93-31471   CIP
Manufactured in the United States of America

ISBN: 0-87951-605-4
135798642

To the memory of my father

CONTENTS

Contents

Hervey Allen, you know, the author of the big best-seller *Anthony Adverse*, seriously told a friend of mine who was working on a biographical piece on Allen that he could close his eyes, lie down on a bed, and hear the voices of his ancestors. Furthermore, there was some sort of angel-like creature that danced along his pen while he was writing. He wasn't balmy by any means. He just felt he was in communication with some sort of metaphysical recorder. So you see the novelists have all the luck. I never knew a humorist who got any help from his ancestors.

James Thurber

One

ROOTS SCHMOOTS

'A lot of Jews who think they're Jewish are not,' Lenny Bruce used to sweet-talk his audience, 'they're switched babies.'

I thought of that one a long time before Lenny Bruce did, but it never struck me as funny. I suspected I was a switched baby because I didn't *feel* Jewish. Somewhere out there in the gentile badlands, in the killing fields of Pendlebury or Harpurhey, the kid who was really me was singing 'Gentle Jesus, meek and mild,' and following the Virgin in the Whit Sunday walks, sure in his heart that he wasn't Christian.

The fact that I looked Jewish made no difference. I had read that people can come to resemble those they live with. I lived with a couple who called themselves my parents. Why couldn't I have come to resemble them?

I must have been about ten before I discovered that none of my Jewish friends felt Jewish either. We couldn't *all* have been switched. I gave the idea away a good fifteen years before Lenny Bruce was getting laughs with it.

But that didn't address the problem of how it felt not to feel Jewish. Had somebody said then, 'Don't look for it . . . it will look for you . . . and find you when you're least expecting it . . . not in a blinding light but as a slow, unfolding conviction of ancient certainties, of quiet in disquiet, of the self-possession available only to the dispossessed' – I wouldn't have believed him. Nor would I have known what he was talking about. You don't deal in quietudes when you're ten. Feeling Jewish had to mean, if it meant anything, feeling fiery and holy, like a zealot.

Feeling Christian meant not minding living in a prefab and dying early of malnutrition. I wasn't a zealot and I would have minded living in a prefab. By eleven I was agnostic.

So the question of roots never entered into it. You can't feel rootsie if you don't feel treesie.

Very few of us felt rootsie then. The times did not favour retrospection – not with new worlds to build and old sins to be forgotten – and we, the unswitched, were very much children of the times. Our grandparents, or our parents' grandparents, had come over with chickens in their baggage fifty years before, fleeing the usual – some libel or pogrom or another, some expression of peasant irrationality or another, brewed up in some Eastern European *shtetl* or another – that was as much as they cared to remember or to tell us. And in truth that was as much as we cared to know. We had been Russians or Poles or something – why split hairs? – and now we were setting about becoming English. Roots we didn't think about; tendrils we needed. You don't look down when you're climbing.

This is not to say that rumours of our foreignness didn't reach us. We may have sneaked our way into local Church of England grammar schools and worn uniforms that made it look as though we had crucifixes embroidered on our hearts, but school assembly every morning reminded us, and reminded those who weren't us, how far we still were from being them. *They* assembled, we messed about in upstairs class-rooms. *They* sang the praises of famous men – famous *Christian* men – we picked holes in the Ten Commandments and did refugee imitations under the haphazard supervision of prefects of our own kind. *They* diapasoned the school song, made the field ring again and again with the tramp of the twenty-two men, we hid in desks so that the SS shouldn't find us.

Sometimes, although there were twenty-two of them to one of us, we made our disharmony heard above their tramping. Then, the music stopped, the headmaster cleared his throat, and in the pause before he threw his voice up into our bolt-holes two thousand years of theological acrimony unravelled. 'If the Jewish boys are unable to concentrate on their own prayers, would they at least do us the decency of permitting us to concentrate on ours . . .'

It was never comfortable trooping out on to the balcony for the post-hymnals. Under normal circumstances – under normally abnormal circumstances – exposure to those alien upturned faces was unnerving. But after a reprimand we lined the parapet more naked than the damned; and had we been charged, as in a sense we were charged, with any of the acts of larceny or other schoolyard criminality reported that morning, we would have confessed our guilt without reserve, and asked for a hundred other offences, not excluding deicide, to be taken into account. Russo-Polack wretches that we were.

You can't exactly call this persecution. Persecution is when you're forced to join in other people's hymns. The worst we suffered were sensations of ambiguity. We were and we weren't. We were getting somewhere and we weren't. We were free of the ghetto and we weren't. We were philosophers now and not pedlars, and we weren't. If we had any identity at all, that was it: we countermanded ourselves, we faced in opposite directions, we were our own antithesis. But we couldn't lay all the blame for that on school. Things were just as contrary at home.

It's possible I idealize – I hope I have the heart *to* idealize – but I picture the house of my childhood as a haven of forward-looking sunny secularity. It's true we sometimes had Leo Fuld on the recorder-player, sobbing songs of diaspora and homelessness – 'Tell me where can I go? Every door is closed to me . . .' But we didn't sob the rest of the time. We weren't swathed or fringed or turbanned. Communists and atheists came to visit. We went boating on the Sabbath. My father, as a young man, had coals in his eyes, burned to be a participant in every revelry and recreation going, and looked as English as George Orwell or

3

D. H. Lawrence, without the malnutrition. I don't recall any family rambling or cycling, but we *could* have rambled or cycled, so many resemblances did we bear to the cheerful, thoughtful, self-improving, gentile lower-lower middle classes of 1950s Manchester. And yet, had any authentic gentile rambler peered late through our particular windows, he would have beheld scenes of such primitive industry that he must have supposed us to be tinkers from some part of Turkey not mentioned in any atlas. For, like many Jewish families of that time, ours was a market family – coffee-tables showing *Swan Lake* under glass paid for me to become an intellectual – and when we were not sitting in a circle on the floor, straightening out and putting into bundles the banknotes which my father shook like confetti from his market apron, we were making up bags of discoloured chocolate to be thrown free, as crowd-pullers, from my father's stall; or counting out plastic poppet beads from a hessian sack and popping them together to make necklaces; or stylishly arranging a sponge, a facecloth, a toothbrush and a shoebrush in a see-through bag on which we then stapled a label saying HOLIDAY KIT, to be sold the next day to gentile cyclists who were looking for that very thing to fit inside their saddle-bags.

To this day I have indentations in my thumbs which I allow people to suppose are injuries associated with the craft of writing, but which are in fact the marks – the stigmata – of all the poppets that I popped more than a third of a century ago. To this day I am unable to pack a suitcase for a holiday without picturing our old production line – my sister on the facecloths and sponges, my brother on the brushes, my mother on the see-through bags, my father on inspection, and me on the stapler. To this day I don't know whether there is more shame than fondness in the recollection.

I never did know. That was part of the condition. We were and we weren't. Thinkers and tinkers. Peasants and poets.

But what's true of the general must be truish of the particular.

Families become attached to the means whereby they seek to change their conditions. You can easily get a millionaire to cry over his first corner-shop. And it's quite possible that we – even without riches to justify nostalgia – were never happier than when we were weighing out those streaky chocolates, and slipping one into our mouths for every six in the bag.

Had my father been a successful businessman I would doubtless be more unequivocally sentimental about his first enterprises; since he wasn't, I can be more unequivocally sentimental about him. Any old person can succeed in business. It takes flair to fail. In his heart he was right not to grasp the opportunity to become the country's largest producer of phosphorescent hoola-hoops, six months before the craze swept Western Europe and the Americas. Of course no one was going to climb inside a plastic ring and shimmy; that millions did only testifies to their unimaginativeness, not his. I knew whose example I had to follow when an entrepreneur pal of mine invited me to invest with him in an obscure northern rock band called, with an uninventiveness unusual even for that period, the Beatles. 'Save your money,' I advised him, after watching them falling over wires in a cellar-bar discotheque. 'Sanctimonious in sentiment, shallow in ideology, monotonous in execution . . . don't go near them.' I still hold to that assessment. A chip off the old block.

So that when I hear tell of Jewish business acumen I go hushed and scratch my head. Have I come across such an animal? I suppose I must have, but I don't associate it with either of the seemingly contradictory tendencies that characterized the Jewishness I didn't feel. We were and we weren't all manner of things, but the one thing we never were or weren't, to my sense, was shrewd. Shrewdness and acumen, whether for business or for anything else, were simply not in the equation. If you're shrewd you don't espy the major choices of your life lying between a well-turned English sentence and a sponge-bag.

But that's not the go-ahead for saying that we lack astuteness.

Or that we're hard to satisfy. We do and we don't. We are and we aren't.

In the end misdescriptions work in your favour. They eliminate everything you're not. Be called a Judas tree or money-wort for long enough and you start to identify the plant family to which you really belong. This is how you get treesie. It doesn't matter that you don't *feel* you're a laburnum; be told that you're a laurel or a lime and you'll *know* you're a laburnum. Getting rootsie follows, without your having to do very much about it, in due course.

My own progression from thinking I must have been a switched baby, so Jewish didn't I feel, to knowing myself to be so exclusively Jewish that I barely had room to know anything else, was not entirely welcome to me. Jew, Jew, Jew. The word hurt my eyes. Friends – even Jew, Jew, Jew friends – began to wonder whether I had any other subject of conversation. Just before he died, my father asked me how far I intended going with all this. Did I mean to end up a rabbi? He wound imaginary *tefillin* – the masochistic phylacteries of the Jews – around his wasting arms. 'You're not doing all that stuff, are you?' I shook my head. The monomania was intellectual, I told him, not religious. He looked relieved to hear it. Three weeks later I was wearing *tefillin* in mourning for him.

It has, of course, occurred to me that I might have been returning to the bosom of Abraham in the mind as a sort of preparation for my father's return to the bosom of Abraham in body. I was in Israel when I learnt of the severity of his illness, and I feared for him precisely because it seemed I was being far too well prepared for something. If a higher hand was steadying me, my father had better watch out.

All that was fancy. There is no higher hand. What we call readiness is nothing other than the intrusion of mortality into the carelessness of youth. Besides, my being in Israel, my decision to go literally on a Jewish journey, had more scepticism in it than any but the most subtle of unseen forces would have permitted in an agent of its will – and who has ever heard of a subtle higher hand? I had been feeling rootsie, I don't deny that. Aggressively rootsie. Rootsie-tootsie. But there was an undertow to my rootsie-tootsiness. I had been brought up to notice pain, and I had Jewjewjew pains in my eyes. Pains like those you get when you've stopped arguing with yourself. Was that what my Jewjewjewishness was, then – the fruit not of middle age and maturation but merely of singleness of purpose? Had Jujujudaism dumped on me the way Cacacatholicism dumps on other writers, as a punishment for forgetting that I had been most the thing I never knew I was when I was my own antithesis?

You can't force a fight with yourself if you're not in a fighting mood. But you can always hit the road. Go rooting around, since I was feeling rootsie, not just in the backyard of my own ancestry, but wherever the word that was hurting my eyes had some pertinence. Go on a Jewjewjourney. Not as the famous black American, who felt compelled to re-root himself in Africa, went on his; not with the ambition of repossessing the sensation of belonging, but rather with the much more voluptuous expectation of repossessing nothing.

Does that sound nihilistic? It isn't meant to. There is giddying romance in the idea of homelessness. It's out of envy for our homelessness that so many artistic non-Jews have tried to pass themselves off as us this century. In peacetime, naturally. So there is absolutely no contradiction in the idea of a Jewish journey in pursuit of loss. To tell the truth, I couldn't wait to buy my tickets. Once I had decided where I meant to go. That's to say, once I had discovered where those Russo-Polack great-grandparents of mine had come from.

Two

BECALMED BUT *KOSHER*

Lithuania.

I don't do my excitement justice. Lithuania!!!

After all that 'Somewhere in Russia or Poland, now get on with your homework' disincentive, evoking vast and anonymous interiors, backwardness too dark and shameful to bear thinking of, it turned out I was a Litvak.

A Litvak!!!!

Of Eastern European Jews, the Litvaks were the most distinguished for intellectuality. The reputation carried a cavil in its wake. Were we, perhaps, a touch too dry, we Litvaks? A spot too sceptical? Litvaks are so smart, the Ukrainian novelist Sholom Aleichem observed, they repent before they sin. We were not as emotional as we might have been, in other words. I knew where I stood on this: with my back resolutely turned on sobbing Judaism, ecstatic Hasids, fiddlers on roofs. The fiercest opponents of Hasidism, that dionysiac extravagance brewed in the vast and anonymous interiors of Russia, fashioned from a backwardness too dark and shameful to bear thinking of, were us, *Mitnageddim*, Litvaks. In 1772 we excommunicated Hasidim's adherents, noting among 'their thousand ugly ways' a predisposition to 'act as if they were cartwheels, with their heads down and their feet up'. No more somersaults, we said. I'd say the same today. And no more exposed fringes either. A man is not an article of furniture. Haberdashery does not make holy.

So that was what I was. A Litvak. A somewhat too sceptical Lithuanian. Good. Excellent. I had always suspected as much.

It was my mother's side of the family, the only side Jewish law reckons you can trust, that yielded this information. When I got my father's lot to go through their drawers the best they could come up with was Kamenetz Podolsky in the Ukraine, nearer to the Black Sea than the Baltic. After Lithuania this felt regressive; a bit too close for my liking to the old somewhere or other it was better not to talk about in the depths of sobbing, somersaulting Russia. Nor could I put faces to the place. I had never looked upon my Kamenetz great-grandparents in the flesh — only very recently have I seen photographs of them — whereas Bobbe and Zayde, from Lithuania, I remembered vividly. They kept chickens in the backyard of their house in Hightown — perhaps descendants of the very chickens they'd brought with them in their baggage. They pinched my cheeks and gave me pennies when I was taken round to see them, fussing over me in Yiddish. I had the smell of their parlour in my nostrils still — a sweet, overpowering smell of varnished wallpaper and spiced rugs and slaughtered hens and old persons' cardigans and waistcoats. And boys' bewilderment. In a sense I had already been to Lithuania.

So in the same sense I could be said to be going back. That settled it. Now all I had to do was find out where Lithuania was.

History beat me to it. No sooner had I begun to assemble maps — not easy to find — and contacts — not easy to find, either — than Gorbachev let himself be walled up inside his dacha, tanks caterpillared towards confrontation, the world bit its nails, and states with independence from Russia on their minds became the last places persons not paid to live dangerously wanted to visit.

I would have to postpone. For how long was anybody's guess. A month? A year? Another half century? I was in a luggage-buying mood and couldn't wait. If the east was out then I'd go west. Who wouldn't rather go west than east anyway? I'd go to

New York, try out my theory that for Jews New York out-Jerusalemed Jerusalem, enjoy the spirit made word, eat Jewish, talk Jewish, fight Jewish, forget about being Jewish Jewish.

Then history – if that's not too grand a term for it this time – intervened once more. A phone call. From the BBC. Only radio, but still the BBC. Religious Affairs, wondering whether I'd like to take part in a programme with Dr Jonathan Sacks, the Chief Rabbi elect, planned to coincide with his inauguration a month or so from now, the subject for discussion being . . .

'Judaism,' I hazarded.

Deferment of my plans apart, it seemed a good omen. I had taken some interest in the Chief Rabbi to be. I had read his Reith Lectures, a passionately argued defence of Orthodoxy, not so much denouncing as bewailing the moral and spiritual failures of enlightenment, in language that was too calculatedly drawn from ordinary life for my taste. 'We no longer talk of virtues but of values, and values are tapes we play on the Walkman of the mind.' *Walkman of the mind*, Rabbi? I had listened to him on *Desert Island Discs*, noted his double starred first at Cambridge, and calculated that he must have been four or five years younger than me. I'm not saying I was in competition with him – you don't compete with Chief Rabbis – but if, on the very eve of my journey of the spirit, I was being given the chance to wrestle with him on radio, like Jacob with the angel, I had to grab it, hadn't I?

I'd live with having to put off travelling for a few more weeks. After his encounter with God's emissary, Jacob had his name changed to Israel, was guaranteed safe passage, and received promises of untold blessings for his seed. You lose a few weeks without complaining for windfalls of that sort.

There was another reason for agreeing to the broadcast. I believed it would smooth my way somewhat, in my arrangements, if I mentioned it. Guarantee my spiritual bona fides. Make me *kosher*.

Becalmed but Kosher

I had a cousin in Manchester whom I'd been meaning to ring for some time, to ask if she would help me penetrate the Lubavitch community, whose heartbeat could best be monitored, I'd heard, in Brooklyn. She had married a Lubavitch herself – she was Kamenetz family, not Litvak – and had children of her own studying in Crown Heights, at the very feet, as it were, of the famed Lubavitcher Rebbe, and some would say Messiah, Menachem Schneerson. I hadn't seen or spoken to her for twenty years or more, and although we had been teenage friends, even romantic teenage friends within the limits of cousinhood, I had taken fright when she became Orthodox and I remain frightened of her Orthodoxy to this day. It was one thing, as a Litvak among Litvaks, to rout the Hasidim in 1772; it was quite another to stand up individually to all the paraphernalia of Hasidic pietism – the beards, the coats, the wigs, the prams, the aggressive modesty. Now, when I rang, I could at least drop the Chief Rabbi's name into the conversation to demonstrate that I wasn't entirely lost to paganism.

'So what will you be doing with him?' she asks me.

The emphasis is on *you*. She is the mother of eight, at the last count, and a grandmother – she has become the mother of eight and a grandmother in the twinkling of an eye – but she still has a girl's voice, a Manchester Jewish girl's voice, a touch wonder-struck, a touch suspicious, a touch conspiratorial in its suspicious-ness ('I bet you don't know what *you're* doing on the same programme as him, either'), a touch old before its time and a touch young after it. Ah, the Jewish girls who were always mothers, the Jewish mothers who were always girls, of my youth.

'What do you mean, what will I be doing with him?'

'You're not going to be rude?'

'Why should I be rude? When am I rude?'

There's no answer to this. She could say plenty, but she says nothing. Except, 'He seems an interesting sort of person,' or

11

something like that. But I am sure, whatever precisely she says about the Rabbi, that she adds, 'anyway'. The Manchester *anyway* – meaning, 'He's what he is and you're what you are. You'll be rude because you can't be anything but rude, and because that's the family view of you.'

Rude cousin Howard!

The phone is hotter in my hand than I bet it is in hers. All she has said is 'anyway'. But I am remembering her at her piano, a blooming girl with her own hair, bare-legged, bold, full of laughter, not as she was when I saw her next, standing demurely and obediently, shaven and covered up, on a wooden stage bearing branches and Bibles, a little outdoor tabernacle meant to suggest vines and fruitfulness, waiting for a boy in Orthodox dress who feigns a struggle on the way to meet his bride, his path strewn not with roses but with some still more difficult flower, for it is a great deal a young Hasid in a black coat must give away when he becomes a husband.

Is she thinking that this is what I'm thinking, and is this why she thinks I'm rude? Am I a view of her she can do without? Or is she the view of me that I *can't* do without? What it comes to, *anyway*, is that the Chief Rabbi is all well and good but I should remember that her spiritual headquarters – her phrase – are in New York, and if I want to find out more about that I should talk to her husband, with whom she'll be holidaying in Llandudno in a few days' time, and I'm welcome to visit them there.

So that's where I begin. Not Lithuania. Not the Lower East Side. But Llandudno.

There are Hasids on the lawn. Handsome, blazing men with beards black like ovens and teeth whiter than coriander seeds – my cousin's sons, my cousin's sons-in-law, my cousin's husband. She's been busy since I saw her last, but she is so unchanged that

I do the most natural thing and kiss her on each cheek. No one stops me. I have a sense that the menfolk are even touched by my gaucherie. But when it's over, my cousin says, 'We're not supposed to do that, really.'

It is one of those melancholy, late summer days that make you wish you were in England when you are somewhere else. And I am somewhere else: on the borders of Wales and Kamenetz Podolsky. It is hot and dry; after a wet summer the hills are looking parched already, almost as yellow as they are green. I can see the beach from the garden. In the glare of orange sunlight, figures trudge towards the water, carry pails, paddle, like characters on an old postcard. I am dizzied by the sense that everything outside the garden belongs to the past, and only these eighteenth-century Russian somersaultists are the present.

My cousin's husband asks me when I last put on *tefillin*. I take a deep breath, and subtract the age I was when I was *bar-mitzvahed* from the age I am now. 'Thirty-six years,' I confess.

He is not shocked. The Lubavitch make a thing of rescue operations. He'll have met men who haven't bound themselves in leather for far longer than my measly thirty-six years. But he would like me to do him the favour, since he is my host, of putting on *tefillin* now.

'Now?'

He smiles. They all smile. It is a smiling creed, Hasidism. That's why we Litvaks excommunicated it.

'Here?'

'We can go inside.'

And we do. Without the faintest murmur of complaint from me. Not for a moment does it occur to me to say, 'And when you are a guest in my garden I will ask you to do me the favour of removing your *yarmulke* and your Polish stockings and your *tzitzits* and any other religious articles you have concealed about your person which may offend my rationality.' Annoyance with my own pliancy will come later.

13

As it turns out, the experience is strangely sensuous, dreamy even. He has gentle fingers, my cousin's husband, light but firm. Seven times he binds my uncovered arm. 'Relax,' he says. 'It isn't necessary to hold your arm so rigidly.' We are standing by the window, looking out across the garden to the flickering ochre sea. A shaft of amber light strikes my knuckles where the strap has been wound around to form the Hebrew letter *shin* – *shin* for *Shaddai*, the Unfathomable Almighty One. Suddenly I see that stray sheep have come wandering off the hills and are contemplating the pastures of this very lawn. One by one, they leap the low stone wall. I go limp in my Lubavitcher shepherd's hands.

'Your soul could easily have come from a higher source than mine,' he explains to me once we are back outside, discussing Cabbalistics in deckchairs beneath the scrutiny of the Great Orme.

I wave away this spiritual egalitarianism with what is meant to be a deferential gesture. A rude cousin knowing his lowly rank in the hierarchy of souls. It is something I do in the presence of religious men. And will do again when I meet the Chief Rabbi, if I am not careful.

'It's true,' one of the sons-in-law puts in. He is American. Teaches in the Crown Heights community, and so knows whereof he oracles. 'Opportunity is all that explains our degree of Orthodoxy, not election.'

I watch the sheep, not all of which have leapt back out again, and I wonder what I will do if one of them approaches me. The Scriptures permit me to eat sheep, as I remember, but am I allowed to pat them?

I am surprised by all the soul talk. I have always commended Judaism for its preference for materialism over metaphysics, for the visible over the unseen but that might just be *my* Judaism

I'm commending. Certainly, Kamenetz-Llandudno Judaism assumes more coming and going of the spirit. Take the story of the One-year-old Soul and the Rebbe's consolatory ruling on infant mortality.

The general behind the particular truth is that souls which fail to fulfil their benign purpose the first or second time around are sent on a descent again to see if they can do better. Appealed to by a father grieving over the death of his one-year-old child, the Rebbe personalized it thus: The soul of an earlier person descended in the form of your dear departed because, although it had previously perfected itself in good works, it had been brought up for the first year of its life by a gentile . . .

(Not a word do I say. Not a sound do I make. I was a switched soul myself, once upon a time.)

. . . In every other way fulfilled, the poor soul had to do a year with a Jewish family before it could reascend to bliss. Which condition, you must assure yourself, you and your dear wife have made possible, by keeping a *kosher* house.

Behold the wisdom of the Rebbe.

I have been reading about this Rebbe. As a result of a road accident in which a car belonging to the Rebbe's entourage has knocked down and killed a black child, savage fighting between Orthodox Jews and blacks has broken out in Crown Heights. According to the blacks, a Jewish ambulance helped the Jewish driver and ignored the black child. According to the Jews, the blacks are anti-Semitic. In the course of this Tom Wolfian bonfire, attention has been focused on the Rebbe and the Messianic fervour of his followers. Here in the quiet of Llandudno, amid stray sheep and faded yellow bathers, I think it safe to ask about the Rebbe's powers.

And am vouchsafed first-hand witnessed wonders that are meant to make my individual hairs stand up, like quills upon the untrusting porcupine.

Has the Rebbe not promised us a year of wonders, and

have we not seen walls tumbling in the east, and Iraq defeated?

Did he not advise the Israeli people to shun gas masks during the Gulf War, and had not gas masks caused more deaths in Israel than had Scuds?

Did he not, only a couple of days ago, advise a Lubavitch delegate to return to Russia, even at the height of danger, and have we not read, only this morning, that the coup against Gorbachev has been defeated?

Even my cousin, who once played me Mozart, has a marvel to unfold. Did not the Rebbe, during one of his Sunday-morning dollar ceremonies in Crown Heights, give a pregnant petitioner two dollars instead of the customary one; and lo! was she not the bearer of twins soon after?

'So it is not out of the question for you,' I ask, 'that the Rebbe is the Messiah?'

They look at me steadily. No one will quite say that. And no one won't quite say it either. We have fallen quiet enough to hear the ancient sounds of holiday-makers by the water, above which the sun is beginning to leak fire.

My next question, although it's only a reworking of the last, proves to be less difficult. 'So if there's going to be a Messianic revelation,' I ask, 'how soon do you think it'll be?'

My cousin's American son-in-law – therefore my nephew-in-law twice removed? – consults his watch. As soon as that.

They drive me to the station in their Volvo. All Hasidic groups – all *frummies*, as you are allowed to call them only if you are Jewish yourself (*frum* meaning devout) – drive Volvos. The usual explanation is that Volvos are the cars best suited to the size of *frummy* families; multitudinous on the grounds that seed-spilling is a sin, and because someone has to replenish the numbers of the broken-backed Jewish people. In Volvos the future of Judaism is borne along our motorways.

An alternative explanation is that *frummies* turn their eyes to

God so much that they are not safe on the roads. Since they believe that God is looking after them, it doesn't strictly speaking behove them to worry about their driving. But just in case – as a sort of nether-world insurance – they pack themselves in cars that boast the best protective chassis.

This is no reflection on my *frummies*, who drive me safely to the station and part with me so warmly – notwithstanding the strict distance my cousin keeps this time – that I begin to understand why the Lubavitch do as well as they do at winning errant Jews back to the bosom of the Jewish faith. They make you feel it might be comfortable there.

A sign outside a snack-bar on the platform says, WHY NOT TRY ONE OF OUR HOT BACON ROLLS? I am not hungry – I have eaten *kosher*-ly on the lawn – but I am peckish. Do I dare to try a hot bacon roll after where I have been, what I have seen, who I have been with and what I have done?

I pace up and down the platform. I pop my head into the snack-bar. I circle the sign itself three times. Do I dare?

I dare not.

One–nil to Lubavitch.

Before it leaves Llandudno, the train does a little beach tour to show you what you're missing or to remind you what you'll miss. After dropping me off, they were going boating, my Lubavitchers, and I fancy I can see them now in a Volvo dinghy, sailing beyond the sunset, their black coats flapping, their wigs lifting, their fringes flying – a boatload of hopeful souls heading for *Shaddai*.

But I am angry with myself, and by extension with them, by the time I reach London. I feel I have given too much away this afternoon. I should not have put on *tefillin*. I should not have deferred to them in matters of the spirit. I should not have listened patiently and smiled while they addressed folksy Hasidic homilies to me about water wearing away stone and kettles that maintain their heat because they are plugged into the Rebbe. I should have tried that hot bacon roll.

I am no better than a peasant in the presence of purple-frocked priests, so willingly do I cede moral authority. And I a Litvak!

It is out of this complex of irritations that I decide to follow up an event currently troubling Jewish consciences in north London, not least because it is a seemingly private matter between Jews that has made it into the gentile press. The old dread – being shamed before the gentiles. And what shame! In Crown Heights, Jews and blacks are fighting; but you expect that in America. What you don't expect are Jews stoning *one another* in Stamford Hill.

Orthodox Jews, to boot. The kind to whom I cede moral authority.

A little girl – the daughter of *frummies* – has been molested. A young man – the son of *frummies* – stands accused. The community sees it as an internal moral matter, a case for a *frummy* rabbi to preside over. The parents of the molested girl come to feel that the community expresses insufficient outrage and makes insufficient judicial progress. They appeal to the secular authorities. And for that they are stoned. Cries of '*Moisrim!*' – 'Informers!' – are heard on the streets of Stamford Hill. We are back in the *shtetl*.

From the Religious Affairs people at the BBC, with whom I am still in contact regarding my forthcoming wrestle with the Chief Rabbi, I learn of Martin Braun. He has involved himself in the Stamford Hill affair by rescuing the twice-abused child and her family from the righteous mob. I am told that he sees the merits of exposing this matter to air and light, and is willing, no, eager, to talk to whomsoever will listen.

I ring him. Llandudno was an overture. Now I am off. I am started. I get his daughter, who is understandably cautious, and who takes my number.

My wife is cautious too, and worries that I have given my number. She is worried all round about this enterprise of mine, this coming journey, this coming book, and this business in

Stamford Hill. I have given my number to a humane man (as I've been assured), but what if the humane man is attacked by the fanatics, and the fanatics find my number on him, and come for me?

Touch the Jewish issue, touch it only internally, as here, and even a Catholic girl from Perth begins to think of madmen coming for me. If you are too publicly, too demonstratively, Jewish, people come for you. That's that.

Martin Braun calls me back. Although he doesn't know who I am, he is at once Hasidically familiar with me. 'There is a saying,' he says, in response to my concern for the distress he must be feeling, 'that no man's beard ever grows grey worrying about another's troubles.'

I disentangle the Yiddish as best I can, and mutter some compliment to his bravery and benevolence. 'When you're carrying other people's problems up a hill,' he says, 'they are not so heavy as your own.'

So this is to be our procedure. I make a statement, he answers with a proverb.

He is from Hungary. He knows troubles. Communist Hungary toughened him up. When you've done Hungary, you can handle Hendon. (That's *my* proverb.)

Tough or not, he has a lot to say. What's happening in north London could have been foretold. The molesting of a child and the community's ring of protective secrecy around the molester are merely the surface of the problem. Things are deeply wrong within Orthodox Judaism, and have been going wrong for a century. Chief among the problems are the Germans. Although a minority in Stamford Hill, the German Orthodox are assertive and assured, and are easily able to sway the less sophisticated. They have brought over from Germany methods they acquired from the Nazis – crowd control, propaganda, hatred . . .

All this and more in the first ten minutes on the phone to an unknown caller. I cannot digest so much passion, so much history, so much Yiddish, without seeing its source. I arrange to meet him in the flesh, tomorrow. He gives me his address. He will be expecting me.

When I get there he is out. A woman in a ginghamy folk-scarf, suggesting piety in moderation, answers the door. Two younger women, whom I take to be her daughters, flank her watchfully. Apparently Mr Braun has not left any messages or mentioned anything about an appointment. But I can come in and wait if I like.

I decline, out of a strange and sudden mistrust of myself. Something sleepy and backward about the street, something innocuously Hebraic about the house, upsets me. The women are kind and Quakerish. I feel as though I have been kissed by a sort of innocence, and want them to be spared the danger that is me. I'll walk for a bit and wait for Mr Braun at a distance, where I can do no harm.

Out on the streets of Stamford Hill, where stalk the Stoners for *Shaddai*, I find that I have used up my day's allowance of compassion. I have not been here for many years, and I am astonished to see how far advanced is the Orthodox revival. Moth-white, snoods askew, wigs worn like Dutch girls' hair-dos in kids' comics, their bodies packed shapelessly into long and colourless pinafores, lest alien eyes should ransack them for clues to the whereabouts of their generative organs, the mothers of the retrogressive Jewish revolution push their teeming prams from *kosher* shop to *kosher* shop. Like all extravagant essays at modesty, these fail of their first objective. As you pass, all you notice are their generative organs.

You don't have to look for long to see that the male Hasids enjoy the better part of the purity bargain. Chain-smoking scuttlers aside, the majority of the men stride straight-backed, proud of how they look, with a swagger that is available only to the sexually vain. Not much of a prize, you would have thought, those furtive, chalky, clapped-out wives; but they are obedient, chaste, ritually impeccable, and breed betimes. Besides, patriarchy is not all that choosy. What matters is to be sheikh in one's own sheikhdom.

Standing outside a *kosher* bakery, I espy a warrior Hasid, a towering *frummy* prince with his *tallis* – his prayer-shawl – worn like a tabard beneath his waistcoat, his shirt crisp white, his black trousers tucked into his socks, keys dangling from his belt (keys to what – his Volvo? his wife?) and over his shoulder, in a leather holster, a mobile phone. He leaves with his challa – the sweet, milky, braided loaf over which believing wives bend and close their eyes on Friday evenings. I watch his fringes sway like plumes upon a Horse Guard's helmet. A soldier of the faith.

When I finally return to Martin Braun's, two and a half hours later, I find him, just returned himself, chock-full of apologies. I am the third person he has let down today. The press are badgering him. He is badgering rabbis. These are busy times in Stamford Hill.

He asks me if I mind watching him eat, which he does from a low leather settee, a plate of dried-out chicken (all the life and goodness having gone into the soup) on a coffee-table by his knees. Assorted children attend to my needs. One brings me water. Another a plate of kugel, or tasteless suet-pudding, the baby-food beloved of all Jews. A further child brings me a serviette. An earlier brings me lemonade. Thus I learn what it is to be a sheikh.

Martin Braun talks as he eats. In accompaniment to his words, the child who brought me a serviette bounces a balloon.

'I don't stop thinking or hallucinating over my tortured Jewish experience,' he says. 'I live the problem of Orthodoxy; I live the shortfalls of other parallel groups in Judaism – that doesn't mean I have a cure, but I sense things. I point out problems. As I am, I am another ghetto phenomenon. I think the ghetto has its

Martin Brauns always; people who choose to stay in the ghetto and meanwhile to study the world surrounding them . . . to be born sometimes with a defect in their fear-producing organs. I've never been frightened or intimidated. I've never cared about my standing in the community, whether I'm more popular or less, whether I'm liked or hated for the time being.'

'And which are you now?'

He falls back in the settee and rubs his *yarmulke* into his head, as though it's a wet sponge. He is reddish in colour, not Esau-red – he is not a biblical-looking man – but gingery, with a gingery beard and hair cut in a gingery fringe. His tie has red spots on it, and his braces, which he sports like a gambler, are blood-red.

'Which am I now?' He laughs. He has a curly mouth and is able to laugh in more than one direction at a time. 'Slowly they are learning that I am not as malicious or as vicious as they thought I was. So they start taking liberties. I wish I'd kept to my original image of a very dangerous man.' He laughs again. At me and away from me. 'Do you know what they call me? The Sheriff of Stamford Hill.'

The phone rings. My guess is that it's a journalist. Rather than appear to be listening, I smile, against my nature, at the balloon-bouncing child, and let my gaze take in the room. It affects me as the exterior of the house did earlier in the day. There is some melancholy here, such as one associates with any attempt to live a serious and upright life without the support of a church or an academy. The loneliness of self-achievement – perhaps that's what I'm responding to.

There are many paintings on the walls. Paintings with religious subjects – rabbis, Passover feasts – but not Orthodox kitsch. A more modern portrait of a lady sits on an easel, leaving me to wonder whether it is being worked on, or just displayed like that. I wonder, too, whether it is a portrait of the woman who opened the door to me in a head-scarf. Am I in a love-house?

22

When I turn to Martin Braun again, I see that he has slid further down the settee and has encouraged his *yarmulke* to fall over one eye, much as a pirate might if pirates wore *yarmulkes*.

To the journalist – it must be a journalist – he is saying, 'Those German Jews, they don't know – forgive me – they don't know where to fuck off. They – the ultra-Orthodox ones – contaminate our religion. They have no honour, no generosity, no prettiness. They come to the court – yeah, yeah, to the trial – in those plant-pot wigs, to put off people with open minds. They're there first thing, so they can take all the seats, staring with hostility at whoever isn't one of them.'

What he doesn't say to the reporter – what he says he *wants* to say but can't – he says to me:

'Child-molesting doesn't bother these people, it isn't seen to be an enormous sin, it can't be grasped by them as such, because they cannot conceive of any innocence to be molested, and because the very idea of molesting a young person is so close to what they do anyway in their educational methods.' He sees my eyes opened very wide. 'Yes, I am saying what you think. The indecent physical behaviour is a kind of manifestation of what is spiritually – no, educationally – going on in the schools and *yeshivot*.'

This is so much what I, as a Jew who values Jewish obstinacy not Jewish obedience, want to hear, that I am stumped for a response. What I would most like to do is wave a balloon, but I cannot take it from the child. 'So, um, leaving aside the particular passions of this specific fight,' I stutter, 'and I can, er, see the passions with my own eyes, are you saying there's a crisis of Orthodoxy?'

Correct me if I'm wrong, but are you saying there's something wrong with the Catholic Church, Mr Luther?

The other Martin – Martin Braun – towels his face with his black velvet *yarmulke*. 'Sure there's a crisis. You know, there's a very sweet analogy which I love to use. There was a madman in

Warsaw who was going round the streets saying, "Warsaw is dead!" Someone says to him, "Come on, you can see people coming and going, what's that?" He says, "You don't understand. They're all dead, including the undertakers, so there's no one to deal with them. Meanwhile they're just walking around."'

The walking dead – is that what I've been looking at in Stamford Hill? A noise in the passage interrupts my thoughts. There have been noises in the passage all along – children congregating, cousins, visitors, members of the molested little girl's family, the molested little girl herself – but now there is a special noise in the passage which tells Martin his wife has returned. He calls her 'Mommy'. 'She's my best friend,' he tells me. 'As long as I have her and a herring I am happy . . .'

He shows her to me. I have to swivel in my chair to see her hovering in the passage. She stands like a girl, awkwardly, in her own house, a mother of ten (eight surviving), but still a girl standing to be admired by a visitor.

Is 'Mommy' the woman who opened the door to me earlier? Is she the woman in the portrait? It is hard to tell, so idealized a picture of Jewish womanhood/motherhood does she present.

Having returned from one errand, she is about to go out on another. Does Martin want anything? He thinks about it – a prince in his own principality. 'Mommy,' he says, 'just get me a Cornetto . . . ach! no – I'm *flaishik*.'

A Cornetto? Do I hear right? Is that Yiddish? Hungarian? Hebrew? – קאורנאטו.

No it's just Cornetto, as in Walls Ice Cream. I am so untutored in the ways of Orthodoxy, so ignorant of its degrees of prohibition, that I am thrown by every incidence of ordinariness. Out on the streets of Stamford Hill, where the dead walk because there are no living undertakers to bury them, I have this very day loitered by the exits to supermarkets to spy on what the *frummies* have in their baskets. Ariel! They wash with Ariel! Andrex! They are allowed to use Andrex! And now Cornetto. What, it is written that they can lick a Cornetto! Except that they can't if they are *flaishik* – meaning that they have eaten meat – because a Cornetto is *milchik* – meaning what it sounds like.

'See,' Martin says, after his wife has left, 'I'm just a boy.'

What I don't say in return: 'Is this a Hasidic trait, this euphoric infantilism?' But I know I'm on the trail of something, whether I keep it to myself or not.

And then his mother rings. She is deaf, so he must yell at her. He booms down the phone, roaring with laughter, red with the effort, overcome with pleasure and coyness. I feel that I oughtn't to watch, but I'm unable to look anywhere else. After five minutes he is almost full length on the sofa, yelling and laughing, rubbing his *yarmulke* all over his face, in a sort of lover's embarrassment, partly to hide it, partly to dry it.

'She's so sweet,' he says, after he's put the phone down. 'Eighty-three and so sweet.'

He gets up and shows me a photograph of her – a woman who has known rural ways, a cow-breeder I think he says. And another photograph of them together, both red, both laughing, both happy so long as there is herring to eat.

So now I have met his two mommies. Now I am in touch, after an hour-and-a-half's acquaintance, with his past and his future. His continuity.

Jewish continuity! Wherever one looks at the moment, one sees the thing that would never have seemed possible fifty years ago, euphoric Jewish continuity . . .

Would my mood have changed so radically, would I have swung so violently from affection for my people to the other thing, had Martin Braun not mentioned to me, at his gate, that he had lost money recently by going into the property market at the wrong time, and now sold promotional ball-point pens for a living?

Would that have done it on its own, or did it take the drive back, through wholesale-warehouse and mean-goods-manufacturing territory, to dump me like a sack of plastic poppets into the old damnable small-business blues – *my* continuity – *petit peuple tristesse?*

I knew this part of London from the days when it lay between my stall on Cambridge market and the bag factories, often owned by *frummies*, from which I bought. Being back in it reminded me so forcibly of what, at successive stages of my life, I had tried to forget that I had to pull over, wind my window up and commit my depression to paper. It was that or crash. Here, without any cleaning up, is what I wrote to avoid a traffic ticket:

So here I am again in purse and wallet country . . . briefcases, holdalls, canvas football-bags – the swag that's forever associated in my mind with being Jewish. Cheap and ugly objects, made for others, for others' tastes, never one's own; Jews always second-guessing the gentiles, making little Hollywoods, little Broadways, returning gentile ideas to the gentiles, giving a Jew's idea of what is gentile back to the gentiles, wherever they go. Is there a Jewish manufacturer anywhere who is making anything for himself? Anything that he likes? Anything that he would like to own? What does a Jew like to own? A nice house. (He doesn't build houses.) A fast car. (He doesn't manufacture cars.) A good watch. (Does he make a *good* watch?)

This is what is so appalling about Ratner's recent confession that what he sells is crap. He blew the gaff. Not on the fact that he sold crap. Everyone knows that. But on the fact that he knew he knew. That it was done mindfully, calculatedly, proudly, with a scorn both for his buyers and, more importantly, himself. He opened the Jewish soul up for inspection. For whosoever makes or sells what he knows to be crap, what he wouldn't want for himself, admits his self-hate. He does not deal in what is lovely because he believes his place is with what isn't. He is wedded to ugliness. And he cannot provide goods of value for himself because he does not consider himself worthy of providing them. He wants what gentiles make, because what he makes is only for gentiles and therefore no good. What a knot! What a sequence of scorn for others proceeding from scorn for oneself, and admiration for others proceeding from an inability to admire oneself. And the more one makes what isn't worth making (or selling, or swapping, or importing) the tighter wound becomes the bind – the more contempt you have for those you provide for, the more contempt you have for *what* you provide, and the more you know that the only things worth having come from those you thought you held in contempt.

Feel good at any stage of that!

And yet I cannot get past the instinct that I must begin where it began for me – not just with the whole family popping plastic poppets, but with the poppets themselves, those hideously coloured beads, shaped like symbols of simultaneous male and female sexuality, a protuberance at one end, a hole for a protuberance at the other, hermaphroditic junk, entire unto itself. If a Jew doesn't have a sack of these in his background, if he hasn't weighed and bagged discoloured chocolates or put a stapling-gun to a HOLIDAY KIT, then he isn't really Jewish. Keep your concert piano-playing; a Jew is not a Jew until he has bound himself to his people in vain, unbeautiful, unimaginative, unproductive, self-defeating activity. Martin Braun with his ball-point pens – there's a Jew!

The Irish taxi-driver who takes me to Broadcasting House for my wrestle with the Chief Rabbi says, 'These are my last two days.'

I am too tense to wish him well in his next job. Only after I get out and run into the Rabbi in the foyer does it occur to me he might have meant his last two days on earth. I could have engaged him in timely eschatological conversation and gone on to radio touched by the mysteries, but I blew it.

The Rabbi recognizes me before I recognize him. I see to that. 'Howard! Howard Jacobson! What are you doing now? I've

27

been a hermit for the last few years. What are you up to? What have you been doing since *Coming from Behind*?'

'This and that, Rabbi,' I say. 'And you?'

We've never met before, but two Jewish boys from Cambridge can quickly cut the ice. He has minders, I don't; otherwise our talk is democratic. I am surprised how young he looks, how dapper, and – all right – how handsome. He has black hair and a short black beard, going silver-grey. A good colour for a Chief Rabbi. His suit is silver-grey, too; more like an accountant's than a prelate's. But when he wishes to express disapproval he is able to flood his face with blackness, and then you do not doubt who has legitimized his agency.

As we walk the corridors of the BBC together, I try not to cede moral authority. I am a handful of years older than him. I was preaching to congregations of ten thousand at a sitting at Sydney University when he was just turning up unsure at Cambridge. Seniority apart, I owe it to Mad Dog not to cede authority. Mad Dog is the *nom de rage* of someone who writes me deranged rabbinic letters with a Golders Green postmark. In the beginning he saw me as a rebellious and prophetic Jewish figure who could lead our people to deliverance; but since I ceded moral authority to the Bishop of Durham on television he has begun to address me as Howard Poodleson. Assuming he is allowed a radio, it is inconceivable that he will not be listening to this broadcast. I can hear him out there.

But it isn't easy, holding on to your moral authority in the company of one who has bathed in the *Shekhina* and talked with You-Know-Who and walks with a minder. I feel it seeping away, ceding itself, glugging out like the last of the water from a water-bottle punctured in the desert at midday.

Then he tells me that he read for the bar, for a day, after his two years lecturing in philosophy at Middlesex Polytechnic; but the one law lecture he went to was so boring he gave it away. So: he looked around a bit, the Rabbi, before bumping into God.

A little authority leaks from him and returns to me. *I* didn't look around. *I* always wanted to be a novelist and a critic, even when I was fulfilling the other side of my Jewish destiny and selling purses and wallets on Cambridge market. Vocation-wise, I've got it. Now it only needs me to try out on radio that I'm more godly than he is too – more godly, that is, for not being godly at all. Dostoyevsky stuff. Coming to God by way of sin. Judaism has its Karamazov figures. Jacob Frank, for instance, who was born in Podolia in 1726, sold *shmattes* for a living, and held that it was only by transgressing the actual Torah that one could honour the Torah of Emanation, that only those who had descended into darkness could ever ascend into the light.

But I'm not so confirmed a sinner that when I'm introduced on air as an assimilated Jew I can wear the title lightly. Assimilated? Me?

It doesn't go the way I want it. I have always known that there will be other people on the programme but I haven't paused to consider how their presence will compromise the idea of combat. Stupid of me. Jacob did not engage the angel with the help of experts from other fields.

In a brief pre-recording pep-talk, the producer tells us we will try to record as live though he expects that we'll run over. There'll be some editing, in other words. 'Good,' says the Rabbi, 'I'll be needing to retract.'

'Retract now,' I say. Ha! ha!

It's a fatal error. What fuelled the Rabbi's joke was an anxious ambiguity at the heart of his position – child of the Enlightenment, child of Israel; private Jew and public Jew. What fuelled my joke was nothing but the naughtiness of the congenitally deferential. A punch, no, not so much as that . . . a tap, from a crouching position.

Some wrestle.

The Rabbi's technique, after one of us has spoken, is to sit on him, or on her – for there is a her here, despite Orthodox misgivings – and apply the homiletic hold. 'Let me tell you a story . . .' 'Let me give you a clearer example of what I mean . . .'

Submit? Submit yet?

After a homily a fable; after a fable an analogy; after an analogy . . .

Submit? If we were still alive we'd submit.

I don't lay any discrete blame on the Rabbi for this. The Bishop of Durham did the same. And he didn't have the excuse of being Jewish.

But it is alarming how blackened becomes the Rabbi's countenance when, from playing dead, you effect a mini-resurrection and try an arm-lock of your own. Black fire issues from his eyes. His skin tightens and embrowns, as though charred from proximity to the Word. Moses will have looked the same, when he came down from the mountain.

A scorpion would not have scrupled to attack the prophet's feet, nor would a sand-flea have feared him; but is it my ambition to bite so low? I cannot descend to mere irritancy, even if it is as an irritant that I've been hired. I back off, I give way, I cave in, I *cede*.

After the broadcast a number of the maimed and suffocated stay behind to lick their wounds and swallow air. Another rabbi, with whom I fancy I've been getting on, sits by me. His eyes are bad and he has – he had when he came in – a broken arm. 'You know that point you were making,' he says, 'about Jews who intermarry ending up probably the best Jews of all . . .'

I move close to him. I know him to be a thinking, amusable, open-minded cleric. 'Yes,' I say, athirst for love or approval from my own people. 'Yes . . .'

'I think it's bullshit,' he says.

*　　*　　*

30

Becalmed but Kosher

I leave for America early the next morning, queasy with the certainty that I have been rolled by two rabbis in a single afternoon.

My wife is under instructions to tear up the envelope addressed to Howard Spanielson the moment it arrives.

Three

PEOPLE WHO NEED PEOPLE

JESUS REIGNS SUPREME proclaimed a flyer in the rear window of the cab that picked me up from JFK. That was cool. I had no hang-ups about who was winning so long as the driver got me quickly to the Carnegie Deli on 7th and 55th.

I was giving myself just one night in New York before heading north to the Catskills for the High Holy Days – or, to be less WASP about it, to the Borsht Belt for Rosh Hashanah – and, although I was coming back, I wanted Jewish America between two slices of rye, and I wanted it now.

For all that I've never actually had a good time in New York, or ever met anyone who's actually had a good time in New York, I cannot keep from sentimentalizing it, not so much in the mind as in the spirit. Spiritually I lean to New York, turn my soul to face it, exactly as Orthodox Jews incline to Jerusalem. And for the same reason. We both believe we are magnetized, like compass needles, by home. Except that home for the Orthodox means the place of final return, whereas for me it is the place of vagrancy perfected. A universal alienation.

And where everyone is alienated is not everyone at home? Ah, how sweet and seductive is that sophistry. I fall for it and don't fall for it every time I watch Woody Allen talking sex and angst in a Broadway Deli; every time Isaac Bashevis Singer is accosted at his table by a refugee from the old country saying, 'Are you Mr Singer the novelist? Mr Singer, have I got a story for you …'; every time Mel Brooks or Jackie Mason distils the soul of Judaism into a pickled cucumber or a cake.

Let the politically correct worry about stereotypicality; to poeticize the bagel is not to trivialize the faith. We isolate such symbols in exile as an act of the deepest reverence. We return their symbolic function to them. And I knew that no observance of ritual soon to be foisted on me in the Catskills would be as hallowed by the heart as this dash by taxi, straight from the airport, straight from being rolled by rabbis, to the Carnegie Deli.

Enjoy! . . . Enjoy! . . . ENJOY! . . . I could read the exhortation to spiritual nourishment flashing on the electro-diode screen from across the street. Gargantuan . . . GARGANTUAN . . . GARGANTUAN . . .

If the EDS doesn't get you, a tout does. 'You wan eat?'

I wanned eat.

The system is to kidnap a customer from off the streets then hand him on down into the bowels – I choose the word carefully – of the Deli. From the tout to a maybe manager, from the maybe manager to a just perhaps head-waiter, from the just perhaps head-waiter to a who knows table waitress – all of them simultaneously black, Chinese, Hispanic and Jewish.

'You wan drink, honey?'

I was jammed into a corner, my space and light stolen by a plate of assorted cucumbers – Polish, sweet and sour, new green – so . . . so *GARGANTUAN* that I couldn't be certain whether they were food or an installation by someone of the school of Koons. Did I wan drink? I wasn't here yet. Yes, perhaps a little wine . . .

'Beer's the only wine here, honey.'

The black waitress, once I could see her above the cucumbers, looked more Jewish than any Jew I had ever met. I subscribe to all Lost Tribe theories. Wherever I go I encounter Jews who don't know that's what they are. This one had all the mannerisms of the Jewish metaphysic, right down to the instantaneous peremptoriness, the psycholeptic impatience that comes from fearing you will miss the last cattle truck out of Minsk.

Beer would be nice, I said, and a pastrami sandwich, and a plate of corned-beef hash. Sure, with an egg on. Coleslaw? Sure, why not. Yeah, and bread. And while you're at it, more cucumber.

Before I had even started on my sandwich, the electro-diode screen was urging me to finish off with CHEESECAKE ... HEAVENLY SOUR CREAM ... BIGGER AND BETTER THAN EVER ... AFTER YOU HAVE TRIED IT ... TAKE SOME HOME ... TO THE FAMILY...

Sometimes BIGGER AND BETTER THAN EVER appeared without any defining reference. Only a pedant would have cared what. As long as it was bigger and better.

SMALLER BUT JUST AS GOOD might have been more to the point. It is humiliating not being able to finish a sandwich. At a table behind mine a woman was refusing a doggy-bag for her hash; but yes, she would take the coleslaw home in a plastic cup for her housekeeper. Smiling but weary, as though exhausted to be proven right yet again, the black Hispanic Chinese Jewish waitresses moved from table to table dispensing take-away containers.

Even without cheesecake and sour cream, I was in heaven. This was not like eating *kosher* in England. Not surprising, since the food here was not so much *kosher* as *kosher*-ish – ersatz *kosher*, *kosher* freed from the rules and restrictions which usually make you wish you were in another restaurant, eating something that didn't have matzo balls in it, or that wasn't mashed and strained and puréed, as though for Jewish babies. And there was no wizened little watchdog from the Beth Din sitting in a corner either – no ancient guardian of the Orthodox palate, such as you find in English *kosher* delis, hovering like a chaperon over the promiscuity of your digestive system, spoiling your appetite, and making you feel that eating is not a pleasure but a penance, a mortification of the duodenum which you misperform at your peril.

I was home, in heaven, in the Seventh Heaven of the Jewish mystics, the soul's original abode, whither it returns after the body's death or while the body is still alive but racked with ecstasy.

How many heavens do the Cabbalists count? If the Carnegie Deli was seven, then we're into double figures with the Concord Resort Hotel – the last of the gargantuan GARGANTUAN GARGANTUAN *kosher* rest-and-recreation centres in the Catskill mountains, a couple of hours' drive into New York State, zipping north from Manhattan.

This was Iroquois country once, but then – to compress history – the Jews came. We make too much of cultural differences. The Concord Hotel abuts on Kiamesha Lake, and I defy anyone to tell, from sound alone, whether Kiamesha is Iroquois for a good place to be, or Yiddish. Either way, the Jews too are now leaving the Catskills. Just after the last war, when money was short and few could afford air-conditioning, the Catskills offered cheap and easy respite from the heat of New York in the summer. You could swim there, play tennis, eat *kosher*, go to the synagogue, find a nice wife for your boy, and watch famous Jewish comedians making jokes about everything you'd just been doing – all under one roof. Now, everyone has air-conditioning and a condo in Miami; a nice wife you won't find anywhere, and famous Jewish comedians you can watch on television. Under cover of darkness, the ultra-Orthodox are wheeling in, taking over some of the old camps, hiding their modesty behind high fences; but as a place for smart, easy-come easy-go Jews who like to run into a few city temptations in the mountains, the Catskills have had it.

Which doesn't stop three thousand of us turning up from all over America for the Jewish New Year.

'Three thousand!' a fellow-Concordian exclaims to me at

intervals as we stand queuing for registration, as restive as conscripts. 'Three thousand!' He keeps feeling the back of his neck, as though he is both hen and butcher, testing his readiness for slaughter. Everything seems to exhaust him – queuing, old age, driving, travel, holidays, his wife's luggage, which, even as we speak, is being unwound from the boot of the Buick like a tapeworm. For exclamation, though, he still has strength. 'Three thousand! Three thousand they're expecting! Today!'

'It's a lot,' I agree.

'A lot! When I first used to come here they had five! Three thousand! Next year it'll be two!'

'It's not many,' I agree.

'Not many! Just make sure you get a nice table! You don't want aggravation with your table! The Ks are good! Get Irving Cohen to put you on a K! Tell him I said!'

Irving Cohen's reputation is international. I first heard of him in Manchester, from a couple he'd brought together. He'd taken a look at each of them separately, as they queued for their table numbers, assessed their personalities, and colour-coded them into a happy marriage. In the Catskills, Cupid is a round, seventy-year-old *maître d'hôtel* called Irving Cohen.

'Are you telling me that romance is what drives the Borsht Belt?' I'd asked the expertly matched pair.

'Sex,' they corrected me. 'And food.'

Looking around the hotel with my own eyes, it seems that old age is what the place is really about. Already every armchair in the foyer and the lobby and the various lounges has a form recumbent in it. As I thread my way through the sticks and walking-frames I castigate the Manchester couple for their misinformation, then I remember that it was some time since they were here and that life is a game of Consequences. What is old age, after all, but the price we pay for food and sex?

By the time I join the queue which will end in my old age, it is hundreds strong. There are still four hours to go before we actually need a table to sit at, but nobody is taking any chances. Rumours are rife. There is no food in the hotel. All the waiters have walked off the job. Fears shake us as though we are a convoy of refugees, prey to one disappointment after the next. Another country is not going to take us in and feed us.

Behind me, a couple of women, born in the Bronx, are having a Never Again conversation.

'Roosevelt, the biggest anti-Semite of the lot. We didn't know. When he died we sat *shivah*. Now we find out the truth. Roosevelt was to blame. He could have got our boys to bomb those camps.'

'Sure. Look at Crown Heights. It's a keg of fire. They're sitting on dynamite day and night. All the blacks know is shoot, shoot.'

'Listen. I wanna stay with my Jews. I wanna live with Jews only. Excuse me, but the others . . . they shop on Friday, they play golf on Saturday. I play golf on Sunday. I couldn't be socially friendly to them if I wanted to.'

The closer we get to the head of the queue, the less abstract and philosophical we can afford to be. Once in sight of Irving Cohen's pegboard, which is the length of three grown men – six, if you take the bowed clientele of the Concord as the norm – we throw ourselves into a panic of specific wants.

'I come here every year. I always have B6. My father had B6. He met my mother, *alevasholem*, at B6.'

'She's in a wheelchair. You can't get a wheelchair to that table. What's she gonna do – eat alone?'

'Mr Cohen – excuse me, Mr Cohen – that's too near the aisle. I know that aisle. It's too busy. You get spilled on by the bus-boy in that aisle.'

Simultaneously bored and harassed, like a god at a chequer-board, Irving Cohen pulls a coloured peg from one hole and plugs it into another. Pink for a girl. Blue for a boy. Brown for a . . . what's brown for?

His memory for faces is reputed to be phenomenal. He can recognize you from your grandparents whom he brought together in 1940. If he has never seen you before he can work out where to put you from a snap assessment of your marital and economic status, your intellectual pursuits, your sociability and your appetite.

When it comes to my turn, I am careful not to give away my country of origin. I have heard that there is a peg to correspond with the code G U – Geographically Unsuitable – and I am fearful of ending up at a table full of other people it is not worth anyone's while getting too attached to. I see his eyes open and close once behind his spectacles. I feel the way a guiltily glowing lump of radium must feel when a Geiger counter passes over it. A slip of paper is handed to me, showing my table number. I am among the Hs. I have no way of knowing how good the Hs are, but I've heard only rhapsodic things about the Ks and I can estimate for myself that I am at least not too far from them.

There are almost as many phones in the Concord as there are armchairs with recumbent figures in them. Unable to sever the umbilical cords that tie their husbands to the city, the women are turning up for dinner on their own, in a sort of universal pet that suits the short, taffeta frocks they wear, the black stockings, the ankle-chains, the teetering heels. I climb the *Gone with the Wind* staircase in their company, like a judge amid a field of startled poodles.

A Latin American waiter welcomes me to my table, as yet empty.

'Hi. My name is Alex. I'll be looking after you. You here for Rosh Hashanah?'

The bus-boy, Luis, introduces himself similarly, and asks the same question. In my marvelling at hearing Hebrew pronounced Hispanically – which is no more surprising, really, than hearing it pronounced Mancunianly – I fail to observe that Alex and Luis need to know the duration of my stay so that they can calculate how big a tip they can look forward to. Five dollars a meal for the waiter is the suggested rate, three for the bus-boy. The reckoning begins from now.

Sweet *kosher* wine is on the table – Concord Grape – and a glass to drink it from that is no bigger than Thumbelina's reticule. We are not a guzzling people. A melon is also waiting. As are twenty pieces of cutlery and every colour of horseradish. While wondering many things – whether I ought to wait for others; whether there will *be* others; which colour horseradish to put on my melon; how come the diaspora has made no inroads into the ancient Israelite assumption that wine and treacle are interchangeable – I become aware of an embarrassing scene unfolding beneath one of the great chandeliers, a table or two from mine. Among the Ks, if I'm not mistaken.

An older-than-middle-aged transparency of a woman, in a poverty-pale cardigan and an inappropriate blue stole, stands wringing her hands. That expression is normally hyperbolic; but not in this instance. Truly, as though it is a wet tea-towel, she puts one hand in another and presses, squeezes, screws it. She is engaged in an argument which she knows she cannot win, and doesn't mean to win, with a man whose job it seems to be to find extra chairs, make extra spaces, and otherwise, as it were, sweep up after Irving Cohen. It is plain he knows her. Otherwise he would not be using her so rudely. This is not Borstal. She is, after all, a paying guest. But he is having none of her.

'You're not going to aggravate me,' he warns her, meaning to turn on his heel but transfixed by the degree to which she is aggravating him.

'It's you that's aggravating me,' she cries. Her hair has been dyed pink, and is so thin it looks as though someone is shining a torchlight through candy-floss.

He raises his hand. Not to hit her but to block her out. He is a big man, with the presence of a bouncer in a high-class establishment. He may know his way round casinos. 'No,' he once more warns. 'Oh, no. Not again. You're not going to aggravate me again. Not this time.'

'How do you like this guy?' She appeals, with no expectancy of sympathy, to the dining-room for three thousand, filling at the rate of a hundred every ten seconds. 'He says I'm aggravating him!' Her voice is shaken-up Brooklyn, as unsteady as a bridge.

She has not wanted to sit where she's been put, this seems to be the problem. Or then again maybe she has. Whatever is amiss, she ends up with me.

Before taking a seat she has to cover the chair with tissues. She has about a dozen of them, ready, in her bag. In the act of sitting she disturbs them, and unbeknown to her they flutter and lie useless at her feet.

'They say I can't sit there,' she tells me. 'I was sitting there for lunch ... I always sit there. But they say it's Chester Reuben's table.'

I ask if Chester Reuben is important.

'Yeah. Chester Reuben. He's from Chicago.'

I wonder if he's a hoodlum.

'He's a travel agent.'

Already, seeing who's joined me at the table, Alex and Luis have lost their friendliness, Rosh Hashanah or no Rosh Hashanah. They too are not going to be aggravated again.

She introduces herself. 'I'm Mini.'

'I'm —'

'You from Australia?'

'No, but —'

'The cantor's from Australia.'

She isn't sure about this table. It isn't her usual table. Will she be turfed off this table next. Did I *hear* that guy? I laugh. Tell her it will be all right. Encourage her to think of it as a singles table. Who knows, we may have it to ourselves.

40

She shifts in her seat, careful not to upset the tissues which I alone know are no longer under her. She tells me how long she's been coming here, how much it costs, how she knows everyone, even Chester Reuben. 'The food's good,' she says. She notices Alex. 'He looks good . . . Hey? What's your name?'

Alex can't believe his luck.

He's saved by new arrivals at our table: Esther and Saul, coupled as only a mother who has lost her husband and a son who has never had a wife can be coupled. They don't so much join as stalk us. 'I sat where you're sitting,' Esther hisses into the back of my neck. 'This afternoon I sat where you're sitting.'

She is only just not a dwarf. Her nose is only just not the mythic scimitar denoting Jewish evil. Her eyes are only just not balls of molten lava, rolled from hell.

'I'll move,' I say. But I have already eaten melon. I am into the fish. I have unfolded my napkin. I have a bread plate with bread broken on it. A wine glass. A water glass. My cutlery is in disarray. I am, in short, established in the seat. 'If you insist,' I say, 'I'll move. But it's complicated.'

Her son, Saul, who is bachelor dark, bachelor slight, bachelor watchful under a *yarmulke*, and almost a hunchback with the stress of being a son, pulls a face, as though to say, If he won't be a gentleman, he won't be a gentleman . . . leave it.

And she leaves it. Sits two seats to the left of me. Squirms. Wriggles. Complains of the angle. Complains of her back. Complains that she can't see. (What can't she see?) And moves one to the right, where she can hiss and boil in my ear. 'I liked your seat.'

'I'll move.'

'Nah.'

'Let me move.'

'Nah. This'll do. It's the pain. The pain's awful. But this'll do.'

Saul is attached to her by invisible wires. When she grimaces, he shifts. When she speaks, he starts. Now he shrugs. It's an extraordinary shrug, starting at his *yarmulke*, taking in his eyes, his nose, his hump, and not finishing until it has reached his feet. The great shrug of Judaism. I die inside, observing it, realizing the weight of dejection it thinks it can throw off.

He asks for wine. To read *Kiddush* from the printed form, waiting in the centre of the table.

'Good *yom tov*,' says Mini.

'Good *Shabbes*,' Esther corrects her.

'I mean *Shabbes*,' says Mini.

Esther catches my eye, as though to say, Who's this *nebbish* of a woman at *our* table?

I'm prepared to collude. To make or break whatever alliances are going. Now I'm here I'm here. I'll sink with the rest of them.

'You're so spiteful,' Esther suddenly spits at me.

'Spiteful?'

'So spiteful – not moving.'

'I've said I'll move.'

Her eyes are pools of evil. 'So spiteful!'

Saul shrugs. At me? At her?

'He's a doctor,' Esther tells me, amiably now, confidentially, as though we'd been discussing friendly affairs all evening. 'He specializes in Gerry Atkins.'

I look puzzled. Have I heard of Gerry Atkins? Is it a method, a technique, like Alexander?

'Don't you know what that is?'

'No.'

Saul overhears me confess my ignorance. 'Old people,' he says. He talks quietly, so that you have to lean forward to hear him. Saul's revenge. Eventually you too will have a hump.

'Oh, geriatrics,' I say. 'I didn't catch the word.'

He shrugs. I didn't catch the word. Shows what sort of person I am.

'Gerry Atkins!' Mini exclaims. 'You don't know what Gerry Atkins is!'

Esther glistens at me. She has found her purpose. To stop me talking to Mini. 'The pain's so awful,' she says.

A bottle of seltzer water is brought to the table. Esther seizes it. I notice that she has tiny hands, tiny even in proportion to the rest of her. The fingers are so small there is no room for nails. I see that she has painted the tips of her fingers. Or dipped them in strawberry cheesecake. Either way they resemble the bloody stumps that befall nail-biting children in *Struwwelpeter*, the punishment meted out by Mr Snip-Snip.

The seltzer water fizzes when Esther opens it. Mini catches some of the spray and dries herself with a tissue, of which her handbag contains an inexhaustible supply. 'I'd like some seltzer,' she says.

'I'm keeping it for later,' Esther tells her.

'I can't digest my food without seltzer water,' Mini says.

Esther asks me if I've seen the cantor's wife yet. She pulls a face at me. 'She's . . . you know?'

I don't know. Deranged? Deformed?

Esther pulls another face. Shows me her brown moustache. Bends her nose from the inside. Lays her pygmy fingers on the table. 'You know . . .'

I think I have it. 'Too glamorous?'

Something passes across the pools of evil which are Esther's eyes. 'I didn't wanna say it,' she says. Could that something be a smile?

'I get ill if I don't have seltzer,' Mini says, her voice stretched and swaying, like a hammock.

Esther loses her temper. 'Have this, have this since you're *nudzhehing*.' And she impels the bottle across the table with the heel of her little hand.

Just as I think we are about to explode, Alex arrives to take our orders for the eleventh course.

'He's good,' Saul says.

'He's very good,' Esther agrees.

'They're both good,' says Mini.

'Very good,' Saul agrees.

'Last year,' says Mini, 'we had a waitress.'

'Was she good?' Esther asks.

'Very good,' says Mini.

'You'd have to be good to be as good as these two,' Saul declares.

'These two are very good,' says Esther.

I sit back in my chair. Not all the expected three thousand guests have arrived yet, but the two thousand seven hundred and fifty who are here are well into their meal. On every table seltzer bottles are being fought over, stuffings compared, soups disparaged, food returned, second or third helpings requested – sometimes second or third helpings of dishes that have been returned – but on one matter there is complete accord: how good the waiters are. Is this in the hope that the saying it will make it so? Or does an agreed no-go area, a fixed point of judgemental uniformity, free the room for dissension on every other single subject?

'There are no girls on this table,' Esther says to me, out of the blue.

'There's Mini,' I whisper.

Esther nudges me with her elbow. Creatures of unsurpassed malevolence bathe and dart in the brown pools of her eyes. 'I said girls,' she says.

I point to the empty places. 'Maybe tomorrow,' I say.

'Last year I sat with Saul and three mothers with three sons. Not a single girl. We complained to Irving Cohen. But he wouldn't budge. "At least half a girl," one of the boys complained. "At least give us half a girl!"'

I look at Saul, who is shrugging himself inside out, and decide that half a girl would be too much for him.

Out of the corner of my eye I see that Mini is wrapping cake in tissues and stuffing it in her handbag.

*   *   *

I hadn't understood, when I read on the hotel notice-board that Ralph Levene, THE COUNTRY'S LEADING AUTHORITY ON HAIR REPLACEMENT, would be in the Sun-Lobby at 8.45, that we would have to walk through his lecture on the way out from dinner.

But this, I am bound to assume, is what I've done, when I stumble blindly into a table laden with dead gerbils, and look up to behold an ape-like man, standing with his feet apart, consenting to have one of these gerbils combed into his eyes. 'Well?' demands the person doing the combing – he speaks through a microphone and wears a dying weasel himself – 'Well? Would *you* know the difference?'

'Yeah, immediately,' a woman who no more means to be here than I do, calls out over her shoulder.

She is smart, within the taffeta convention, and thin, within the convention of being fat. Although she is walking on carpet, the spikes of her heels click.

'What d'ya mean you can tell?' Ralph Levene – for such I must take him to be – insists on being told. 'C'm back here! What d'ya mean you can tell?'

The twenty bald heads of Ralph Levene's audience turn to question the woman. What does she mean?

She stops. Revolves. Not at all nonplussed by the attention. 'You can tell,' she laughs. A cruel, weasel-killing laugh. 'You can always tell. It looks like something you wipe your feet on.'

Ralph Levene goes from apoplexy to spasmophemia. 'C'm back here,' he shouts, not certain now which hand holds the microphone. 'Don't tell me you can always tell. I own the largest hair replacement company in the United States. Half the men you've loved have probably been to me. C'm back here. Feel my hair. C'mon, c'mon and feel it. This real hair? Do you think it's real? Well I've got news for you . . .' And tossing the microphone from one hand to the other, he tears off the wig which no one in the room has ever supposed he is not wearing, and struts like a transvestite stripper – 'See! Totally bald! Totally! And you know who made me get one of these? – my wife!'

The twenty hairless heads of Ralph Levene's audience turn again to witness the effect of this revelation on the weasel-killer. But she is moved only to more mirth. 'If I had a wife who wanted to wipe her feet on my head, I wouldn't advertise it,' she laughs.

I follow her down the *Gone with the Wind* staircase, enjoying the rustling of her taffeta and the stabbings of her heels. She wears, I notice, a gold chain around her ankle. *Under* her stockings.

A difficult channel to negotiate – grooming.

It's the last Saturday – the final *Shabbes* – of the old year.

And I do what I have not done, what I have not been able to bring myself to do, for over a quarter of a century: I attend morning service at a synagogue. It is the hotel synagogue, a small conference-room made over temporarily to worship. I trust that there is a facilitating congruence in this, a coincidence of accommodation, for I too am made over only temporarily to worship.

I shuffle my feet, adjust my *yarmulke*, and push open the door, to see ... that they are still here! The old men with spectacles and bad-tempered faces, who all seem to know one another, unhappily, as gamblers in a betting-shop seem to know one another, and who do not seem pleased to see me.

Thirty years on and four thousand miles from home, and still they are here, substituting the fear of man for the fear of God, staring me down, staring me out. How many times have I taken the furthest of far seats, and looked into their skinny old necks, made vulnerable if not venerable by prayer-shawls, made to look like boys' necks again, scrawny, without much hair, ears too prominent, skull-caps kept in place by hair-clips? How often?

And still I find them formidable, cabbalistic, exclusive. A secret society of widowers and pensioners. I imagine it, of course. They wish me good *Shabbes*. They give me prayer-books. They make room for me on their benches. They're just frail little men. But I am still the outsider. Their power still works with me. Probably *only* with me.

And still working, too, is the old revulsion and fear when the scroll comes out of the Ark and is walked around, up and down the aisles, for the congregation of the enfeebled to kiss with the fringes of their *talaysim* – to me an idolatrous thing, although it's language itself they're kissing, words, words, but an idol none the less, a pagan thing for all that, I am bound to feel, because of its shape, because it's a *thing*, because of the ecstatic way it's carried, and because it has ears, bull's ears, goat's ears.

The object and the response are too primitive for me. Kissing paper – this takes us too far back. There are worse things to kiss, I know. And most religions kiss them. But can we not have it that we kiss nothing? That aversion to idolatry on which we pride ourselves, we Jews, ought it not to include an aversion to the Word as well, when that Word has been wound on rollers and fashioned to resemble a ruminant?

To my surprise, for I have not been in a synagogue for half a lifetime, and have never been in an American synagogue at all, the service suddenly takes an English turn.

'May he who blessed our fathers, Abraham, Isaac and Jacob, bless and protect the President and the Vice-President of the United States.'

I'm here, in a makeshift tabernacle in the Catskills, to bless Dan Quayle?

When the blessing is extended to Yitzhak Shamir and members of the Knesset and the brave soldiers of Israel, I am less surprised. But less surprised is not unsurprised. This is my first brush with what is called, in America, Conservative Judaism. Apart from the unwelcoming dodderers and the Word-kissing, I'm finding it hard to see just what is being conserved. Another of the contradictions of being Jewish purely in the intellect opens before me. I'm shocked by how much the modernity, the actuality, the naming of names even unto Quayle, take from the divine mystery of the service, even though I don't much care for the divine mystery of the service. Mouldering stands the edifice of ancient Hebrew, but, if it's Bush and Shamir who will appear when the walls totter, I would rather the walls stood.

The presiding rabbi yells out a sermon taken, as it were, from contemporary life. His subjects are Operation Desert Shield; the Intifada; Australia (where, like the cantor, he has officiated); a toy called GI Joe, and the significance of its being designated a doll for import duty purposes; Crown Heights; Al Sharpton and Jesse Jackson.

'And I tell you this, Jesse Jackson, we Jews are not against colour. We Jews are proud to integrate into our community twenty thousand – count those, Mr Jackson – twenty thousand Ethiopians . . .'

He screams this, tub-thumper to tub-thumper. And he isn't even American.

There is speculation about Rabbi Alony in the corridors of the Concord. Is he from Dublin? Sydney? Cape Town? Cheshire, England? In most cases, American confusion over accents can be put down to an insensitivity of the ear unequalled anywhere on earth. Only adders have worse hearing than Americans, and they at least take the precaution of shunning society. But Rabbi Alony's broth of howls and vociferations would give Eliza Dolittle's mentor pause. Let us grant that he is a citizen of the world.

His theme, as opposed to his clamour, is the mystery of God's promise to make the children of Israel like the stars of the skies and the sand of the sea. What can this mean since we are so unpopulous?

'And since six million of us died in the Holocaust,' a member of the congregation calls out.

'Thank you,' says Alony, who is more of a toast-masterish than an apocalyptic rabbi – 'thank you, I'll come to the Holocaust.'

All in good time, the Holocaust.

We are to understand it, this stars promise, this sand business, not as being about numbers. We are the stars in our brightness and steadfastness; and we are the sand, in the sense of being a gritty substance, in our defence against . . .

What?

Remembering where he was a rabbi last, and swept up in a tide of grit, Alony free-associates from God's promise to Abraham to the Sydney Opera House. 'If you want to see a beach, forget the beaches you know here. You've got to see an Australian beach.'

Which reminds him of stars, which reminds him of Israel, which reminds him of sand, which reminds him of God, which reminds him of himself, which reminds him of his sermon, which reminds him that he was in Israel only recently, where he saw . . .

He is off again, throwing out his arms, spitting at the congregation, hurling words as though they are rocks at the furthest wall, against which I cower, fearing for my hearing.

'I saw Hasidim, ladies and gentlemen, in their heavy shawls, and Sephardim, and Falashas, and Jews from Iraq, and Jews from Iran, and Jews from Syria, ladies and gentlemen, praying together at that wall . . . And so I say to Jesse Jackson . . .'

It is thrilling in its way. I do not know what any of it means, but it is thrilling to be gritty like the sand, to be a single grain in the great sandbag of Rabbi Alony's populist eloquence, holding back the waters of whatever it is.

Esther has taken to calling me Harold and to kissing me.

And to saying, 'Harold, knowing you is so important to me. My son says you're a very nice man. This is for you . . .'

49

And she reaches up to me with her bleeding stumps, and I bend from the knees, but we still can't meet until I am pulled down further, so that she can grasp my hand, wish me good *Shabbes*, good *yom tov*, and keep my hand between hers, and then kiss me, not on the cheeks, not on the cheeks, but smack on my lips from which for an hour or more she seems to hang, a malignant dwarf suspended by a hellish glue of lipstick, spittle and terror.

I am getting ahead of myself. There is too much happening at the Concord – too much noise, too many events, too much food and food-associated activity – for a single pen to record with any historical accuracy. Time here is not as it is elsewhere. What you think you did yesterday you won't in fact be doing until tomorrow. This is Jewish time. Next year in Jerusalem, but we're already there. If we play our cards right with the Pharaoh he may let us go, but he already has.

'Every day,' said the Maggid of Koznitz, 'man shall go forth out of Egypt, out of distress . . .' Time past and time future are all contained in Jewish time present.

Breakfast. The breakfast before Esther kisses me. Mini is now universally accepted as beyond the pale. The table, augmented by a civilized realtor and his family from Sacramento, turns its back on her. The waiters walk away while she is talking. No one can take the aggravation. In a temple devoted to wants, Mini wants too much.

This morning it is decaff. 'Louis . . . Louis! Decaff!'

'It's Luis,' Esther snarls at her. 'Lui*ss*.' She hisses the esses. '*S-s-s*. He's Mexican.'

'Louis!' Mini cries. 'Decaff!'

Luis is deaf to decaff.

She tries for Alex. 'Alex, are you feeling better? You feeling better, today?'

Alex, too, is deaf.

'He doesn't answer. I asked if he was feeling better. Yesterday he said he wasn't feeling too good. Today he doesn't answer.'

I suggest that he still isn't feeling too good.

'How do you get decaff around here?' she asks Barney, the realtor from Sacramento.

He calls Alex and gets her decaff.

'I've got family in Sacramento,' she tells him.

'You told me yesterday,' he says. This is your reward for helping Mini. 'I still don't know them.'

It's cruel. Mini is suffering from poverty. Her clothes are old. The sleeves of her jacket are frayed. The stole she is never without is not just threadbare but actually looks as though someone has taken to it with scissors. (A waiter?) A suspicion crosses all our minds that she might be here on charity. Could there be some sort of bursary? A Concord Convalescence Scholarship? It's cruel, and we know it, but we cannot live with the aggravation.

Esther's kiss comes after Alony's atomization of the Jewish people into particles of particles of grit. Although there is no interval to speak of between breakfast and the morning service, a banquet is laid outside the makeshift synagogue. Herrings. Chopped and fried fish. Sponge-cakes. Macaroons. Tumblers of whisky. Thimblefuls of red treacle.

It's as I'm backing away from the banqueting-table – or, to be truthful, as I'm regaining my balance, having been pushed from the banqueting-table, and narrowly escaped falling into a wooden waste-paper basket containing the lace doily-like veils which the women borrow to pray in – Esther gets me, calls me Harold, describes the pain she's in, shows me her bad leg, tells me how much I mean to her, and climbs aboard my lips.

Saul, of course, is by her side. When is he not by her side, bent at the neck, hunched at the back, devoted, ashamed, glowing, wincing, a hoop of love and humiliation, his mother's faithful companion, her toy-boy, her pride and her punishment?

I see him shrugging while she grapples me. Not the complete inside-out shrug, but a substantial shrug for all that, leaving only his head from the ears up showing above his shoulders. Because so much of his face is hidden behind his sternum I cannot tell whether the shrug is competitive or brotherly or stepson-ish.

'Harold, you weren't next to me this morning,' Esther says, the moment I release her.

'I noticed,' I say.

'That realtor and his wife were in our seats when I got there. I asked them to move but they said it was their wedding anniversary and they wanted to be together. And Saul kept kicking me under the table. He wanted I should be quiet. So I let them stay. It's my seat but I let them stay. You were nice to me. You said you'd move.'

Has she forgotten she called me spiteful? Or is this a subtly spiteful way of reminding me? I throw her an understanding look, to be on the safe side.

'But . . . eh!' She hits the air with her little hand, as though to say, There are some horrible people in this world, Harold, if you exclude you and me.

Seeing another kiss coming, I back into the macaroons.

As the sun goes down on *Shabbes*, making it all right to be secular again, I take my seat at a lecture to be given by Rabbi Alony, entitled C'MON, FORGIVE ALREADY.

Lecture is the wrong word. Alony himself disowns it. 'I just want to share some thoughts with you. I'm not lecturing. I just want to share.'

Sharing for Alony means never having to lower your voice. He has pumped up his lungs for the evening. And is in demonstrative mood. He bawls individual hellos at us. Introduces people who arrive late. Bids them welcome. Insists they sit down. 'It's a thing I've got – a *mishegaas* – I can't bear to have people standing while I'm talking.'

Some of the people who arrive late he knows. Another rabbi.

The hotel astrologer. The social organizer. His own wife, to whom he publicly acknowledges debts of gratitude too multitudinous – I fear more sand and stars here – ever to repay. He loves her. She's his *neshomeleh* – his little soul.

There's something not right I think about his Yiddish. He keeps breaking out in it as though it's second nature to him, as though it lives at the very tip of his tongue; but it feels rehearsed and artificial, poorly pronounced, without either the comic or the mournful cadences intrinsic to it. To my ear his music is all wrong; his accent is all wrong; his pitch is all wrong; and his thoughts are all banal.

'Why do people do certain things in life?' he wonders.

We wonder, audibly, with him. Some of us even think we know.

He's pondering a recent case in which Woman A killed Woman B because Daughter B was chosen instead of Daughter A to be head high-school cheerleader. Contrary to everything I have ever supposed about America, this apparently isn't a common occurrence.

'Why do people do such things? Why? Why?' He is shouting again, throwing his head back, appealing to the curtains, to the light-bulbs, 'Why . . . WHY . . . WHY?'

A moment of calm. A moment to collect ourselves.

'I haven't got all the answers,' he goes on, just as I'm thinking that he hasn't got any of the questions, 'I wish I had. It's the $64,000 Question – what's it all about. Basically, people are the same everywhere. They have the same hopes, the same aspirations, the same fantasies, the same bubbles that burst . . . and you ask yourself in the end . . . WHAT'S IT ALL ABOUT?'

This is all preliminary to his theme. 'Don't . . . live . . . with . . . *baroygis*.'

Don't live with anger.

He has a story of a daughter who hasn't spoken to her father for eighteen years, and now he is dying of a heart complaint, and she doesn't know how to talk to him.

'Anger – see! Bitterness – see!'

We see. We know the situation. We've all got a father we haven't spoken to, out of *baroygis*, for eighteen years. We all *are* the father who hasn't been spoken to, out of *baroygis*, for eighteen years.

Alony goes biblical – folksy biblical. The story of Joseph and his Coat. He shrugs. A you-tell-me shrug. What's the *mishegaas* here? 'What's it all about? A coat? The father loves the son a bit too much. He wants to give him something nice. A coat. A coat of many colours. So? But the brothers get jealous. They want to leave him in a ditch. Then one of them decides to sell him and what happens? FOUR HUNDRED YEARS OF EXILE! All because of *baroygis*. FOUR HUNDRED YEARS. For what? Why do we do these things? Have we got nothing to eat? Haven't we got a bite? WHAT'S IT ALL ABOUT?'

Living. His new theme. Living is what it *should* be about. His voice rises unnaturally to that queer rabbinic nasality – that Sinai sinusitis – to which Jewish clergymen the world over are mysteriously subject. 'Living is pulsating. Living is great. Sorry, Mr Segal, who wrote *Love Story*, but living is having the vitality to say you're sorry.'

Why, I wonder, since we're on to whys, has Judaism descended into a folksy form of relationship-guidance counselling? On my first morning in New York, before catching the bus to Kiamesha Lake, I watched a Lubavitcher-sponsored television programme in which a comedic-philosopher rabbi, called Manis Friedman, exhorted me to 'go with the flow'. I was too rigid, he told me. I had a rigid idea of what love and marriage were about, and if they didn't measure up I said forget it. But what did I mean when I said that? What did I *think* life was all about? What had happened to looseness, flexibility, trust? Take it easy; take it easy – one *mitzva*, one good work, at a time. Then the television flickered and Manis Friedman's hour was up. But here I am again on the receiving end of Talmudic agony-aunt advice. Is this Hasidism at work? Proving that Judaism is more than just exegesis of the Torah? I twitch my Litvak antennae. I remember I am a *Mitnaged*, an opponent of things populist.

I notice that the cantor's wife – the one who is too glamorous for Esther's taste – has taken the seat in front of me. She has long blonde hair which has been sprayed with a fine mist. Many women here who are not cantors' wives sport the same look. It is as if you have been out walking in the early morning, immediately after a dawn-perm, and the dew has settled on you. A guileless dew. So it's a child-of-nature look, suggesting sky-kissed innocence as much as glamour. Maybe it's manna. Maybe this is how the wives of the children of Israel looked after they left Egypt. Maybe, in their hour of need, in the waste wilderness of Zin, in the howling Midbar, God leaned out and did their hair for them.

I return my attention to Alony and discover he too has God on his mind.

'What was the first response to God's ordering of Adam and Eve out of the Garden of Eden?' he is asking.

A large red-headed woman essays an answer. 'A primal scream.'

'Not a bad effort,' Alony concedes, but it's not the answer he's looking for. The answer he's looking for is – suicide.

He waits – as he has no doubt been taught to wait at rabbinical college – for our surprise to die down. Hit 'em with a near sacrilege, then placate 'em with a commonplace.

Mortified by God's verdict, Eve prepares to end it all. But God sends her the wherewithal to cry, a.k.a. a tear, newly crystallized in heaven. Saying, in so many words, 'What's the fuss? So you're losing paradise. It's not the end of the world. Cry. You'll feel better.'

Rabbi Alony's God has Rabbi Alony's gift for homely expression down to a T. 'Don't ... live ... with *baroygis*.'

Just as sand had the rabbi dashing between Bondi and Tel

Aviv the other day, so now God's invention of the tear has him tearing between laughter and dejection. So much activity plays havoc with his pronunciation. He blames the French existentialist writer Albert Camussss for our loss of zest for 'the sheer fun and frolic of life'. He reminds us of the number of synonyms for fun we can find in *Roger's Thesaurus* Useful bloke, Roger.

'What's happened to good old fashioned laughing? People are frightened to show their true feelings. Everything is plastic these days . . . your Visa card . . .'

We mutter our assent. We are tuned into banal maxims. We breathe them in, take deep gasps of them, like air. 'Beaudiful,' I hear someone near me exclaim, 'this is beaudiful.'

Alony lets the current of our enthusiasm bear him to new heights of nasality, like an eagle with a cold. 'Don't hold in your anger, ladies and gentlemen. Life is to be lived, life is to be loved, life is to be caressed, to be preserved, like a fresh stream in the forest.'

'Beaudiful, beaudiful.'

We are nearing the climax. We know we must be nearing the climax because wisdom cannot have many more depths to plumb. But the rabbi has one more mix of myth and *Midrash* for us.

God dispatches three angels to bring back from earth three objects 'which we don't have here in heaven'.

One brings a rose.

One brings a sunset.

One brings a baby's serenity.

But the rose withers by the time the angel gets it back.

And the sunset fades to dark.

And the baby . . .? Well, it cries and pulls a face, but the mother (how did the mother get here?) soothes and caresses it, and soon, soon, serenity returns.

Tossed in a sea of Ahs! I find fault with the story. I question the angels' flight time. Their ignorance of earthly transience. The inconsistency of their being instructed to bring back something heaven doesn't have with the choice, by one of them, of serenity – does heaven, then, not know serenity?

But, like all critics, I am out of step with popular sentiment. Better attuned – for does not 'rabbi' mean 'master' and does not a crowd love to be mastered? – Rabbi Alony launches himself into his finale. 'People who need people, in the words of Barbra Streisand, people who need people . . .'

There is no faltering, no hesitation. All around me singing breaks out. '. . . are the luckiest people . . . in the world.'

Trouble at the dinner-table.

Mini is sitting in a sea of protective tissues, asking Alex and Luis, neither of whom is replying, why her fish is so fishy. And Esther is demanding her seat back from the Leventhals, the realtors from Sacramento.

Saul is aflame with shame. If he could shrug himself invisible, he would. He is doubled up, grinding a hole in the table with his forehead, to disappear into. Out of the side of his face he pleads with his mother. 'What . . . are . . . you . . . doing?'

She? *She* is doing nothing. It's the demons and the *dybbuks* of the dining-room that are doing all the doing. They set on me, too, as I turn up late from Alony to behold this fracas, and they are the reason that, the moment the Leventhals move, I move with them, denying Esther my propinquity.

'Harold!' she cries with a dismay that would touch my heart were I not *dybbuk*-driven, 'you're not sitting in your seat!'

I make jokes about democracy, about going the rounds of the table, chair by chair, so that everyone can have a share of me. But Esther kissed me this morning, and showed me her leg, and this is her reward.

'He's not called Harold,' Mini says. 'His name's Howard.'

This is her revenge for Lui*ss*. It's war between them now.

'Harold, I'll kill you,' Esther says, and blows me a kiss across the table. It flies like a poisoned arrow.

Mini nudges me. 'Try the grapefruit. The grapefruit's good. You should try it.'

There is no horseradish on the table tonight. Esther calls Alex. He gives her red and walks away. Esther wants white.

'I want white!' she screams.

Mini tells the table she needs roughage. Roughage is good for her. She wonders whether squash make gas.

'Depends on you,' Jean Leventhal says. 'All depends on you.'

'I make a lot of gas,' Mini says. 'It's called diverticulosis.'

She looks at my fish. What kind of fish is that? Is it good? Hers was fishy. And fat. She's got to watch that. She can't have butter. 'Louis! This is butter – I gotta have margarine.'

'I want white horseradish!' Esther screams.

'Alex! Louis! I gotta have margarine!'

I turn to the Leventhals. Usually with the Leventhals there's the chance of conversation. They've been to university. They've made the great escape from the breast. But tonight the demons of the dining-hall have got them too. When they pause from the food it's only so that they can talk about the food. Have I tried the brisket? It's good. Have I tried the poppyseed cake? It's good. Have I tried the brisket and the poppyseed cake together?

The Leventhals have a daughter. Although she has been at the Concord for a couple of days, for the duration of six meals, I haven't yet seen her. She spends her time on the tennis courts or in the gym. She is just divorced, so she needs all the tennis she can get. She lives in Los Angeles now, where she teaches mime. Barney and Jean are hoping this week in the Concord with them will take her out of herself. Somehow or other I get the impression she is beautiful.

And now, quite unexpectedly, here she is. Swinging her California brown legs under the table. Dark. Intriguingly tragic. Sun-kissed. Mime isn't my subject, but I'll try anything that gets me off the verbalization of food. I lean towards her, just as Alex delivers her a plate of poached fish. 'Mmm,' she says. 'This fish – it's so go-o-o-d.'

I cannot go on swimming against the tide. I take in her fine, almost African, profile. She is what gentiles have in mind when they moisten their lips around the word Jewess. Her name should be Naomi, not Lesley. Yes, I decide. She is. Indubitably she is. Good enough to eat.

The Catskills may not be what they were, but at the Concord's Imperial Room you can still get to see Joan Rivers or Jackie Mason or the Diceman if you pick your week carefully. Coming for Rosh Hashanah is not what you call picking your week carefully. We get the comedian Jack Eagle and, as an hors d'œuvre, Holly Lipton, a voluminous *schmaltz-chanteuse*, seventeen stone of sequin and stiletto and what used to be called 'It', a movable feast of thighs and breasts and belly wrapped, like the cakes Mini smuggles from the table, in a confection of drapes and gauze. A *bar-mitzvah* dress, I suppose you have to call it, for many a boy has read his portion of the law while his mother weeps in an outfit such as this.

I find myself, in the showtime dark, at a table next to Beverley, who claims she has her own cable TV show interviewing people 'in the news'. I have seen her about the hotel, wearing Huck Finn trousers that stop half-way down her calfs, and end in fringes. A sixty-five-year-old river urchin. Tonight, she tells me, because it is too dark to see, she is wearing a slinky number, very short skirt, slits in the sleeves. Why not? She is a widow. No kids. Believes in taking a positive attitude to life.

She whispers in my ear – I face the stage, she faces me – beating out phrases of hot breath in time to Holly Lipton's music. Her earrings clink against my cheek.

Holly herself has come down from the stage and moves amongst us. She brushes past an elderly man. 'You Jewish?'

What does she think? This is the Concord, isn't it.

'Then leave my breasts alone.'

We all laugh. Beverley bitterly. It's a joke that runs deep. Only gentile breasts are made for playing with.

After a medley from *Cats* – oh, my people, my people, what will you applaud next? – Holly Lipton wishes us a good new year, a happy Rosh Hashanah, and delivers us a message: 'Just go for it.'

Beverley is telling me how she fell in love on the QE2, but her husband wouldn't give her a *get*. A *get* is a religious divorce, something you must have if you want to remarry in a synagogue. She was wildly in love, more than a shipboard romance, but her husband wouldn't give her the *get*. So she gave up the man. Then her husband died. The story of her life.

But at least she's going for it tonight.

Jack Eagle, the comedian, tells jokes about food. After eating and talking about eating, we're now laughing about eating. Tomorrow, while we're eating, we'll be talking about laughing about eating. Where Holly Lipton was the quintessence of all that is woman in the Concord, Jack Eagle is paradigmatic Borsht Belt man. He is short and barrel-chested. When he goes to buy a suit they measure him and say they've got nothing for him. 'You're toddler 44, sir.' One thousand five hundred toddler 44s in the audience throw back their heads and go purple.

Forget about those tall, blond, blue-eyed guys, he tells the women, they're only interested in other tall, blond, blue-eyed guys. Besides, they've got no balance. They fall off the bed. Whereas, whereas, girls, put a little fat toddler 44 in the middle of your mattress and he'll stay there.

We laugh at that. Beverley bitterly.

Jack Eagle's material is even-handedly offensive, as befits a comic. First the enemies of the Jews – 'That Yasser Arafat, with his sheet on his head, that's what I'd like to do to him: *sheet* on his head.' Then the Jews themselves – 'You seen those Hasids?

Their women are so plain, if they held a beauty-contest no one would win. And they're always driving so fast. You know where they're going? To get their *tzitzits* cleaned. Hey, did I just hear someone laugh? I drop a word in Yiddish and you respond; that's unusual for the Catskills these days.'

But I'm thinking it might not be such a good idea telling jokes about the way Hasids handle cars, just two days after the Israeli kid in the Lubavitcher Rebbe's entourage, who knocked down and killed a black child, is acquitted of dangerous driving. A sudden reminder that I once did have a life outside the Concord. That I was once a cautious English Jew who worried whether saying such-and-such or such-and-such was such a good idea. Jews in America are not so frightened. They show their heads above the parapet. But I am still taking cover, despite – or is it because of – what Beverley is doing with her earrings against my cheek.

Trouble at the breakfast-table.

When it's all over, Esther hisses at me, 'Harold, I could kill you.'

'Why?'

'Because I love you.'

But she mouths to me, 'Because it's your fault.' And to the Leventhals, 'He took sympathy on her.'

But all I did was ask Mini why she was holding her arm rigidly in front of her, as though saluting the President and Vice-President of the United States. I am not to be blamed if she told us.

'You need heat on it,' Saul said.

Mini disagreed. 'I need ice.'

'My son's a doctor,' Esther put in. 'If he says you need heat, you need heat.'

'Heat! Where am I gonna get heat here?'

In the dining-room of the Concord this sounds like a complaint. 'Alex! Louis! Get me *heat!*'

As a consequence of which, neither Alex nor Luis came near our table for the whole of breakfast, leaving us with nothing to eat but baked herring, fried herring, pickled herring with cream sauce, lox, brisling sardines, boneless sardines, Mueslix, Raisin Bran, Cheerios, matzo, griddle-cakes, grape jelly, strawberry preserve, honey, cream cheese, cottage cheese, Muenster cheese, and cold coffee.

Otherwise, it's a busy social Sunday morning. Busy, but not fast. We are heavier and more sluggish than when we arrived. Those who came emaciated have puffed out nicely. Those who came puffy are catching their breath against walls. Those who came in Zimmer frames are now in wheelchairs. Lourdes must look like this at weekends.

Outside the dining-room, people are examining slides of last night's photographs. Dozens gather round a table and put little squares of plastic to their eyes, and laugh.

In the library, Gus Carayas is giving a mini-seminar entitled THE SENSUOUS SPINE. The wheelchaired are the first to arrive to hear him. Gus Carayas practises and purveys the Carayas Technique. He is flexuously vertebrate, wearing the moustache you would expect, and the sleeveless blue singlet you would wear yourself if you looked like him. He is accompanied by anatomical charts and a skeleton. He has a phrase for the condition most of us are in: 'Living physiological rigor mortis.'

No one has the strength to argue.

'You have taken the foundation of everything you do in life,' he tells us, 'and you have stopped it performing its prime function.'

Next door, Morris Katz is painting a painting in five seconds flat. Morris Katz is listed in *The Guinness Book of Records* as 'the most prolific painter in history', with over eighteen thousand paintings painted and sold to date. Only Picasso comes close.

'Paint fast, sell cheap' is his motto. Morris Katz's motto, that is, not Picasso's. And it seems to be working. In the time it takes Gus Carayas to explain how a single muscle dies, Morris Katz has whipped off a *shtetl*-full of melancholy rabbis, a six-picture series of Hasidic fiddlers leaping into complementary corners of the canvases, a couple of Jerusalem dreamscapes, and a specially commissioned dentist, all stretched, stapled, framed and raffled as we watch. 'Every work,' he guarantees us, 'has its own personal integrity.'

The legend WORLD-CLASS PAINTER is printed across his shirt. 'You make a bid,' he invites us, in an accent which is both Polish by birth and Polish for comedic effect, 'and I'll up yours ... UP YOURS!'

The same people who laughed like drains at Jack Eagle's airless and ill-favoured *frummies* now purchase sentimental likenesses of them to hang on the walls of their condominiums.

Never presume to know a Jew by what amuses him. Or by what makes him cry.

See how juicy we look, we Jews, this Rosh Hashanah morning. A new year, another twelve months of temptation, and we are up and about early in our Sabbath best, ready, braced, as plump as summer fruit. The young women, round and oily, hoicked up on to their heels, loving the height, the precariousness, the danger. And the young men, soft and dark, wearing their prayer-shawls slung insouciantly over one shoulder, the defence-forces of Judaism. So juicy. Now I know why their fathers, who wrap their *talaysim* tightly around them, like winding-sheets, seem always to be as dry as Passover cakes. In their youth they over-expended their sap.

No side conference-room doubling for a synagogue this morning. For Rosh Hashanah we gather to hymn the Vowelless One in nothing less than the Imperial Room itself. Where Holly

Lipton heaved her breasts there now stands an Ark of the Covenant, a choir, a conductor, a cantor and Rabbi Alony.

I miss the first half of the service in admiration of my people's
juiciness and because I am distracted by a row going on between
half the congregation and whomsoever you blame when things
aren't right. The issue is prayer-books. There aren't enough. It's
a scandal – I actually hear that word: SCANDAL. Congregants
pound the aisles. Peer covetously at prayer-books in other
congregants' laps. 'You finished with that?' someone asks me,
the second I look up from the page. Not a pretty sight, a congregation that would be holy but is denied access to the Word.

A shrug – *the* shrug – starts to do the rounds, passes down one
row and up another, like a fire taking out a forest, a line at a
time. 'No books! Rosh Hashanah and there are no books!' We
throw our hands in the air and jolt our heads into our shoulders
with so much ferocity it's a wonder we don't break our necks.
There are shrugs and shrugs. 'Shrug it off,' we sometimes say,
remembering that the shrug can be a gesture of forgetfulness and
indifference. That's a different shrug. *This* shrug is an eternal
flame. Never forget. Never forgive. Live, live in exasperation for
ever and ever, amen.

By the time I have regained my concentration, Rabbi Alony is
telling a joke. The great plastic Ark of the Covenant is closed;
the flags of Israel and the United States hang solemnly on either
side of the *bima*, the pulpit; wherever there is room to stick a
Star of David a Star of David has been stuck; the Imperial Room
is full to overflowing, three thousand souls, running with the
juices of redemption – and Rabbi Alony tells a joke.

There is this miser. Bets ten dollars a day on the lottery.
Ten dollars a day, every day. Then he wins ten million dollars.
His wife finds out before he does. His heart is weak. How does
his wife break the good news without also breaking his heart?
Goes to the rabbi, saying, 'Rabbi ...' (Funny, how often in
these stories the ungodly consult a rabbi.) 'Rabbi ... his heart is

weak ... you tell him ... but be careful ... if you're too sudden, it'll kill him.'

So the rabbi calls the miser. 'I hear you bet on the lottery,' he says, gently, gently.

'Every day,' the miser tells him. 'Every day I bet ten dollars.'

'And what would you do,' asks the rabbi, 'if you won ten million dollars?'

'Rabbi, I'd give it all to the synagogue,' replies the miser. 'Every dollar.'

And the rabbi dies of a heart-attack.

We love it. The Rosh Hashanah joke. And Alony loves it that we love it. There is even a trickle of applause, as if we have forgotten where we are and think it's the Freddie Roman Show.

Alony smiles and shows us the palms of his hands. Caring/sharing. Sharing/caring. And after the humour, the *schmaltz*. We say goodbye to the old year (Goodbye, Alony) with all its faults, and welcome in the new year with apple and honey. Sweetness. 'May the coming year be sweet to you.'

We taste it from his lips, the apple and the honey. A sweet, rabbinic kiss, from him to us.

It's a gift we don't all have, I must not deny it, the gift of being able to kiss three thousand simultaneously, with a single pucker.

When the service resumes I find myself exactly where I was all those years ago, when I last put on my suit for Rosh Hashanah. Still the words slip by; Hebrew and English alike, still they won't adhere. Baffling, these hopeless, repetitive yearnings for a King who is apparently crucial to my faith but who, in American English anyway, seems suspiciously to belong to another. Who is this King, unto whom there is no one like? It's all too Christian. We are just inches from Redeemer-talk.

Only one line will stick for me. 'And iniquity shall shut its mouth.' The rest glide Christianly by.

We are supposed to be people of the Book. Words are meant

to be our strong suit. But all I can find in the High Holy Day Prayer-book is hysteria and weeping: 'There is none like our God; there is none like our Lord; there is none like our King; there is none like our Deliverer'; and acrostics – 'According to the Cabbalists, the forty-two words of this poem represent the name of God, which is composed of forty-two letters.'

Nothing in the liturgy gives greater proof of the rabbinic idleness into which intellectual Judaism declined than these holy mathematical ingenuities. 'There are 245 words in the *Shema*. When the reader repeats . . . the number of words is raised to 248, corresponding to the 248 parts of the human frame.' To go searching for God in numbers is the price you pay for too long an exile from the world of flesh and blood. I fear this Judaic passion for abstruseness and distortion the way some men fear an hereditary disease.

It is music, at last, that draws my attention from the footnotes. The cantor, whose wife is too dewily attractive for Esther's taste, sobs like Mario Lanza. The choir is more restrained and therefore, in the end, less Jewish. We are all pulling in different directions. Only the blowing of the *shofar*, the ceremonial ram's horn, unites us. No Jew, however lost, is deaf to the power of this ancient mountain reveille. Some difficulty in the sound, some reluctance in the instrument to yield sound, some obstruction in the blower and the blown – whatever the special obduracy of the music is, it's Jewish. And today it is commemorating the birthday of the world, awakening us to another year of God's creation, calling us, like a goatherd, to the resurrection.

We murmur as one after the blowing of the *shofar*. It has taken something animal to make us human.

Later in the day, it will take something human – Mini's need for a bread roll – to make us animal. But first there is *Tashlich*, to cleanse us of our sins.

You need water for *Tashlich* – 'And thou wilt cast all their sins into the depths of the sea' – and this is where Kiamesha Lake, whether you pronounce it as Yiddish or as Iroquois, comes in handy. We troop out of the hotel, with Alony at our head, past the gymnasium and the forty tennis courts, all quiet today, feeling for the symbolic crumbs in our pockets, the sins which we will sprinkle on the lake, for all the world like pagans placating the demons of the sea.

No doubt it was the routine paganism of the custom – now you're a sinner, now you're not – that caused the Jewish school-men of the Middle Ages to discourage it. Only recently, in an age that likes to collect religious practices, has it returned to favour. You can see why it goes down well at the Concord. Or would go down well at the Concord were there not quite so much mud at the fringes of Kiamesha Lake.

A woman I've been admiring all day, a baby-doll grandmother in a blue and white sailor suit, which incorporates a lacy choker for the neck and a matching lacy garter or, to be more exact, a garterlet, for the ankle, speaks for us all in our sinfulness. 'I ain't gonna ruin my shoes in this.'

There is another impediment to atonement. Tracks in the mud.

'Are these an animal's?'

'Sure are.'

'Pretty big animal.'

'Looks like a bear track.'

'A bear track!'

'You're in the mountains, honey.'

'Again I won't sleep tonight.'

A ripple of curiosity disturbs the lake: what kept her from sleep last night?

But at last Alony finds a wooden jetty, and there we gather in the grey light, like Swedes on the morning after a house-party of the soul, to empty our pockets of our transgressions.

When it is all over, the bread is gently borne back to the edge of the lake, where it gathers – little ovals of rye – and seems to flower like water-lilies.

It is New Year's Day, creation is five thousand and however many years old, and outside my room I hear two porters voicing the frustrations of gentile staff in *kosher* hotels the world over.

'D'you know what I'd give anything for? A pork chop.'

'Me too. I haven't had a pork chop in eight weeks.'

At the supper-table – for some of us the last supper of the stay – Mini is complaining that she hasn't had a bread roll for almost as long. 'Alex! Louis! Louis!' Unable to catch a waiter's eye, she expostulates with the air, her voice swaying like a suspension bridge in a gale. 'I keep asking the guy. What do you have to do to get a bread roll round here? Louis! Alex!'

Esther is beginning to glower. 'It's Luis. Lui*ss*.'

'I'm calling Alex.'

Esther blows me a kiss across the table. For Rosh Hashanah she has painted her lips into a perfect crimson O. The kisses she blows me stutter my way like smoke-rings of blood. 'How d'ya like this woman,' she hisses at me. 'She says she's calling Alex.'

Saul, though, is in expansive spirits. He has his New Year suit on. And a white *yarmulke*, to show he means to begin the next twelve months spotless. Next to him sits Lesley Leventhal, black like a handmaiden to a Pharaoh. Unable to play tennis or lift weights today, she has brought her sizzling limbs to dine with us. Mini once asked me, in reference to Saul's medical credentials, whether he is psychological or physical. Tonight, he is unequivocally physical. For Lesley he de-concertinas.

Hearing Mini still wailing for a roll, he rises, takes a bread roll from a serving-trolley, carries it over to Mini, and deposits it, with a flourish, on the pile of matzo and pumpernickel and sponge-cake she has already accumulated. It is a gesture at once gallant, ironic, exasperated, kindly and manful. Really, he is bearing a bouquet to Lesley. There is love in the roll. So we all expect Mini to enjoy the charade, accept the roll, wrap it in a tissue and thank him. But we have forgotten the precautionary measures Mini takes every time she sits down. We have forgotten Mini and germs, Mini and purity, Mini and mirthlessness.

'Hey!' she shouts. 'That's wrong. You shouldn't have done that. You shouldn't have used your fingers. That's wrong.'

'You don't talk to my son like that,' Esther seethes. 'You don't even belong to this table. You're only here because no one else would have you.'

'That's a nasty crack.' Mini's suspension bridge comes to grief in the tempest. Her voice vibrates like snapping cables. 'Did you hear that crack?' She appeals to me. 'Wasn't that a nasty crack?'

I notice that Lesley has taken refuge inside the darkness of her features. That Saul has turned the colour of his mother's lipstick. And that Esther is shaking her little nailless fists – one at Mini, one at me for talking to Mini. The *dybbuks* of the dining-room do not rest on Rosh Hashanah. I feel them lifting me from my chair, directing my hand to Mini's already contaminated roll, carrying me round the table to where Saul sits shrunken, and depositing the roll on to Saul's plate.

When I am my own again, I see that I am back in my seat and that no one is amused. Both of Esther's fists are now aimed at me. 'You know what, Harold?' Saul says to me. 'You're all air.'

This is the first time he has ever called me Harold.

But in the morning, over breakfast, we are all friends again. Mini cannot believe I only want coffee. 'How do you like this guy? He only wants coffee.'

They all want to know how I can only want coffee.

'Eat something. Have cake.'

And Esther is blowing me kisses. 'Harold,' she says, 'have you finished your book yet?'

69

'It's close,' I say.

In the evil pools of her eyes I see the reflection of last night's shame. 'Harold, I could finish it for you now.'

I laugh. Seeing me appreciative of his mother's malignant pleasantries, Saul gives me his card. 'Come and see us when you're in Brooklyn.'

'And when you're in Sacramento,' say the Leventhals.

'I got family in Sacramento,' Mini says.

If I am not mistaken, there are tears in our eyes when we take leave of one another. Was there ever a time when we did not eat at the same table? Will there ever be a time when we can eat in the company of someone else?

As I leave the hotel I catch sight of Saul, taking the air on his own. This is the first time I have ever seen him not in the company of Esther. And I notice that he walks with a perfectly straight spine. How many other hunchbacks, I wonder as I travel back to Manhattan, are hunched only in the company of their mothers?

Four

A LITTLE BIT CUCKOO

On a recommendation from the *Jewish Travel Guide*, published every year by the *Jewish Chronicle*, in London – 'one of the most colourful sights' etc. – I go for a Friday afternoon ramble through New York's Jewellery Exchange district to watch the Hasids come and go, talking of ... Well, not Michelangelo. More Maimonides. But what rhymes with Maimonides?

> On 47th street the Hasids take their ease,
> Talking of Maimonides

– except that ease is the last thing they take. They bounce and lope and dart, dodging traffic, dodging one another's cigarettes, in and out of the exchanges, which are organized like the Chelsea Antiques Market, labyrinths of booths where you can get a stone set or buy a single earring.

Business is slack. Hence the eyes that find yours, through window panes, even before you've decided you mean to enter. I am pleased that it is not the Jewish jewellers who pounce. In the main the Jewish stall-holders – who are not Hasids but have Hasids as their customers – are too busy with their cholesterol-free salads, or with their Hasids, to be interested in you, who are clearly not a dealer. As usual, it's your own people who most make you feel excluded.

An American-Chinese girl with broad Mongolian cheek-bones and a wrist full of silver bangles rattles herself at me. If I were a Red Indian I'd give her Oregon, but as I'm from London I have nothing to swap.

'London. How nice. Maybe you'll take something back.'

I explain, pompously, that I am here to take back only impressions.

'OK,' she says, since there's nothing else doing, 'let me give you mine.'

And she does. Whatever I want. Business? Slow. Hasids? She corrects my Hebrew – should be Hasidim. But OK, if I'm trying to put a bit of western air around what is already eastern enough, that's fine by her. So where were we? Hasids. 'Well, we don't deal with them. That's because they don't deal with us. We don't sell to many Jews, if you want to know the truth. They go to their own regular dealers.'

Do I detect criticism? Sniff. Sniff. Like a beagle on the scent of a hare, I'm after it. Attitude.

But no. Wrong again. 'We all respect one another here. We all get on with it.'

Maybe it was my own attitude I was smelling. I hate to hear that my people are still keeping themselves separate. We have a ritual word for it: *Habdala*. Separating what is Sabbath from what is not Sabbath; what is light from what is dark; what or whom is chosen of God from what or whom is not. The Jews are so separatist, one of us has said, we will not even mix metaphors.

Back on the street I Hasid-watch once more. And am struck by:

How tall they can be.

How burly.

How sexually vain.

How many ways there are of wearing *payess*, the sideburn-locks which advertise the separation of the very devout from merely the devout:

(In ringlets curled forward.)

(In ringlets kept to the rear.)

(In ringlets wound around the ear.)

(In ringlets wound partly around the ear.)

(In ringlets wound and wound again, tightly around the ear, so that from a distance the *payess* resemble a terrible aural growth, something that has crawled *out* of the ear and means to take over the entire face.)

How many ways there are of wearing the hat over the *yarmulke*, whether the intention is to conceal the *yarmulke* or to offer enticing glimpses of it.

How many ways there are, since we are speaking of enticements, of having the fringes of the *tzitzits* hang out of the pants.

How frail they can be.

How white.

How lithe.

How nervous.

How quick.

But in *all* cases, how soft and red and even feminine their mouths are, like the insides of a pomegranate. And what a shocking contrast that red softness makes with the prophetic beards and the dark suits and the jewellery boxes and the intense business purpose.

Juicy Jews – even here on 47th Street, between 5th and 6th.

Do I mean *even* here, or *especially* here?

Perhaps what's shocking is me – my innocence. That's to say, the innocence of my expectations and requirements when it comes to what is holy. I am shocked by how much and how publicly they smoke. I am shocked by how frequently their attention is seized by what is not divine. I like to know where I am with people: they are pious or they are not. And if they are pious, I like them *only* pious.

I watch to see if they are an object of exceptional interest to anyone else. They are not. The parcel-vans neither dodge them nor aim at them. The taxis are equally democratic. The cops come and go. Blacks come and go. Hispanics come and go. And so do the Hasids. This is as much a Jewish street as it is anything else. I see a sign pointing to Radio City Synagogue. On the

73

mezzanine floors of the exchanges there are *glatt-kosher*, that is *über-kosher*, nosheries. This is Hasid country. The only person watching them is me.

I am beginning to feel conspicuous, an enemy to my own people, and I am on the point of putting away my notebook and leaving, when I catch the strains of decidedly *glatt-kosher* music, something in the style of '*Hava Nagila*' only without the subtlety, coming either from a ghetto-blaster turned up to full volume or the public-address system of an ice-cream van. It turns out to be a Mitzva Tank, one of the several dozen rented trucks which the Lubavitcher Rebbe has ordered to tour the fleshpots of Manhattan with the intention of luring lapsed Jews back to Judaism.

Just in case the music is not enough of a lure, the rebbe has also ordered the liberal use of exclamation marks. TEFILLIN ON BOARD! the truck proclaims. And, L'CHAIM! TO LIFE!

Not only are we people of the Book, we are people of the Exclamation Mark. This comes from having a God whose first words were in the imperative mood – LET THERE BE LIGHT!

The Mitzva Tank is parked directly outside the Diamond Horseshoe. Which is hard on the jewellers within, who may not want to hear Hasidic melodies played through speakers capable of recognizing only two notes. At a second-floor window across the street a bunch of Hispanic kids has appeared to protest against the noise. They are trying to listen to a horse race or a baseball game on the radio, but they can't hear past the Mitzva Tank. A wonderful reversal of who is usually drowning out whom.

From the back of the Mitzva Tank a small army of Hasidic boys dismounts and scatters. Each is armed with Messianic literature – HELPING TO BRING MOSHIACH; FROM EXILE TO REDEMPTION; MOSHIACH – BE A PART OF IT! *Moshiach* is the Messiah, who may or may not be resident in Brooklyn at this very hour. But whether he is or he isn't, his decision to reveal himself will depend on enough Jews putting on *tefillin*.

It's the Hasidic boys' job to scour the streets for those very un-*tefillined* Jews who are keeping the rest of us Messiahless. But they are too young for the task. They lack the nous merely to tell a Jew from a non-Jew. I know, because they swarm past me, although I'm lingering suggestively, and pick on black postmen and drunken Irishmen to ask, 'Are you Jewish? When did you last lay *tefillin*?'

Enthusiasm gets you a long way, but there is no substitute for experience.

At last, on my twentieth circuit of the tank – short of humming '*Hatikvah*', I don't know what else to do – a ginger Hasid with a broken accent accosts me. Am I Jewish? When did I last lay *tefillin*? Will I lay them now?

I tell him I am here to observe, not to lay.

'Does that mean you're not Jewish?'

He's Israeli. He's been here four years, studying. I wonder that he, an Israeli, has come to study Judaism in America. Shouldn't it be the other way round? He shakes his head. It's a *mitzva*, he tells me, to be close to the Rebbe. Holiness-wise, Messiah-wise, Crown Heights is where it's at.

He is excited by the number of people who are turning up from all over the world this weekend – the last weekend before Yom Kippur – to see the Rebbe. I tell him that I intend to be among them. That I too mean to collect a dollar from the Rebbe's own, aged hands. In which case, he reminds me, I should be preparing for the experience by leathering-up. He's not pressing – he'll do me in the street if I don't fancy climbing aboard the truck – but my time is running out.

I thank him. His eyes blink with that dry melancholy common in ginger people, a postponed sorrow that crosses the species divide as unmistakably as does a cat's. The bond that I feel with all Jews, even ecstatic ones, is loosed only when they're ginger. Though we are not together, we shake hands. But I cannot tell which of us feels sorrier for the other.

Now that I am not waiting for them to notice me, I have the leisure to take in the teeny-proselytizers. They are not an engaging sight. I follow the progress of a little fat one, as he badgers Puerto Ricans about the last time they put on *tefillin*. Like the criminally obese at the Concord, he is already distorted from the hips down. His feet turn outwards, his knees point in, locked together. He wears dirty Reeboks, but can barely walk in them. Fringes dangle from his shirt. On his way to hector a Tibetan monk he espies a man selling snakeskin belts from a cardboard box – three for five dollars. He stops, with his mouth open, and stares.

'Talk to me in Hebrew,' the man says to him. 'You should have more Hebrew.'

But the kid's only got Brooklyn. And would love three snakeskin belts.

I ponder buying him a set, in return for a promise that he will never again be so impudent as to ask grown men what they believe. But it occurs to me that he might not actually know what the snakeskin belts are. It's possible he thinks they're fancy *tefillin*.

Apart from the Hispanics in the second-storey window, who can't hack the racket, nobody is making it difficult for the Mitzva Tank commandos. No one minds being stopped. Most people, Jewish or not, politely accept the literature. I marvel at the tolerance. And even begrudge it the Lubavitchers, for they are granted what they cannot themselves grant.

In accordance with which thought, one of their own, one of their *nearly* own – a tall Hasid who is obviously not Lubavitch – pauses, looks at the tank, looks at who's manning it, and proclaims authoritatively, 'Too loud!' He shakes his head and walks off, muttering '*Meshuggeners!*' to himself.

So that's two instances of intellectual disapproval I've counted. One from him and one from me. And we are both Jews.

*   *   *

76

Because I can't go on circling the truck and then refusing the truck's services, and because, for all the exclamation marks, nothing much is really happening here, I tear myself away and go in search of something neither *kosher* nor *glatt-kosher* to eat.

But just in case – I don't know just in case of *what* – I return a couple of hours later, as the tank is preparing to beat the *Shabbes* traffic, and see an odd and unexpected sight. A Jewish tramp. A Hebrew trash-and-can collector, big and bent, wearing a *yarmulke*, and a T-shirt which bears the legend USED, and track-suit pants which are too short – stylized too short – and one red sock and one green sock, and baseball boots. These too are stylized. This is a trash-and-can tramp with style as well as faith.

He is a bear of a man with a big round soft face, and spectacles.

I overhear him haranguing a cop. 'I didn't like what he said – "A Jew should be seen but not heard." I didn't like that.'

He's running to keep up with the cop.

'You shoulda punched him,' the cop says.

'Yeah – then you'd have locked me up.'

He stops the conversation, even though that means losing the cop, because he has seen a can going into the trash-bin. He lowers himself into the bin like a hungry grizzly raiding the suburbs. On the way up he finds that he is looking into the eyes of a couple of black city dudes.

'Go back to Brazil,' he says. They laugh. He laughs. 'Poison darts,' he says. 'The kind dames use.'

I don't so much as start to figure out what that means. Sometimes you just have to accept that you're in a foreign place.

He is about to slip into one of the jewellery exchanges but is spotted by a security guard. He exaggerates changing his mind, and bounds down the street, arguing with everybody.

I switch my attention to a vaudeville-prophetic figure, a regular Jewish old-timer with a mission, a cross between George Burns and Isaiah. 'Don't burn your money,' he calls out to a smoking Hasid. 'Don't get drunk,' he shouts into the window of a bar. 'You Jewish?' he asks a group of Hispanic construction workers. 'Me neither,' he laughs.

He's got my disease, the Lubavitch disease, the street disease. You Jewish? You Jewish? You Jewish? Jew Jew Jew . . .

I observe a trio of Hasids dodging a police horse. They look horrified as it backs towards them. Mere mortal fear, or *halachic* terror, ritual angst? Is it permissible, according to Torah, to be touched by the wrong end of a horse on the eve of *Shabbes*, when your hands have been in contact with jewellery?

I scoff at Hasidic instability but I can scarcely claim stability for myself, out here on Jew watch. Jew Jew Jew . . . I espy the jew in jewellery. Jew Jew Jew . . .

Suddenly, a commotion in the vicinity of the impure horse. A man has gone down on the sidewalk. A fit. There is a woman bending over him, resting his head on her Filofax, stroking his cheek.

A crowd forms in seconds. A perfect circle. An instantaneous colosseum. No one does anything. The cops just look. One rings for an ambulance on his walkie-talkie. The young man on the sidewalk is devoid of all colour. He writhes and foams. The cops watch. The Hasids watch. The horse watches. I watch. The can-collecting Jew returns and wrings his *yarmulke* – still arguing with a cop. It's as if he warned this was going to happen.

I feel unaccountably upset. Or maybe it's not so unaccountable. A hot day in the Jew and Jewellery district of New York. A crowd brutally mixed and curious, without any stabilizing culture, without any common attitude or humanity save tolerance – you do your thing, I do mine – and without, it would seem, any knowledge of first aid. (The woman is still doing it all herself.) And something about the horse, something about the horse and the mad Jew, adds to the upset. The tragedy of too few words, and the tragedy of too many.

In the end, one of the cops decides the crowd around the

foaming man is too big. Too big even for Manhattan's diamond quarter. He uses his horse to describe a clearing circle; and because what he is doing resembles an exercise in a military tattoo, another crowd assembles to watch it. But finally both crowds are dispersed. The man comes round. Looks up. And cannot make any sense of where he is.

He is not alone. In tears, in *near* tears, I leave the scene and flag down a cab. And guess what? The driver is Jewish.

Russian Jewish, to be precise. Mikhail Polonsky.

I give him an address but tell him I don't really know where I'm going.

'Neither do I,' he says.

'I'm new to the city,' I say.

'Me too,' he laughs.

He's from Leningrad. Been here a couple of years. So he's one of those who can thank Gorbachev for his freedom. But why here and not Israel? He's surprised I cast the question in that form. Here is where Russian Jews want to be. The problem for many is that America is not able to take them. His friends have had to go to Israel. (*Had* to go?) And he is feeling cut off from his old connections. As soon as he's made a bit of money, that's what he'll do with it – take a vacation in Israel to see his friends.

And is he pleased to be here?

He shrugs. He has an engaging smile. Russian warmth and all that. And Russian silver in his mouth, the work of Russian dentists. He is an engineer, he tells me. I am not surprised: was anybody who has left Russia ever anything else? But now he has to drive a cab. That's not so terrific.

I ask about Brighton Beach, the neighbouring suburb to Coney Island, once home to the humour of Neil Simon and Woody Allen, but now known as Little Odessa. Mikhail Polonsky doesn't like it. Ukrainians go there.

79

Aha, I say, do I detect some social finessing here?

That could be a difficult sentence for a Russian who has only been in America for two years, but he gets it, and throws me a silvery smile through his driving mirror. Leningrad was a city of culture, he would have me know. He is used to theatre, opera. Being Russian does not have to mean strolling the boardwalk in your shirt sleeves, spitting out sunflower seeds.

(So *that's* what I'm going to find at Brighton Beach.)

I ask him about his Jewishness. He tells me that he sends his son to *yeshiva*, which in this country need not mean rabbinical college but simply a school where things Hebrew have primacy, and after that he will see. If his son turns out to be a believer, well and good. As for him, he can't believe in any god; it's too late. There have been too many years of enforced disbelief. Going to synagogue two or three times a year is enough. But he wants me to understand that he likes it when he does go. He likes covering his head and shoulders and rocking from side to side. He performs the ritual while we're driving through Central Park. 'Rocking – like this.'

We discuss Yom Kippur, and the great test of whether you really are a disbeliever when you say you are. Yom Kippur sorts atheist men from agnostic boys. Is he the lost Jewish soul he says he is, apart from rocking twice a year, or will he go without food that day? Is he, like many Jews who hedge their bets, a closet faster?

He is evasive at first. He says it was only Pesach and Rosh Hashanah that he kept in Russia. But then he flashes me one of his silvery grins. 'I won't eat,' he says.

I am surprised to learn that although he must be six or seven years younger than me, and grew up in circumstances far less propitious to Judaism, he speaks Yiddish. His family kept it alive so that they could talk among themselves and not be understood. 'A secret language,' he explains.

The secret language of the Jews. A light kept burning

underground during all those years of atheism. I'd be touched if I wasn't alarmed. For where people speak a secret language, how can suspicion and fear of them not multiply?

We are both sorry when we get to where I'm going. 'This is good for me,' he says. 'I get no chance to practising my English.'

I'm upset again. It's one of those upsetting days. After I leave him I wonder why I didn't get him to drive me round and round and round Manhattan while we talked. It would have been good for both of us.

Hoping to drive out the upset of the day with ugliness, I sit up late in my hotel room and search for porno on the television. Some Nordic filth would do the trick, a bunch of Germans playing out their primordial arrestation in the urethral.

But there is to be no escaping my subject. When I finally locate the noxious channel it is to see Al Goldstein, editor of *Screw Magazine*, putting a finger up to the screen and saying, 'Fuck you!' This preparatory to his more general theme tonight, which is why Jews can't be like the Mafia and be called, say, Al the Mouth.

'I'm Jewish, so I don't have a nickname. Jews don't have nicknames. Well I wanna fuckin' nickname. I wanna be Al the Kike. That's what's wrong with these Hasids. That's why there are these fuckin' troubles at Crown Heights. (And fuck you too, brother.) You show me a Hasid with a nickname and I'll show you a Hasid with a scar down his face.'

The oblivion I sought in unindividuated zones and fluids won't come. Instead I must hit the pillow wondering why Jews think it's so funny to say, 'I'm Jewish,' whether they add 'And fuck you' or they don't. The comedy – the comedy to *them*: the comedy to *us* – must reside in the release, in the act of saying the unsayable.

Jew Jew Jew . . .
I go to sleep, counting Hasids.

It's been a steaming Saturday in the city. Mid-September but too hot to go out of doors. The news is all about record highs in temperature and record lows in relations between America and Israel. Bush has just postponed loan guarantees to Israel because Israel keeps putting up settlements in disputed areas to house the friends of Mikhail Polonsky.

If Bush won't guarantee the loan, the tens of thousands of Polonskys arriving every week won't have anywhere to sleep. If the Israelis don't stop giving the tens of thousands of Polonskys who arrive every week somewhere to sleep, Bush won't guarantee the loan. The epithet 'anti-Semite' or 'near anti-Semite' is beginning to be used of Bush in the Jewish papers.

I'm beginning to miss England, where no one's seen a Jew or heard of Israel.

By early evening the weather has calmed. Now it's just very hot. Ideal for a descent into the SoHo art-markets under the Virgil-like tutelage of Peter Schjeldahl, art critic for the *Village Voice* amongst others, and a friend in the sense that I once wrote about him admiringly and he doesn't know how to break it to me that I admire him for all the wrong reasons. It's a bit like Schweitzer keeping company with Hitler because he thinks he's a humanitarian, and Hitler not having the heart to disabuse him. Except that Schjeldahl is nothing like Hitler.

This is the beginning of a new term in the New York art world, so tonight's a big night. The first Saturday back at school after the summer hols. Where has everybody *been*? What has everybody been *doing*?

Peter is sleeked down, ready to move – an art critic to go – in charcoal pants and black suedes and a denimish shirt, open. The first time I wrote about him I said he reminded me of a younger and more Swedish Enoch Powell and had a voice that could be imagined calling the cards at an all-night poker game. He looks less like Enoch Powell tonight – more Donald Sutherland – but I can still hear the cards.

He propels me through the Village into SoHo, all the while discoursing on Lilith, the first wife of Adam. He mentions that he'd seen some work on Lilith and been struck by her potential for anti-heroine sexual-outlaw status – a possible for the fashionable reversal of good and bad. He'd mentioned this to a Jerusalem curator – you can now see why Peter has brought up this subject: he is writing himself into my book – anyway, he mentioned this to a Jerusalem curator who said, 'No – absolutely not. There is nothing, repeat *nothing*, to be said for Lilith. No playing fast and loose with morality here, no perverse deconstruction of the myth.'

But later Peter re-encounters an old flame, one-time wife of an Orthodox rabbi, but now a radical feminist academic lesbian for whom Lilith is, of course – of course! – a symbol of female power. Didn't Lilith refuse to adopt the prone position in congress? Wasn't Lilith created in the very same moment as, and absolutely independent from, Adam? Wasn't Lilith the avenger of female wrongs?

Hypocritically I raise the question of babies (for the myth also has Lilith devouring them in the night), and wonder whether a baby-eater can really count on much of a future in any lasting pantheon of womanly bravery. But Peter is no more swayed by this objection than I am. The whole point of an art world is that it's a place where you can forget about babies.

And art.

We slip in and out of lofts, Peter deliberately admiring objects of the slightest worth and lightest whimsy in order that I should be finally convinced that he is not the austere retroverted moralist I insist on taking him for. A pile of fibres, painstakingly extruded from a pillow, one by one, lies inert on a gallery floor, like a wig for someone leonine. (Norman Mailer?) On the wall are two crumpled pieces of A4 paper. Peter draws my attention to the astonishing effort and concentration that has gone into crumpling the two sheets identically – a crease here exactly matches a crease there; a bump, a bump; a fold, a fold; a contusion, a contusion. Wow!

On a little shelf a sculpture made of Lifesavers, glued together and sucked to effect a shape reminiscent of glued-together Lifesavers, sits in proud testament to infinite patience and nullity of thought.

'Hypnotic,' is Peter's verdict.

We brawl over minimalism. Peter likes what's left out. I like what's left in.

'What's left out can be more eloquent than what's left in,' Peter says.

'Silence may be a social virtue,' I say, 'but it does nothing for art. Art should teem.'

'Art should what?'

'Teem.'

'Teem?'

'Yeah. I'm a teemer.'

'That's because you're English,' Peter says.

I want to say, 'No, that's because I'm Jewish' – but remember that in this world Jews are busy shedding their proliferations, cooling their heat, making themselves less. It's a reason to be an artist, it seems, if you are Jewish, to simultaneously advertise yourself and shut yourself up. It's the aesthetic version of assimilation – becoming as silent as a WASP.

This could be why I take a step or two back whenever I meet Jews in the visual arts: because I fear their contribution will not be Jewish enough.

With Schjeldahl I at least know where I am.

'I came to New York to be Jewish,' he once told me.

'Did you make it?'

'No.'

'What were you before?'

'Porcelain-sink Lutheran.'

'And now? Since you haven't made it across as one of us?'

He paused. He wasn't sure he wanted to be *that* un-Jewish. 'A certain transformation has occurred; but a certain gulf remains.'

It takes me a little while to put it together – the fact that just about every gallery/space/loft we go into is run by a Jew. This isn't Jewish how I like it. This is slow-drawl, camp Jewish, retreating, high-toned, not very sense-of-humourish Jewish.

The pallid women gallery-owners whose walls and wine we absorb are also Jewish. Slips of things in black frocks the size of handkerchiefs. Black-haired – the perm a sort of metaphor for boredom. White-faced. Very, very red-lipped. And unamused. I cannot believe in such girls as gallery-owners. It's the brevity of their outfits. Where do they put their money? You feel you could blow them naked and penniless.

Ought I to understand them as an extension of the minimalist ethos? It's what they don't wear that's impressive.

Out on the street – for there are no cable-cars in SoHo as yet, connecting one loft to another – Peter runs into Mary Boone, a dealer almost as famous for making the painter Schnabel as for making herself. I notice with pleasure that we are standing outside Leo Fucking Castelli's Gallery – Leo Castelli, who is also famous for making Schnabel, having been made famous himself as Leo Fucking Castelli by an Australian art-dealer who referred to him in those terms no less than a hundred times in a single moon-drenched Venice night. Of such legends is the art world composed.

Mary Boone is diminutive, smiling, polished, the colour and consistency of a chestnut, wearing a figure-hugging purple silk suit (where does *she* conceal the takings?) and airing a little brown breast. All the girls are doing that in New York this steamy September: letting a little brown breast show. Not crudely, not in the old-fashioned prospect-down-into-a-canyon manner, but deviously, in silhouette or profile, through the gap between buttons or through a drastically foreshortened sleeve, so that you can, as it were, weigh it.

'You look terrific,' Peter says.

She smiles in agreement while I weigh the breast. About one ounce.

Since we keep running into the Jewish sculptor Joel Shapiro, and his wife, the painter Ellen Phelan, who isn't, we decide to sit the *danse macabre* out for half an hour and drink Negroni on the pavement. SoHo is all pavement restaurants at this hour. From the most unpromising doorways and alleys, tables are hauled out, laid with stiff linen tablecloths in a twinkling by waiters in stiff linen aprons, and, where there was nothing but empty street five minutes ago, now there is wine and conversation and food from French Martinique.

This is what I have come for – to eat, drink and talk amid the roar of the metropolis. This is what God always had in mind for us when he chose us. This is what Moses missed out on and I haven't.

Ellen Phelan has a high ironic tone, *de haut en bas*. She drawls out a sort of street-talk of the intellect. She has an air of looking at things as though they are all below eye-level for her. Save, of course, Schjeldahl (but then I've got him wrong), she is the drollest person I've met in SoHo. But I am unable to repeat any of the droll things she says because she has to go on living here.

Joel is more comfortably amused. Enjoying being middle-aged and successful. The highest felicity given to man. Or woman, for Ellen Phelan is enjoying it too.

We talk Jewishness. *I* have to work if no one else does. Joel isn't Jewish-Jewish. He comes from a political/philosophical/intellectual family, which held left-wing views if not actually Communistical ones. A background like that, he doesn't need to remind me, is hardly compatible with slavish Orthodoxy.

And he has married Ellen, an Irish Catholic. This is usually the way when Jews marry gentiles – it's a Catholic or nothing. Why bother with half measures? I tell him that I have married a Catholic myself. We order more Negronis and, so to speak, swap wives.

He doesn't go to the synagogue. But so that I shouldn't think he is completely beyond the pale, Ellen tells me that she has made a *Seder* – a Passover dinner – for his mother, who also comes for Christmas. But that, of course, only proves that *she* isn't beyond the pale. It's an observable fact of mixed marriages that when a Catholic woman marries a Jewish man the Catholic woman becomes more Jewish than the Jewish man. The point I was struggling to make the day before I left England, on radio with the Chief Rabbi: don't worry about the Jew that marries out. It's the Jew that marries in you've got to watch.

I know they are the wrong people to ask, but I ask them, anyway, to recommend a synagogue where I can find refuge and spectacle on Yom Kippur. Joel reckons the socialite Temple Emanu-El on 5th and 64th will take some beating, but it's members only on Yom Kippur and they'll be checking. We agree it would be a wheeze for me to be turned away by My Own People on the Day of Atonement. I give the idea serious consideration. Joel won't be going himself, but he enters into the spirit of my anticipated jubilant discomfiture. I try them with Leo Fuld – 'Tell me where can I go . . . Every door is closed to me . . .' But they are too high-toned for it. They think I've made him up.

Whatever he says about observances and ritual, Joel is at pains – no, that's too active for SoHo: he is moderately concerned – to have me understand that he doesn't for a moment consider himself not Jewish.

'I'm Jewish – there's no question about it. It's a fact. It's a fact of me and of my work. But I don't have to go to Temple Emanu-El to prove it.'

So we sit out in the SoHo night, a couple of Jews, a would-be

Norwegian Jew and an Irish Catholic whom any Jew not fringe-fixated would be proud to call his wife. Already, a tradition I would like to see initiated is coming to an end: Peter is not bothering with any more of these Saturday night openings, Joel neither; Tuesday afternoons are better, they agree, quieter. But I hold on to this sweltering Saturday night, sitting in the street, smelling French Martinique food, watching the bright young aesthetes and connoisseurs go by in their pocket handkerchief frocks, as a peculiarly *Jewish* thing to be doing. Right down to the denying of all but one's most basic, intractable, inalienable Jewishness.

We most are, when we most protest we're not.

And therefore we are most not, when we most protest we are.

Back at Schjeldahl's place, the Miss America competition is on television. When Miss Kansas appears, Peter confesses that he is in love. (*Now* will I see he's not a moralist!)

But Miss Honolulu – or is it Miss Hawaii? – lifts the title, and my evening with the country's most austerely exacting but now inconsolable art critic is over.

I have come by the name David Mikhailovich, and by his telephone number, through ringing up the Long Island Committee for Soviet Jews. I want someone who lives there to take me around Brighton Beach; and I want that someone to be Russian and Jewish and newly-arrived and English-speaking and articulate and good company. David Mikhailovich.

I take the subway.

That is not a sentence to deliver lightly. I have not on this visit, and I have never on any previous visit, taken the subway. Too terrifying. I have read the literature and I have seen the steam rising. I know what goes on down there. But today is

Sunday, and everyone says the subway is the most efficient and dramatic way of getting to Brighton Beach, and it's early enough for the muggers and rapists still to be in church, and, besides, I've locked my credit cards away in the hotel safe.

Leaving aside the rats on the rails – slow, fat and *kosher*-fed – the experience falls below expectation. The trains are clean. A happy family atmosphere prevails among the passengers. And when at last a crime does occur, it is characterized by urbanity and good manners all round.

The disturbance is quick and almost noiseless. A slender Chinese-American paterfamilias, off with his kids to Coney Island, is suddenly on his feet. A dapper, grey-haired man who has been sitting next to him is on his feet. It looks for a minute as if it's a nearly-fight – a staring-out, hold-me-back stand-off whose cause is a too careless collision. But the Chinese-American is startled, holding his wallet and, you could almost say, amused.

'C'mon,' he says. 'C'mon, c'mon.' He appeals to the train, showing us that something is missing from his wallet. 'Ten dollars!'

In return, the grey-haired man, respectably dressed in a clean white linen jacket (white!), shows us his hands. Empty. 'C'mon,' he says.

But a suspicious leather bag – suspicious because, well, suspicious – hangs over his shoulder.

'C'mon,' says the Chinese-American.

'C'mon,' says the dapper thief.

There is nothing the Chinese-American can do. He still has his wallet open, for us to see. He is still half-amused as well. He can't get over the thief's audacity.

And the thief, meanwhile, is off down the carriage, putting space between him and the crime, yet unmistakably scrutinizing our possessions. For all that he is protesting his innocence – 'C'mon, c'mon' – and, preparing himself for a quick exit at the next station, he cannot *not* look, intellectually, as it were rhetorically, for an easy pocket to pick. Platonic mugging.

Long after he has stepped on to the platform and disappeared in the crowd, we are still staring after him, mesmerized as much by our own impotence as by his effrontery. For the ripped-off oriental in the carriage we have neither time nor sympathy. In a go-get-'em society, the getters have more to teach us than the got.

The excitements of the city. I am exhilarated the second I get off at Brighton Beach. It may be Sunday but the shops are open and everybody's out. By everybody I mean the whole of Russia. You can smell borsht. You can smell the sea, too, and just see it, a block away. The train itself runs through the middle of the main street, not across it but *with* it, the tracks raised up so that you can choreograph car-chases underneath. It's a noisy, brutal, ugly intrusion into the life of the street, but energizing. Here is might. Here is movement. Here is the way in and the way out.

I am early for my appointment with David Mikhailovich, so I do the boardwalk. Given the choice, one would always do a boardwalk in preference to a pier or a prom. The word's more invigorating and so is the experience. From a pier you fish; from a prom you look out to sea and think of death; but along a boardwalk you bounce. You rattle the boards.

There is more life on the boardwalk than on the beach. This is partly the beach's fault. There are too many litter-bins on it. A nation should know that its trashphobia is out of control once it starts trashing its public places with trash-cans. But there is another reason why almost no one is on the beach here. This is Little Odessa. These people don't come from a beach culture. They don't have the clothes for it. I saw more nudity last night, in the serious art salons of SoHo.

The temperature is rising, but few concessions are made to the idea of aeration. The prevailing style is Americanized-peasant:

on the men, dark trousers, baseball caps made of heavy materials in heat-absorbing colours, striped or faintly floral shirts for going visiting in. On the women, turbans.

Under shelters on the boardwalk – and shelter from the sun seems to be what everybody wants – the men play dominoes on boards that are balanced on the backs of benches. The dominoes are slapped down, expressively, passionately, with a noise that resembles the striking of an opponent's face with a glove. This is how Greek and Turkish expatriates throw down cards in the cafés of whichever city in the world they've washed up in. I've seen Italians playing chess with the same venom on Clapham Common. You pound your sorrows out in parlour games.

Excluded from dominoes, old women fill up the benches on the boardwalk, their faces protected by umbrellas but the rest of them shamelessly exposed, manifestly enjoying sitting with their legs apart and their bloomers showing, which appears to be the supreme consolation of being old if you are a woman.

A few run-down Russian restaurants offer hamburgers and shashlik. I can see the Ferris wheel of Coney Island in the distance, like a mirage, a floating Jerusalem of old Jewish jokes and fast-talking Jewish comedians. It was in such places that a new Enlightenment was achieved for Jews just arrived from the Volga and the steppes. But we are starting again in Brighton Beach. Here the atmosphere is dour, suspicious, poor, rural.

A dead smell rises from the beach, where a family stripped down to vast bathing-costumes is trying to find room to lie out between the trash-cans.

I veer in my boardwalking and am nearly knocked down by a Russian woman in print drawers riding a tricycle. She laughs and says, 'Oooops!' in a Russian accent.

It's all vaguely circus-like and oafish. Were a bear suddenly to turn up playing a balalaika, I would not be bemused.

*   *   *

David is waiting for me, as arranged, at the junction of Brighton Beach and Coney Island, by a bank. I observe him, for a while, without knowing it's him, for he is accompanied by a woman, of whom there has been no mention. Left to our own devices, it's possible we will go on not knowing that we are each other; it appears to be the woman, at any rate, who makes the decision that I'm me.

David is not what I expected. Not bushy and silvery like yesterday's taxi-driver, and not knock-about Chekhovian like the boardwalkers of just now. He is trim, lean, handsome, compact, brown – brown in the way it was stylish to be brown ten years ago: stressed-out brown, tanned from good business-trips, tanned into the very furrows of your forehead, tanned deep into the bags under your eyes.

He wears an almost effeminately spotless, well-pressed pink shirt and fawn slacks and elegantly light, Italian-looking shoes, the kind you have to have dinky feet to even bother trying on.

The introductions are botched all round. 'Mr Jacobson?' he asks, and I say 'Yes' but forget to add 'Howard'. And he forgets to mention that there is a woman with him, and that she has a name, and I forget to remind him.

He points to a bookshop across the street. BLACK SEA BOOKSTORE INC. 'I thought we'd go there first,' he suggests, 'so you can ask any questions.'

This then is the reason for his uneasiness, if not for mine. He's been planning me an itinerary, and now he's anxious about whether he's planned me the right one. What did I want to know, he'd asked me on the phone. I didn't know, I'd told him.

It's a bit of a set-up situation – that's what's worrying us both. We're Russians, after all. We believe in spontaneity.

As we're about to cross the street the woman says, 'Excuse me. I haven't been introduced. I'm Margharita. He's some gentleman, this one.'

We laugh. He laughs. I laugh. She laughs. But we're taking

our time getting the fundamentals right, and as we cross the road, me in the middle, we collide into one another. This becomes a pattern which I get to like, me being bumped on both sides. I take this to be the famous Russian warmth and tactility. I even initiate some of it myself, rolling into them both as we negotiate the traffic, to show that I have Russian in me too, despite being a Litvak. With hindsight I acknowledge I may have given them a much more tactile time of it in the streets of Little Odessa than they are accustomed to.

Margharita is tall and good-looking in the Roman-nosed style of Eastern European. Romanesque, I suppose, is the word for her. But would-be *à la mode* Romanesque. She wears a white-and-black polka-dot dress, with a grand collar, hinting at cleavage but not delivering. She wears black stockings and high clicking shoes in polka-dot patent. Strappy shoes. Glamour shoes.

There is a dated air about her, as there is about him, but they are not generations out of it, they are just not of this very minute. Which makes them immediately likeable. Only the vapid know how to dress with precise contemporaneity.

Margharita's good looks owe much to the functioning of her intelligence. There is life in her eyes. There is mirth in the click of her heels. Very quickly she has taken over the prime social role; she is the one doing most of the talking; she is the one doing most to break down what is left of our social stiffness. Now we are in the bookstore, David is at a loss to remember why. As am I. But Margharita is pulling books off the shelves, telling me that she has no time to read Russian literature now, that she must give all her time to reading English; but whereas at home she would have read the classics, Tolstoy and Dostoyevsky and Pushkin, here she can manage only the lighter stuff. So she is on Danielle Steel at the moment. Her English teacher tells her that that's the best way to do it. I disagree with her English teacher, but don't say so. Give them Henry James, is my position. But then I am more out-of-date than David's tan and Margharita's patent polka-dot shoes. Out-of-date and passingly irked – I haven't come to the BLACK SEA BOOKSTORE INC in Brighton Beach to hear about Danielle Steel.

A woman working at the store is too embarrassed to talk. She has been in the United States only three months, and people asking questions still hold terrors for her. But a great, distantly smiling man of granite, a man seemingly made of elephant-hide, raps out some information. It's like a history lesson. Speaking highly formalized English, as though rehearsing his answers for an examination in the history of the Russian book trade in America, he tells me what it had never before occurred to me to wonder about.

'Largest collection of Russian language books in America. Imported from . . . by . . . now he is . . . millionaire . . .'

The noise he makes is perfectly synchronized with the movements of his lips, but it seems to be coming from another part of him. Maybe the same part that I'm listening with.

What I gather is that, largest collection of Russian books in America notwithstanding, not many Russians in Brighton Beach are interested in buying Russian books, because Russia is the past and their eyes are fixed on the future. Learning English, becoming American, is what they care about. Exactly like my great-grandparents. Fifty years from now there will be kids here astonished to discover that their families came from Odessa.

As with being Russian, so with being Jewish. It's not a priority. I notice a couple of shelves of Judaica, low down and hard to find. As far as I can make out, most of the volumes are published in Israel and few look as though they've been touched let alone opened. So is there no hurry, then, to catch up on all that Jewish culture which Soviet socialism stifled?

What I have to understand, David tells me, as we leave the shop, is that, for the majority of them, Jewishness has been an identity felt only negatively, a matter less of harbouring a faith than of living with a hindrance. I am not to mistake him: he is and always has been proud to be Jewish himself. But that pride has been partly obstinacy. You take pride in the stamp in your passport which limits your rights to travel, and your access to the highest institutions of learning (for there were always quotas on Jews), and your capacity to win promotion and trust. Since you have no choice, you become bloody-minded. That, though, is not to be confused with feeling the pull of Hebrew ritual at your heart. Being a Jew for David has meant being thwarted, not being a believer.

There is some bitterness in him. He is still a thwarted man. In Russia he was an engineer denied preferment; in America he is an engineer denied employment. It casts a long shadow, the Jewish stamp in his passport.

Out on the street we run into a little boy got up horribly in *yarmulke* and *payess*. Were he in a Thomas Hardy novel he would hang himself on account of being old before his time. How does David regard such demonstrative Jewishness as this? He pulls the face I would expect him to pull. The pink shirt and the Italianate shoes point to the limits of his interest in the Asiatic. But Margharita wants to chart a path of changed and still changing impressions: what it was like to encounter uncouth Orthodoxy for the first time, with Russian eyes, and what it is like now, seeing members of her own family flirting with it.

'First of all it is very funny. I felt I couldn't stop to laugh first of all. You know, in Borough Park they go without pants . . . just like a black stocking. It's funny. But now, I think, it's just . . . now I'm proud of them.'

'Proud?' I don't know who asks the question – David or me. Maybe we both do.

She answers us both, anyway, laughing and letting us take turns at falling into her.

'I am proud of them, yes. You know what? It's not easy to go like . . . I'm sorry . . . like a little bit cuckoo. Everybody makes fun of you but you don't care because it's your way and you respect yourself and you're religious and you're proud of yourself. I'm really proud of them. I can't be like them. I can't change myself now, but I try to grow a little more close to my people. I want to know as much as I can, you know. And learn, and really enjoy it. I am proud that I am not ashamed any more, like I was there. Very often it was uncomfortable, you know, to say that I'm Jewish. I always said so, because I wouldn't give a chance to people to say something bad about Jews. I don't really look . . . I mean my face is not very . . . specific like a Jewish face, and they started to tell me, "Oh, you know what Jewish people" blah blah, and I always used to interrupt them to tell "Sorry, Jewish people not . . ." But I didn't feel very comfortable.'

Meanwhile, she has a son and a nephew both going to *yeshiva*. And becoming Orthodox? I cannot disguise the eagerness of my curiosity. It is astounding to me that Russian Jews should be struggling out of the eastern darkness only to emerge into a still more labyrinthine obscurity in the west. 'And becoming Orthodox?'

'My nephew, yes. You know that he kisses the Torah? It's *tzitzits* all the time, and a *yarmulke* almost to the bath-tub. And my sister in one way she is frustrated, but in other ways she's proud of him because he likes it and believes in everything, so in that respect he is my nephew. Sometimes we have argument with him, but anyway it's his way.'

'Aha,' I say, 'but he's just your nephew. It's easier with nephews. What happens when it's your son who takes the Torah to the bath-tub?'

'Probably he will change me a little bit.'

'What if he wants to change you a big bit?'

'It's not easy. But if I think about the other options, that he could pick up the black girl probably, I would rather . . . you know, to see him in the religious family with ten kids and something like that.'

'Ten kids rather than one black girl?'

'Exactly.'

We head for the boardwalk, pausing to look into the Shorefront Y, a sort of Jewish school and Jewish social club and Jewish YMCA (if that's not a contradiction in terms) combined, where new immigrants can come and get help filling out forms, and meet others similarly bereft, and assemble for bus-trips, and learn slowly how to disappear into the community. A chorus-line of little Jewish girls is falling over and crying in ballet-tights. 'Not Bolshoi,' Margharita says, 'but give it time.'

Then on to the boardwalk which, if anything, looks more Black Sea than it did earlier, and which Margharita fails spectacularly to negotiate on account of her heels. One moment she's talking vivaciously at our side, the next she is gone, sucked down into the spaces between the boards. The old women call out from under their umbrellas, telling her to try the section where the planks run in straight lines and not diagonally, but this becomes an exercise akin to tight-rope walking. We offer to take an elbow each and hover her to our destination. She refuses. Not the way ladies behave in Odessa.

What you do do in Odessa, David explains, echoing Mikhail Polonsky, is chew sunflower seeds while you're walking. 'I show you.' And he is off to a charred Russian take-away from which he returns a moment later bearing warm, freshly roasted seeds in a brown paper bag. You take a handful, put them in your mouth, and spit out the husks.

I observe that the only public places in England where it's acceptable to spit are cricket and football pitches. 'This we don't do in Moscow,' David assures me. 'It's a southern Russian tradition. Ukrainians – they have no sophistication. They are not from the city. Look around. Babushkas on the benches. We're in the country.'

There now ensues a bout of ill-advised horseplay between David and Margharita – ill-advised on Margharita's part, at least, given the lack of sympathy between the boardwalk and her shoes. What is at issue here is David's Muscovite superiority and Margharita's Odessa open-heartedness, her Kishniev kindness. He's a snob, she says. She's a peasant, he says. I hold the sunflower seeds while they sort it out.

I feel distressed for them. In horseplay you see what lovers enjoy in each other, but also what will separate them at last. Suddenly, they look fragilely bound. They didn't come out of Russia as a pair. They met here. At the Shorefront Y, for all I know. And they have that tender transience about them, such as you see on children who become friends on their first day at a new school, sensing that next term they will have forgotten each other. I don't know what I'm doing, caring about their future. I've only just met them. But I am enjoying myself, and if they break up they will fracture my memory of the day.

We stroll back down the boardwalk, spitting sunflower husks, and picking Margharita out of the cracks. I am being taken for afternoon tea, Russian style, at Margharita's sister's apartment. I am to meet the family. But first we call into a Russian supermarket whose windows rattle whenever a train goes by. It is sumptuously stocked, more a food bazaar than a supermarket. The food is Russian – vats of herring, pickled cucumbers as big as your arm, tins of caviare and sticky cakes I don't recognize. Margharita tells me that when new immigrants first come to this bazaar, and see the eastern food they are familiar with available in western quantities, they faint.

'Right here,' she says. 'Right where you're standing.' And I have to take her arm to prevent her giving me a demonstration, full-length, polka-dot frock or no polka-dot frock, between the pickles.

I nearly faint myself when I see the table that Margharita's sister has prepared for us. Traditionally, this is when hospitality is supposed to mean something, when the hosts can ill afford it. But I am more comfortable when there is an air of disdain and devil-may-care around food. I bleed, as I eat, for the family's

cramped apartment, and their fallen condition, and their uncertainty about the future, and their pleasantness to me, who
will be gone in an hour and who will be laying his head on
pillows that probably cost more to rent for a night than this
tenement costs for a month.

Margharita's sister, Nina, is smaller than her, less Romanesque,
with a face, in Margharita's parlance, more specific Jewish. She is a
mechanical engineer but works in Manhattan in some other
capacity. Specific face, non-specific job. Her husband, Boris, is
also a mechanical engineer – there are enough engineers in this
room to take Brooklyn Bridge apart and reassemble it in an
afternoon – but he has no work. His disappointments have not
sharpened him as they have David. He has no edges. He sits in a
cloud of melancholy, fingering his moustaches, a kind man fretting over the past and the future. When David insists he never
believed a word of Soviet ideology, saw through every syllable of
it, Boris shoulders that burden of gullibility that someone has to
carry. His face crumples, remembering how easy it was to accept
the unacceptable. He looks as though he would like to sit here
for the rest of his life, a stone's throw from Coney Island,
blaming and then letting himself off. In another room his son,
Margharita's nephew, is kissing the Torah.

As I rise to leave, Nina notices that my back is stiff. It appears
they have not yet been kind enough to me. Nina knows backs.
That's what she's doing in Manhattan, giving back massages in
a beauty parlour. If I ring Nina's Nails – owned by another
Russian Nina – I can fix an appointment. In the meantime she
does me on the sofa that is in normal circumstances home to
Boris and his sad reflections.

When she finishes with me I am unbowed, taller than I've
been in years. Which is another reason for crying when I leave.

Tonight I do not ransack the cable stations for porn. That
message, exclamation-marked all over the Mitzva Tank –

99

L'CHAIM! TO LIFE! – was in fact a flyer advertising a night-long Hasidic fund-raising television programme, to be beamed all over America by satellite from Los Angeles. CHABAD TELETHON. And I am sitting up in bed, with a straight back, watching it.

Chabad, which is the more spiritual word for the Lubavitcher movement – Lubavitch itself simply being the name of a small town in Russia – is an acrostic formed from

> CHACHMA meaning wisdom,
> BINA meaning understanding,
> DAAT meaning knowledge.

So this promises to be a weighty telethon.

The master of ceremonies is Rabbi Baruch Shlomo Cunin, a West-Coast Hasid with personality and rhythm, who kisses his male guests and keeps his overcoat on all night. It's Rabbi Cunin who Morris Katz, the world's fastest painter, must have had in mind when he did his HASID LEAPING INTO ALL FOUR CORNERS OF THE CANVAS SIMULTANEOUSLY.

There is no containing Cunin. 'And now a special human being, a dear, dear friend of mine,' he explodes, as the actor Jon Voight appears in a *yarmulke*. 'Isn't he great? Let's hear it for him!'

Jon Voight would seem to have a special relationship with Chabad Lubavitch. He speaks of 'whirlwinds of knowledge'. Baruch Shlomo Cunin becomes a whirlwind. 'I'm a firm believer,' Jon Voight goes on, 'in this source of energy that keeps the just justly.'

Rabbi Cunin becomes such a force and gathers Jon Voight up into a Hasidic waltz.

They ask us to hear it for each other.

'Sing to life, never give up trying,' sings Ron, an Israeli entertainer in a blue silk suit and a brooch instead of a tie.

A Little Bit Cuckoo

> Share it with one another,
> Reach out to your brother.

Ron wrote this song, we are told, especially for the telethon.

At the bottom of the screen a never-ending list of sponsors and their pledges unfurls. *Mr and Mrs Forshpann, North Holly-wood: $180; Mr and Mrs Jeremy Schwartz, Jericho: $180; The Oberfests of New York: $500; Mrs Murray's grandchildren, Hollywood: $180; The Katzs of Culver City: $1,800; Mr and Mrs Mordy Bershtel: $180; The Lehavis of Tarzana: $180; The Jacques Mouws, Los Angeles: $2,500; The Lefkowitzs of Encino: $30* . . . (Only $30!)

The actor Richard Benjamin turns up, rather more expectedly than Jon Voight, to my mind, and asks us to keep the pledges coming. In return, he can promise us entertainers who 'will sing and play their hearts out for you'. It's that kind of a Jewish night – everyone performing just that bit harder.

Moishe Yes, a fiddler-on-the-roofer, sings the first country-and-western circumcision song I've ever heard. 'This song is for my kids and for your kids,' he prepares us, just in case we were thinking of sending them to bed. He takes it for granted that we will all know that a *mohel* is the ritual circumciser.

> That's my boy, just seven days old,
> With the rabbi all around him and the *mohel* . . .
> > That's my boy.
> That's my boy, with his *tallis* and *tefillin*,
> That's my boy – just thirteen.
> > That's my boy.
> That's my boy, now he's underneath the *chuppa*,
> That's my boy . . .
> > That's *his* boy!
> That's his boy, with the rabbi all around him
> > and the *mohel* . . .

A woman who has had a serious accident, been confined to a chair and told not to have children, describes how she went to the Rebbe for help. Now she has six. SIX! We all clap. Cunin becomes an instrument of percussion and then introduces one of the woman's sons as 'a miracle!!!'

Mel Carter – another male singer, for of course there can be no female singers on stage tonight, modesty purity and pudicity and all that – sings a Gulf War song he wrote himself.

> Raise the world's voice as one,
> Sing louder than the gun.

Deliberately or otherwise, his *yarmulke* falls off when he reaches the line,

> The hour has finally come.

The Kaminzkies of Sherman Oaks: $1,800; Mr David Fluhstein, Flushing: $180; The Pruskies of Beverly Hills: $180; The Litts of Woodland Hills . . .

Every time the current total is flashed on the screen, Rabbi Cunin does a dance. I try to remember that the money is going to good causes. Drug rehabilitation, for example. No strings attached. You don't have to be Jewish. But Mordechai Ben-David's plea to the Jewish God,

> We ask our *Shem*, please bring those old times back.
> Some day we'll be together: some day we'll be sheltered and warm

has me reaching for my remote-control gun. Back on Channel 35, some Nordic American's 'sweet pussy is on fire'. I suffer a crisis of conscience. Filth or faith. I bleep back to find Cunin screaming, 'Three and a half million dollars! Oy!' Whereupon six Chabad Lubavitchers – all male, not a sweet pussy in sight – dash on to the stage and embroil Jon Voight and Charles Durning in an hysterical whirl.

I opt for sleep.

*   *   *

And wake, early, with a back worse than it had been before Nina fixed it. I decide to visit her at Nina's Nails on 43rd Street, just a few blocks from my hotel, and which I can therefore approach on all-fours, without having to crunch myself into a taxi.

Nails are big business in Manhattan. There's a booth on every block, usually with an Anglepoise lamp in the window, and a woman in a semi-surgical smock waiting for you to bring your fingers in. It all manages to feel vaguely sexual while being entirely respectable. Just like this visit I'm making.

There are no customers as yet in Nina's Nails, so the staff are doing one another's. The Nina who's the proprietor is not so much made-up as startled by colour, in the way that Russian women athletes sometimes are. She has a ribald eye. Would I like a manicure after my massage? I feel as a sailor must, on shore leave in Novorossiysk. But, not having been at sea so long, I decline.

The other Nina shows me the way to a little cubicle. 'Hanging your clothies there,' she says, 'leaving your underwears. I am back.'

When she returns I am almost asleep, and stay that way. The radio plays light classics. Nina's fists roll up and down my spine, like bags of marbles. She is strong for a slight woman. And good at what she does, considering she is a mechanical engineer. She turns me over and grinds the marbles into my forehead. I don't know why that should give pleasure, but it does.

We talk about yesterday. About David and Margharita. About Boris and herself. About the strains of being in America at last, after all the struggles associated with escape, and finding oneself poor.

'Our years they are going so fast,' she says.

If my eyes weren't already watering, they would water. What a gift for melancholy these Ukrainians have. I am momentarily ashamed of being an intellectually strenuous Litvak.

She is going to make a career of massage. She is going to get a diploma in shiatsu. There's money in it. So Boris won't have to become a taxi-driver. 'I dream there will be golden time in my life,' she says, 'when my husband gets job.'

It's too much for me – years going so fast, golden time . . . I am ageing and away from home myself. My subject is supposed to be Jewishness, not upset. And I am determined to resist the *schmaltzy* conclusion that they are the same. That way telethons lie.

I leave all the Ninas to their nails and walk up Broadway, straightened in the back but lumpy in the throat.

Five

A JEW HOLIDAY IN HYMIETOWN

'Sweat city!'

The weathermen are waxing poetic over New York's freak hot spell. 'The air has body in it.'

It is 8.30 p.m. and still eighty-seven degrees in the street. I am waiting outside my hotel for Howard Felperin, a professor of English literature I know from other days and other countries, but who saw me in the street and called my name the night I left Schjeldhal inconsolable in SoHo because Miss Kansas hadn't made it. Tonight is Monday, and on Monday Woody Allen plays a saxophone or something in a jazz-band in Michael's Pub. Howard and I are going to catch Woody.

Howard arrives at the same time as the gaudiest, stretchiest stretch limo either of us has ever seen. This limo is stretch and stretch again. The interior is lit to resemble a night-club and a casino. We can just see the cocktail bar and the decanters and the croupiers.

A couple of German tourists, Germanically in love, gazing hungrily into the eyes of other couples to gauge the chances of two becoming four, inspect the limo with us. 'You ever seen anything so *vulgar*?' Howard asks them, camping up his New York drawl.

The Germans rattle out a laugh.

'I thought Mercedes was bad,' Howard presses. 'I thought Mercedes knew what vulgar is – but *this*!'

The Germans laugh again, uneasily. They know there's a joke here and they know it might be against them, but they can't quite get the measure of the war that's still being fought in the heart of this least Holocaust-conscious of Jews.

Preparatory to Woody, Howard suggests a drink in the hotel bar, a steel slinky dive for steel slinky kids. We talk *eros*. Howard is hot. Looks Mephistophelean in a slick summer suit which he wants me to admire. The girls are wound rather than dressed – swaddled. A black girl wears a snake-marked leotard as though it's a second skin. She has no secrets from us. Sweat city.

We walk the dozen or so blocks to Michael's Pub, still talking *eros*, the decline of the western world's education system, the end of English studies, and Howard's realization that after a career ostensibly devoted to the slippery French game of puns and echoes known as deconstruction he has all along been a stern Anglo-Saxon Leavisite. Too late, I tell him. You can't have the good times *and* hope to save your soul. He should know that; he's Mephistopheles.

If anything, the night is getting hotter. People rummage like rats in the rubbish. Pester us. Glare at us. Stretch out in shop doorways. I remark that the most boring thing about dossers is how early they go to bed. Howard thinks that 'go to bed' is not quite the phrase for it. Pedant. 'OK, turn in,' I say.

Not that Howard is in humanitarian spirits. His theme is human dross – the appalling creatures who inhabit the streets, a new insect life, ingesting the trash. We're blade-running.

In Manhattan you have to stop for traffic-lights every one and a half seconds. I elaborate a theme of my own: the staccato quality of New York talk has developed from needing to pace your thoughts between lights. You have to think by the block, muse between intersections, and then get your conclusion in quick while the lights are against you. Hence the major influence of Jewish talk on American talk. Jews think naturally by the block, are accustomed to speculating between regularly spaced obstructions and catastrophes. There is never the time to fully develop thought, to ponder, to meditate. Everything has to be got out fully formed, fast.

And we exemplify this very truth, we Howards, as we cross the streets – two middle-aged Jewish men in sweat city, hitting each other with perfectly timed portions of crisp speculation. *Portions* – the portions of the law, verses of the Pentateuch. They too fit nicely between lights, exactly a block long.

Michael's Pub is in a dead street and affects a dead, half-timbered Englishness. The interior wood-panelling brings back memories of cocktail-lounges *circa* 1959. There are a number of youngish people at the bar when we arrive, though *at* the bar suggests the wrong sort of accustomedness. It would be more accurate to say that they're backed *off* the bar. They are not *habitués* of the place or of drinking. They are tourists of the spirit, and they all look like Woody Allen.

From a back room you can hear jazz and applause, sudden eruptions of solo clapping, also *circa* 1959. You can just see a few tables, and waiters moving about, but you can't see Woody because of the screens and curtains that have been put up to protect his privacy from mere starers at the bar.

A sign says, ONLY COMPLETE RESERVATIONS SEATED and a velvet rope enforces the law, whatever it means.

Howard quizzes a Latin who mans the rope.

'It means if you four you must be four,' the man tells us.

'OK,' Howard says, 'I get it.'

'Have a drink at the bar or leave,' the man tells us.

'OK,' Howard says, 'I get it.'

I don't get it. Inside the room that counts, the room that's roped off, people are applauding and whistling, Woody's instrument (whatever it is) is blowing, and we have to stand at the bar?

I notice that the Latin relinquishes his watch to a pugnacious white-European American in glasses. A couple of Woody Allens ask if they can just have a quick peek into the sanctum.

'You can leave,' the man tells them.

But at least he is intelligible. I tell him how far I've come for tonight, what I am up to, where I was born, where else I'm going, in return for which I want him to tell me what ONLY COMPLETE RESERVATIONS SEATED means, since I'd like to be seated.

'It means you can't say you're four if you're not,' he says.

'Four what?'

'You can't reserve for four and then come as two.'

'What if you are two?'

'You gotta come as two.'

'We've come as two.'

'You gotta reservation?'

'No.'

'Then you can't come in.'

'Can we make a reservation?'

'No.'

'Because?'

'Because we're full.'

'What about later?'

'You mean at eleven?'

'Yes.'

'You gotta reservation?'

'No.'

His attention wavers. 'Buy a beer at the bar or leave,' he tells a little Woody in a *yarmulke*.

'Can I make a reservation?'

'Name?'

'Felperin and Jacobson.'

'For two?'

'For two.'

'And you'll be two?'

'We'll be two.'

'I got it.'

So we go and wait in the front lounge, which is badly lit and desolate and feels like a back lounge, and we agree that the secret of life, which we have both cracked, is to learn the Art of Losing Well.

At about 10.30 there is a disturbance in the street. Until now it's been quiet outside. We're in a business area. There's not much to bring you here at night, saving Woody on a Monday. A few black and Hispanic kids have been sitting on the pavement or draping themselves around concrete stumps, wearing bandanas and looking menacing, but not making trouble. Michael's Pub is not a hot spot.

But now something is happening. We look up. A stretch limo is outside, as vulgarly overstretched as the one Howard baited the concupiscent Germans with a couple of hours ago. We think we discern civilian bodyguards, and secret policemen, scattered among a press of people in summer shirts or tuxedos, one of whom is the second sentry at the velvet rope, the man who tells people to drink at the bar or leave. Excitement mounts, inside the pub and on the sidewalk. Autograph excitement. Famous-face excitement. For there, *there* in the heart of the crowd, looking small and frightened and not much pleased, wearing dark clothes and preparing to enter the vulgar stretch limo, is Woody! – Woody in a stretch limo fit for Noriega.

I just catch the familiar squashed expression – haunted, quizzical, oppressed – see it for longer than I actually see it, as is always the way with faces made familiar by celebrity, and then it's gone.

The blacks and Hispanics in bandanas look on. I wonder if they know who he is.

Howard and I now have to face that that's it. That the reason we have been able to wheedle a reservation for later is that there is nothing to reserve for. We can take it. The Art of Losing Well. But others who have not been able to see Woody play go around asking those in the know whether it really is all over for the night.

A beautiful South American girl, who has been sitting on her own in a white tailored suit and white stockings – she lets you see they're *stockings* – is close to tears, her lips swollen with blood and rage and disappointment. 'Won't he be playing here again?' she asks a group of jazz-groupies, who *have* seen him.

They shake their heads. She bites the inside of her mouth. She doesn't have to tell us for us to know – she must fly back to Buenos Aires tonight. This is the last night of her freedom. In the morning she will be married to a millionaire rancher who will never let her out of his sight. She has missed Woody for ever.

Woody the *schlemiel* with women!

'Oh, to be short and Jewish and near-sighted,' I say to Howard.

'But you already are,' he reminds me.

'Oh, to own a stretch limo, then.'

The night falls away. People drift off. The blacks and Hispanics in bandanas go and sit somewhere else. The few Woody look-alikes who are left strike desultory attitudes with the Mia Farrows they are* dating, not knowing what to do with the rest of the night. Howard and I decide to give Michael's Pub away. I am not too disappointed. I never did much care for jazz.

We pace back the way we came, measuring our thoughts to suit the traffic-lights.

Howard is back in New York after twenty years. He has been in Australia, which is how I come to know him. We have both given English literature to a people who have not always known how to show their gratitude. He thinks New York has gone to the dogs, but he will stay if the visiting-professorship at NYU turns into a permanent job. He's had Australia, wonders who'd

* were

miss it if it fell into the Pacific. I don't bother to say I would. I can see he is charged by *eros* – *eros* in New York.

We stop off at the Stage Deli, an affair of bright lights and brass rails and none of the authentic hurried seediness of the Carnegie, for all its boast that it serves the most famous pastrami and corned beef in New York. Fame, as we've seen, isn't everything.

I eat hash. Howard eats something like a bacon sandwich. And talks cars. 'I'm not interested in a car to get me from A to Z,' he tells me, lengthening his vowels to suit the hour. 'I'm interested in the erotic experience.'

Well, well – who'd have thought it? So Howard is my erotic Jew, the kind I grew up with in Manchester, the kind I went to Cambridge to forget, the kind who became market-men and fancy-goods wholesalers and furriers and car dealers, not college professors of a deconstructionist persuasion.

I take a look at Howard's face. Deconstructionists love to play with philosophical uncertainty – doubt, *aporia*, undecidability. But this is a *texte* that reads easy. A naked face, intense bleeding brown eyes, fleshy protuberances. A face in need of some protection, he must feel, for he wields his hands like defensive weapons, shielding himself from interruption, from unwelcome information, from whatever promises to stop the expression of *him*. He attacks with them too, attacks the space between you, warding you off, warning against trespass.

It must be tough if you're a woman in Howard's company. It must be bruising.

So he's like the Jews of my early acquaintance in this regard, as well: he's a warrior of his sex.

Like Joel Shapiro, he was not *bar-mitzvahed*. Like Joel Shapiro, he had a father who was a Marxist. We are both breathing onions, hot, a touch *louche*, drunk . . . We can't be a pretty sight. But a feeling of appropriateness assails me, a feeling of being in the right place, a sense of justified worldliness, a conviction that while Jewishness cannot be *only* this, it must, to be true to its own richness, include this.

I am suddenly ashamed in advance, lest Howard should ever find out that I put on *tefillin* in the shadow of the Great Orme.

On the subject of *tefillin* – I am taken aback, the next day, by my American agent's never having heard the word. She's Jewish, her name's Grossman, and she doesn't know what *tefillin* are. Or, if she knows what they are, she doesn't know what they're called. This is New York, she reminds me.

It's *erev yom tov*, the day before Yom Kippur, but a business day for me, a day for meeting agents, television people, writers, publishers; so Jews spill out of cabinets and filing systems. Jews ignorant of *tefillin*. Phylactery virgins.

In the studios of WNET I run into the man who produced the Abba Eban series *Heritage*. He is a glistening Sephardic Jew, with smiling Spanish and Portuguese eyes. There is a blue-black gloss on him, a patina so lustrous you want to stroke him.

Another Jew who does not observe, he will be keeping Yom Kippur as an act of fondness to the memory of his father, whom he loved and admired, and who would have wanted him to fast. His own children are not much into it. They will probably marry out. Does he mind? Yes . . . He becomes pensive. Yes . . . he thinks he does mind. He won't fight it. No use battling the inevitable. But he minds. 'I think of the past,' he says, 'and all those Jews who went through what they did in order to *stay* Jews . . .'

It's an end-of-the-line melancholy he's looking at. The struggle endeth here.

He can't go on talking to me. He has to leave work early, to make it home before sundown. Most of New York is doing the same. On Yom Kippur eve special trains have been put on to get the faithful – the more or less faithful; the faithful to the memory of someone else's faith, at least – home to atone for their sins.

As for me, I mark the fall of darkness on the city, the commencement of the great penitential fast, by sitting in the mezzanine restaurant of my hotel, eating chilli. I hold this to be only moderately sinful. I don't eat a *lot* of chilli. And it's not as though I've gone on the town, *looking* for food. I just let the food come to me.

The Paramount Hotel is noted, since its face-lift, for high design and cool interiors and clientele to match. The desk clerks and bell-boys wear Joseph Tricot black, and have their hair styled by conceptual artists in SoHo ateliers. Downstairs in the lobby, where people come to pose and be posed to, a hundred nut-brown girls with white faces and red lips flit like a plague of locusts. They buzz and nibble. They would be crisp and nutty to the taste. You would crack your teeth on them.

A solitary boy, sulky and transparent, wearing the finest of fine-cut black T-shirts, is concealed among them. And it is him the waiters at my mezzanine table immediately spot.

'*He's* gorgeous,' they agree.

Sodom and Gomorrah. Strike Lord! There are worse crimes than a bowl of chilli on Yom Kippur.

The day does not break apocalyptically. But you can tell it is not just any day. You can tell this is not the Day of Atonement in a gentile city.

Because I think this will be a good time to reach him, I ring Professor Louis Schmier in Valdosta. I have read some articles by him on Jewish life a hundred years ago in the southern states. I am toying feebly with the idea of heading south, after New York, but want to be dissuaded. You can always count on an academic for that. He is not able to talk to me. He is just off to the synagogue. You are meant to be in *shul* all day on Yom Kippur. The phone thrills a little in my hand. Fancy that – they're in *shul* right now in Valdosta, Georgia.

Down in the hotel café – I will go to *shul* myself, by and by, but there's no hurry; I bet Felperin's not hurrying – I settle in to a quiet read of the papers. *The New York Times* is full of the US–Israeli conflict over loan guarantees. There is talk of Bush addressing the nation on the subject. The story proceeds at a calmer rate than some of those I've been reading in the more excitable of the Jewish papers. BUSH BULLIES LITTLE ISRAEL was one heart-tugging headline. 'Never in our history has an American President been so biased against an allied democratic country, Israel, as is George Bush . . . Some Middle East refugees are calling the President, *Butcher Bush*.' There is no talk of Butcher Bush as yet in *The New York Times*.

A story in the Metropolitan section catches my eye: Al Sharpton in Israel, trying to serve a summons on Yosef Lifsh, the young Lubavitcher Hasid charged with knocking down the black child in Crown Heights, but not indicted. Sharpton is making something of a crusade of personally nailing Lifsh, but also something of a hash. He finds himself in Ben-Gurion Airport just as it's closing for Yom Kippur, and can't do much but come home. 'Go to hell, Sharpton,' an Orthodox woman shouts at him, as he's leaving the duty-free shop.

'I already am in hell,' he replies.

Later, *The New York Times* succinctly reports, Mr Sharpton 'went on to say that he was referring to the airport'.

New York Newsday is less nice. A front-page photograph of Sharpton carrying his overnight bag is captioned 'I AM IN HELL. I AM IN ISRAEL.'

In order to capitalize, presumably, on the stirred Judaic emotions of the day, the *New York Post* also carries a front-page Jew–black-related sensation.

I RAN WITH LYNCH MOB
Crown Heights witness tells how angry gang killed Hasid

'What was the mob yelling?' columnist Mike McAlary asks the witness.

'They were saying, "No peace. No justice."'

'What else?'

'"No justice. No peace."'

'Anything else?'

'"Kill the Jews."'

The young black McAlary is interviewing was originally held by the police after the murder, but then released. McAlary asks him whether he goes to school.

'Uh-huh. I go to Thomas Jefferson. We got off tomorrow.'

'Do you know why you have the day off school?'

'Uh-huh. We got a Jew holiday.'

I take the air.

On Yom Kippur, New York manages to be at one and the same time open and shut.

A surprising number of shops are shuttered. Not just the *kosher* delis, but video shops, computer stores, even the TWA desk in the airline booking office on Broadway. But theatre-land is packed. The queues at the reduced-ticket-booth snake twice around Times Square, and Neil Simon's *Lost in Yonkers* is playing to a full-house matinée.

Forty-second Street, though, has never felt scarier. There seems to be more than the usual number of blacks sleeping rough, and those that are upright look angrier than they were yesterday. The anxiety may be all self-generated, because I fear the consequences of today's tabloids, every one of them rubbing at the sore of black–Jewish relations. There was an alliance of sorts, once, between the two. In the civil-rights marches of the sixties Jews and blacks walked together. 'The Negro identifies himself almost wholly with the Jew,' James Baldwin had written. The Passover story, the long exile in Egypt, as slaves, was capable of a black interpretation; while those socialist Jews that Joel Shapiro and Howard Felperin are proud to have had as fathers found their own cause in the black struggle. In his famous list of what is Jewish and what is *goyische*, Lenny Bruce has Eddie Cantor (born Edward Israel Iskowitz) as *goyische* and Ray Charles and Count Basie as Jewish. We weren't just interchangeable, some of us were more the other than we were ourselves. But then came Israel's military victories, and the Black Muslims, and Farrakhan's traducement of Judaism as a 'dirty religion', and Jesse Jackson's ill-advised reference to New York as 'Hymietown', and affirmative action, that well-meaning principle of social interference that gnaws at the heart of a Jew's instinctive belief in meritocracy, however socialist he is.

And now, as the papers don't scruple to observe, the two groups are brawling in their own backyards.

On a corner close to the Port Authority building, where at any time you walk in fear of your life, the Heirs of Esau are gathered, dressed in pantomime velvets and Ali Baba turbans, surrounded by the proofs of their claim to be one of the Ten Lost Tribes of Israel – a worn print of a black King James I, quotations from Malachi 3:6–11, a parody painting of Jesus as a white hippy, and a collecting-bucket asking us to SUPPORT YOUR NATION: ISRAEL.

'We're gonna come out here killin',' their leader feels we ought to be warned. 'We'll have to kill a lot of white men, 'cos there is no faith, no salvation, without adversaries. And all *you* wanna do' (this to a couple of brothers standing idly and sceptically by) 'is get down on your goddam knees and clean white men's shoes.'

The demagogue is studded and chokered and gauntleted like a biker. Except that every stud contributes to a pattern of the Star of David. The Nubian slave that guards him has Stars of David tie-dyed into his cloak. The others have them embroidered on their shawls, or appliquéd on to their boots.

'I'm a Jew myself,' the demagogue proclaims. 'I'm a descendant of Abraham, Isaac and Jacob. They were black men.'

A white thug passes and calls him a goddam nigger – casually, just by the by as it were, not bothering to raise his voice.

The pantomime genie is not fazed by that. 'Tell me something I don't already know, brother.'

But who will tell me whether any of this means trouble or not?

Taking no chances, I hurry back to my hotel, put on a suit, and hail a cab. 'Sixty-fifth and 5th,' I say. 'Temple Emanu-El.'

The driver is dark and glowing, not black, but black enough for me to want to try out his responses to today's headlines.

'I shouldn't really be taking this cab,' I say, sneaking up on my subject, addressing it laterally. 'I should really be walking, today being . . .' (Will he understand?) 'Today being what it is . . .'

'I hope you're fasting,' he says.

I shake my head. 'I've just had lunch.'

He wags a finger at me. 'Tut-tut.'

'I know,' I say, remorsefully. I look at his keen brown eyes, and his bristling moustache. His ID identifies him as Yehia Mansour. I imagine that, come Ramadan, he is unfailing in his observances. 'I know,' I say again. 'I know.'

'At least I hope you've done *Tashlich*,' he says.

'*Tashlich*?'

'Cleansed your sins at the water's edge.'

I'm not going to say, I *know* what *Tashlich* is, especially as I've known only since last week. And I'm not going to say, How come *you* know? I check his name again. It's still Yehia Mansour.

'I realize this is New York,' I say. 'But you still make me ashamed. You know more about my faith than I do.'

He's pleased to have surprised me. He gives me a comprehensive smile, a play of light across his darkness. 'That's because I'm half-Jewish.'

117

'What's the other half?'

'Egyptian.'

'That must be hard for you.'

'You don't know how hard. I have an Egyptian father and a Jewish mother. I don't hate either of them. How can I take sides?'

'Your mother comes from –?'

'Palestine.'

He doesn't say Israel. 'That's hard,' I concede.

But if I think that's hard . . . 'And I have an American Jewish wife.'

'So are *you* fasting?'

'How can I fast when I'm driving? And I can't afford not to drive. I got a big sum owing on the cab at the end of this month. My wife doesn't understand. She says that if I drive today she's taking the kids and leaving. She doesn't understand. I don't like seeing debts accumulate. Yom Kippur doesn't have to be special. I do no wrong today if I pray to God. If I'm a good man and ask for forgiveness, why shouldn't He forgive me?'

'He should,' I say.

'If I'm a good man the rest of the time, why should today be special?'

'It shouldn't,' I say.

Somehow or other, although it was me that began the questions, and although I go on asking him about Crown Heights, and what the papers are saying, he is the one that has gained the interrogative upper hand.

'I see it this way,' he says. 'Why should the ambulance have picked the black kid up? Wasn't it a Jewish ambulance? We pay for this service, don't we? The black kid was the city's responsibility, wasn't he?'

'Yes,' I say. 'Yes. Yes. No. Yes.'

'It's not as though the guy hit him deliberately, is it? Look – there's two black guys and there's two white guys, if I lose control of this car I don't choose which I hit, do I?'

'No.'

'Right. It'd be an accident. And he didn't mean to hit the kid. Why would he have done that? For what reason? To bring trouble to himself and his people?'

'No.'

We reach Temple Emanu-El, where I've promised Joel Shapiro I'll go to be turned away by My Own. There are crowds outside, on the sidewalk, on the road, wearing white carnations.

'That's the custom,' Yehia Mansour tells me. 'You gotta wear something white. To suggest cleanliness.'

I don't have anything white on me. Except maybe a bit of cream cheese still in my beard.

I'm suddenly not in the mood for being turned away by My Own. I would rather go on being peppered rhetorically by Mr Mansour. So I get him to drive me further uptown, to the Park Avenue synagogue, which was mentioned to me yesterday by a clever cat-like Jewish girl at WNET. Park Avenue on East 87th she'd recommended. Anyone who is anyone will be there to hear Cantor Shlomo Carbackle.

She'd been so convincing that, although I'd detected the wicked mischief of invention in her eyes, I'm still half-expecting to hear Cantor Shlomo Carbackle when I get there. If they'll let me in.

'OK, let me ask you this,' Yehia Mansour continues, only too happy to go on driving and asking; 'if a car hit me and Bush, who'd the ambulance pick up?'

'Bush.'

'Right. Bush. That's the system, right?'

He tells me that Jews are the city's biggest and most sympathetic employers of blacks. That blacks are his friends. That blacks have no reason to complain of Jews in New York. But that Al Sharpton is concerned to whip up trouble. And people are always prepared to believe that Jews make too much money.

He's wild with Sharpton. Full of Sharpton's 'I'm in hell, I'm in Israel' crack. He believes the papers shouldn't have printed the story. He believes Sharpton owes the Jewish people an apology. He believes a crack like that is especially derogatory on Yom Kippur.

But what do I think of Sharpton?

I'm not thinking anything about Sharpton. I'm thinking that I don't know what I think. What are they worth, these opinions of Yehia Mansour? Do I measure what he says about blacks and Jews against statistics? Can you quantify the ebb and flow of relations between social groups? Can you *prove* sympathy? I want to believe my driver because I want to believe him. And I'll trust him on blacks because I originally took him to be blackish. But I'm aware that what passes for truth in this speeding yellow cab will fly out the doors the moment I open them.

He won't rise to any speculations about the future. Can't tell me whether there's serious trouble coming, what will happen next in Crown Heights. He's picking at different knots. The half of him that's Jewish has taken over completely from the half of him that isn't, and he's off, away on the do-you-ever-see-a-Jew-on-the-streets-begging theme. As a question. Well, do I?

And who shoots the cops?

What are the jails full of – blacks or Jews?

Who employs the blacks when they come out?

Who doesn't raise too many queries about their criminal records?

'Blacks,' I say. 'Blacks. Jews. Jews. Jews?'

I don't know how I'm going. He doesn't tick me. No time. Too many queries . . .

And who pays them better? They complain about low pay, but why don't they look around and see who pays better?

We are at Park Avenue synagogue. He drops me discreetly round the side, and wishes me good *yom tov*. It's only after he drives off that I remember to wonder whether his wife and kids will be there when he gets home.

*　　*　　*

There are crowds here too, but not in white carnations. Maybe on Park Avenue we're already cleansed. Security is tight but I get through by looking harmless.

I take up a seat next to a young woman with a drooping expression, somewhat stylized, like Eleanor Bron's. She has thin legs, which she holds tightly together, and flat knees, but I'm not noticing – I'm not conceding Rabbi Sacks' point about the unprayerfulness of one's thoughts when women are present. 'You should know, Howard,' he'd challenged me on the radio. 'You're a novelist.'

I'm still thinking about that, about what a novelist is pre-eminently qualified to know about women and unprayerfulness.

Whether the Park Avenue synagogue is at all a prayerful place on Yom Kippur, I am unable to decide. Prayer certainly seems to be afoot – that's to say, if the congregation were Claudius and I were Hamlet, I would have to think twice about doing it pat, and dispatching him to heaven. An organ plays. The choir sings. Light filters celestially through stained-glass windows. And sober reflections seem to occupy the minds of the congregants.

It's all so well mannered we might as well be in an Anglican cathedral. There's the rub. It may be prayer, but it isn't Jewish prayer. There isn't the babble. There isn't the wild individualism, everyone going at his own pace, rocking to his own rhythm, praising the *Shekhina* in his own good time.

The fact that I've never been comfortable in synagogues of the kind this isn't does not mean that I am bound to be comfortable in synagogues of the kind this is. The service is conducted in English and phonetically spelt Hebrew. The woman next to me – whose name, I see from the pass she carries in her lap, is Ruth – phoneticizes scrupulously. The man in front of me is wearing a *yarmulke* and prayer-shawl borrowed from the communal *yarmulke* and prayer-shawl table in the vestibule. Is any of this right? Shouldn't we be chanting Hebrew Hebrew at different speeds? Shouldn't we have our own *yarmulkes* and *talaysim*?

I have *my* own!

The rabbi's name is David H. Lincoln. His sermon is mainly to do with raising money. There are various bits of paper on the seats, pledges and envelopes that come with your pass – the pass I don't have. The cards are designed so that you don't have to write on them. (No writing on Yom Kippur.) They have flaps representing different amounts of money. You fold down the flap corresponding to the sum you're willing to pledge, and hand it to a man who comes round with a receptacle.

Israel is the other subject of the sermon. Our reasons to be satisfied with the realization of our dream of a national homeland. Why we have to modify our prayers, somewhat, in the light of this realization, for we cannot pray one day to have what we have already. How we are to proceed in view of what Bush . . .

There are quiet expressions of acknowledgement, but no deep murmurs of assent or anxiety, and no vulgar responses of the Concord kind. This is not Barbra Streisand territory.

We read prayers for the dead in English. For our parents. For those whom we joined in holy wedlock, 'sharing all our deepest interests, thoughts and emotions'. For those whose 'attributes and qualities are immortal'.

That does it for me. *Deepest interests, thoughts and emotions? Attributes and qualities?* We are in a house of God and we have descended into computer-dating talk. Single-ese.

But, *but*, against everything I hold dear, I have to acknowledge that the act of praying, the act of remembering the dead whose deepest interests and emotions we have shared, does seriously affect the congregation. Next to me, Ruth is having a hard time of it. Breath catches in her narrow chest. Wherever I look, people are crying. Quietly. Not wailing, just drying their eyes, reservedly.

So, the poetry might not be up to much, but it works. It is possible to touch the heart in American-English. And only I – on eternal vigil for vulgar usage, safeguarding the purity of a service I never attend and the sanctity of passions I don't mean to yield to – only I am out of it. Denied the consolations of communal feeling, thought and emotion.

I look at Ruth's legs and leave.

Out on the street, I observe a skill I have never seen before. You walk out through the gates of the synagogue and in a single movement, assuming your *yarmulke* is your own and you're still wearing it, you remove it and, *while* your arm is describing its natural downward arc, you hail a cab.

It goes: synagogue – street – *yarmulke* – cab. One action.

In England you don't drive to or from *shul* on Yom Kippur. Here, on Park Avenue, you don't fuss over trifles. In a Cadillac parked at the very gates of the *shul*, an old guy in a white cotton suit sits holding his prostate. He is either doing deep-breathing exercises or having a heart-attack. Nobody is concerned for him. Today would be a good day to die. And outside a *shul*!

'You know what gets me?' a crone in a *yom tov* frock that is too short for her is saying to a companion – 'They don't know anybody, but it's all, "Hello, how are *you*? Kissy-kissy."'

Her companion is male, bored, irascible. Hardly what you would call shriven. 'Yeah,' he says. 'Yeah. Yeah.'

As they are about to cross the street they are accosted by a couple identical in dress, age and temper. 'Hello,' they say to one another. 'How are *you*?' Kissy-kissy.

At a respectful distance from the synagogue – nothing I can do: training – I catch a cab to Temple Emanu-El. Done Conservative; now I'll do Reform.

Security is more serious here, even if the worship isn't. Men in black suits and white carnations guard every entrance and exit. An emergency ambulance waits outside, its engine purring, ready to go. If a black child were to be knocked down right here, I wonder, right outside this great moorish-romanesque edifice, would the ambulance go to his aid?

I pace up and down, unwilling to try the security system, which will surely not give, but frightened in case it does. I don't want to be inside another *shul* today.

Temple Emanu-El – perhaps it's because the place sounds as though it's a couturier's that there is so much suffering for fashion among the – no, congregation is not the word – among the clientele. Briefer are the skirts of the matrons than the days of man's happiness on earth. And higher are their heels than his sorrows. I cannot estimate exactly the age of the woman who clicks out of the temple on nine inches of diamanté stack, her eel-unsteady legs enmeshed in silver lamé stockings, her gold Richard III hat tilted Tudorly on the flamingo nest of her hair, but I read it in the consternation of the ambulance men who watch her every step. Older than the century, their faces say, older than our grievances, older than our sins.

The male worshippers fall out of the temple's various exits, blowing hard and sweating. They are in open-necked shirts. Their white carnations have expired and gone grey. Some of them feel called upon to apologize, to explain their dishevelment, or just their appearance on the street while the service is still going on. 'Hot in there,' they say. 'Phew.'

But isn't that the point of today? That you suffer?

Out of sorts and sick at heart, lamenting the Orthodoxy I do not have a minute's time for when I see it, I cab it back and ring Felperin. Two hours later we are sitting in the Top of the Sixes, a 5th Avenue cocktail-bar with cloud and vapour views, discussing banal liturgical English and the obstacles in the way of any modern child's getting himself a basic religious education outside the ghetto.

Howard tells me one of those university horror stories that all academics now relate. He has reason, in the course of a class on Shakespeare, to mention Moses. Blank faces all around him. 'No one know Moses?' One single black girl puts her hand up. A boy complains. What gives here? How can he be expected to have heard of Moses? 'I'm Jewish,' he says.

Howard sighs. I sigh. We sigh together, high up among the Sixes, two ageing thinkers atop a rotting city, two secular Jewish philosophers presiding over the death of faith and faith's appropriate language.

'Eroticism,' Howard says, much later, 'is the expression of insecurity. Eroticism is inversely proportional to material security.'

I'm not sure whose fault it is that we're back on eroticism. But these remarks of his are in response to my observation that the blacks I've noticed in the streets of Manhattan are more engrossed in the bodies of passing women than any other men I've come across, except Jews as we used to be. Eroticism has passed, I said, from us to them.

So if I'm right in my characterization, and Howard is right in his analysis, does that mean that the heat we prided ourselves on possessing, we fifties and sixties Jews, was nothing but a fleeting consolation for not yet having power? Were we juicy only because we weren't sure we were safe?

We ponder this, belatedly, atop the Sixes.

Six

CRÊPE-HANGING

After the pallor, the passion. After Park Avenue Synagogue, Mineola.

To Long Island to meet Lynn Singer, who runs the Long Island Committee for Soviet Jewry. It was Lynn Singer who gave me David Mikhailovich's name and therefore, in a sense, a massage. I wish to thank her in person, and also in person enjoy some of the deep-voiced Jewish mirthfulness – the *haimisheh vitsikayt* – she exudes on the phone. The only catch is having to get to Long Island.

I go by Long Island Railroad, taking the train to Mineola. Jamaica is hereabouts. And Babylon. And East Hampton, which may not sound exotic but is the birthplace of John Howard Payne, the composer of 'Home Sweet Home'. Payne was the grandson of Aaron Isaacs, one of the first Jewish settlers in Nassau County; and, although Isaacs couldn't wait to marry out and baptize his children, thereby effectively de-Hebraizing whomsoever came after him, I am still able to derive satisfaction from the idea that 'Home Sweet Home' is a quarter Jewish. We need a few more songs like that. They make a change from 'Tell Me Where Can I Go?'

Musing on the train about the wide divide between the urbane, absorbed Jew of New York and the omnipresent Hasids, it occurs to me that religion is not the issue, but that what is still being played out is the old dilemma – to be seen or not to be seen. To make oneself distinguished by becoming invisible versus securing one's safety and bondedness by becoming as

126

conspicuous as possible. Both positions are paradoxical, both were tried out in pre-war Germany and, as adherents of both will tell you, both failed.

A couple of black women are philosophizing in the seat behind me. 'I'm not mournin' – I'm not mournin' no cop no more,' one of them says. 'They're rotten killin' bastards. I don't mourn when a cop gets killed no more. What goes around, comes around.'

'You have to see nothin' and know nothin',' the other agrees. 'That's the only way to survive in this world. When I see it, I just keep walkin'.'

So they've got the same problem around visibility.

A rogue taxi-driver picks me up from Mineola station and takes me the couple of miles down Old Country Road to where Lynn Singer does her thing. He marvels over my accent and tells me that the chicks in England may be O K, but here in Nassau County they're strange – strayinge.

'What do they do?' I ask.

He finds that funny and repeats it a few times. Then says, 'They're not interested in what a man's got between his legs. Only how many bucks he makes.' And laughs.

The Long Island Committee is in chaos when I arrive. Bankers' boxes all over the floor, and Jewish women with their heads in them.

On the phone, Lynn Singer has advised me to get here early so that I can witness the welcoming of a refusenik, hot from the plane. But at the moment the traffic seems to be going the other way. For reasons unknown to me, it would appear that the Long Island women are posting themselves to Russia.

'Blame the U J A,' Lynn Singer tells me.

'I've never been good on initials,' I say.

'The United Jewish Appeal. You don't know the U J A? They're the biggest agency, the *gantser machers*. We do the work getting the refuseniks out, they get the credit. That's the way it is. They know how to suck in the funds. We've never been more needed, but –' Her hands go to the heavens; this is one for the Almighty to pass judgement on.

'You're folding?'

'Folding!' (Am I mad?) 'We're moving to smaller premises. Thanks to the UJA.'

No one hates a Jew or a Jewish organization like another Jew or another Jewish organization.

Lynn Singer rolls her eyes, twists her shoulders, shows the UJA her back. She swivels in her seat, full of thoughts, full of fire, full of resentments, full of energy, full of humour. She is a power-pack of a woman, with exuberant breasts and extravagant features. Nature was in no mood for understatement when it made her; and she runs with the gifts for immoderacy she's been given. She can position her eyes in any part of her face, dropping them like a landslide to indicate sorrow, flying them like kites to suggest joy. Her lips are heavy, in conflict with each other over sensuality and humour, but capable of putting a pout together if it will help. She wishes you to see that she has flirted herself out of a few tight corners in her time. 'Why thank you,' she says, when you pay her a compliment. She flutters her eyelids, and dares you to think of her as a flutterer.

We sit squeezed into a corner of a large conference table, the rest of which is being used for packing. Higher and higher the bankers' boxes pile. Every now and then she has to break off conversation to make decisions about keeping or throwing, or the phone rings and she has to tell a newly arrived Russian that she can't give him references or guarantee him into an apartment. 'That's N A Y A N A. No – N-A-Y-A-N-A. The New York Association for New Americans. I'll give you the number . . .'

She slithers an eye. See how much there is to do? Would UJA offer such a service?

But I am not to suppose that her duties stop at the clerical. She is an operative in the field. From 1981 to 1988 she was banned from entering the USSR. She tells me how she was, as it were, taken into custody by four KGB men for abusing USSR hospitality. They came to collect her from her hotel room. Would she go with them, please? She most certainly would not. 'I am a respectable Jewish matron,' she told them. 'I don't go off with one strange man, let alone *four*. My husband will not be pleased to hear about this.'

It's a wonderful thing, Jewish respectability. Ribald in the utterance, but woe betide you if you presume on its suggestiveness.

Lynn Singer, the respectable Jewish matron, pouts, straightens her skirt, pulls at her lime-green blouse. All her clothes are too tight on her. Nothing can contain me, her wardrobe says. It's all funny and it's all not. She can pass from supreme drollery to supreme sentimentality in a second. On the wall there is a photograph of her giving the first book of refuseniks' names to Menachem Begin. A framed sentence from the lips of Moshe Dayan hangs beside it. 'All we ask is that you feel Jewish. Because then you will do what one Jew does when another Jew is in trouble. You will help.'

Why do I gag at the sentiment when it's printed and hung, but not when it's made opulent flesh? Lynn Singer is all help. She sits like help's personification, fretting and pouting, in a sea of paper. Perhaps it's her capacity to go back the way she's come – from supreme sentimentality back to supreme drollery – that saves her.

She tells me about a refusenik she's been helping, who gets his permission to leave but then decides that he would like to buy some paintings in Russia to sell when he gets to America. He clears it with the authorities. All above board. But as he's due to catch his plane in Leningrad he's stopped. They make a fuss. He makes a fuss back. And involves Moscow customs.

'Moscow customs!' She squeezes her lips and looks at me out of the side of her face. I am supposed to know what involving

129

Moscow customs entails. 'The *schmuck!*' she says. 'So now he's being done for attempting to smuggle national works of art out of the country, and he's expecting me to help him.'

'The *schmuck!*' I say.

Which only causes her eyes to go into a landslide. 'If you ask me, the Jews are in big trouble in Russia,' she says. 'More and more are going to want to come out, but Russia's afraid of the brain drain. And is the west going to say that there's no persecution now? So will the Jews lose their refugee status? If they lose that, and they don't have a first-degree relative living here, they've had it. I don't know. I don't like it. Not just in Russia. I don't like it here. Maybe it's the atmosphere again of 1937 . . .'

The conversation moves, as though on chicken-fat, from Russia to Israel to New York back to Israel to Bush. Where it pulls up awhile.

'For Bush to take on the Israeli government,' she says, 'is heinous.' She pronounces it with a full Brooklyn neigh – heighnous. 'It's heighnous to me.'

The Long Island women come out of their boxes to join in. One of them has just read an article by a Jewish journalist, supporting Bush's stand. 'I'm sorry,' she says. 'But for any Jew to criticize Israel . . . It's different if they're not Jewish, but for any Jew to pass criticism – I'm sorry – but it's unforgivable. They're not real Jews.'

(The old question: Who's a real Jew? My answer: Whoever doesn't ask the question.)

Lynn Singer has been lobbying senators about the loan guarantees. She shows me some of the replies, on White House paper. Polite. But not promising much. She curses selected senators. 'Supposed to be a friend of Israel. A real anti-Semite that one.'

I'm bought a turkey sandwich for lunch. The women eat salads out of plastic containers, and berate Bush. A wry, humorous, hectoring, resigned atmosphere prevails. An atmosphere of women. Lynn empties two sachets of pink mayonnaise on her lunch, then complains they've given her too much salad.

'I feel like a crêpe-hanger,' she says, once the food has been cleared away.

I don't follow her.

'I thought it was just initials you weren't good on. A crêpe-hanger. The woman who hangs up the black in a house of mourning.'

Prognostications of doom again. The signs everywhere. Bush. The rise of anti-Semitism in Europe. The recession. The troubles at City College in New York, where a black lecturer is stirring it against the Jews. The lack of father-figures in the community – in the black and Jewish communities. The lack of role-models. The decline of the Jew in American eyes, dating from the Vietnam War, when many of the intellectual agitators against the war were Jewish. And maybe – who knows – the wearing thin of the Holocaust factor.

She's tired. Her husband wants her to take a holiday, somewhere unassociated, where there's no refusenik business to be done. 'But I can't,' she says. 'I feel it would be wrong to stop.'

I like the idea that she has a choice.

Just as I'm thinking it's time I let Lynn and her women get back into their bankers' boxes, the refusenik I'd been promised arrives. He's not just any refusenik, allowed to leave at last by a more benign administration; he has escaped, bearing names and carrying whatever classified secrets an ultra-high-frequency physicist carries.

He is here with his wife, who got out a year ago, and an interpreter. Because he has been in America only a couple of days, and because he has a fastidious curl to his mouth, and dresses particularly, even primly, and because his wife is still emotional, and has been beautiful in a gypsyish way, but is losing it, palpably losing it – I fall to wondering about the strains of such a reunion. Can it ever live up to all that's expected of it? Will they make it as lovers and companions now they've pulled off their great escape, or will the escape itself turn out to be the high point, and all else a disappointment?

Everyone is upset. Lynn Singer has been here many times before. She met Sharansky, after all, the famous day he arrived in Israel. But she is affected by the physicist's gratitude, by the formal speech of thanks he makes her in Russian, and by the fragile tableau to which we all contribute.

His name is Mikhail Finkel'shteyn, and he is from Saratov, on the Volga. He brings worrying stories about the five thousand Jews in Saratov. He fears a volcano – a walcano. This year, on April 20th, Hitler's birthday, the KGB warned Jews to expect a pogrom. And sure enough, on April 20th, there were troubles – insults, desecrations.

His wife looks at him while he speaks. She is carrying too much weight. And her hair, though a beautiful lustrous black, is thinning. Does she recognize him? Does she fear him? Does she *know* him?

He tells us of his escape. He deposits a thin briefcase on the table. I am blithely taking notes when Lynn halts me, halts all of us, to suggest that it may not be such a good idea for me to be recording how Mikhail got out. My pen freezes in my fingers. Mikhail's secrets are safe with me.

Not that I can follow any of it anyway. I never have mastered the spy genre. The moment an unnamed third party enters, collects the papers, goes on ahead, and arranges to meet X, I'm lost. I actually do not have a clue how Mikhail made it out, or what ultra-high-frequency physics is if it's not hi-fi, or whether there's anything telling in the slim briefcase. Life is what Jane Austen, not Len Deighton, sees. Even Jewish life. And the extravagant human drama which turns me cold, here in Mineola, Nassau County, is about a curling mouth, and a once wonderful head of hair now losing its amplitude – not passwords.

Once they have gone, but before I do, Lynn Singer expostulates us into another mood with an anecdote about the time she was asked to transport a Sefer Torah – the scroll containing the law – from a town in Pennsylvania to a settlement in Israel. The Sefer Torah had been brought to Pennsylvania by a Russian rabbinical family, and was now to be returned to a community coming from the very Russian *shtetl* that had originally owned and worshipped it.

'Imagine! A Sefer Torah! I say I'm honoured. Honoured! Such a *mitzva*! I ring up El Al. "Fine," they say, "we'll arrange for it to go in the hold." The hold? Excuse me. This is a Sefer Torah we're talking about! "Madame, baggage is baggage. It's the hold or nothing." I go on up the line. Each person I talk to is more senior than the rest. Same story. "Madame, baggage is baggage." At last I get someone very very. Don't put the phone down, I say, or I'll be over in a taxi to sort you out. He asks me to hold on. Five minutes later he's back on the phone. "Madame, the captain says he'll be honoured to give the Sefer Torah a seat next to you."'

Her face erupts. She loves a triumph. Every button on her blouse quivers for her, taking the strain.

'So – I flew to Israel with the Sefer Torah sitting next to me, in a seat belt.'

I go to shake her hand. She holds me off. She isn't quite finished.

'When I get to the settlement – and we'll not discuss that I'm not allowed to participate in the service, because I'm a woman, but a woman was good enough to bring it over in a seat belt – when I get to the settlement and the Sefer Torah is being unpacked, I see one rabbi standing aside and watching and shaking his head. You can imagine, I'm wondering if I've done something wrong. Finally, he comes up to me. Do you know what he says? – "Now can you get my congregation one?"'

I laugh. 'And can you?' I'm careful not to laugh too much. There could be tears in this one. Jewish helping and all.

But it's all right. Her eyes are away like kites. 'I'm looking,' she says.

Mineola is like L A in that you can't ever hail a cab, you have to ring for one. And the cab-driver that comes to take me out is as rogue as the one that brought me in. No. Roguer.

'Woooooooow!' I am no sooner in his cab than he sees a girl. No one special, just a regulation girl.

But hang on. It doesn't begin like this. It begins with me saying, 'Forest Hills, please.'

And him. 'Again.'

'Forest Hills.'

'Say that again.'

'Forest Hills.'

'Just one more time.'

'What's the problem? Is there no such place?'

'No – the accent.'

And then it's, 'Woooooooow!'

'You guys are hot round here,' I say, trying for idiom, and trying to shed my accent, otherwise I'll be repeating everything. 'The driver who picked me up earlier was talking girls before I told him where I was going.'

'You know why? The girls in Nassau County are the best in New York.'

'That's a tall order,' I say.

He waves away my objection. 'The really good ones you see in New York come from here. They may work in New York but they live in Nassau County.'

We stop at lights. Three blacks cross in front of us.

'We got the brothers here too – most of them got attitudes.' (A-tit-toods.)

He takes a detour, for which there will be no charge, no sir, and swings into a parking lot that has meters in it. He puts a quarter in a machine. 'This is my other car,' he says. 'They'll give me a ticket even though I'm on city business. They can see it's on city business, but they still give me a ticket.'

'City business?'

He thought I'd never ask. 'I'm a cop. I just do this on my day off. I'm in narcotics.'

Wooooooooow! Lucky me. I got me a cop. And I got him for quite a while if I read my map of Nassau County right.

So I get him going. 'What about this Crown Heights business?'

'Well, let me tell you – it's true.'

True? What's true?

He detects my hesitation. He's not a cop for nothing. He's certainly not a cop because he looks like a cop. What he looks like is a cab-driver. But then he is in narcotics. 'The Hasidim do get favoured treatment.' That's what's true. 'We're told to go easy on them.'

'And do you?'

'Sure. But it's gonna have to stop. The brothers see, and say why don't you give them parking tickets when you give 'em to us? It's one law on one side of the street, and one law on the other. And if you can't pick up any fines on one side then you gotta pick up more on the other.'

'And it's going to change?'

'Has to. We're gonna have to say to the Hasidim, That's it.'

I try to see the drama in my mind's eye. A cop in a cop car winding down his window and saying, 'That's it, Hasid.' Meanwhile the Hasid's scouring his soul to be ready for *Moshiach*. So he gets another fine – the Messiah will pay it. And the Rebbe will make an acrostic out of the ultimatum. *That's* and *it* – numerical equivalent twelve, for the Twelve Tribes, the complete Jewish Nation. Where's the joy for the brothers in any of this?

To the driver I say, 'Did you object to giving the Hasids favourable treatment?'

'Not really. They run a more peaceable neighbourhood. And they're hell to arrest anyway. They know their rights. And they're tough guys. They look after themselves. They're ready for it. It's easier to pick up a black. The Hasidim are more aggressive. And they can overdo it, let me tell you. I've seen 'em half-kill someone for trying to get into their car. And that's not right. A car's just a car. You don't kill for it. This is getting your values mixed up.'

I enjoy that. In this great democracy of a-tit-toods you never can say who's going to judge the values of whom.

'So that's it for the Hasids?'

'Things will go quiet now. We'll fix it.'

He's a 'Nam veteran. A fluent talker. Long hair, balding on top. He wears glasses to drive in, which give him a somewhat studious look, but his shoulders have been worked on and his arms are pumped up. I decide he could be dangerous, mainly because he has so many thoughts.

He reckons the city's had it. He's sorry for the blacks. Things were going well for them. They were improving their lives. Then crack came along. No – it's not that they're all on it. It's that smart black kids who would have been going to college now see their way to earning hundreds of dollars a day selling the stuff. In fact, it's mainly whites they sell it to.

No. The city's not what it was. 'I remember the good old days,' he says, 'when they shot you for a cigarette. Now they just shoot you.'

He wouldn't mind retiring. Enough now, of writing tickets on black streets.

I don't say, Hang on, I thought you were in narcotics, now you're talking like a traffic cop. He might be easy to upset.

We've made it to Forest Hills. He wishes me well. Tells me to be careful. It's dangerous out there. I tell him that he should be careful himself. That it's even more dangerous where he goes.

'Yeah, but I gotta gun,' he calls back.

*   *   *

Crêpe-hanging

Every Sunday morning since he initiated the custom in 1986, Rabbi Menachem Mendel Schneerson, the seventh Lubavitcher Rebbe, has held a sort of maundy court at the movement's headquarters on Eastern Parkway, Crown Heights, not to wash the feet of paupers, and not to give alms exactly, but to be the cause, as it were, that alms are given. A blessing is bestowed and a dollar is conferred on every petitioner. And that dollar, augmented as the receiver sees fit, is then passed on to charity.

It was at this ceremony that the pregnant woman alluded to by my cousins in Llandudno received two dollars instead of one, and lo! was delivered of twins.

Since it is Sunday, and since I am in New York, and since I have thought of nothing else all week – for the Rebbe might just be the Messiah, and you don't get to meet one of those every day – I join the queue.

My preparations have been thorough if not meticulous. I have people to meet when I get to Crown Heights. Connections of connections, who will show me what to do, and at what time, and employing which demeanour.

Yesterday, because I knew today would be a *yarmulke*-ish experience, I spent the afternoon in a drugstore looking for the right clip to keep the *yarmulke* in place. I have never been an admirer of the hair-pinned *yarmulke* look – the rakish, Talmudic-pioneer, man-about-town-but-Orthodox style of being Jewish. It seems to me you wear a *yarmulke* or you don't, and, if you do, you wear it on the crown of your head, not concealed somewhere in your anterior curls. Wearing a skull-cap like that makes it the equivalent of a string bikini.

But now I'm calling on the Rebbe, and will be a long time, by all accounts, standing in the line. I don't fancy having to check that it's still there every thirty seconds; and I don't fancy the stiff neck that comes with balancing it while trying to look indifferent, or at least accustomed, to its presence. So it's a grip or a slide or a bobby-pin or whatever.

This isn't easy for me to do. I creep about the drugstore in a condition identical to that in which I once went after condoms, when condoms were merely preventatives of life, not death. I circle the hair area – I am reasonably at home with gels and fixatives – then close in on brushes and headbands. I reject plastic, anything with ribbons or bobbles. I would like tempered steel, a couple of tiny rapiers. In the end I panic-buy a bulky spring-loaded Afro-perm roller with spikes. It's either that or condoms.

I don't go back on the purchase. Instead, I resolve to find a way of burying what I've bought in my scalp, so that the Rebbe won't notice it. There is just the possibility, anyway, that I want to look foolish and feel uncomfortable.

The old deference trap opening its jaws.

I have not negotiated this part of Brooklyn before. Not overland. There are areas here blacker than I have ever seen. A black neighbourhood in Britain means that there are blacks in the streets, hanging on to the edge of an alien culture. Here the streets are given over wholly to the black community's concerns. Black food shops, black boutiques, Gospel bookstores, Baptist churches, and something called The Gospel Den, offering Needles, Sermons and Accessories. It's the accessories that always tell you you're in a foreign land. I wind the windows of the cab down to get some air, then wind them up again when I hear drums beating in a park. I look back to see it is a black boy-scout jamboree.

But the moment you cross the line, which is Eastern Parkway, it is all Jews.

The cab drops me in a residential quarter. It's by no means a slum, or even a ghetto, if you think of ghettos medievally. There are more houses here than tenements, and there are trees by the roads. Yet you know, by some oppression in the air, by the unnatural quality of the quiet, that there is teeming life within.

Crêpe-hanging

I press a bell. A little English girl answers it and stares at me. Behind her in the hall her brothers and sisters, her mother, her aunts, her cousins, stand and do likewise. Other faces appear from doors. White-faced, but not fashionably white-faced, women. Multitudinous children, uncertain whether they are themselves or their siblings. I smell milk. By the time I have found the right apartment, I have grasped that this is a Lubavitch-only block.

I meet Shmuel and Aviva, my connections' connections – a lustrous couple, half my age – and at once set about ceding the moral high ground and betraying most of my beliefs. For their behoof, I slag off the Conservative service I attended at the Park Avenue Synagogue. But I make the mistake of slagging it off for the wrong reasons. They stare at me in a sort of contained wonderment as I satirize the help-yourself-to-a-*yarmulke* table, and the poor quality of the liturgical English. You're fiddling, their looks say. You're pettifogging.

'There are bigger objections than that,' Shmuel finally cannot keep from telling me.

I glimpse some of the objections he means in the glances he exchanges with his wife. They are big all right.

I suddenly miss Felperin. Maybe I should mix only with academics. But I'm here to please. I'm scrupulous about touching. I don't touch any woman. I'm not sure I ought to touch the baby. (How old, before the no-touchies start?) I try to show how Jewish/scholarly I am by describing the books I found and bought yesterday. One on the Baal Shem Tov, the father of Hasidism. The trouble is, yesterday was *Shabbes*.

In a rare show of free-thinking, Aviva tells me how hard it is for Orthodox women at this time of the year, with one *yom tov* following another, and so many meals to prepare in accordance with *Halachah* – according to Jewish law. She leads me to her stove – not by the hand, not by the hand – and demonstrates what you can and can't do with the gas-taps on *Shabbes*, and what you can and can't do with the gas-taps on *yom tov*. I'd always thought you couldn't do anything with them on either, but apparently there are subtle differences, which I'm unable to follow, relating to turning down and turning up. And to before and after. And to during.

It seems to me that Felperin and I got it right. We went out for a meal.

We discuss the situation at Crown Heights. I've already done a little exploratory work on this subject. When I was ringing around among my connections, one young bull Lubavitcher aired his views on blacks. 'They're animals. They're inferior. They think they've got a chance to take something from us. They'll learn. They'll learn in time.'

'Sounds threatening,' I'd said.

But then the voice had fallen away into Jewish inconsequentiality. 'Eh, threatening . . .'

Today, Lubavitch speaks a mite more temperately. Today, the talk is of how poorly the blacks are led. How there is no black leader, no so-called Reverend, you can liaise with. They change their minds. They fight among themselves. They are hopeless. They don't work hard the way Jewish communities do. Or the way other immigrants do, come to that. They can't make it happen for themselves, because they have no community spirit, and no stomach for labour and enterprise.

Leaving everything else aside, there is one element missing from this diagnosis. Pity.

And the future? Aren't the kids scared by the violence?

'They're used to it. Some of them have been accosted by blacks and told, "We're just waiting for the police to go, then we'll get you." But we're not worried.'

What the not being worried is based on, if these threats are true, is hard to say. Divine protection? Acrostics?

The apartment is given over in every essential to child-rearing and Lubavitch Judaism. A picture of the Rebbe hangs on the wall. The only books on the shelves that aren't prayer-books are volumes of commentary on *Mishna* – the six orders of the code of Jewish law. There is a *mezuzah*, for kissing, on every doorjamb. A *menorah* – the seven-branched candelabrum whose symbolism is dear to the hearts of light-conscious Lubavitchers – on every horizontal surface. Not an object or a sentence that doesn't perform the holy function of reminding you that your mind is not your own.

The surprising thing is that Shmuel and Aviva manage to accept the idea that every waking moment of their lives – and many a sleeping one – is governed by a ninety year old's regurgitations of ancient precepts, without themselves looking musty. Shmuel is lithe, athletic even, with good teeth and bright eyes and a fervid personality. Aviva broods darkly, her fine bones shown to striking effect in the regulation modesty-long dress and snood. In their own way, give or take a tassel, they are a snazzy couple.

With time to kill before the dollar-queue forms, Shmuel takes me window shopping on Kingston Avenue, which may sound Jamaican but is in fact Kamenetz Podolskian. Because it is Succoth, the Festival of Booths, there is an agricultural flavour to the merchandise. There are palm-fronds on sale everywhere, green wands and twiglets, and the *etrog* – the citron, or lumpier lemon. Few shoppers are not carrying some if not all of the foregoing – the fruit of goodly trees, branches of palm, myrtle and willows of the brook: the wherewithal to rejoice before God seven days.

Even without this ritual harvesting in the middle of Brooklyn, Kingston Avenue is remarkable. I do not lightly invoke Kamenetz Podolsky. I do not mean you see Eastern European faces here. What I mean is that it is a *shtetl*, a Russian village, an entire Lubavitcher settlement, out of time and out of place. Not by virtue of clever scene-shifting. There are no chickens in the street. As far as the mortar and the traffic are concerned, we are still in New York. It's the concentration of human purpose that is anachronistic; the unvarying style of dress, the identity of mien, the singleness of mission, the agreement as to height of hats and length of beards and width of prams. Above all, it is the atmosphere of expectation. The imminence.

You can cut the imminence with a knife.

'What time is the Rebbe giving the dollars?' Shmuel is continuously stopped and asked. Everyone is stopped and everyone is asking. The question is feverish and means something else. It means, How long before *Moshiach*?

We call into a Judaica shop, at my request, because I am drawn to its apocalyptic chaos. All the stores appear to have been stocked by a man with St Vitus's dance in a blindfold, but this shop is tumultuous on a grander scale, as though it doesn't merely suspect but *knows* there are greater things in the wind than window-dressing. No respect is shown to the consequence or holiness of any item. *Yarmulkes* lie on the floor, *tefillin* spill from their boxes, the fringes of *tzitzits* and *talaysim* trail on the linoleum, where you tread on *Mishna* and *Gemara* if you don't lift your feet.

And nobody bothers but me, the unbeliever.

Only the walls retain some order. For the reason, perhaps, that the walls are given over to likenesses of the Rebbe – an old man with a white shovel-shaped beard and hard eyes. We are not meant to be a likeness people; likenesses have been forbidden us. It is one of the supreme virtues of Judaism – thou shalt not worship the image of thyself. But the immodesty of these walls knows no restraint. Giant posters of the Rebbe. Framed snaps of the Rebbe. Scrolls, bookmarks, key-rings of the Rebbe. If I have dreamt place-mats and coasters it is a dream that will by now have come true. There is even a clock for sale, a laminated board showing the Rebbe outside the World Headquarters of Lubavitch, just around the corner from here, with a dial on either side of him, one in English numerals, one in Hebrew. In this way you can read secular time and Messianic time synchronically.

I pick up a plastic *Shema* doll, made in Hong Kong. The *Shema* is the great Hebrew prayer proclaiming the singleness of God. No rebbes, just God. When you pull the string a music-box recites the prayer, and the doll, an Orthodox little girl with hair like her mother's wig, covers her eyes.

'Cute, eh?' Shmuel says. He can't hide the father in himself. Or the boy. He has gone toothy over the dolly. Wet beneath the beard.

How long ago was it that he and Aviva stood in a circle of radiance, exchanging glances over my incapacity to be anything but frivolous?

I put a small conundrum to myself: how is it that austerity on matters of religious faith and ritual almost invariably accompanies laxity in matters of art, music, proportion, tact, ethics, manners, civic probity, passing decency and whatever else you can think of that isn't religious faith and ritual.

But to Shmuel I say, 'Yeah, cute.'

Just as I am picking up a *Chumash* from the floor, where it lies among a spillage of Hasidic dance tapes, Shmuel signals that it's time to go.

'Is the Rebbe giving dollars now?' someone asks him. The shop becomes a tuning-fork, struck by a giant finger.

If it was Kamenetz Podolsky before, it is the Urals now. I have been told there are one thousand five hundred Lubavitcher families living in Crown Heights. But how big is a family? Assume fifteen, and now imagine that they are all out.

It is another hot day. The sun bakes the faithful in their black coats. Shmuel gets a swing up as we walk, presumably to cool himself. There are beggars on the streets. Jewish beggars. Until today I have never seen one Jewish beggar, now I am having to brush my way past hundreds.

Outside the Lubavitcher World Headquarters, which I cannot now look at without imagining a clock on either side – one telling terrestrial time, one heavenly – crowds are milling. Trestle tables are set up like market stalls, selling more pictures of the Rebbe, *Moshiach is Coming* literature, *Moshiach Has Already Come* cassettes. *Tefillin* are of course available.

Already the women are queuing. Subdued and pale, they stand in a line that will wind upstairs. When we queue it will be downstairs. On no account must the two queues intertwine. Every woman is in a snood or a *shaytl* – the tipsy wig. There can be something fetching about a snood – perhaps it's the way it suggests the weight of the hair it conceals. But the wigs, worn wearily and askew, are standard Diana Ross: straight, shiny, false.

Pull a string and the women will cover their eyes.

I am taken down – I stress the preposition: down, down, down – into the *shul* of the Lubavitcher headquarters, where the dollar-queue will form, and here I behold a sight which beats even Areyonga in the Central Australian Desert for uncouthness, for outlandishness, for other-worldliness beyond any imaginings of other worlds. The *shul* teems and shudders with men and boys in every attitude of Hebraic, and to my eyes pre-Hebraic, worship. Men rocking, men hiding their faces, men hooded in *talaysim*, men shrouded, men enveloped paler than their own ghosts, men with their sleeves up like junkies, winding their *tefillin*, men pacing, men whimpering, men worshipping the Ark, men lost in Torah, men cradled in God's hand, men watching, men listening, men arguing, men coming and going, men laughing and joking, men smoking, men and boys – and here's the most startling thing of all – men and boys begging, begging in the synagogue, banging you for money, pulling at your sleeves for charity – *tsodekeh, tsodekeh* – offering to pray for you for money, to pray for your parents for money, selling you raffle-tickets, shoving them into your pockets, into your breast pockets

– a *mitzva*, a *mitzva* – except that that's not the most startling thing of all, because the most startling thing of all is that they're selling gold watches down here.

I try to hold on to my nerve. Jesus lost his sense of humour and proportion in the temple, and I am determined not to lose mine. I am in a place at one and the same time worshipful and transactional. Well and good. I disagreed with the Chief Rabbi when he questioned man's capacity to be prayerful in the presence of women; I am intellectually bound to be as sceptical of the power of other distractions. Not least because no one here – no one here who chooses not to be – is distracted by them. Those who would be rapt, stay rapt. Those who have a line through to God, keep talking. So is there a problem? Is there any justification, outside of one's own self-importance, for overturning the tables?

I grew up in a domestic version of this mayhem myself. So did all my Jewish friends. We did our homework with the television on. Judaism is separationist in every regard but this: we believe there is no distinction between the world's business and the business of the spirit. We are not ascetic. We are not monastic. We serve God here. It was retrogressive of Jesus, it made the world itself a less holy place, to say we serve Him somewhere else.

I buy a raffle-ticket.

And I join the queue.

Shmuel leaves me. He is not dollaring it himself today. But he would like it if I come and see him when I've got mine. He'd like to hear how the experience has affected me. Before he goes, he tells me to note the precise minute I meet the Rebbe, because it's all being videoed and if I can give them the time I'm on, they can give me the video of it. By 'give' I take him to mean sell.

Which is fine by me, if not by Jesus.

Before me in the queue are two blue-collar Russians, just in from Leningrad. They wear peaked caps, like early Bolsheviks. Men in black coats and black hats accost me, accost anyone, accost one another. I shake my head. I don't speak Yiddish. When they get to the Bolsheviks they drop into Russian. In the main, it's only the boys who speak English; otherwise it's all Yiddish, Russian or Hebrew. And I'm beginning to get sick of it.

The babble.

And, despite my best intentions, I'm beginning to get sick of the pushing. The queue doesn't move. Unless it's moving in the wrong direction. After thirty minutes the queue in front of me is longer than when it started. But wherever I am in the queue there is always someone who wants to push past me, by me – where it is possible, *through* me.

There is some compulsion, and I can't decide whether it's ethnic or geographic, to get very close. The hand extended for charity actually grazes your chest. The pleading, dishonest eyes almost enter your own. A fringed, rancid boy in shoes so filthy he must have sent them away to be filthied, asks me if I'd like to rent his *tefillin*. I shake my head.

'You laid today?'

'Yes,' I lie.

He doesn't believe me. He makes his eyes do that deathly dance Hasids call joy, presses his shoulders against mine, and laughs.

'People like to lay *tefillin* before meeting the Rebbe,' he lisps. 'It feels a better preparation.'

'I've just told you I've laid,' I say. 'You couldn't be better prepared than I am.'

He laughs again. He's so near to me I don't know whose mouth is whose. It's possible I lose consciousness for a second or two. But I don't fall. There's nowhere *to* fall.

Benches are being moved out of the room. Long benches and tables. Someone has waited for the queue to be at its densest before giving the order for this. It means we can all pack in a little closer. Become one people. Become one person.

An amiable black janitor in a red felt top-hat calls out, 'Watch your backs – working man! – working man!'

He wears a track-suit and running-shoes. His shoes may be worn and discoloured but they are still, after mine, the cleanest shoes in the *shul*.

The Hasids make a poor fist of getting out of his way. He is asking for a motor-awareness from them which they do not possess. Watch their backs? Which are their backs?

The black janitor reads the physical incompetence and panic his way. 'The Rebbe got plenty dollars, man. He got plenty dollars.'

Shmuel returns. He wonders if I've prepared a little something to say to the Rebbe. That way the Rebbe will be able to personalize his blessing of me. Maybe if I explain it to him, he'll bless my project.

'Explain it?'

Shmuel laughs, brushing away a beggar. 'Just briefly.'

Then he's gone again, before I can try him with, 'I was feeling kinda rootsie, Rebbe, so I took me on Jewjewjourney.'

Every ten minutes or so a hush descends. Everyone stands on tiptoe. You can see black hats jumping. You feel fists in your back. It's not out of the question that someone will climb you.

But what are we straining to see? The Rebbe? A miracle? There are people around me who do this once a week, yet they too don't know what's going to happen next, what may appear, what may be performed.

There is hysteria in the air, an absolute conviction that we are in the presence of the marvellous.

After the hush and the straining, nothing. And now the begging and the pushing and the fervid praying begin again.

I am struck by the amount of reading that is going on. Solemn, absorbed, obsessive, oscillating reading. No one is amused by anything he reads, or struck afresh, or surprised into meditation. No one pauses to think again about what he's read, or to formulate a difference with the author. No one takes notes. This is reading of the sort that gives a bad name to reading. This is reading that countermands everything that reading is meant to be for. The only other place I have seen such self-abased, volitionless, uncritical engrossment in books is the London Underground, where wives, mothers and serving women submerge their immortal souls in sagas of Shopping and Fucking.

Meanwhile, the books themselves – those that are not in the hands of rocking worshippers – lie strewn about the *shul*, piled any old way on tables, thrown on to shelves, their spines ripped, their pages loose, their covers hanging off. They contain the unmediated word of God; they are kissed when they are closed; and we are the people of the Book; yet they are treated, as objects, with less reverence than a schoolboy shows his comics.

It is getting hotter and more desperate. More and more men have rolled up a sleeve and are wearing boxes on their foreheads. The room has become smoke-filled. The Bolsheviks in front of me are getting through bag after bag of potato crisps. Wherever there is a rail or a table or someone else's back to support them, men are rocking. I feel the floor sway.

Another hush. A hundred black hats go up. I prepare for the usual subsidence, but this time we are on the move. Rapidly on the move. Men I have not seen before, sleeker men in sleeker beards, are hurrying us along, and shouting at us – no, screaming at us – 'Come on . . . come on, quick! Quick!' And pulling at us. Actually taking us by our lapels and shirts and tugging us. And a queue that wouldn't make it out of a football stadium in under fifteen minutes is disappearing in seconds.

'Come on! Come on, quickly! Quickly!'

The orders are so peremptory and so delirious that I wonder if we are under attack. Have the blacks come for us?

Or is *Moshiach* here? Have we prayed and smoked so hard this afternoon that he is convinced of our readiness at last?

'Come on! Move it, move it!'

It's so fast that the configuration of the queue has changed. The plebeian Russians who were in front of me have vanished. I don't recognize anyone before or behind me. I have never until now seen any of those I am being swept along with. An ancient terror grips me: I will meet my maker or His agent in the company of strangers.

The orderlies, or disciples, or whoever they are, are still chivvying us like sheep. Then suddenly we are not on the same level, we are propelled up steps and on to a balcony or platform, and I see the Rebbe, shovel beard and hard eyes, propped up on a sort of lectern, looking exhausted and expressionless, and I see bearded men all around him, Lubavitcher security, hit-men of God, one of whom is doing the videoing and another handing the Rebbe dollars, counting them out like a croupier from a clean deck, while the rest keep up the bodily harassment – 'Come on! Hurry it up!'

Until the crowd in front of me falls away, as though into an invisible crater, and it is my turn. The Rebbe mutters something, apparently to himself. I think better of saying, 'Rebbe, you don't know me, I'm an English writer, a Jewish writer, here to ...' And it's over, all over in the blinking of an eye. I have my dollar and am out, heading for the light, still hearing the disciples behind me yelling at the lame and the halt, 'Move it! Come on, move it!' – and I am thrust into a sea of clutching hands, begging-bowls, boxes, collecting-tins, all hoping for the dollar I have not a second ago received from ice-cold fingers.

I am appealed to, pleaded with, muttered at, cried over, stroked and kissed, by beggar-women in Ukrainian costume and beggar-men with the pallor of Siberia on their faces, dozens of them on every step, moaning and rattling, trying me in Hebrew and Yiddish, making the irresistible appeal, Jew to Jew – *tsodekeh,*

tsodekeh – only here, today, it's eminently resistible, because Jews don't beg in my understanding of Judaism, and because I need air.

Earlier in the day I had asked Shmuel and Aviva whether I would be able to find an appropriate charity for my dollar. Now I understand why they had laughed at me.

Of course, the dollar you multiply by whatever you can afford and give to charity is not the *actual* dollar. The actual dollar, the blessed dollar, the Messianic dollar, you keep as a souvenir. No sooner do you beat back the first wave of beggars than you find yourself waylaid by tradesmen wanting to sell you polythene sleeves to store your dollar in. For two dollars you can protect the one dollar. Or you can have it sealed and plasticated, turned into a place-mat with a date and a picture of the Rebbe. I shy from that, but buy a key-ring with the Rebbe's likeness on it, for two dollars and fifty cents.

And still the beggar-women in their peasant scarves and woollen ankle socks keep coming at me and crying; and still the venerable old men in beards show me their upturned eyes and search for my humanity in the universal brotherhood of Yiddish. And only the negative example of Christ's sanctimoniousness keeps me from kicking over tables.

I cannot go straight back to Shmuel and Aviva's. It's a part of getting older that you are no longer able to throw yourself from one trial to the next without a sleep, or at least a long pause. Now it goes, frying pan . . . punctuation . . . snooze . . . fire.

Passing a Jewish bookstore, I think I will call in to remind myself of the wit and rationality of my people. I'm aware of the wit trap. I accept that a faith, or a nation, cannot go on making itself pleasing by virtue of its jokes against itself. 'In Jewish mockery,' the Yiddish critic Ba'al Makhshoves wrote, 'one can hear the voice of self-contempt, of a people who have lost touch with the ebb and flow of life. In Jewish mockery one can hear

. . . the sick despair of a people whose existence has become an endless array of contradictions, a permanent witticism.'

I have come away, quit my fireside and my peace, fully prepared to engage with this criticism. Alongside the permanent witticism, the permanent worrying. After the mockery, the melancholy. What if the Jewish joke is just another self-inflicted torment on the Jewish people – the mind paying back the body for all the tremors the body registers, for the inadequately secure housing it provides?

No shirking this, I know. But after where I've been today am I not entitled, for old times' sake, to a spot of innocent philandering with the mind?

I look on the shelves for Saul Bellow, Philip Roth, Isaac Bashevis Singer. Nothing. Joseph Heller, then; S.J. Perelman, Lenny Bruce, David Mamet. Nothing. No Martin Buber, either. No Isaiah Berlin. No Freud. No Amos Oz. No Yehoshua. No Woody Allen. No Norman Mailer. No James Baldwin.

In the world of Jewish Orthodoxy these voices do not speak of anything commendably Jewish. In the world of Jewish Orthodoxy a good book is Manis Friedman's *Doesn't Anyone Blush Anymore?* subtitled *Reclaiming Intimacy, Modesty and Sexuality.*

The body may be covered in Crown Heights, but it is winning all the battles there are to fight against the mind.

I open a Yiddish–Hebrew–English dictionary at an entry explaining the meaning of a Yiddish word thus: 'To rub the face of a child with urine, so removing the evil eye . . .' Whereupon I decide I had better get Shmuel and Aviva over with.

'Well?' they both want to know. 'How was it?'

'Interesting,' I say.

'Interesting?'

I look for another word. 'Mmm . . . interesting.'

They look at each other from within their circle of pure, blushing radiance. I am naive enough to suppose they fear they may have let me down. In fact, the one who's doing the letting down is me.

'Didn't you find it inspiring?' Shmuel asks at last.

I remember my manners. This is how it must always be in the company of believers. You must remember your manners, for they will never remember theirs. Whoever would have a social life must stick strictly to the company of sceptics.

They are surprised it was so rushed that I couldn't exchange a word or two about my project with the Rebbe. But I should rest assured that he would have grasped what I was about. For he is a remarkable man, who misses nothing.

I say that it was my impression he missed a great deal today, that he looked tired and out of it, and would much rather, if you ask me, have been somewhere else. For which, of course, I don't blame him one iota.

Aviva shakes her head. We are reaching that sad and inevitable stage in a conversation that has God and the supernatural in it, when one of you realizes the other comes from Mars. Aviva shakes her head, imparting an exquisite thrill to the two ping-pong balls on aerials which grow out of her snood.

The Rebbe is never tired, she tells me. 'Rebbe,' a woman who had been queuing for a dollar half a day once asked him, 'how do you do it, standing here for five or six hours? I am younger than you, I have not been here anything like as long, and I am exhausted. How do you do it?'

'Imagine counting jewels,' he told her. 'I am counting jewels. And no one gets tired counting jewels.'

I make some self-disparaging remark, to the effect that as jewels go I doubt whether I would have coruscated much in the eyes of the Rebbe. Another permanent witticism. Only I leave out my observation that the Rebbe's eyes are dead eyes.

Twang! go Aviva's aerials. 'He will have blessed you,' she

says. 'He knows what he is doing. You got your blessing whether it looked like it or not.'

And she is off, up up and away, into the clear blue yonder of Rebbinic wonders . . . Iraq . . . Communism . . . Scud missiles . . . Ethiopian Jews . . . babies . . . gas-taps . . . modesty . . . *Moshiach*. . .

Twang! twang!

Seven

HIGH SOCIETY

In Philadelphia, for no other reason than that I have fans here. Four fans to be precise.

If I had four fans in every major city in America I would consider myself to have a readership.

And these are not just any old fans, the kind that send you blank pieces of paper to sign, or write to say that they would read your laundry slips if you cared to forward them; no, these are distinguished Philadelphians, or adopted Philadelphians, who have fans themselves. Bernard Jacobson is the musicologist for the Philadelphia Orchestra. Laura Jacobson resembles, she tells me, a heroine in one of my novels. ('In what regard?' I ask. 'In regard to hair,' she says.) Bea Wernick is a bassoonist. Dick Wernick is a Pulitzer-Prize-winning composer.

As a rule, it doesn't strike me as seemly to append people's prizes to their names. Least of all on introduction. But Dick Wernick is a fan.

When Bernard wrote to me to say that if I was ever in Philadelphia etc., he wasn't to know that I already had a plane ticket in my pocket. It occurs to me I may be a trifle previous.

'So what brings you?' they all want to know. Beneath the question is another one. What would bring *anyone* to Philadelphia?

By way of a short-cut I show them the Rebbe's dollar in its plastic sleeve. We are sitting at a round table in a Chinese restaurant, so the dollar does a perfect circle before returning to me, like a lesson in basic economics. But no one knows what the dollar is; and when I tell them, an expression of mild disgust does the same perfect circle.

Hasidism is not what they mean by being Jewish.

'What is?' I ask.

They look at me as though they are wondering how quickly they can renege on being my fans.

'To tell you the truth,' Dick says, 'I'm not particularly or identifiably Jewish.'

To my eye, he looks particularly *and* identifiably Jewish. But I'm on Jew watch. And in appreciative spirits. I like the white goatee beard he wears and sometimes tips at an acute angle, as though it's capable of listening. It's a satyr's goatee, allowing that a satyr may be fastidious. He is clearly amused by the satyr in himself, a reflective man who enjoys reflecting on his appetites.

He is also, it should be said, a Litvak. From Vilnius.

So he's got that over me. He's from the capital whereas I'm from the muddy provinces.

Bea the bassoonist is a Jew of the other sort – a Sephardi. The daughter of socialist Jews with a Sicilian background, she gave up the name Messina to become a Wernick. She gets very close to me to tell me this. Which she should do. It's an intimate business, changing your name. I would like to tell her I can smell Sicily on her, but that would be too intimate. She is the sort of woman who invites indiscretions, so long as they are comic. Lively, ironic, confidential, musical, given to the conversational arts, capable of making you feel you are the centre of all her attention and the epicentre of all her mirth, full of fun, full of talk, full of listening, maternally voluptuous, scornful, an intellectual élitist – she too doesn't think she is particularly or identifiably Jewish.

'What about you, Bernard?' I ask. 'Are you take-it-or-leave-it, as well?'

'Well, I had Christmas trees when I was a kid. And I didn't

have a *bar mitzvah*. I held out against my parents' wishes. Not that they were Orthodox. I come from the sort of background where my mother worried about having bacon in the house in six-week cycles.'

'When I heard about the Christmas trees I was shocked,' Laura says. Laura who is like one of my heroines in regard to hair.

At Christmas, when the kids from Bernard's first marriage come to visit him, he gives them trees.

'And I insist that they have Hanukkah candles as well,' Laura says.

She is his second Jewish wife. And I, who stop short of Christmas trees, have had one-and-a-half Catholics. Who can fathom faith?

I am having the time of my life. Once we get the Jewish fundamentals out of the way – once I have professionally justified being here, that is – I am able to settle into the Chinese food, the cold beers, and the accolades you idly imagine for yourself when you have written one of those paragraphs which you know that only a handful of intellectuals in centres of excellence such as Philadelphia are ever truly going to understand.

When the meal is over they will be taking me to hear the Philadelphia Orchestra. We will, of course, have a box. The orchestra is their world. What's a box to them? It's a pity that Muti is ill with viral tonsilitis. We're not sure what we're going to make of his replacement for tonight, the Czech conductor Zdeněk Mácal, now resident in Los Angeles, but it should be interesting. Muti rates him.

I sit back in my chair, taking care not to sit too far from Bea, and breathe it all in. I am *really* having the time of my life. The motto from my fortune-cookie falls into my saucer. 'The joyfulness of a man prolongeth his days,' it says.

I am looking at the possibility of making it to ninety, having the time of my life, when a sixth and, as far as I'm concerned, uninvited person belatedly joins our party. His name is Jamake Highwater. He is a Red Indian of the Blackfeet people of Canada. And he is here, as a guest of Laura and Bernard and Dick and Bea, because he too is only in town a few days, and he too is a writer, and he too, it seems, has fans.

There is a Mythos Festival currently on in Philadelphia, and Jamake Highwater is running it.

For all I know he may *be* the Mythos Festival.

Jamake Highwater, as coincidence would have it, went to school with Susan Sontag. Since we haven't been talking about Susan Sontag, this doesn't seem much of a coincidence to me. But we haven't been talking about the late Joseph Campbell, the anthropologist, either, but it is nevertheless brought to our attention as a matter of some relevance that Joseph and Jamake were good friends.

'Are you an anthropologist, then, as well?' I hear one of my late fans inquire.

Jamake Highwater is everything, knows everyone, and has been everywhere. He is very handsome, if you like a face to be hewn from rock. His skin is the colour of dark olives. His hair is so black it is blue. It is cut tribally, to resemble a mop. He has a necklace of stones around his neck. He wears a check shirt, a black jacket, grey corduroy trousers, and running shoes. He knows everyone everywhere, and everywhere is where he has just run from.

He tells a story of being at a PEN meeting – does he say he is World President? – where Norman Mailer boasts that his new book has sold forty million copies worldwide. 'That's nothing,' Susan Sontag says, 'mine has sold two hundred.'

Still at the Chinese table, we purr over this elegantly anti-populist sally, a touch uncertain, for all that, how it relates to Jamake's main point, which is that we cannot go on talking, as artists, to people who already agree with us.

He mentions the names of a few thousand people who agree with him on this point, poets, painters, playwrights, set-designers, dancers, critics. I think I hear Peter Schjeldahl's name making it on to the list.

'You know Peter?' I ask, gutturally.

'Sure. He was at the beginning of the SoHo thing before it became a place where people take their Guccis for a walk.'

I don't say, I asked you if you knew him, not knew *of* him. I'm too busy trying to see if Bea and Laura think it's cute that a Blackfoot should feel so at home with white vernacular.

On the way to the concert hall we discuss the column Jamake writes for the *Christian Science Monitor*. Is it true, Dick wants to know, that he is forbidden to use the word 'death' in his copy? Yes, it is. Nor can he use 'contagious' or 'infectious'. Not even as in 'infectious smile'? Not even then. How about 'catching'? Nope, no 'catching'. So what do you do with a train? Jamake doesn't quite see the problem. We laugh carelessly. And I notice something about Jamake. He's at home with Blackfoot culture, he's at home with American culture, he's at home with high culture and he's at home with low culture, but he's not at home with jokes.

Ensconced in the box, the Jacobsons and the Wernicks reflect on the sorrows of life in Philadelphia – a life, they maintain, without any culture. I make a question mark of my face and a basket of my arms. In five minutes from now one of the world's greatest orchestras will strike up. The auditorium is full. The women in the audience have had their hair done. The men do not wear earrings. No culture? Here?

'Look around carefully,' Dick tells me. 'Everyone's old . . .'

'Or, at least, not enough people are young,' Bea puts in.

'They talk during the music,' Dick says.

'They cough too much,' Laura adds.

'They walk out,' says Bea.

'Whereas in Europe . . .' says Bernard. But he is careful not to gloat. In six months he and Laura will be gone. He is quitting Philadelphia for the Hague.

Jamake Highwater isn't sure about Europe. He is even less

sure about England. 'Name me one contemporary British composer ...' he says. 'Name me one contemporary British painter ...'

I am saved from having to compile a list by the arrival on the platform of Zdeněk Mácal, a figure who seems to have too much sag in him, who seems to bend at the middle like one of Dickens' love-sick clerks. This is more or less Dick and Jamake's verdict on his conducting too, judging from what he gets the Philadelphia to make of Dvořák's *Othello Overture* and Mozart's Serenade in D Major K329. But after the interval comes Mahler's First Symphony, and something in Zdeněk Mácal's Czech origins rises to the alternating Hebrew despondency and jauntiness of Mahler's music. For a half an hour or so Philadelphia becomes Eastern European, rural, uninhibited and Jewish. We abandon ourselves to the folk-melodies, and the orchestra which looked asleep during the Dvořák plays with all the wild zest of a klezmer band.

Almost before it's over, the audience is on its feet. A tumult breaks around our heads. The blood runs cold in my veins. And I am about to ask Dick what he means by accusing this audience of passionlessness when I realize that he is not just on his feet but leaping in the air. 'Wonderful,' he cries, 'wonderful to hear a twenty-year-old Jewish kid take the *shtetl* and shove it up Cosima Wagner's nose!'

Dick, who is not particularly or identifiably Jewish.

Only later, after a standing ovation, does the critic reassert itself over the Jew. 'A bit ragged here and there,' he says. 'But the raggedness suits the piece.'

There is perspiration in his goatee. There are coals in his eyes. Deny it all you like – it is a wonderful thing to be a Hebrew, even in Philadelphia.

It is a wonderful thing to be a Blackfoot, too. 'I thought I knew everything there was to know about that piece of music,' Jamake whispers to me. That's how good Mácal was. He saw something Jamake hadn't.

We go backstage (Bernard and Laura and Bea and Dick exchanging kisses and handshakes with the second violin and the timpanist) to congratulate the conductor. He is on a grander scale than you would know from the box. The hips are still Dickensian-clerk-slender, but his face has an unexpected Bohemian cragginess. He is excited, sweating. But then, who isn't? He carries a large glass of water and a towel. Had I ever been asked to guess what a conductor carries after a performance that has brought the house down I would have said a large glass of water and a towel.

Laura calls him maestro. I shake his hand and thank him. Jamake shakes his hand harder and thanks him longer. Dick talks about other versions of the symphony. Apparently there is a rogue movement which Ansermet always included. Dick and Mácal agree that it is better left out. Jamake thinks so too. Still breathless, Mácal tells us that he was born thirty miles from Mahler's birthplace, and therefore knows what the horns are doing in the piece. When he was nine, in 1945, Mácal could hear the military trumpets blowing in the nearby villages. Mahler would have heard the same trumpets.

For a moment or two we fall silent so that we can let the sound be passed on down, from Mahler to Mácal to us. We are individually emotional, receiving our inheritance.

Guess what?

Jamake is Jewish.

'Highwater,' I observe, 'is not a very Jewish name.'

It turns out he isn't Jewish in that sense, isn't *Jewish* Jewish. It turns out he isn't Jewish in the Lost Tribes sense, either. The idea that Indians were Jews enjoyed some currency in early Puritan America. It raised the hopes of those who believed that the Second Coming was dependent on the conversion of the Jews, but who could see that the usual Jews of their acquaintance weren't easily convertible. A better bet seemed to be the Indians. So stories abounded for a while of explorers coming upon Indians who were able to recite the *Shema* in Hebrew. But Jamake isn't claiming these sorts of origins. What actually happened was that he was adopted out of the Blackfoot tribe of Canada by a kindly Jewish family from the San Fernando Valley.

'So you weren't *bar-mitzvahed*?'

'I wanted to be. I asked to be. But my foster-parents took one look at me and said, "You cannot be a Jewish boy!" '

We all look at his granite face, surmounted by its blue-black mop. No. There is nowhere in his features for a joke to hide, therefore no, he cannot be a Jewish boy.

But the surprising thing is that Jamake, who has written about everything everywhere and in every language for every publication and every television channel, has *not* written about being a Red Indian who was adopted by Jews from the San Fernando Valley and who wanted a *bar mitzvah*, for anyone.

'I didn't feel I could,' he says. 'I hate racism.'

We are in Bernard and Laura's place, sitting in comfortable chairs, drinking wine. But we all shift to the edge of our chairs together. 'Racism? How would it be racism?'

'I cannot tell the stories I have to tell,' he says. 'People will be hurt by them. They will misinterpret them.'

'Who will?'

He pauses. 'Everybody will.'

'If you mean the Jews will,' I remind him, 'you should never forget how much they love satire against themselves.'

He is quick, and sore, with his reply. 'Only when *they* make it,' he says.

An invisible thread linking Bernard and Laura and Dick and Bea and me, but not Jamake, vibrates infinitessimally.

Still harping on what he could an' if he would, Jamake tells us that he has one of the best Jewish accents in America, but won't use it for fear of causing offence.

'Show us,' we say.

He can't.

'Go on,' we say.

He can't.

'Please,' Laura says.

Only if we promise not to take offence.

'We promise,' Laura says.

He shows us.

I take offence.

Nor is it one of the best Jewish accents in America. In the Concord it wouldn't come among the first three thousand.

Because I have been so good at sharing what should have been a glorious evening for me with someone else, the god who looks after these things has prepared a last treat for me. Jamake, it appears, is not an old friend of Dick and Bea's. He has met them for the first time only tonight. And, at an hour that those of us who are not Blackfoot would find rather late for such a question, he asks Dick – Pulitzer-Prize-winning Dick – what his name is and what he does. Picture, then, his shame, when Dick tells him.

'I knew I should have known.' He hits his face with the heels of both his hands. He changes colour. 'I knew I should have known. I knew I knew . . . your name is so familiar to me . . . your face . . . your work . . . I know your work so well . . .'

It is a name-dropper's nightmare. Here he is, having spent an entire evening in the company of a name to conjure with, and he hasn't once dropped it because he didn't once know it was in the air.

But you will, Jamake. You will.

Just before we go, Laura bethinks herself of something that's been on her mind. On the subject of Indians and Jews, and Indians being one of the Ten Lost Tribes. 'That could explain,' she says, 'why Jewish women like Indian jewellery so much.'

*   *   *

There is another justification for being in Philadelphia, if justification outside Jamake is needed: Reconstructionism. The third of the three primary liberal movements in Judaism in this country, Reconstructionism, is not exactly on the lips of every Jew I meet, but I have heard tell of it. Unlike Reform and Conservative Judaism, I gather, both of which originated in Germany in the nineteenth century, and were the offspring of the *Haskala*, the Jewish enlightenment, Reconstructionist Judaism is American, home-grown in every sense except that its creator, Mordechai Kaplan, was born in Lithuania. I take that to be a guarantee that the movement will not be without its intellection. 'The spiritual regeneration of the Jewish people demands that religion cease to be its sole preoccupation,' Kaplan wrote. But that was not meant to be an invitation to a spiritual free-for-all. 'Our position,' he also said, 'is that those *mitzvot* which, in tradition, are described as applying "between man and God" should be observed, in so far as they help to maintain the historic continuity of the Jewish people ...' Sounds folksy, but not as folksy as Alony. Reconstructionism, I decide, might just be Streisand-free. And what does any of this have to do with Philadelphia? If you want a Reconstructionist education, Philadelphia is the only place you can get it.

I have been given the name of Jacob Staub, Dean of the Reconstructionist Rabbinical College, but when I call I can't get him. It is still Succoth, the Feast of Booths, and the college is closed. So it's not *that* Reconstructionist.

But I am. In order to find out a bit more about a movement which claims to have over one hundred thousand adherents in North America – that's roughly a third of the number of Jews there are of all persuasions in Great Britain, after all – I decide to reconstruct my travel arrangements, put off flying to Los Angeles for another day or two, and stay in Philadelphia, taking care to give the Mythos Festival a wide berth.

Armed with a guidebook to Jewish Philadelphia, lent to me by

Laura and written by Esther M. Klein, a native Philadelphian who, at the time the book was published, directed an annual Passover and Hanukkah *Kosher* Cooking School, I hit the Jewish sights. But I have forgotten Succoth again. The Jewish sights are closed.

Outside a darkened Jewish Museum, on David Ben-Gurion Place, I find room on a bench, otherwise peopled by poor, sleeping blacks, and give myself up to ethnic loneliness. Out there in the suburbs, the Jews are in their *succahs*, their bowered booths, eating fruit and rattling their wands of willow. Elsewhere, Bea is practising her bassoon, and Bernard is administering linctus to Riccardo Muti. Every now and then a pony and trap rattles past, bearing tourists to or from the Liberty Bell. A tramp on the bench next to mine is having nightmares, frightening the squirrels. I permit myself a couple of sighs, deeper than exile, and am ready to see what is written on the few memorials hereabouts, the only things Jewish that are available to me on yet another festive day in this interminable season of festivals.

A carved semicircle of stone, guarded by four white marble pillars, sculpted by Buky S. Schwartz, commemorates Jonathan Netanyahu, the lieutenant-colonel who died leading the Entebbe Raid. An inscription taken from the Second Book of Samuel sends my soul soaring out of the state of Pennsylvania.

> They were swifter than eagles. They were stronger than
> lions. The bow of Jonathan turned not back.

The B'nai Brith statue of Religious Liberty, executed out of a single block of carrara marble by Sir Moses Ezekiel, is less stirring. Not surprising; Jonathan Netanyahu was a man, Liberty is a concept.

A youth personifying Religion holds a bowl of inextinguishable faith, like *latkes*, in his left hand, while with his right he seems to be supporting a low ceiling. Like Liberty, he boasts features of an Anglo-Saxon cast. Only the eagle of Democracy, making short work of the serpent of Tyranny, looks remotely Semitic.

'Sir Moses Jacob Ezekiel (1844–1917),' Esther M. Klein informs me, 'was the first American plastic artist to enjoy world fame ... In 1874 he won the coveted Rome prize for a bas-relief "Israel" never before awarded to a foreigner. This B'nai Brith statue was considered his masterpiece.'

I make my way towards the Liberty Bell and the Constitution area, wondering how well Jamake knew Sir Moses. I don't stay long among the Liberty paraphernalia of Independence Mall. It is a banal but unavoidable truth that monuments to democracy lose their gloss in proportion as the number of beggars in their vicinity increases. And anyway, a bell is just a bell.

I hail a taxi, since everything I want to see is closed, and ask to be taken back to my hotel. The driver is dark and prickly, and has a spectacular scar running from his right eye to his right ear. A war wound, I decide. The bow of Jonathan ...

He asks me if I've enjoyed the old area. On a Jonathan-fuelled hunch I say that I'd actually been trying to get into the Jewish Museum, but it was closed. 'Ah, Succoth,' he says.

My luck with taxi-drivers, if not with festivals, is holding. I was right about him being stronger than a lion. He is an Israeli, fourth-generation, a Yemenite. His father was among those who air-lifted the remaining Jews out of the Yemen in 1940, in the bold operation code-named Magic Carpet. Swifter than eagles.

He isn't mad about Philadelphia. 'It's too mellow,' he tells me. That's his exact word. *Mellow*. We savour it together in the Philadelphia traffic. 'There is nothing to raise your passions here,' he says.

I don't mention Mahler. Or Bea. Or Laura. Or the Mythos Festival.

He lives in a Jewish area of the city because he likes to be

surrounded by Jews. He likes to see them going to *shul*. 'It
touches your heart. You know what I mean?' But he wishes the
Jewish community was more demonstrative. Take this business
with Bush. He wishes the Jews of Philadelphia would be more
open about how they feel about that. Go public. Make some
noise.

'It sounds to me,' I say, 'as though you want to be back in
Israel. Why aren't you there?'

I don't think I imagine that his scar becomes more livid.
'I'm always being asked this,' he says. 'By American Jews
especially. They feel I'm letting them down by being here.
"Then go yourself," I tell them. They don't understand what
it's like there. They can't imagine how hard it is to go there,
learn a new language, learn new customs. It's a tough place.'

'Isn't that the point?' I say.

He takes his eyes off the road to look at me. 'You been there?'

'No,' I laugh. 'I haven't had the nerve. But I'm going, I'm
going.'

He wants me to be clear about something. He isn't dis-
illusioned.

I nod. I get it. You don't argue the merits of a country with a
man who has received a scar in its name.

But it's precisely the army that's the problem. 'I was a full-
time soldier for three years,' he tells me. 'That's a long time.
And it's not as though those years come when you are twenty-
seven to thirty, when they wouldn't matter quite so much. They
come between school and university. You go in a boy and come
out as a man. They're lost years. They're the time when a man
or a boy can lose his way. Crucial years. And then, when you
come out, they do nothing for you. Nothing. Listen, it's not that
I begrudge those years. I wanted to serve. It's important. I knew
what we were fighting for. I was proud to serve. But . . . but . . .
It's hard in Israel.'

And now, to make things worse, there's the problem with the

Russians. The Israeli government gives them tax incentives, housing benefits. It doesn't matter how clearly you understand the need for Russian immigrants and their skills, you still don't like to see them getting hand-outs when you've just been sent home from the army with nothing. In the long run they'll make Israel a different and a better place, but meanwhile, yes, there is disgruntlement.

And him? Will he go back? His eyes dance. He is a boy still, whatever he says about having lost his boyhood to the army. A boy with an enviable, pulsing scar running from his cheek to his ear. Yes. He will go back. Someday. Yes, he will.

I shake his hand and tip him inordinately. My effort for Israel.

I watch him drive away. He has found something fatherly or confusedly patriotic in me. I seem to be touched that he is a Yemenite. That he is Jewish and has African hair. Perhaps I am simply touched that there is such a thing as a Yemenite.

A doorman who has bothered us while we were parked outside my hotel talking – opening the door and then slamming it because I wasn't ready to alight – feels the edge of my wrath. I have to do something with the emotion I feel. It's either strike or go around gulping. Swifter than eagles, I approach him and stare him down.

Does sir have a problem?

'Yes,' I say. 'Sir wants to see your name.'

It's Scott. OK, Scott. Big trouble. I'm already annoyed with this hotel. They kept me waiting twenty minutes when I arrived because, they said, they'd lost my reservation. They didn't fix my coffee machine, even after I'd rung housekeeping twice. An ice machine outside my room churns enough ice for the whole of Philadelphia, day and night. Ring room-service or reception and they say, 'Mmm-hmmm,' as if they're imitating a Southern mammy who's heard all this a million times before. And now Scott has come between me and my Yemenite Israeli brother.

167

You're in deep shit, Scott!

The only thing they have done right in the Terrace Restaurant of the Wyndham Plaza Hotel is find the colour to suit the spiritual condition. I sit deserted on this shore for lost souls, marooned in maroon. The chairs are maroon, the tables are maroon, the serviettes in the wine glasses are maroon, the food is maroon, the waiters are maroon, the pain in one's forehead that throbs in time to the tinkling elevator music is maroon.

The Terrace Restaurant is supposed to be open until eleven, but at ten-fifteen the waitresses are crowding me, pushing me to sign my bill before I have finished eating. I lose my temper. 'What do you want?' I ask. 'Blood?'

'Mmm-hmmm,' they say. 'Aah-haaah.' They'll take blood. So long as it's maroon.

No one is left but me. Scott is wandering the lobby in his uniform, showing me that he is still in employment. The invariable world-over sad sacks are at the bar, sipping cocktails through straws, twirling the tiny Chinese umbrellas, wondering why, when, where ... At ten-thirty the hotel feels like a long-haul aeroplane after the movie is over and the lights have gone out. I can hear the drone of the engines.

A lone pair of heels clicks across the marble. The men at the bar are too tired, too old, to look up. Phones ring. Lifts ping. A woman kisses two men goodnight. 'Take care.' 'Thank you.' 'Take care.' 'Thank you.'

It's over for another night in Philadelphia.

'Tomorrow's gonna be another long day,' one fat man, breathing hard from getting out of a taxi, says to another. Conferees. Dressed for *après*-conference good times. Which they haven't found. Far from home and it hasn't happened. Now the despondency. Post-congress *tristesse*.

Out of suits, the conferees look like plumbers. I'm the only person in the hotel who looks like a conferee. And I have no conference to go to.

No one Jewish is about. Help.

A Reconstructionist prayer, composed by Mordechai Kaplan:

PRAYER FOR SUSTENANCE

I thank, Thee, O God, for the gift of life and for the wherewithal to sustain it.

Restrain my hungers from becoming extravagant, and hold back my desires from exceeding the bounds of justice and equity.

Banish from my heart all care and anxiety. Imbue me with confidence in man's inherent goodness. Let me not feel that my world has come to an end, if I have to turn to my fellowmen for help.

The old problem – toss out the snarling God and you're left with a citizen's charter.

But it gets me through a bad night at the Wyndham Plaza, and, since it is, in a manner of speaking, a Philadelphian prayer, that might be all it was ever intended to do.

Desperation is a marvellous thing. Succoth or no Succoth, I'm not staying another day in Philadelphia, but nor am I leaving without talking to somebody in the Reconstruction business. So, in despite of all natural law, I just somehow come to know, I just somehow come to possess, Jacob Staub's home telephone number.

'The best I can give you,' he tells me when I call, 'is phone time.'

'I understand,' I say. 'It's Succoth. Phone time is fine.'

He takes me through the basics. The Center of the Federation of Reconstructionists was started in the early fifties. The college of which Jacob Staub was an original member and is now dean was founded in 1968. There are currently sixty students enrolled. Of which half are women. The course lasts between five and six years. Twelve students graduate as rabbis each year.

'Not rabbis that would be recognized by the Orthodox body of Judaism, I take it?'

'We enjoy adversarial relations with Orthodoxy,' he tells me.

He is quietly spoken, gently humorous. His accent is New Yorker made lenient, perhaps, by the Quaker breezes of Pennsylvania. I picture him, since this is all of him I am going to get, as wearing a tweed suit and a red polka-dot bow-tie. A W A S Pish sort of Jew. But with a steel-grey beard, like Jonathan Sacks's, to show that he isn't an art critic.

'The college is committed,' he explains, 'to the principle that rabbis need a secular as well as a religious education. Jews in this country enjoy a dual allegiance; they honour two civilizations, and therefore we offer training in two civilizations.'

I observe that it is my understanding of Orthodoxy that it too, in England and America, accepts the necessity of dualism.

He pauses to say something to his family. I fall to wondering whether he is speaking to me from the *succah*. I see it, elegantly plaited, at the bottom of a long garden. Everything is there that should be there. The *lulav* and the *etrog*, the willow and the myrtle and the lumpier lemon. But the children are golden-haired and pug-nosed. Little *goyim*. Such is the tyranny which an ancient faith exercises over even its least compliant members: let anyone mention innovation and you at once imagine treason.

'We define Judaism,' he says, returning to the phone, 'as the evolving religious civilization of the Jewish people.'

'Evolving?' Now *his* nose is just a rounded blob of clay.

'Yes. Reconstructionists are very traditional in ritual, but in a non-*halachic* way. Our view is that our Jewish heritage is humanly, not divinely, ordered. When *Halachah* is impossible to observe, especially in relation to many laws involving women and ritual, then changes are made.'

'So it's flexible ritual?'

'Our phrase is "creative ritual". The code word for us is *revaluation*.'

I'm at home with the language. Give or take a *Halachah* this is Eng.-Lit.-Speak, Cambridge *circa* 1960. It is not entirely out of the question that Mordechai Kaplan was influenced by F. R. Leavis. We were Reconstructionists of sorts, back there in the early sixties. We too were a puzzling blend of the conventional and the heterodox. Mollified, apologetic even, I ask if there is a Reconstructionist community outside of the academy. Are we talking letters here, or are we talking life?

It's not what you call a searching question. He's not likely to go against life. And he doesn't. 'Oh, we have a very exciting community. The last thing we are is coldly intellectual. People come to us precisely for the warmth of community, for *haimish-ness*.'

'And these rabbis you produce – do they go out to their own synagogues? Are there Reconstructionist synagogues?'

This is the only time he lets me down. 'Yes indeed,' he says. 'And they are very much centres of Judaism, of Jewish life. They are structured as participatory decision-making institutions . . .'

I suddenly remember that I have read about these community synagogue-centres, and that they were the occasion for a famous jibe when Kaplan first came up with the idea. *Shuls* with Pools, they were called. I don't mind the pools. It's the phrase decision-making I find hard to take. One of the best arguments for God is that He took the decision-making process out of our hands, thereby removing all necessity for using the phrase.

I make one last attempt to get Jacob Staub to meet me, to give me contact time as well as phone time, but he can't. That other participatory institution, the family, requires quality-time paternal input. But he gives me the number of a young English woman who is studying at the college – Helen Glanz – and I call her.

She's shy but amused to get my call out of the blue, and pleased to hear an English voice, so, well, why not, yes, she'll meet me in my maroon hotel lobby, and is here, just as she said she'll be, in half an hour flat.

She's even more shy in the flesh. Intelligently shy. Shy because, when all is said and done, it's foolish not to be. Her eyes are weepy, leaky. I can't tell if she is short-sighted. And there is a slightly Indian-subcontinent look about her, which turns out to be because her mother is from the Indian subcontinent.

She's a doctor, an MD. A real doctor, someone useful. She was in St Louis doing post-real-doctoral work when she heard about the Reconstructionist college. She's in her second year here. But lonely. She hints at a broken relationship. She has three years of study left but she's thinking hard about returning to London and finishing her rabbinic training there. That's what she wants to be – a rabbi with her own congregation.

Her shyness and her loneliness, yet her gameness in coming out to discuss her life with a perfect stranger in a hotel lobby, her personal hesitancy and her professional courage, all contribute to an atmosphere of extreme dejection. She weaves some melancholy around us both, which I am powerless to shake off. But it is she who suggests that we drive to Fairmount Park, 'one of the largest verdant city parks in the world,' according to Esther M. Klein; and it is she who finds us a bench to sit on in the sun.

It is a lovely warm day, with just a hint of autumn in the air. Only the very tips of the leaves are browning. Squirrels run across our feet as we talk. Things haven't got any less melancholy. We sit, awkwardly, two Jews adrift, discussing acquaintances we have in common in London. But at least the summer hasn't given up the ghost.

She talks to me about the Reconstructionist course she's doing. How it shades off, for some students, into New Age philosophy. There are *Shabbes* services where they sit around in circles, massaging one another's shoulders and analysing the prayers, word by word. It's *gestalt*, study-group, caring sharing Judaism.

Her services, when she becomes a rabbi with a congregation of her own, will be partly in Hebrew, partly in English. I tell her about my Park Avenue synagogue experience, and what happened to the lining of my soul when the 'attributes and qualities' of the beloved dead received their dues. Unlike Shmuel and Aviva, she grasps the enormity of the crime. I do not tease her with Kaplan's 'Restrain my hungers from becoming extravagant.' She doesn't look strong enough for banter. And anyway, she is quick to tell me that Reconstructionists are concerned to have new and powerful translations done for them. By poets? Yes, by poets.

A major issue, though, is how to translate the venerable sexist language of the Scriptures. Or rather, how not to translate it. How to prise the Divine free from divine chauvinism. I watch the squirrels. There is her strength to consider, but there is also mine. Even when I'm in tip-top health and not languishing in Philadelphia I don't accept that the word 'sexist' is allowable in adult company. And that's to say nothing of what's allowable in the company of the Divine.

She explains some of the ways Reconstructionists are rethinking *Halachah*. Thus, *Kashrut*, the whole business of what's *kosher*, takes on board issues of humanity and ecology. We can prohibit tuna, not on the say-so of the Torah, but because we disapprove of the way they are fished. A new category of considerations has been born: the eco-*halachic*.

I don't know. I try to shake my head internally, so that Helen doesn't have to see. I don't know. This has more of Mordechai Kaplan's justice and equity and inherent goodness in it than does the gas-tap neuroticism of Orthodoxy; but why not just go eco and drop *Halachah* altogether?

'And what about morals?' I ask. 'Where are you on ethics?'

She blinks a few times. Her watery eyes worry me. *She* worries me. I feel she needs taking care of. Ought I to ring her parents when I get back? Your daughter the rabbi is low and lonely in Philadelphia. She's on something. Reconstructionism.

She is surprised, actually – this in response to my morals question – how tolerant the movement is of gays. But she thinks adultery is frowned upon.

You never know where you are with Jews and adultery. The word is out (I can say no more than that), the word is out that the Orthodox are the worst of all offenders against their own purity code. Manis Friedman, the same Manis Friedman of *Doesn't Anyone Blush Anymore?* fame, tells a homiletic tale of a woman adulterer who goes to the rabbi to confess her infidelity. 'I'll talk to you tomorrow,' the rabbi says. Come tomorrow, he says, 'Yes?' She says, 'About yesterday's matter . . .' The rabbi says, 'I don't remember anything from yesterday.' Moral: every heart has its secrets.

Does Orthodoxy know something Reconstructionism doesn't?

Ignorant of either, the squirrels go about their business, not minding that our feet are directly in their path. They brush our ankles, like feathers on springs.

'You know,' Helen says suddenly, 'one of the reasons I agreed to meet you was that I recognized your name. I've read all your novels.'

My spirits rise. Now I've got five fans in Philadelphia. Or, assuming I lost one to Jamake, I've still got four. Small things like this tip the balance of a day, ease a disconsolate morning into a serene afternoon.

'Do you mind talking about your work?' Helen asks.

I shrug. Not something I care to do, but today, in the warm sun, among the hoarding squirrels, in one of the largest verdant city parks in the world . . .

'Because,' she goes on, 'I've always wondered how you came to the decision – I think a very brave decision – to write *The Rape of Tamar*?'

I go very still. So still I disturb the squirrels. I didn't write *The Rape of Tamar*. She has the wrong Jacobson. She is thinking of Dan – *Dan* – Jacobson.

I don't have the heart to tell her. I can't risk those leaky eyes. Instead I embark on a long and rather subtle exposition of how I found the courage necessary to write *The Rape of Tamar*.

Eight

SENSELESS BEAUTY

The balcony of my almost-Beverly Hills hotel, overlooking Pico Boulevard, is twice the size my room was in New York. That's the upside. The downside is that it's overlooking Pico Boulevard. More calming to the spirit would be a balcony overlooking the M25.

But it is high up at least, and I am glad to be on it in the company of a bottle of Californian merlot, relaxing after a long flight. The sky tonight is magnificent – livid, reddy-brown, ribbed like a vast beach, angry, growling, intermittently lit by lightning. Spectacularly speckled charcoals and even turquoises, all in motion, colour rolling over colour, preside over the limitless spread of lights, hills, houses, communication masts. Truly it is a Hollywood night, cataclysmic, a disaster movie of a night. But not God's night. This sky is emptied of all divinity. It is incontrovertibly human. A sky made by motor cars, sulphur, buzzing air-waves, people who need people. An imitation sky, a backcloth, marvellously unconvincing. If this city is struck down it won't be God's doing. The place is top to bottom autonomous, self-generating, self-destroying.

In my experience you are always surprised when you wake up still alive in Los Angeles. Since yet again I do, I celebrate with a staccato burst of telephone calls. I have fixed nothing in advance. I mean to do LA on the hoof. But there are always preliminaries. I'm not expecting things like Succoth to stand in my way. This is California. Still and all you have to be certain that people are not out of the country before you set off to see them. The freeways run for long distances in all directions in this town.

I learn something very quickly about unbraced, easy-going California. No one is unbraced or easy-going. Nowhere on this journey so far have I encountered such wariness. No one, absolutely no one, is coming out to play. Every relaxed take-it-as-it-comes West Coast rabbi is phenomenally busy. The shysters and mountebanks whose job it is to talk to anyone at any time are suddenly bashful. A wall of secretaries, trained in scepticism, stands between me and every Jew in Los Angeles.

The Simon Wiesenthal Centre passes me down the line – from the director Rabbi Hier's office to Communication, from Communication to Research. Research I don't want. Research I do myself. The University of Judaism puts me through to its souvenir shop. Jews for Jesus wish me *shalom* and then listen like spiders. When I explain that I'd like to meet someone who can describe the movement's activities to me – I don't say that I am curious to observe by what act of moral prestidigitation they seek to reconcile the irreconcilable – a warm woman's voice says, 'I'd like to present that to our ministry staff.' Only the Gay and Lesbian Alliance, accustomed to strange requests in strange accents, is helpful. They give me the telephone number of Beth Chayim Chadashim, voted best gay synagogue by the LA equivalent of *Time Out*. When I ring the synagogue I am back in warinessville. But they can't stop me coming along, Fridays at 8.30 p.m.

Are they in their cars too much, these people? Are they simply unpractised in any art save that of lane-changing?

The sun shines, the palms sway, the avenues run dusty into the hills. The place smells like Sydney. It bakes, it cooks at a similar temperature and gives off a similar odour of sweet urban sizzle, of solids burning, of gases leaking, of flesh browning on a spit. But none of this does anything for the city's temperament. New York is better behaved, is less socially cynical. Here, you encounter a dead fall – not a dying fall, it has already died – every time you pick up a telephone.

Given that nothing else is doing, and that I took this hotel precisely to be in walking distance of the Wiesenthal Centre, I decide it was rash of me to refuse Research. I ring again and speak to Rick Eaton. From him I gather that Research was what I wanted all along. Research is where it's at; Research is where the Nazis are logged and nabbed. Will he talk to me in the flesh? Yeah. Now? Yeah. It's not camaraderie exactly, but it's an advance on anything I've had so far. And besides, Rick Eaton has reason to be cautious – I might be Mengele.

I walk out on to Pico, into the heat. Something has to be good here, and this is it. Forget the knock-you-down heat of New York, forget sweat city; the sun here is insinuating, even when you've got your back to it, even when you're in retreat, it creeps around and cups your face, a hot hand caressing each cheek.

I don't have too long to enjoy it. In less than five minutes I am at the Yeshiva University of Los Angeles, housing the Menachem Begin School of Jewish Studies and the Simon Wiesenthal Centre – correction, Center – for Holocaust Studies. Next door, a new building is under way – The Simon Wiesenthal Center Beit Hashoah Museum of Tolerance, architects Starkman and Vidal and Christensen.

A Museum of Tolerance – what a simultaneously grand and anticlimactic ambition.

A Museum of Tolerance! What do you put in it? What do you show? Or will it stay empty? Will that be its eloquent point?

There's no easy access to Holocaust Studies. You have to push buttons and then confront a secretary. A notice on her desk says PLEASE DO NOT INTERRUPT RECEPTIONISTS WHILE THEY ARE ON THE TELEPHONE.

I take my notebook out while I'm waiting. 'Is this a touchy town or is this a touchy town,' I write.

Rick Eaton comes out to find me writing. I drop my notebook. He is no friendlier in person than on the telephone. I don't know what I expected, but somehow he isn't it. He is lean, tallish, with pitted skin and weepy Helen Glanz eyes, and a rather chilling beard, cut like a Scandinavian's into a sort of ridge, a disapprover's beard, more a disfigurement of the flesh than a decoration for it.

He escorts me past a film-crew who are interviewing a survivor, and sits me down in a nondescript office, full of filing-cabinets and books, of which I note only a German dictionary, a number of volumes of the *Encyclopaedia Judaica*, a *Who's Who in Nazi Germany* and a biography of Kurt Waldheim.

After telling him what I'm up to – which, since I don't know myself, is an unconscionable time finishing; and which, incidentally, he attends to with fearsomely cold concentration – I ask him what he does.

He begins by talking to me about *haters*. *Haters*? I notice his verbal italicization. A *hater* is more than a noun coined from a verb; a *hater* is clearly a known type here, a person familiar and recognizable to Research, a distinct subspecies of individual. A *hater*. Like a psychopath or an arsonist. Someone definable by many more characteristics than just the accidents of whom or what he may end up hating.

And where you have more than one hater you have hate-groups. Rick's job is to keep an eye on these hate-groups. In a sense, to infiltrate them. To be around their activities. To keep tabs on their literature, to subscribe to their magazines and news-letters, to know who they are and what they are up to, and how they might be changing their procedures, and where necessary, 'to put up road-blocks'.

The cop phraseology is not fortuitous or fantastical. A cop is what he is. An undercover agent.

I ask him if he has ever taken a risk too many, if he has ever felt in physical danger. He shakes that one away. Not really. On the other hand he doesn't go putting himself on television or otherwise draw too much attention to himself. 'There is a degree of sensible prudence,' he says.

He takes me through the current villains. David Duke, the one-time Klu Klux Klansman who may well end up senator for Louisiana. Tom Metzger, the leader of White American Resistance, who has his own public-access cable-television programme, *Race and Reason* ... He pauses to tell me that he was in Metzger's home the other day, walked straight in by the side of a British film-crew making a documentary. This is what he calls 'keeping channels of communication open with the haters'. Knowing where to locate them, knowing how their breath smells. If you need intimate information on the *dramatis personae* of the Fascist theatre, Rick Eaton is the man you turn to.

Or there is Aaron Breitbart, the senior researcher. I am not prepared for Aaron Breitbart. He appears suddenly in the office, an overweight man in a *yarmulke* (Rick Eaton does not wear a *yarmulke*), and immediately begins talking to me. Although his dark hair is beginning to grey, he has a boy's face, somewhat cherubic lips and a boy's sad eyes. But it is an amusable face, framed if not for mirth, at least for registering that mirth exists, a talker's face, a face for expressing, where Rick's is all for suppressing.

Perhaps because he can see that I am more comfortable with Aaron Breitbart's face, Rick Eaton, on a pretext of business, removes his.

'This is not the kind of job that it's easy to go home from,' Aaron Breitbart tells me. 'You don't easily get over the horrors. Put it this way – I don't go back to the family and watch Holocaust movies on TV.'

He sits back in his chair, magisterially, and crosses his ankles. His legs are white. Always the sign of a reflective man.

But his theme for the moment is relief, the lighter side of the Nazi-tracking business, and it's in that spirit that he vouchsafes me a glimpse of what they call their 'Crazy File'. Letters from people finding anti-Semitism behind every bush; from people discovering a terrible significance in numbers – their neighbour's age multiplied by their neighbour's telephone number; one from a dentist who believes he was a Holocaust victim in another life, and who dreams the SS is after him. Fairly often it is hate mail, people contesting the Holocaust, or people pretending to be sympathetic but who are trying to catch the Wiesenthal Center out – 'I have this friend who was an engineer in Germany in the 1940s and *he* says there were no concentration camps; how do I explain to him that he's wrong?'

'In other words,' Aaron Breitbart glosses it for me, 'give me some information that I can refute . . . go on . . . put your foot in it . . . give me a quote that I can use against you.' He smiles his mischievous choir-boy smile. 'I can't prove it empirically, but I can always tell when an apparently innocent request for information is one of those. There's always some little give-away, something that tells me it's wrong.'

Like a swastika at the head of the notepaper.

While I am trying to get a look at more of the crazy letters, the phone rings. Someone believes his next-door-but-one neighbour could be SS. Aaron asks the suspect's age. And what the caller knows about his biography and movements. Usually the suspect is too young to have been an actual employee of Hitler's. As on this occasion. 'He could do with being a bit older than that,' Aaron tells the caller. 'But keep in touch, and if you have further reason to be suspicious phone me here, direct, on –'

I ask what the grounds for suspicion were.

'The usual – a foreign language. He thinks the suspect might be speaking German.' We both laugh. 'Most times a few questions dissuade the caller or the writer from pressing further. But everything that seems worth looking into is looked into. You never know.'

He has dark eyebrows which contradict each other. One is shaped comically into an interrogation mark. The other is an underscoring, heavy and final. Whatever the conflict inside, as a conversationalist he is emollient. His lips make a wet sound whenever they meet, so that his sentences are punctuated by a sort of moist percussion. It is like listening to someone talking by a brook.

He heaves his bulk forward in his chair. Jews and their overdeveloped sensitivity to anti-Semitism remind him of a joke. Hymie Greenberg goes for an interview for a television announcer's job. Afterwards, his friends ask him how he got on. 'Th-th-they d-d-didn't g-g-give it t-t-t-to m-m-me,' he says. 'M-m-m-must b-be anti-s-semites.'

Rick arrives back, perhaps because he has overheard our laughter and, Scandinavian beard notwithstanding, wouldn't say no to a laugh himself.

They put on a double-act for me. Apropos the work they do checking who is keeping company with whom, which so-and-so is seen supporting which such-a-one, how come X is suddenly spending time with Y. 'Sometimes we are accused,' Aaron says, 'of promoting guilt by association.'

'But our defence,' Rick puts in, 'is the duck test.'

'The duck test?' (That's me – the straight man.)

'Yes,' says Rick.

'The duck test,' says Aaron.

'We like,' says Rick, 'to make a *shiddach*.' A *shiddach* is a match, a matrimonial bringing-together.

'We like putting like with like,' says Aaron.

'And the duck test is . . .' says Rick.

What they say next they say together. '. . . that if it walks like a duck, makes noises like a duck, and communicates with a duck . . .'

I've got it. '. . . then it is a duck.'

By rights I should have gone by now. These are busy men, and they have already sung and danced for me. But I can't tear myself away. I have the feeling that if I stay they'll open more files for my delectation and improvement. Or another call will come through from a crazy. Or the KKK will try to bust us. This is it, I decide. This is the place. This is the power house.

They read my mind. Aaron goes rooting for a letter. His voice reaches me from a filing-cabinet. 'The spiritual grandchildren of the Nazis are much more dangerous than the Nazis themselves,' he says. 'The original Nazis are few and old. But their heirs are young . . .'

'. . . and numerous,' Rick adds. 'And they don't just make you sick now, they make you bored!'

Aaron has found what he was looking for – a letter from a deranged European woman who distributes material such as this across America. In this particular instance she is accusing the Jews of pharmacological evil. The Jews, she claims, are poisoning the rest of the world with drugs. It is the Jews, for example, who put the tannin in tea.

Aaron shakes his head and lets a great sigh inconvenience his body. 'Pharmacodynamic anti-Semitism now! Fortunately the words are too long for anyone to take any notice. Hate has to be brief to work.'

I know a closing-line when I hear one. I get up to leave. But Aaron has one more little surprise for me. He pulls a brown envelope out of his drawer and empties the contents on the table. Swastikas. Swastika arm-bands. Swastika badges. And unsigned membership cards of the National Union of Socialists.

'These are so that you can . . .?'

'Yes,' he says proudly, making a soft wet sound with his lips.

Our eyes meet over the droll picture of Aaron Breitbart in a swastika, rolling along to a Nazi get-together, and passing himself off as a gauleiter. I am prepared to swear that in his picture as well as mine he has omitted to remove his *yarmulke*.

But just so that my last impression of him shouldn't be the wrong one, he introduces me to something he calls the Irving Syndrome. Irving is the name of the quintessential, soft, stay-out-of-it Jewish boy. Lie low, don't mix in, keep your nose clean, don't let the *goyim* notice you're there. Aaron, even though his legs are white and he taught Hebrew before he hunted Nazis, is no Irving.

'The one thing I don't try to keep,' he says, 'is a clean nose.'

'I wish I could say the same,' I say.

That's the other thing about Irving – he's a crawler.

Back on Pico, I decide to do what no one does in Los Angeles and go walking. Tough, if I scare the motorists.

I am soon among the Jewish shops, the *kosher* restaurants, the synagogues. It's not like New York. It's more like Prestwich or Golders Green. New York is one giant *kosher* but not too *kosher* deli, open to everyone. Here on Pico I'm back in a ghetto.

A gift-shop sells I'M A JEWISH-AMERICAN PRINCESS aprons, and LITTLE FRESSER bibs, and I LOVE, or rather I ♥ ZAYDE T-shirts. An Electrical, Plumbing, Rooter and Drainwork Shop has a picture of the Rebbe hanging in its entrance. The hardware stores all have Persian or some other Middle Eastern script on their fascia boards, and specialize in samovars, vacuum-flasks and lunch-boxes – whatever will keep food and drink cold or warm, and dispense liquid from a tap. Are there nomads here? Is Pico Boulevard Bedouin?

The food shops and nosheries offer variations on a more familiar Middle Eastern theme. There is a Nagila Pizza House. Charlie's Kosher Delicatessen sells Sinai Corned Beef. You can get Sabra Salad in the sandwich-bar. The A A A Flag and Banner Shop has the Israeli flag wound around its counter as around a bier.

Whatever the tone is here, I hadn't counted on it. I had expected beach-Judaism. And, while this isn't exactly backs-to-the-wall minority paranoia, there's an excitability about the neighbourhood which I don't associate with sun and surf and everything I've heard of West Coast assimilation.

Senseless Beauty

A white hacienda synagogue offers CRASH COURSES IN HEBREW. What's the hurry?

A notice on the door of a Kosher Pizza Nosh Deli gives the shop's business hours as *10.30 a.m. to 8.30 p.m. – Saturday (after Shabbat) till?* – but adds a telephone number for EMERGENCY CALLS. Emergency calls? I need a pizza . . . quick! quick! Get me *kosher* pizza!

A sign in the window of Dove's Kosher Bakeries says HELP WANTED! It's closed, otherwise I'd rush in to see if they're all right. But ought I to be breaking the door down? What if the baker is being held hostage in there?

On a fly-poster announcing an appearance of Yigal Ben Chaim, 'one of Israel's best *chazanim*' – that is to say, cantors – someone has scrawled in red ink (blood?) 'Nancy/Mark Telem – I'm in the bar at Hymie's fishmarket. Find me. Dora.'

Soundlessly, without there being a soul on the streets, the Pico end of Beverly Hills envelops me in its agitations.

Which is fine by Aish HaTorah, an Orthodox outreach organization that sits imperturbably on Pico Boulevard amid the ferment and uses its windows to offer comfort to the stressed-out and the bewildered.

Do you go to the synagogue out of guilt? Do you have the 'what page are we on in the synagogue' blues? Join Rabbi Dov Heller for 'Understanding Prayer and how the Prayer-book works'.

If your blues are not prayer-book centred – correction, centered – Aish HaTorah can still help.

LOVE LIFE
ENCOUNTER THE SOURCE
LEVEL 2:
THE ULTIMATE EDUCATIONAL EXPERIENCE

The only catch being that you still have to join Rabbi Dov Heller.

I stand outside the building, which resembles a funeral parlour, and scratch my head. Is this the beach-Judaism I've been looking for? Is this a house of ill-repute passing itself off as a *yeshiva*? Or – and am I at last beginning to understand Jewishness in LA – is it a *yeshiva* passing itself off as a house of ill-repute?

A blown-up extract from an article in the *Jewish Journal of Greater Los Angeles* is displayed in the window like a rave restaurant review.

> Men and women, ranging from 22 to 44 . . . are lined up in Pico Blvd hoping to get into the Aish HaTorah Center's 8 p.m. weekly Love Life Encounter . . .
>
> Participants are directed to tables seating 10 each. Only candles light the room.
>
> Smiling, red-headed Rabbi Stephen Baars greets the group and tells a couple of funny stories . . . He talks briefly about tonight's subject, *commitment* . . .
>
> People linger and talk. Some leave as couples.
>
> 'I wish women's lib never happened,' says a pretty woman in her 30s. 'It did women a lot of damage.'
>
> 'Men want an old-fashioned woman, yet they want us to be equal,' adds a tall, slender blonde.

Bad journalism. You can tell from what she says that she's a tall, slender blonde.

And I, slow as I've been about it, now see what the Aish HaTorah Center is up to. Aish means flame. Nothing can stop those men and women, ranging from twenty-two to forty-four, from burning. They'll burn whether there are Love Life Encounters or not. So let us at least contain the fires. Aish HaTorah exists to keep Jewish desire Jewish.

That's how it looks judging simply from its windows, anyway. If there's something I've missed they can put me straight about it when I confront them. Which I decide I might just as well do while I'm here. Right now. West Coast informally. Without a by-your-leave. While I'm hot.

*   *   *

There is no one senior available to talk to me. The usual *lulav* and *etrog* alibi. If they're rabbinic they're in a booth, thinking on God's bounty. But the secretaries or helpers or second line of command – they're hard to place hierarchically, because they're not English – get excited about the idea of enthusing over the Center to a stranger. As long as I understand that they are only etc. etc. And that they are not authorized etc. etc.

One of them, a tall, slender blonde in her thirties, apologizes for not having any flyers to give me. 'I'm so angry,' she says. 'I'm so angry about those flyers.'

It's as if she's been waiting for just this eventuality, for someone like me to walk in off the street and put his finger immediately on the very weakness in the organization that she's been campaigning to remedy for she doesn't know how long. No flyers! God, is she angry.

But it's the other one, the darker, quieter one, the Orthodox one in the snood, who sits me down and, in between phone calls, tells me what she can.

She is called Hanna Kenner. Hanna pronounced Channa. There are a lot more Hannas pronounced Channa around than there used to be when I was the right age to be collecting young women's names. This is the consequence of *ba'al tshuva* – the return to Orthodox Judaism. The secondary Jewish names we always had, the names we were circumcised and *bar-mitzvahed* and married by, are the names by which returnees are now choosing to be known in their secular lives too. Hence the number of young men called Baruch who have suddenly appeared.

Hanna wears no make-up. Just as Aviva didn't. I'm just beginning to understand that wearing no make-up, as Hanna and Aviva wear no make-up, is a species of arrogance. Look at the unmade-up beauty of my skin. Observe my virgin freshness. God-kissed, that's what my flesh is. God-kissed and husband-cherished.

A species of arrogance and a subtle form of flirtatiousness. Sit before a married virgin of the Orthodox return movement and willy-nilly you are drawn into the drama of her sexual choices. Let the topic of conversation be what you will, slowly, ineluctably, the legend of her chastity or fidelity or restraint edges across the table, as transfixing as a cockroach.

Anyway, Hanna – for we have not been speaking specifically of Hanna – shows me her sincere, faithful, unroving eyes, and tells me about Aish HaTorah: how it was started by Noah Weinberg, an Israeli; how the organization in Israel has taken over the very last available site facing the Wailing Wall for its headquarters; how the new thing is the Discovery Seminar Program (DISCOVERY – WHERE THE PAST MEETS THE FUTURE); and how the two most successful programs staged here in Pico Boulevard are 20-Something – 'We have really tremendous outreach to young people,' she says – and Love Life Encounters.

Since they are what got me in here, I quiz her about the latter. All this stuff about candles, commitment, couples . . . What are we talking here, Torah or romance?

'People get very involved,' she concedes. Then, just in case I may have the wrong idea about her – 'I don't myself. I'm married.'

'So it *is* a meat-market?'

She winces slightly and plays with her fingers. There's something of the nun about her. Anyone less of a meat market-woman you cannot imagine.

'To young people who don't have much of a Jewish identity,' she says, 'some of the greatest challenges facing them are to do with dating . . . So yes, we've had several marriages come out of our programs, especially 20-Something, even though we're not strictly a dating-agency.'

What she says is so reasonable that I find myself wondering what it is I think I am nosing out here, and why I am offering to be quite so morally censorious of it. Of course dating is an issue. Of course it bears on matters of social and religious solidarity.

Not only is there nothing new about religion and romance being yoked together, you could argue that religion exists for no other reason than to ensure the sexual and marital homogeneity of the tribe.

Watching me feverishly taking notes, and hardly being in a position to understand that I am ticking myself off, Hanna suddenly takes fright. I notice that she exchanges glances with the tall, slender blonde in her thirties.

'You mustn't quote me,' Hanna says. 'I'm not senior enough to be telling you what we stand for. I'm only giving you my impressions.'

I promise her that I will not cite her as an authority on Aish ideology. The last thing I want to do is cause her any embarrassment. I won't even make more than a passing reference – this is for the tall, slender blonde – to the fact that they were unable to furnish me with flyers. And anyway, her seriousness and zeal are the best possible advertisements for what goes on here. No one could talk to Hanna and doubt the high-mindedness of the enterprise. Assuming that it is high-minded of a people to insist on having sex only with itself.

Hanna runs up and down the office on errands, her feet splayed, her long floral-print frock flying. 'When I have a moment,' she says, 'I'll give you the names and numbers of the people I think you should contact. But they're all very busy right now.'

'I know,' I say. 'Succoth.'

'Not just that. We've got this raffle going on. We're raffling a '57 Thunderbird . . . so we're all busy.'

On a filing-cabinet by her desk is affixed a message: PRACTICE RANDOM KINDNESS AND SENSELESS ACTS OF BEAUTY.

I am so struck by it that when I find myself on the street I cannot remember whether I took decent and polite leave of the two women.

Senseless acts of beauty! Where am I? Where have I just been? Do they think they are in touch with some irresponsibly plastic paganism in there? How many gorgeous acts of improvidence can you perform, conformably with Torah?

Or with a snood?

After all, I have come out with the very thing I went in for – a renewed conviction that California and Zion, love and law, are incompatible. That all the optimism Los Angeles can muster will never alter what must therefore be an immutable truth: that the only good Jew is a tragic Jew.

For no other reason than that I see a taxi, I hail it.

This is such an unusual event all round that the driver feels obliged to call in to his operator to explain it.

'Don't make a habit of this, three-four,' the operator tells him.

It takes me a minute or two to decide where I want to go. First you get the taxi, after that you worry about a destination.

I decide on U J, the University of Judaism, Mulholland Drive. Partly because I have been told that it is worth a visit in its own right. And partly because I have read in *LA Weekly* that there's a photography exhibition on there – Vanished but not Vanquished: Photos of a Jewish World That Was . . .

I would never go to an exhibition of photographs unless I'm working, so if I go to one I must be working.

U J is a steep ride out of town. By the time we get there we are in the hills, virtually in the desert. A rugged, frontier university. I am relieved. I dread *shtetl yeshivot* which are just no more than holes in the wall from which boys in skull-caps emerge like termites.

U J is modern, athletic, low-slung, strenuously of the place and of the moment, the way I expect a *kibbutz* to look. A *succah* has been built in the grounds, and people wearing *yarmulkes*, but liberated *yarmulkes*, are sitting around in it like pioneers, talking in deep, joyous voices.

I go in through the main entrance and find myself immediately in a gift-shop. I don't know enough about universities in America to be certain, but I have a hunch that it is not normal for a gift-shop to be the first thing you encounter on campus, before reception, before notice-boards, before directions, even, were it not for the *succah* pioneers, before students.

And it is a gift-shop in the best Jewish tradition of gift-shops, full of *tsatskes* and *shmontses*, Judaica kitsch, baubles of the heart, the sacred and the sentimental thrown together without the due reverence for the one or the appropriate contempt for the other.

Since I'm here, I pick up a number of those authentic *yarmulke*-clips I was unable to come by in Manhattan, just in case I find myself in a Messianic-waiting situation again. As I hang on for my change I notice a sign above the till reminding sales staff that there is ABSOLUTELY NO DISCOUNT ON ANCIENT COINS.

I tear myself away from a display of the same sterling silver Hasids I last admired in the Concord, and go wandering. I'm still a sucker for universities. They remain holy places for me. No other institutions tease you with the same promise of books and company and eating away from home. The first thing I wonder about when I arrive in a new city is not what it's got in its museums and art galleries, but what its university is like.

And I have never seen one like this one. Or at least I have never seen one so punctilious in its expressions of gratitude to those who have put up the money for it. There is not a room, not a wall, not a stone, not a step that is not named after someone. A list of the university's founders is done in gold lettering on marble tablets in the hall of what is the SYLVIA AND DAVID WEISZ EDUCATION WING, which is itself, as I understand it, part of the SHIRLEY AND ARTHUR WHIZIN center (dedicated to the JEWISH FUTURE), which is in turn, as I further understand it, housed within the WILLIAM AND FRIEDA FINGERHUT ACADEMIC BUILDING, a sub-branch of NORMAN AND SADIE LEE COLLEGE.

To get from SYLVIA AND DAVID'S WING to the BESS AND ALEXANDER L. BERG DINING CENTER (fed, incidentally, by a kitchen dedicated to the memory of CELIA AND MORRIS I. PELLOW BY THEIR CHILDREN JUDITH AND LOUIS) you have to negotiate the ELIE J. AND RACHEL GINDI ENTRY PLAZA AND LOBBY.

It's like being inside a Russian doll – I suppose I should say a Russian *Shema* doll. You go into one named chamber only to discover that there is another named chamber within it. And no one is promising that the sequence will ever come to an end.

The photos of a Jewish World That Was are exhibited in the Platt Gallery. I am disconcerted by the gentile name. *Platt? Channa and Baruch Platt?*

A video on the work of the famed Russian Jewish photographer Roman Vishniac – born 1897; took sixteen-thousand-odd photographs, of which only about an eighth survive, of a people about to be annihilated – is playing on a television set. Seeing the sorrowing faces on the screen, and the ennobled-by-poverty-and-pogroms portraits on the walls, I am reminded of why I was so enraged by what trespassed on my pity in Crown Heights. Those *schnorrers* and beggars and bums had the same faces as these we've been weeping over for centuries. Were these too, then, just bums and beggars in their time, but willing to stay still long enough for the cameras of the likes of Vishniac to confer some grandeur on them?

Something is wrong with this exhibition. Something is wrong with the way we modern Jews idealize a past we wouldn't touch with a barge-pole if it were offered us again.

I turn in anger from the video and walk straight into a group of photographs of rabbis studying, taken by the Hungarian-born photographer Arnold Eagle. Which only makes me angrier.

Why is Jewish study always made to look so soulful in these sorts of photographs, so unrelieved, so unvarious, so fucking miserable and desolating? What is it about *Jewish* books that makes absorption in them such an invariably heart-rending business?

What a sell! How have the Jews done it, how have we persuaded not just ourselves, but gentiles as well, that anguish and lamentation and self-abnegation and bodilessness and pathos attach inalterably and exclusively to *our* studies?

You don't see Aquinas looking into a book like that.

Vishniac's photographs are of Vilnius, Warsaw, villages in Carpathian Ruthenia, Slonim, Lublin, Cracow. He is especially partial to snaps of old men carrying books. Fucking books again.

One, entitled 'One of the People of the Book: Warsaw 1938', shows a venerable, white-bearded *frummy* with a stick, carrying four big volumes. It's a photograph everybody knows. Even if you don't know it, you know it.

Vishniac's accompanying text says, 'Books became the spiritual food of Jews. Boys of thirteen could read and write while 90 per cent of the non-Jews were illiterate.'

But what books? Is it any more spiritually nourishing to read lists of forbidden fowl – the ossifrage and the osprey and the vulture and the kite and the owl and the cuckoo and the cormorant and the swan and the pelican and the stork and the heron and the lapwing – than to read Jilly Cooper?

I must be even angrier than I know. For me to suggest that there may be an activity that rivals reading Jilly Cooper for mindlessness, I have to be incensed indeed.

It's not just the books that are doing it. It's the invidious comparisons. Under a photo called 'Jewish Peasant, Carpatho-Ukraine, 1937', I read:

The peasants around were so uneducated that you could

193

not speak with them about anything. Their interest was just vodka, only alcohol to drink. But a Jewish peasant – he was a wise man who knew about life, without having a radio or a newspaper or any information, nothing but his own thoughts and understanding . . .

Sound like any Jew you know? Sound like anyone you know?

But even if there were such a paragon of peasant wisdom, gleaning understanding from the closed university of his own thoughts, is it necessary to rub the vodka-peasant's nose in the disparity? Must the rest of humanity be humbled because a Jew is bright? Hasn't a Carpatho-Ukrainian-gentile eyes? If you prick him does he not bleed?

What a mix and what a mess it is, this dreaming nostalgic hotchpotch of misery and pride, arrogance and *schmaltz*. Who can wonder that it leads at last to the moral confusion of being proud of your misery, of being half in love with the cruelties that have been visited on you.

I pick up a volume of Vishniac's photos. And find that Elie Wiesel has contributed an introduction. As with the pictures, so with the words. Show Elie Wiesel an Orthodox Jew and he sees a 'dreamy Hasid'. Show him a Hebrew teacher and he sees a 'gentle and vulnerable *melamed*'.

On Vishniac's subjects in general: 'He loves them because the world they lived in did not, and because death has already marked them for its own – death and oblivion as well.'

Coffee-table thoughts to suit coffee-table art. But how we love these cadences, we Jews. How smitten we are – far from all harm – with the poetry of our tragedy.

Outside the exhibition, which is the best place to be in relation to it, I overhear a couple of Jewish women slagging off Rabbi Marvin Hier, the dean of the Wiesenthal Center.

'Long before Hier we had a Holocaust Center.'

'Quite.'

'It's not as though he started it!'

'Quite. No. Quite.'

'But from the way he goes on, anyone would think . . .'

'Quite. Quite.'

First the poetry, then the quarrelsomeness. In Los Angeles we squabble over Holocaust Centres.

You mean Holocaust Centers.

Quite.

I'm grateful to the two anti-Hier women. They break into the monotony of the place. They are the only things in the building that don't carry a dedication.

I try ringing for a cab – on the Moses Mendelssohn telephone.

There's a long pause from the operator. 'Where did you say you are?'

I tell him.

'But where is it?'

I give him the address once more.

'Any more clues?'

'Well it's in Los Angeles.'

'Any more . . .?'

'I've already given you Mulholland Drive.'

'And the number?'

'It's a university. I don't know if it has a number.'

And it's a university of what?'

'Judaism.'

'Ju . . .?'

'. . . daism.'

'Could you spell that?'

I spell it.

'I've never heard that word before.'

'Judaism?'

'Never.'

'Never?'

'Not used like that.'

Nine

WE'RE HERE, WE'RE QUEER, WE'RE NOT GOING SHOPPING

As far as punishment is concerned, no distinction is drawn in the Torah between sleeping with another man's wife, sleeping with your neighbour's wife, sleeping with your father's wife, sleeping with your son's wife, and sleeping with a member of your own sex. Ye shall surely be put to death which ever way you jump. The only difference is that sleeping with your own sex, lying with mankind as with womankind, is called an abomination to boot.

Sleeping with a beast doesn't make it as an abomination; sleeping with a beast is just a confusion. Even sleeping with a woman and her mother simultaneously, for which the punishment is fire for all three of you, simultaneously, is only deemed a wickedness.

So there is no excuse for not knowing where the God of Moses and Abraham stands on the question of free and open self-expression for gays.

But where do gays – more specifically, where do Jewish gays – stand on God? It is Friday night. Beth Chayim Chadashim – voted BEST SYNAGOGUE FOR VERY NICE JEWISH BOYS AND GIRLS by Jim Schmaltz for *LA Weekly* – is a mile or two down Pico Boulevard. Nothing else is doing. I can offer myself no reason for not going and finding out.

I arrive a little late, 8.45ish, so as to be able to slip in with no ado. If there are any preliminaries of a confessional nature, I mean to miss them.

A couple of black security guards eye me indolently. I am dismayed that they don't stop me. I'd be more comfortable if they thought I looked out of place.

I clip on my *yarmulke* and edge sideways into the *shul*. It is small, modest, a Friends meeting-hall, with individual chairs, not benches. The room is very nearly full. I estimate seventy to eighty people here. There are so many bits of paper on each seat, it is hard to tell which, if any, are reserved. Someone hands me a blue plastic folder as I arrive. A ring-binder. When I open it I realize that it is the *Siddur*, the Sabbath prayer-book. I get it. We are meant to feel that we are back at school. And that there are no rigidities. The contents of the binder may change. We may put things in ourselves. We may add to the photocopied pages, some of which are illustrated and spell out the Hebrew phonetically. It is like a project.

I am also handed a couple of supplements. Photocopied especially for tonight. *Supplementary readings for September 27th, 1991 and prayers for Succoth.*

We are a movable feast, in other words. Nothing is fixed for eternity. We pray as we feel. On the night that we feel it.

Cantor Croll is taking us through some of the special Succoth customs. He is a Frank Furillo style of gay Jew, slight, with aquiline features, pale skin, a twitchy nervous sense of humour, dark shadows under his eyes. He wears a summer-weight grey suit. And over that he wears his prayer-shawl like a silk scarf. He is talking about shaking the *lulav*, and how he'll be giving it an extra shake at the end of the service. Something for us to look forward to.

'We do things in Reform Judaism that Orthodox Judaism doesn't do,' he tells us. He is stressing positivity. People think that Reform is all about what we don't do. But it is also about what we do do. As, for example, blowing the *shofar* on *Shabbes*. Orthodoxy doesn't do that. But Reform can't see why those who wouldn't otherwise hear it should miss out.

There is a gentle murmur of assent. We are for not missing out. There has been too much missing out.

I look around. I am the only person in a jacket. I did right to wear a *yarmulke*, although there are a few here who don't wear one. I also did right to leave off my tie. I actually have it in my breast pocket, folded, next to my notebook and my passport and my spare *yarmulke*-clip. All the proofs of my insecurity, unaccustomed as I am to being among gay Jews, convinced as I have heretofore been than gay Jews no more exist than do bestialists.

Everyone is in short sleeves, open-necked, Levied, Reeboked. There are maybe a dozen women here. Dressed, in the main, with the same studied stevedore nonchalance. There are more elderly men that I would have expected. But they sit at the back. Front-row brazenness has come too late for them.

The Ark of the Covenant is arch-shaped and appears to be made of bakelite. On the altar wall are two batik bedspreads, in oranges and purples. Part of their design feature is a green oblong motif, suggesting bricks or books, from which emanates a criss-cross of light or maybe conflagration. Bricks on fire. Books aflame. Inspirational thoughts, the shape of lozenges.

Cantor Croll, Don Croll, thinks it would be nice if we wished good *Shabbes* to our neighbours right and left, to the people in front, to the people behind. And if we introduced ourselves in the process.

So it has done me no good, coming late.

I swing from side to side, giving my name, saying, '*Shabbat shalom.*' An elderly man to my left says, 'Hi! I'm Stephen.' He is nearly blind. I've watched him having to raise his ring-binder to within an inch of his face. A young lumberjack to my left is Michael. 'Hi, Michael.' A woman with marvellous, long, fertile hair of the deepest brown turns around. Deeper than the brown of her hair is the timbre of her voice. 'I'm Mary Ann – *Shabbat shalom.*' We grasp arms.

To my great surprise, I am not minding any of this. I cannot claim to be relaxed. There are things to fear still – intrusions and intimacies I cannot even put a name to. But however forced the conviviality (and it may be only me that's doing the forcing), it is preferable to the normal hostile individualism of the synagogue. Togetherness, that's what we've got here, togetherness before God. 'Hi, God, I'm Howard.'

There is, as how could there not be, a degree of *de rigueur* possessiveness. One man holds his arm aloft, like Liberty, only it is not a torch he holds but the shoulder of the man beside him. Another massages his neighbour's neck. Strokes it and then squeezes it. Squeezes and then strokes it. It is hard to tell whether the action is meant to give relief or pain. Naive of me to make a distinction. I stare, mesmerized by the single green stone set in silver on the little finger of the squeezer's claiming hand.

Cantor Croll, meanwhile, remains painstaking in his explanation of the service. This means this. That happens because . . . No one is to feel excluded. Religion may be a mystery, but there will be no mystification here. He spells out the Hebrew. Have we got that? He gets us to sing along, coaching us in the melodies. So what, if the sound we make is not beautiful? At least it's *us* that's making it. At least we're giving it a go.

And that includes me. For the first time, for the first time ever, I sing along, as best I can, in a synagogue.

We stand, we turn to the door at the right to welcome *Shabbes* like a maiden, we bow, one or two of the congregation even rock a bit. 'Stand or sit, according to your custom,' Cantor Croll suggests.

Tonight we don't have a rabbi. Tonight we have a Service Leader. Michael Main – bearded, red-faced, unashamedly vulnerable, a Jew of the kind that teaches creative writing in small universities or libraries. He has just been to a rabbis' camp in upstate New York and he wants to tell us about the experience. 'I love New York,' he begins. This isn't a sermon. It's more of an offering. A sharing. That moment in a creative-writing course when the leader reads out what he's been writing. 'It was so emotional up there,' he says. 'And so spiritual. By Wednesday we were already saying, "*Shabbes* is coming." I don't live like that in my normal life.'

We all know about that. The hour when you are taken out of yourself. The insight hour. The epiphany.

We want more from Michael but we have to wait. First, the lighting of the *Shabbes* candles. In a Jewish home it is the woman who lights the candles. The husband will either be at her side or will join her later, once he has returned from *shul*. Either way, the kindling of the lights is heavily associated with the ideals of family. So there is a poignancy not lost on anyone in this room, when Phil Starr and Michael Simental are called up to perform the ritual, 'In honour,' Cantor Croll announces, 'of their seventeenth anniversary.'

We let off little gasps, like damp fireworks. 'Seventeen years!'

Not nothing, seventeen years, in these precarious times.

Phil and Michael take their places at the table. They wear matching woven *yarmulkes*, somewhat Egyptian in style, a fez each, like the Two Pirates. They exchange shy glances as they extend their tapers. Darby and Joan. Baruch and Channa. One is very hairy, thick-set, with a bushy moustache and a stack of black hair. The other – I don't know which is Phil and which is Michael – is tenuous and fragile. Blow out the candles too vigorously and you would blow out him.

More songs. More touching. Because Cantor Croll asks me to, I put out a tentative finger and find the turquoise T-shirt of the congregant in front. He is a fleshy man with a pleated neck and a silver stud stapled through his ear. Someone does something similar, if more affectionate, to my back.

We get to the *Amida* – silent devotion. The prayers are to be found in our blue ring-binders, in Hebrew, English or a mystical version on page 44. 'Or just find the words in your own heart,' Don Croll says.

I turn to the mystical version, where I read of 'food-plants sprouting'; 'civilizations' having 'their genesis'; 'lifelong partners'; 'freedom to be ourselves'. Two lines of verse catch my eye:

> Your children grow
> Heartbeat, bloodflow.

Nothing I can do – bloodflow breaks through the dam of my devotion. I flick through my folder and find more verse, some by Walt Whitman, whom I never took to be Jewish, some by Judy Chicago, whom I never took to be a poet.

Michael Main begins his sermon which isn't. We are back in upstate New York, back in rabbi-camp. A particular rabbi made an impression on Michael Main. A Rabbi Syme. Leading a seminar on the subject of Jews not talking enough about God, Rabbi Syme proposed that his group discuss the time they came nearest to God. No one was obliged to speak. You can't force these things. They just could if they wanted. And Rabbi Syme perfectly understood that there was a reason why none of them at first wanted. 'I know,' he told them. 'I can see from your faces you think, "Heh! – Jews don't do this. Christians do this." You think it's a bit like witnessing, right?'

We all laugh. We laugh at Main laughing at Syme laughing at his seminar-group. Binding laughter. We're all Jews on this one. It's fun, thinking aloud together about the ways that we're not Christian. It's fun just having the word Christian dangled for our delectation like this. It would have been the same had Main made allusion to heterosexuals.

But back to being close to God. Michael Main doesn't mind admitting that he found it difficult to address Syme's challenge. Would rather not have. And only did once everybody else had. His fear, as he reports it, engages with our own. What would we say in his position? When was the time we came nearest to God?

'My answer,' he confesses, 'was that I am still waiting.'

The congregation holds its breath. Some of the men sit bolt upright, releasing their neighbours from their grip, almost losing their *yarmulkes*. I have never seen an audience more alive to a story. They bend towards every word. It is about them, for them, *by* them.

Aren't we all still waiting for God? I wonder if there's going to be more touching. 'Lean across and touch the person waiting for God on your left.'

But what did Rabbi Syme say, in reply to what Michael Main said? We wait to hear. We sway in our seats, heartbeat, bloodflow. Rabbi Syme said, 'King David felt the same – "My soul doth thirst for God."'

'I cannot tell you,' Michael Main tells us, his voice more soothing than a lullaby, 'the degree to which this validated my experience. In one fell swoop he encompassed me into the bosom of the Jewish faith.'

And in one fell swoop Michael Main does the same for us. In no other gathering would the idea of faith being measured by its frailty, closeness to God being gauged by our distance from Him, be given such a responsive hearing. Here, we make a virtue out of our failings. We have to. We bear the abomination charge. And the suggestion that we are near by being far is honey to our ears.

For a moment I think we may get applause, Concord-style. But there is just a susurration of content. The sea of faith flowing back over the shingles of our exclusion.

More singing. We take the shoulders, or the waist, of the person on each side of us, and we rock together, we sway, truly a congregation. There's been a lot of talk of harmony, of the need to rid ourselves of disharmony; well, it's working. We're in it together. We touch, sing, sway and pray. I am as watchful as a snake. Too readily and too obviously, for my taste, do the moustached men in their short-sleeved work shirts divide into those who caress and those who would be caressed. The odour of stale sexual roles infests the service. But then I remember what synagogues are usually like. The old men. The secret rites. The chill. And I go back to swaying.

After the *Shema*, which Croll and Main do together – Croll delivering each word from deep in his chest, rounding it in his mouth as if it has never been pronounced this way before, and Main glossing as we go, so that we get the word and its manifold meanings simultaneously – it is time for *Kaddish*, the prayer for the dead. Those who have died of AIDS, women who have died of unsafe and illegal abortions. Martyrs of the sexual revolution. We are asked to update the solemn list. Since last we said *Kaddish*, more have perished. We bow our heads as the names of friends are called out like a roll-call of heroes, like a litany of sorrows.

And then Croll is back to shake the Succoth plants for us. He does it with fervour, rattling the fronds and explaining the symbolism. 'The myrtle, whose leaves are shaped like eyes that can behold the grandeur and beauty of the universe. The *lulav*, the palm that resembles the human spine, to remind us that we can stand straight with courage and integrity. The *etrog*, shaped like the human heart – may we remember that love is the doorway through which we pass from selfishness to service, and from loneliness to kinship with all the world.'

So *that's* what we're doing at Succoth. How come no one got that across to me before?

We answer Cantor Croll. 'May we serve God by standing up for justice, truth and peace. May we serve God by looking with kindness at every living being.'

After which unexceptionable but not particularly Hebraic blandness, we make ready for *Kiddush*, the ceremony which the early Christians snitched and called Communion. Tiny, frilly paper cups come round, with something red and sweet and ecologically sound lying like a pool of blood at the bottom.

Michael Main pulls apart the challa, the sweet braided loaf

from which the early Christians snitched the idea of a wafer. Under Croll's instructions, one person at the front of the room lays his hand on the challa, and, so that we may all, as it were, touch it together, we touch the shoulder of the person who is touching the shoulder of the person who is touching the shoulder of the person who is touching the shoulder of the person who is touching the challa. In this way we imitate the bread and become an unbroken braid of dough ourselves.

And thus do I touch more people in a single synagogue in a single hour than I have touched anywhere in forty-nine years.

The service is over. I decide to skip the cakes. Serious socializing is now afoot, embraces unsanctified by prayer, and I am feeling impostorish. I am also feeling pedantic, or at least I can feel pedantry coming on, as a substitute for censure. Not that there is anything for me to be censorious about. I have enjoyed the service. I have understood it. I have come to see that there is a case to be made for being treated considerately in a place where contemplation and quietude is of the essence. Salutary to learn that you don't have to be scared out of your wits in a house of worship; or badgered out of your sanity. But if I stay I'll start hectoring whichever stray gay attaches himself to me. Why simplify the immemorial difficulties of being Jewish by boiling them down to a particular fix of your sexual nature, I will want to say to him. Why hit on gay when there are so many other reasons within Judaism for pride and shame, fear and glory, vexation and exultancy? If you were Christian I could understand it, but since you're Jewish . . .

And he wouldn't want to hear that. And I wouldn't want to hear myself say it.

So I ring a cab and wait for it in the street, under the unsurprisable watch of the security men. People drift out of the synagogue. Often alone. The most melancholy get into the best cars, and speed off companionless into the LA night.

Slowly, it begins to occur to me that something or other

worked tonight because the outlawed, embattled, exclusivist nature of the gay community suited the temper of the Jewish service. Who can say? – perhaps I have been close to the original spirit. The simple rituals. The temporary tabernacle. The need to bolster up the confidence of a menaced minority. Are the once-abominated then, today's true heirs? Are the gays the children of Israel?

No cab comes. I decide to walk the couple of miles, feeling safe in my thoughts. Like all the other dark deserted streets and boulevards of L A, Pico is peopled only by short Mexicans in red jackets, waiting to valet-park your car. What life is this they lead? If they're lucky there's another restaurant nearby, so they can fraternize with one another in the night. Otherwise they prowl up and down, waiting for diners; or they sit on collapsible stools, listening for the walkie-talkie to tell them that a customer has eaten and now wants his car. A new form of nocturnal creature. When you walk past them in the darkness they are disgusted by you. You are a person who has nothing that requires valet-parking.

I get back to my hotel room just in time for a telephone call. It is the call I thought would never come. From Jews for Jesus who, when I last spoke to them, were running my request past their ministry.

I am so taken aback by a man's voice saying, 'Is that Mr Jacobson? I hear you're interested in Jews for Jesus,' that I at first assume it must be the hotel operator, being helpful, or being ironic.

But it is in fact Tuvya Zaretsky, leader of the Southern Californian Ministry, trying to get a handle on what I'm after. I'm trying to get a handle on his handle. 'Who did you say?' I ask.

'Yes,' he says, apologizing already, the way you would expect a Jew who is for Jesus to do, 'the name is inclined to go by without lodging. Tuvya Zaretsky.'

Tuvya is like Baruch – a name that suddenly the faithful are all sporting.

But this Tuvya is hardly a *ba'al tshuva* – a returnee to the faith.

I wonder to myself whether Jews for Jesus see it as advantageous to rest the Jewish part of their argument, their first premiss, on a solidish foundation of undeniable Jewish nomenclature. If Tuvya were called Troy Baron his witness might not carry the same weight. So do they actually change their names to very Jewish ones if they are not very Jewish already, prior to their, as it were, changing back again?

Tuvya is pretty busy. Hard to believe, but he is. Why any Jew would want to be a Jesus-Jew when there's so much other leniency on offer, I can't imagine. But Tuvya is in demand. And suspicious. What am I about?

I do my daffy-writer and confused-Jew stuff – I wish *I* knew.

He is speaking on Sunday morning at the University Bible Church, Wilshire Boulevard, corner of Malcolm, just east of Westwood. 'Who God, Which God, Where God' is the title of his sermon. I am welcome to come along and hear him, and talk to him afterwards if I so desire.

'I'll see you Sunday, Mr Zaretsky,' I say. LA or not, I stay formal. Tuvya would stick in my craw.

I'm beginning to miss the chalk-white urban-stressed faces of New York women. I haven't seen one of those sour, crimson, knife-wound mouths for what seems an age. Here the predominant look is nut-brown Mexican slut. A black lace camisole worn over a short flouncy skirt, cut on the bias, and cowboy boots. After that, the face doesn't much matter, but if there is one it is usually Acapulco somnolent. The slut part is post-Madonna – not so much a promise as a remembrance.

Every woman in LA is post-Somebody. I am sitting out on the
street in Beverly Hills – Beverly Hills proper, not Pico – taking
frozen yoghurt and reading Neal Gabler's *An Empire of Their
Own*, the story of how the Jews invented Hollywood and
therefore, in every sense that matters, America. It's a wonderful
conceit. Eastern European refugees cooking up an idea of white,
gentile, picket-fence family decency, selling it to Americans as
their own identity, but still remaining excluded from it
themselves. It makes me alternately proud of my people and
disgusted with them. Because if that is a Jewish tune to which
the Lauren Bacall and Faye Dunaway look-alikes are dancing in
Beverly Hills, then I wish someone other than the Jews had
written it.

I order another yoghurt from Julia Roberts. At the cash desk,
Michelle Pfeiffer takes my money. Even the black women behind
the desk at the post office are all Whoopi Goldbergs. And what
kind of a name is Whoopi Goldberg anyway?

Not that I will hear a word against the Beverly Hills Post
Office. I wish it could be shown that the Jews had invented the
Beverly Hills Post Office. It is quickly becoming my favourite
places in Los Angeles, a haven of humour and efficiency. Whenever one of the Whoopi Goldbergs behind the counter recognizes
one of her Whoopi Goldberg friends in the queue, peals of
laughter break out. 'There's little Wilma! Hi, Wilma, you speed-
bomb!'

'You ready to roll?' Wilma asks, before she puts in her order
for a hundred stamps.

Wilma is going gambling this weekend, in the desert. 'Have
fun Vegas,' her friends wish her, as she leaves.

Whoopi and Wilma aside, it's a joy to be in a post office
which deals primarily with post.

A good reason for leaving England altogether is the English
post office, the sights and sounds you must endure there, the
iniquities and indulgences of the entire social system which you

are reminded of every time you go to post a letter – pensions, child-allowances, social-security payments, TV stamps, penury and charity, hopelessness, hand-outs, inquisitions. Here, you post parcels in the post office and discuss your private life with the FBI.

I have started to come here so often, to give my ears a break from the Jewish music of the boulevards, that I now own enough American stamps to start a small mail-order business.

But I'm a glutton for punishment. It is now fourteen hours – counting the hours of sleep – since I did anything specifically Jewish. And it is Saturday morning. A time to be among one's own. I've heard that there's a performing-arts synagogue not far away, where the congregation strums and stomps and sings and for all I know blacks-up during the service. After what I've been reading in Neal Gabler, it seems appropriate that I should go there and catch what's left of the entertainment.

I check under 'synagogues' in the LA phone-book and find something called the Creative Arts Temple on Santa Monica Boulevard. Sounds right. I ring to find out whether anyone can come along or if you have to be a member of Actors' Equity, but no one answers. I cab it through the wastes of Saturday morning Los Angeles, as charmless as Ramsbottom or Rochdale, and let the cab spill me out at the address I copied from the phone-book, although there is nothing resembling a synagogue, let alone a song-and-dance temple, in sight. It is hot on Santa Monica Boulevard and smells like an oil-refinery. A Chinese tailor's shop is open, but that's all. I peer through the locked doors of an office block and read the name of my temple on a directory-board. It's on the second floor, directly above DICK BANK and directly below DJANOGLY CONSTRUCTION. I put my ear to the glass, but no creative or revellous worship do I hear.

The Chinese tailor is no help. All he can tell me is that there is a temple – 'Temple . . . there . . . temple' – on Santa Monica

Boulevard, back the way I came. I don't try him with creative arts.

The temple he means is the L A Temple of Jesus Christ of the Latter Day Saints, the Mormon headquarters, a vast, Tex-Mex, overweening, spectacularly plain, unimaginatively overpowering, djanogly construction indeed.

Which I determine to scale, else my Saturday will be theology free, and I have become addicted, since I came away, to having God tied up with the early part of my weekend.

It's a climb to the temple, through well-laid-out gardens, shaded by fine, slender-limbed palms. *Lulavs.* I follow the arrows directing me to the Visitors' Center. People in their Sabbath best nod to me. Music is being piped from somewhere: Handel alternating with easy-listening. Perhaps from the same source, an atmosphere of needle-fine euphoria, as cold as steel, is also being piped.

Outside the Visitors' Center are a number of small sculptures celebrating maidenhood's chaste steps to motherhood, and a colossal statue to the family – bronze, larger and lovelier than life, an all-American family group barely able to conceal that slightly Germanic complacency which lurks behind all all-Americanness. This could easily be Nazi art; exhortatory, urging us on to more and more Aryan fecundity. No wonder this country produces so many masters of *kitsch* – put your ear to the marble or the bronze and you can hear the *kitsch* crying to be let out.

Sister Corbridge greets me the moment I walk into the Visitors' Center. If I'm willing, she'll do me a 'presentation'. She is a slip of a girl, in her early twenties at most. She wears a long, shapeless blue garment – no, I must be fair: it *is* a frock – and dark stockings, and simple, flat blue shoes. She has white plastic jewellery in her ears, very plain, mere half-hoops, and a white chiffon scarf in her hair, which is part back-combed and part allowed to fall on to her face, in a fetching fringe. Her eyes are a liquid bruin brown, full of trust and yearning. And her teeth are little-girl exquisite; her milk teeth, is my guess. Thus accoutred, Sister Corbridge sets about telling me how best to live.

I stand with my head fallen on one shoulder, like an old crow, and marvel at the teeny-vocabulary she brings to bear on matters spiritual. She 'levels' with God. That's what's 'neat' about the Holy Spirit – He listens to you and understands your needs. She's noticed how responsive He always is. She hit a bit of a low this morning, as a matter of fact, what with her friend flying to England, but the Holy Spirit was there, knowing just what she needed.

'And giving it to you?'

'Oh yes, He always does.'

She has long nails, lacquered but colourless. She proffers her face as she talks, tilts her chin, exposes her cheek to imaginary blows.

There are illuminated pictures, marking the stations of her presentation, on the walls. We pause before 'Marriage'. This is a big marrying day at the Temple. Sister Corbridge explains that marriage is not entered upon lightly by Mormons. Couples have to talk their marriage out with the authorities, prove their worthiness and affirm their chastity. They are encouraged to desist sexually before they become man and wife, and to marry fellow-Mormons. For her own part, she will not be 'violating her cleanliness' before she becomes a bride.

I don't talk filth to her, of course, even though filth is, in a sense, all she talks to me. But I do hint at the allure of a more variegated personal life than the Mormons advocate. She turns her face and makes a presentation of her unspotted cheek. Except that now there is a spot on it, a roseate suffusion, though whether of shame or temper it is not for me to say.

Freudianly, she describes a recent occasion when she had 'bad feelings' about a particular 'presentee'. Something wasn't right.

She had . . . well . . . bad feelings. And sure enough he suddenly rounded on her, accusing her of being too sure of herself and of inventing latter-day prophets. But the Holy Ghost (the Neat One) gave her the strength to answer him, to calm him, to deal with him, to refute him.

'The Holy Ghost did that for you?'

'And he will do it for you too.'

'Provided I level with him . . .'

More spots on the unspotted cheek. Temper again? Shame again? Pleasure at the strides I am taking under her tutelage?

She has a gift for me, anyway. A presentation within the presentation. A portrait of Jesus.

I refuse it. No room in my luggage, I say. It's a gaudy painting, in hot orangey colours, aspiring to the verisimilitude of photography. In it, the young Jesus is doing his damnedest to look like the young Charlton Heston. Elsewhere, on the walls not given over to family fulfilment, Jesus is being Kirk Douglas or Willem Dafoe. In *Yeshua and the Mormons* he is a pop-star whose name escapes me, warm-eyed like Bambi, with a soft winnowed beard and attitudes to rain forests.

How smart it was of my people to find themselves a divinity who was camera-shy, who said no to likenesses. We may have made mawkish art of ourselves for the cameras of Arnold Eagle and Roman Vishniac, but at least we have obeyed the ancient injunctions of our volcanic God and spared Him the indignities of Disney. I used to think it was our vanity that was at issue in this matter; that we are not to portray God in the image of ourselves because that only perpetuates our self-love. But here in the LA Temple of Jesus Christ of the Latter Day Saints I see that the problem was aesthetic all along. God didn't trust us with the paintbrush.

Sister Corbridge would like to talk to me a little longer about cleanliness. But I say I have plenty to think about already. She asks me if I have enjoyed her presentation. I wonder if I am meant to give her a little gift, and for a second or two think about presenting her with my *yarmulke*. Instead, I do it with words. 'I have very much enjoyed it,' I say. 'It was neat.'

Outside, where the odour of moral cleanliness rises from the lawns like spilt talcum powder, the weddings are going off. A commonplace of being a traveller – you are always watching weddings.

'Congratulations, Jackie and Mary Lou,' a choir of boys sings out, as a bride and groom appear on the steps of the conjugal chapel.

Jackie and Mary Lou are overweight. Most of the happy couples are. It could be something to do with all the desisting they've been doing. You can't desist from everything.

'Everybody come on up,' the groom calls. 'Everybody! Come and join the pictures. Even those who aren't with the party. Everybody!'

I imagine how the family will feel back in Utah when they come to look at the wedding-pictures and find me in them. And on that basis I turn down the invitation.

There are brides and grooms everywhere. Strolling across the lawns, posing under the palms, bending to be wonderful to children. The bridesmaids are all in pink, to match the pink ties and cummerbunds of the best men. And they are all practising to be Sister Corbridge, raising their blameless eyes to me as I pass, showing me their milk teeth. If I linger, they will tell me how to live.

Some of the women – matrons of honour, I take them to be – wear bridesmaids' frocks over cowboy boots. The little nut-brown Mexican Mormon I'm-not-a-slut look.

I walk around to the front of the temple, where there is a pool big enough for every Mormon child in LA to paddle in, and ascend the triumphal steps. A sign says it is open for members only today. I peer in and see a further sign saying TAPE RECORD-ERS AND CAMERAS SHOULD BE CHECKED HERE. Aha, I think, there is secret ritual afoot.

Whatever is or has been going on in the temple, it has involved large numbers of people. A stream of elderly couples issues from the building, the men in white suits and ties, the women in white dresses. Many of the women wear Reeboks. Not for the first time, I remark that this is a town that has trouble knowing what to put on its feet. And when.

Both sexes carry little suitcases, about the size of a flute-case but housing something more sinister than a flute, I am convinced. But what? Hoods? Feathers? Decent footwear?

I stand on the temple steps and look down, past the pool, past the milling couples in white, to Santa Monica Boulevard with its desert strip running through its middle, and its telegraph poles, and its scruffy palm trees, and its stores selling DONUTS (which they can't spell properly), and its 7/ELEVEN hoardings, and its shops stocked with Mormon tapes and videos, and I cannot conceive how there could be a more desolating spot in the whole of Christendom.

Behind me, the temple rises vast and heartless, a breeze-block concrete edifice of no grace, surmounted by a pointing figure in gold, who might be Christ, but who might also be someone more latter-day.

'The purpose of life,' it says on one of the pamphlets Sister Corbridge pushed on me, 'is to find lasting peace and happiness. But where can such peace and happiness be found?'

I know the answer even if the Mormons don't – Rodeo Drive.

In fact, Rodeo Drive, Beverly Hills, is about as interesting as Bond Street. But there are whisperings of a gay march this afternoon, starting in Wilshire, going through Rodeo, and ending up in a nearby park. The reason for the march is that Governor Pete Wilson has vetoed a bill that would have banned job discrimination against homosexuals. In an earlier political incarnation, Wilson had promised undying support for the bill. So the gay community feels betrayed as well as hurt.

And I am here, as an onlooker, because I have gay Jewish friends now – Stephen and Michael and Mary Ann and Phil and Don. We may not have talked much but we have made human chains in the presence of the gay *Shekhina*.

Empty as yet of gays qua gays, Rodeo Drive is given over to those two great nations of boring shoppers: the Italians, who have forgotten what their culture once existed for; and the Japanese, who have never known.

At the corner of Wilshire and Rodeo is Via Rodeo, a Roman stage-set shopping-and-looking mall, *circa* twenty-one hundred BC and AD simultaneously. There is a campanile here, fountains, a little hill, a colosseum, Tiffany's, Porsche Design, Charles Jourdan and Shoshana Romance. A woman clicks out of Porsche Design and puts herself back into her sunglasses in perfect synchronization with her feet. First step, first ear; second step, second ear; door of shop closes, Porsched eyes look up. It is Sophia Loren, aged twenty-two.

Up and down Rodeo Drive proper, Japanese girls are thumping the sidewalk like Sumo wrestlers. They have no attention for one another, they rake every passer-by who is not Japanese for the secret of what to wear and how to look. It's touch and go who is the more inept and out of step, the Japanese in their black rubber suits or the Americans in their diamanté T-shirts and cowboy boots. Between the Italians and the Japanese, the Americans look lost, even in their own city.

But that may be because they are caught, spiritually, between the Mexicans and the Jewish. What chance of attaining chic do you have when you are pueblo Indian below the waist and social secretary of Temple Emanu-El above it? At least the Japanese go homogeneously astray.

Before the march, the cops. One minute it's quiet, just the sounds of Sumo thumping and spurs catching in fabric, the next there are sirens screaming. Police cars arrive from all directions. A riot squad lines up outside the Beverly Wilshire Hotel, shields out, gay-proof visors down. Motorcycle cops, some in khaki, some in blue, ride up and down Rodeo, answering calls on their walkie-talkies. Their marvellously erect bearing is noted by the Japanese shoppers, who immediately straighten up. A helicopter circles overhead. All LA's best toys are out. Rodeo Drive is agog, and then sealed off to traffic.

Whoopi Goldberg, disguised as a traffic-cop, stands at the intersection of Rodeo and Santa Monica, controlling the flow with wrist movements that suggest she plays a mean game of table-tennis. She chews gum, every now and then blowing enormous pink bubbles at motorists who give her trouble.

Three sounds prevail over all others. The whirring of the helicopter blades. The crackling of the cops' walkie-talkies. And the bursting of Whoopi's bubbles.

But as yet no sign of a gay march. All I've seen so far that gives any clue to what may be afoot are two sinuous Asian boys, one wearing a T-shirt that says PRACTICE SAFE SEX, the other with a T-shirt that says ABOVE THE RIM. I take it as a matter of course that in order to have meaning they must stay together.

Then suddenly, from Wilshire, turning right into Rodeo, the march. It's not a gay carnival. No outrageous dressing. Only one marcher that I see shows any propensity to provocativeness. He snaps his suspenders at us. Otherwise, it's an orderly, regular procession of men with rings through their ears and noses, shouting for the resignation of Pete Wilson, and accusing him of lying, of cowardice, and of being 'a closet fundamentalist'.

Of all fundamentalists, I take it that this is the worst sort.

Half-way up Rodeo, the marchers break out into a chant which I have to assume has been especially composed for the locality, although it has a universal application that is not lost on the applauding onlookers:

> We're here,
> We're queer,
> We're not going shopping.

216

We're Here, We're Queer, We're Not Going Shopping

A refrain that cannot be repeated too many times for any of us.

A man I recognize from the gay *shul* walks up and down the sidewalks, confronting the crowds who *are* going shopping. 'Equal rights!' he shouts, meeting each one of us individually, eyeball to eyeball. He doesn't remember me, even though I grasped his shoulder and made a braid with him that connected us to the challa.

Most of the stores close for the duration of the demonstration. In J.-F. Lazartigue and Cole-Haan and Georgette Klinger the staff gather in anxious huddles. Six girls and six boys wearing identical black jackets stand in the window of Armani and urge on the marchers with V signs for victory. Considering how plain the marchers have made it that they're not going shopping, I read this as a mark of unusually disinterested solidarity.

I do overhear one complaint, from a woman kept out of her favourite store. 'I don't understand this,' she says. 'I don't get it.'

But her husband explains it to her. 'They're exercising their constitutional rights,' he says.

He makes it sound gymnastical, an activity equivalent to jogging or walking the dog. Somewhere in here I glimpse the reason everyone in LA wears runners. It has something to do with the Constitution.

Ten

WHO GOD, WHICH GOD, WHERE GOD

Sunday. Ten-thirty a.m. The University Bible Church. Wilshire Boulevard. Corner of Malcolm.

I am come to hear a Jew preach the word of Jesus to Christians.

I hope it is to Christians. A fear assails me in the taxi that, as this is LA, there will be a queue of Jews a mile long, wondering if Jesus is something they should try next. But then I remember that the LA of actuality has not lived up, or has not lived down, to the LA of repute. As far as Jewishness is concerned, at any rate, I have yet to find anything experimental or daring. Even the gay *shul* felt proper.

And things remain proper still. The only Jewish face at the door of the University Bible Church is mine. Tuvya Zaretsky's will be the other, but Tuvya Zaretsky is not here yet.

Churchy people welcome me. Ask me my name. Tell me theirs. It's all very homely. More of a coffee morning than a scene of a terrible apostasy.

Do I know there is a surprise today, a special speaker? I know. That's the reason I'm here. That's the *only* reason I'm here.

It matters to me that they should grasp from the outset that I'm not Christian meat. But this is a miscalculation. The more I stress my interest in Tuvya, the more of a potential convert do I look. If I'm not careful, the whole of the morning's service is going to be a battle for my soul.

218

I peruse the Jews for Jesus pamphlets which have been arranged on a trestle table for my sole entrapment. *Issues: A Messianic Jewish Perspective* contains a piece entitled 'The Day the Rabbi was Wrong', and illustrates its point with a watercolour of a rabbinic Jew appealing to the authority of holy texts while a second Jew looks away in discomfort and perplexity. Jewish? Perplexed? Then this is for you . . .

'Mark grew up in an Orthodox Jewish home, attended a *yeshiva* in New York City and lived his life in accordance with the opinions and commentaries of our great rabbis. Yet, as a small child, he pondered a very unorthodox question about a very unorthodox topic, a topic which no one in his Hebrew school had ever discussed. The question: What if we're wrong? The topic: Jesus.'

Speaking for myself, I've come upon many Jews unimpressed by the teachings of the rabbis – we specialize in being unimpressed – but never one, of sound mind, who thought we may have been wrong about Jesus.

I pick up another pamphlet. *Strange Facts About You, God, and Your Mother.* In a series of scrupulously non-Semitic drawings, the proposition is put that God has a 'perfect plan' for your life and wants the best for you, '*even better* than your mother wants for you'. There is sin in your life, and there is sin – here the pamphlet begs my pardon – in your mother's. But 'God (unlike your mother) did more than just make you feel guilty about sin. He sent Y'shua, the Jewish Messiah, to *relieve* your guilt by – *paying the price* for your sin.'

This is inaccurate. Every Jewish son knows that his mother encourages his guilt only in order that she should have more sin to suffer for herself. Here is why Jesus will never catch on amongst us. We already have a saviour/redeemer/martyr at home.

A grand piano is playing jolly hymns. As I proceed to a pew – a rear pew – I am given a gift. A little red New Testament and a white University Bible Church biro and a bookmark saying, 'Thy word have I hid in my heart'.

The church interior is plain, no ornamentation of any kind, no facilities for elaborate ritual. It has a wooden ceiling from which hang ranch-housey chandeliers, but otherwise nothing that means to be art. A projection screen has been erected where you would normally see stained glass and goblets of blood; and two banks of microphones proclaim the age of the electronic word, one by a lectern, the other by the electric organ.

A Chinese girl takes her seat at the organ, then a guitarist in a Pacific-Islander shirt, then three plain-clothed backing singers. They hymn us to our pews in a semi-revivalist manner, and, once there are about forty of us seated, the lead singer, who is marginally male, leaves his place, mounts the rostrum, switches on a slide-machine, and leads us in singing the words that have appeared on the screen.

> Praise the Name of Jesus
> Praise the Name of Jesus
> He's my rock, he's my fortress.

I decide I don't like the rhyme of Jesus with fortress. It should be fort*russ*. Or Jes*ess*.

The pastor is John M. Whorrall. Plain John M. Whorrall. A plain preacher in a plain red tie. With remnants of a plain breakfast between his teeth.

He thanks the Lord for the 'wonderful day'. Drops the word 'motives' several times, and speaks of the 'clear, meaningful and incisive message of the Holy Ghost'.

Could go a long way corporately, the Holy Ghost.

The main task before John M. Whorrall this morning is to receive new members. 'We are a small church family,' he says, and it is as family that new members are to be welcomed. They have already, although this is not the way families work in my experience, had their testimonies heard. 'We want our new members to have a firm fixation of faith,' the pastor says.

Oh yes he does.

Four people step forward. Three white, one black. For some reason, my heart goes out to the black. Perhaps it's because I think he is the only one with any excuse. They sign a doctrinal statement: 'I have accepted Christ as my personal sin-bearer.' Then they are surrounded by elders and have their shoulders slapped.

'There's an impact of meaning to joining our church,' says the pastor.

Oh yes he does.

A second and even plainer speaker goes to the lectern, forgets what he is supposed to say, recovers himself with a plain joke, and announces Wednesday-evening Bible class on the Song of Solomon.

(*Behold thou art plain, my love; thou hast clear, meaningful and incisive eyes; with one chain of thy neck thou hast had an impact of meaning on my heart.*)

He talks of Wednesday being a boost; it is like putting up a pole to support the middle of the week. I take the week to be a washing-line in this figure, but can't decide whether that makes Sunday wash-day.

John M. Whorrall returns to prepare us for Tuvya Zaretsky. He talks about them in the plural – the Zaretsk*ies* – for Tuvya's wife, Ellen, is amongst us. They are new to the area, but they are very welcome additions. An 'honorary cheque' has gone to Jews for Jesus, in accordance with the practice of the church's mission programme. So: what we are dealing with here is Christians for Jews for Jesus.

'I want you,' the pastor tells his flock, 'to be tuned into a prayerful association to this minority.'

I can't make up my mind what's worse – Whorrall's sentiments or his prepositions.

But an *Ecumenical Guide to Prepositional Usage in Temples and Synagogues* would make a killing in this country. *For* this country. *To* this country. *Up* this country.

Founded by Martin – Moishe – Rosen, Jews for Jesus, Whorrall tells us, 'is a most strategic category of outreach in our missionary work. We are already assuming friendship roles with the Zaretskies. I ask you now to pray for the ministry to our Jewish people . . .'

When we open our eyes the collecting-baskets are coming round. I make a donation, in the normal manner, imagining I'm doing something for a belfry, before I realize I am probably helping to defray the 'honorary cheque' and therefore helping Zaretsky. So I hereby confess that Jews for Jesus is two dollars the richer on my account; and that such is the amount I feel honour-bound to withdraw in kind.

Zaretsky comes to the podium. '*Shalom*,' he says.

Cute, eh? *Shalom*. Exactly what they say to you when you ring. *Shalom*. These Jews. *Shalom*. See – we keep what is essential to our culture alive. *Shalom*.

'*Shalom*,' the congregation replies. They like saying it. It authenticates them. Binds them to the ancient language of the Holy Land. Jesus Christ would have said, *shalom*.

First of all Zaretsky must thank John M. Whorrall, who 'impacted on my predecessor personally'. Then he must thank his wife Ellen who, we must assume, did not impact personally on his predecessor. He points to her, gets her to show herself for the 'wonderful, beautiful, gorgeous, gracious Jewish-Christian' she is.

She half-rises from her pew and smiles, Jewish-Christianly.

Tuvya Zaretsky wears a flecked grey suit and a grey tie. Not quite a business suit. He has big ears. A reddish, non-rabbinic beard. Distressed eyes. And a crumpled face. His forehead is too small or too compressed. He doesn't comb his hair back, but lets it grow down, narrowing his brow still further. He is in hiding.

222

He begins with a brief autobiographical sketch, an account of his conversion, or whatever the word is. He was comfortable in the traditional institutions of his father. Had anyone told him, when he was a young man, that he would end up blah blah, he would never have blah blah. But one day he begins to be troubled. He goes out into the desert. (Sound familiar?) 'I sat on a rock in the San Antonio Wilderness, and asked the God of Abraham, Isaac and Jacob – I wanted to be absolutely certain I had the right person – why . . .'

I don't hear the exact details of what he asked God. I am distracted by a voice behind saying, 'That's what I do. I do that.' And his neighbour replying, 'Me too.'

Which sets me wondering how many people are out there in the San Antonio Wilderness, putting the big question to the God of Abraham, Isaac and Jacob.

I am also distracted by the laughter. They like him. They enjoy seeing a Jewish boy coming clean with them about the pitfalls of Judaism. All those biblical names to remember. All those Jewish names. He opens his crumpled face to them. He wins them. He is giving them the secrets of his heart, the secrets of his father's heart, and *his* father's heart before that. And they're giving him . . .? Well, approval. And a few dollars in a basket.

He's very neat. Very clean. Carefully put together to be just Jewish enough. No fringes. No dirty shoes. No shirt out of shabby trousers. His shirt cuffs are so spotless you could eat your last supper from them.

'I'm heading up our work in South California,' he tells us. A bit about the nuts and bolts of the organization. A bit about the outreach literature on the desk by the entrance. A bit about how we can give when we leave. But he is at pains to warn us against simply substituting Jews for Jesus for our usual charity. A donation to Js for J is not to supplant; it is to be extra. 'We're an over-and-above ministry,' he says, 'and we want you to give in an over-and-above way.'

223

An over-and-above ministry. What does that mean? That we're supererogatory? A luxury? Or is the Jew apologizing again for his existence? Denying his rights? Anxious for you to dissociate him from wealth or greed? Sliding out of your view even as he is insisting himself upon it?

'Droves of Jewish people are coming to faith in Jesus,' he tells us. A lie, I decide. Unless a drove can mean two. 'Jewish people are looking for the truth but we struggle with some of the things that have made truth fuzzy.' One of these things is Y'shua. His theme. 'Confronting people with who is Jesus Christ – who do you think Jesus is?'

An interminable rigmarole, full of biblical contextual analysis of poor quality, now begins. The audience drifts off. I see a few stifled yawns. The drama of droves of defecting Jews is one thing, close scriptural reading they can get on Wednesday, when the washing-line is hoisted. To win them back, he quotes Leonard Nimoy. Someone asked Nimoy if he had any thoughts on why we are here. His answer: 'The question is not why are we here, but *are* we here?'

It's the very question I ask myself as I sit rigid with boredom but curiously angry with the congregation for being bored too. That is, when all is said and done, a Jew up there. You weren't yawning for Whorrall. A little more respect, if you please.

'I wanna stir your hearts with one last thought,' the Jew Tuvya concludes, or at least begins his conclusion. That one last thought is the transfiguration. That 'awesome moment'.

Remember Y'shua's conversation with Elijah and Moses, sent to minister to Jesus on account of their experience of heights? Well, Tuvya can't get over the fact that the disciples fell asleep while Jesus was receiving his guests. 'I would have been so stimulated,' he tells us, not afraid to show his enthusiasm, 'I wouldn't have slept for weeks.'

He gives us his smile, his winning, Jewish smile. The like-me smile. Like me, I'm a good, clever, sweet boy. See my teeth. See the kind twinkle in my eye. Now show me yours.

He winds up with some good-news propaganda. 'We estimate between twenty-nine and thirty-seven thousand Jews believe in Jesus in the United States.'

We have some way to go, Tuvya and I, if we are to agree figures. I'm still estimating two.

He talks about the progress of the outreach programme in Israel, where there are new officers in the field. 'We got a call yesterday. Five' – he shows his hand, every finger spread – '*five* Israelis came to faith in Jesus in that first week of our ministry! But I can't do it all alone. My staff can't do it all alone. We're looking to you . . . Give us a call if we can come and encourage you, and stand beside you . . .'

'We appreciate the very clear Christ-centred message,' says Pastor Whorrall, after Tuvya has finally sold himself down the river.

And that's it. The end of the morning service. 'You are dismissed,' the pastor tells us.

I'd have liked a stronger end. Something in the order of, 'You are damned.'

But it's not all over. There is still lunch, downstairs, in what would be more of a crypt, were this more of a church.

Whither, none the less, I repair with my name-badge stuck to my lapel, and where, like a snake in the garden, I slither from Kurt, who is prematurely grey and fetches me coffee because there is no tea, to Jeff, who is from Washington and is surprised I got here by taxi because he has never *seen* a taxi in LA, to Lona Brown, wife of Hartley, who hears my accent, scrutinizes my face, and then says, 'I'm a Jewish believer, too.'

Her *too* fills me with forebodings. Does she mean in addition to Zaretsky, or does she mean in addition to me?

Either way, I now have to upwardly revise my estimate of Jews who have come to faith in Jesus by one. That's three.

Lona is unmistakably Jewish. A ringer for any number of my Lithuanian aunts, not one of whom, of course, would ever have set foot in such a place as this. She is petite, with a blush in each cheek. She is wearing a simple frock with a vaguely ethnic design on it, possibly Blackfoot, and what I take to be a hair-piece interwoven with pearls. The look is meant to suggest girlishness, an ever-renewable innocence.

The one discordance on her person is the black diver's watch she has around her wrist. But I notice that her husband Hartley has one too, so I just assume that diving is something they do together, when they are not at worship.

I am at a long table with them. Hartley next to me, Lona next to Hartley. So when she starts to tell me how she got here – to faith in Jesus, not to Wilshire Boulevard and Malcolm – I have to lean across Hartley to hear her. I also have to lean across the two matching leatherette cases which Hartley has on the table in front of him. And I have to take my mind from their possible contents.

'I knew something was wrong,' Lona tells me, 'when I was about seven or eight. But when I was eleven I was praying – I always prayed – and I suddenly felt an urge to pray to Jesus Christ. I believed I shouldn't, but I couldn't help it. I asked God for help. "If I'm wrong just ignore it," I said to Him. "Don't listen." So, at the end of the prayer I said an amen in the name of Jesus Christ . . . And the relief I felt! And the peace I've felt ever since! Such lightness. Such lightness, Howard.'

The story complicates now. While she is still a girl, her family moves house. There is something about addresses. 223 North Somewhere as opposed to 223 South Somewhere. (I start to do some pre-emptive mental arithmetic. Can we get to the number of the beast from here?) What this seems to boil down to is that their mail was delivered to the wrong people, who sussed the mistake, returned their mail to them, and in the process asked, the way you do when you're returning somebody's letters, 'Is there anyone here who would like to go to church?'

Lona engages me with looks that are full of meaning. I am to wonder about higher hands.

I do the best I can. 'And?' I say.

'And I said, Yes, *I* would.'

'And you went?'

'Yes.'

'And?'

'And I loved it.'

'How did your parents feel?'

'I had trouble with my father . . . But that's another story.'

Here Hartley, of the Bible-pouches (for that's what I have decided they are), comes into the picture.

'Her father!' he exclaims, creasing his face in what is to be construed as tried patience competing with amused tolerance. 'Her father!'

I'm not sure I'm ready for Hartley.

'And you're a member of this church now?' I ask Lona.

She nods. A serene Jesus nod. She puts her hand to her mouth just long enough for me to read the time from her diver's watch.

'And are you a member of this . . . er . . . organization?' I ask, inclining my head in the direction of Tuvya, who is eating cake and discussing the San Antonio Wilderness with Christians who have always been Christians.

'No. They're more for . . . you know . . . people who are just starting out. Once you've found Jesus it's another matter.'

'So you did it on your own.'

'Yeah. And there were not many of us then.' She has grey, confidential eyes. Eyes like my Litvak aunts.

A pause. A smile between us. Time to move the confessional from her to me.

'And how long have you been a believer?' she asks.

I say I'm not.

She is very disappointed in me. Her grey eyes blink back something – not quite annoyance, and not quite regret, but a mix, a very Jewish mix, of the kind I have seen before in grey Litvak eyes. It's as if the downward path I have taken since I was at the breast, quiescent and yet full of promise, is being charted by a kindly but relentless angel.

I feel, as I am meant to feel, that I have obscurely let Lona down. What's novel is that this time I've failed, not by being too little of Jew, but too much of one.

'So what *do* you believe about Jesus?' she asks me.

I am saved by Hartley, who has collected himself for another assault on Lona's father and on people, well, *like* Lona's father. 'It's funny how often you meet them,' he says. 'They don't know the Bible, they don't even know their history, and yet when it comes to Christianity . . .'

Lona leans across him. She may have been saying amen to Jesus since she was a little girl, but only a Jewish woman could put-in so expertly. 'My father wasn't too pleased about me marrying a gentile,' she says. For a thousandth of a second it's me and her against the gentile. Me and her, understanding what the gentile never will.

The gentile in question, who has a closed and watchful face, and worn-out eyes, goes on with his point. 'You know, he got furious once when I told him that Saul changed his name to Paul. "What did he do that for?" he kept asking. "Why did the name have to change? What was wrong with Saul? I think that's terrible. What was wrong with Saul as a name for a leader?" Do you know, he thought I was talking about *King* Saul!'

He looks at me. He appeals to me. What can you do with a man who thinks Paul was King Saul, and then has the gall to take an attitude to the person his daughter marries. Hartley wants me to despise Lona's father with him.

I try to explain the apparently irrational complex of loyalties and fears that makes a Jew who may be ignorant of either Testament of the Bible anxious about intermarriage. But Hartley is not fashioned to be a listener. The two matching Bible-pouches tell me that.

He has more stories of Jewish ignorance to relate. It isn't that the Jews have no reason to fear prejudice, he concedes; of course there has been prejudice, but (the eternal but), to be so unaware of their own faith . . .

'And anyway,' Lona puts in, 'I don't see how you can be Jewish. I don't see how you can worship as a biblical Jew. Where's the blood?'

I look bemused.

'The blood . . . the blood. The blood sacrifice.'

Hartley agrees with this. They've had this one out. They think as a family on blood. 'The Bible stipulates sacrifice. But modern Jews think they can get round that.'

'But it makes no sense,' says Lona.

It has finally dawned on me. 'Oh, you mean Christ,' I say.

They both smile. Sad but conclusive smiles. Lona's is a Jewish smile, notwithstanding all her efforts to change it; over the centuries she expresses her disappointment in me. Hartley's is more bitter. He's been stung by something, by many things perhaps, else why the Bible-pouches in matching fake leathers, but specifically he has been stung by Lona's father.

We have made many enemies, we Jews, by not showing the rightful gratitude to our children when they bring home Hartleys for our approval.

'So go on . . . what do you believe?' Lona asks me again. 'Who do you pray to?'

I say that I pray to no one. And that blood sacrifice is not a problem. Judaism rejected the paganism which later Christianity had recourse to. Jews turn to the Torah, to law, to help them sort out evil. A refusal of human sacrifice as a means of redeeming sin is at the heart of Judaism. Ours was a revolutionary faith for precisely this reason: we brought evil out of the supernatural sphere into the moral.

Or that was what I *meant* to say. What I actually get out is something much more windily liberal, and ends with my attesting, 'Look, whatever else, I am Jewish, I feel Jewish, I think Jewish, I argue like a Jew, I read like a Jew, I talk like a Jew, I look like a Jew . . .'

Another of those if-only-I-could-have-got-to-you-sooner smiles from Lona. If I only knew how wrong I was. If I only knew the peace of mind I was missing.

But from Hartley – hurt, watchful Hartley – a joke. 'You could always get plastic surgery,' he says.

And I think, 'Bingo! I got me one!'

Scratch the friend of a friend of a friend of a Jew for Jesus, and you find a you-know-what.

And now it's exchange-of-addresses time.

Yes, we mean to go on with this. They do, anyway. Or they *say* they do.

I wonder if they're going to bombard me with mail. Junk Jesus mail. I think of giving them a wrong address, but I am in the house of someone who said he was the Son of God, and that seems to me misinformation enough. I give them an old address instead.

Hartley can't read it. He is almost blind. Too much close reading of the Bible. He holds the paper right up to his face, pokes his worn-out eye with a useless address. I don't laugh. I refuse myself cheap satisfactions.

They give me the address of their son in Phoenix, in case I get across there. They are proud of him. A lawyer.

'Is he . . .?' I ask. 'I know this is a personal question, but is he . . .?'

I simply mean, Is he Jewish or is he what you are? But it occurs to me that she might think I mean, Is he circumcised?

If I had any measure of courage that's exactly what I would say: Is he circumcised or does he have ugly bits hanging off his dick, like Hartley?

But the pastor is smiling at me from the far end of the room,

Zaretsky is smiling at me from the middle of the room, and I
have no courage anyway.

Lona gives me the look of the proud Jewish mother. Her grey
eyes shine. She wrinkles her nose. She could be saying, 'And you
should see the *bubeleh* he's given me, *kayn aynhoreh*!' But what
she actually says is, 'We're very proud of him. He's a loyal
member of the congregation.'

He's a believer in Jesus, *kayn aynhoreh*!

'Of course his grandfather thinks he's Jewish,' Hartley says,
blindly, fondling his worry-Bible bags.

I rise. My Zaretsky hour is at hand. I wish Lona and Hartley
well. They hope I find what I'm looking for. The implication is
that I'm looking in the wrong direction.

As I leave the table, Lona pierces me with one last, silent,
inverted, reproach – an aunt from Cheetham Hill, remembering
what a nice boy I was before I started to take an interest in
Jewish girls.

Now that I'm here, mixing, Tuvya Zaretsky looks less worried
about me than he sounded on the phone. Am I concealing my
contempt so well? Or do I not, in fact, feel the contempt I feel I
ought to feel?

To keep my ire fuelled, I force myself to remember what's
written on one of their calling-cards. 'Pray for Tuvya and Ellen
Zaretsky,' it says, alongside a benign family snap. Then it tells
you who they are and where they've been and that they both
have an M.A. in 'missiology with concentration in Jewish
Evangelism/Judaic studies from the Fuller School of World Mission in Pasadena, California'. I don't mind that. It would be a
poorer world without missiology. But turn the card over and
you read, 'When you pray for Tuvya and Ellen Zaretsky, pray
for their unsaved family members to come to faith in Y'shua.'

I ask myself if I know of any indecency comparable to the
indecency of exposing those who bore you to the compassion of
their eternal theological foes, and my answer is that I don't.

To me, Tuvya Zaretsky's tone is more confidential – let's not beat about the bush, it's more *Jewish* – than it was to those he preached to. There's a difference. And he feels it. I am not them. They are not me. And with me he is not him. Unless with *them* he is not him.

I do not make this up. Even his argument is different. Sure, he is ironical and hurt – he has extremely hurt eyes, a deeply stressed face, and a forehead narrowed, concertinaed with pain – sure, he is ironic about what Jews say about him, how they want to psychoanalyse him, to work out what it was, what happened, what trauma seized him, to have made him what he is. 'But believe me,' he says, 'nothing could have been more normal or more natural.'

OK, Tuvya. Fine. One normal day you went out into the desert, sat on a rock, and said Vich God, Vat God, Vhere God, and came up with Jesus. Fine.

We stand very close. I feel the warmth of his breath on my face. It's hard to listen to everything that people who have found faith have to say to you, but suddenly I realize that he is pooh-poohing the Christian holy days. Christmas? Just an adaptation of a pagan festival. Easter? Passover with variations. 'I often suggest to my Christian friends,' he says, 'that we should have Pesach and Easter combined.'

The tone is different and the emphasis is different. Now it's all about the vexatiousness of getting them (*them*) to see what it is they've grown from, religiously. 'Some of them' (*them*) 'find it hard to grasp that Jesus was a Jewish thinker,' he almost whispers, 'who wanted to reform Orthodox Judaism.'

I ask him where the money comes from to fund Jews for Jesus. 'Do you have a philanthropist?'

'Here.' He extends his hands to take in the crypt. 'From here.' (From *them*.) 'From little basket collections like this one.'

But it's not easy. The money doesn't pour in. 'In the end,' he says, to my astonishment, except that astonishment is far too feeble a word – 'In the end,' he says, to my *bouleversement*, 'we're still Jews and we have to help one another.'

Well, that's *chutzpah*, Tuvya.

I would like more time to scrutinize him. To see what's troubling him. Because I too, of course, believe that there has to be some psychological reason for his embracing a system that is not merely inimical but anathema to his upbringing and faith. No problem about his not wanting to live a life demonstrably Hebraic, but Jesus, *Jesus!* The psychology will be similar, I have no doubt, to that of the Cambridge Communists – gay treason. Turn your father into your fatherland, and sell both to the highest bidder. Make the planet pay for pa.

I sigh, thinking about it. Tuvya sighs, thinking I'm thinking about Jews for Jesus finances. Lona is still eyeing me. Hartley would if he could.

'Finally,' Tuvya says, 'it will be proved through them.'

He points to his children, gathered around their mother. They are golden-haired, preternaturally fair, given his auburn colouring and his wife's darkness. Like children out of science fiction.

Cocoons. Pods. Explosives.

While I am waiting for my cab, at the corner of Wilshire and Malcolm, a van pulls up. A hand beckons me. I recognize the diver's watch. Lona and Hartley.

'Howard,' they call.

I wave.

'Can we take you anywhere?'

'No, thank you,' I say, suppressing, for I know where they're going, 'No bloody fear!'

Eleven

REPULSION

Wearing an acid lemon shirt and toting a leather shoulder-bag, Tom Jones, the singing Welsh miner, has just sashayed past the Beverliz Café, Beverly Drive, Beverly Hills, at an outside table of which I am sitting with a bagel and Neal Gabler's book on Hollywood and the Jews.

I watch everybody. I want to know how true it is that this city dances to a Jewish tune.

Hooray for Hollywood.

It deranges everybody that movies are being made here, *right* here, this very hour, at the bottom of this very boulevard. At the table to my left, as at the table to my right, the only talk is of contracts, production money, development fees, ultimata. 'I told him, if the money isn't here, then I'm not.' The difference between nothing and everything is just inches away, just *inches.*

The first talkie, *The Jazz Singer*, was not just made by Jews, it was about Jews. Cantor Rabinowitz wants his son to continue the tradition of sobbing in Hebrew for a Lower East Side congregation. But Jakie Rabinowitz, otherwise known to us as Al Jolson, has his heart set on a black face and a Broadway career. In the end, Jakie Rabinowitz satisfies the Jews and the *goyim.* He does *Kol Nidre* in the synagogue on Yom Kippur, and 'Mammy' to a full Broadway house the night after.

Think of it – the movies begin with a fable about Jewish assimilation.

And now a black-supremacist who teaches African history at City College, New York, is making the headlines with a demand

234

for an apology from Jewish Hollywood for its negative typecasting of blacks. The black that Jakie Rabinowitz was ready to risk his father's wrath to be was evidently the wrong sort of black.

The right sort of black doesn't sing 'Mammy'.

But neither, Cantor Rabinowitz would argue, does the right sort of Jew.

Tom Jones is back. He has his son with him. They are both eating frozen yoghurts. I can't decide if they are dancing to a Jewish tune. Tom Jones wears black jeans and thick crêpe-soled shoes, like an old rocker (what do I mean *like* an old rocker?) and walks differently from other men.

He doesn't want to be pestered. He's going about his ordinary daily life. The merest flicker in his eyes tells me that he is still curious to know if he's being recognized. I stare at him hard, as an enthusiastic fan would, but in fact I'm only looking to see if he's wearing a *yarmulke*. This is now something I do to all men. I check for a *yarmulke*. And sometimes I see them when they're not there. Mirages. Ghost *yarmulkes*.

I have an appointment at Venice Beach. With a *mikveh* lady.

Mikveh is Hebrew for a pool of water, but it has come by extension to mean a ritual bath-house. Into the *mikveh* is meant to go (i) a Jewish bride on the eve of her wedding, (ii) a Jewish mother on the fortieth day after the birth of her son, (iii) a Jewish mother on the eightieth day after the birth of a daughter, (iv) a Jewish menstruant on the seventh night of the 'clean' period following bleeding. (*If a woman shall have an exudate of blood within her body, for seven days shall she be separated.*)

The only thing I know about *mikveh* ladies is that they are, so to speak, pool-attendants; and I only know that because I have rung one up, on the strength of a recommendation, and spoken to her. It wasn't an easy conversation. Are you a *mikveh* lady; what *is* a *mikveh* lady? doesn't cut much ice with a perfect stranger. In fact, she *was* a *mikveh* lady. But my curiosity suffers no diminution on that account. Between is and was seems to me no great distance where superintending bodily purity is concerned. Once a *mikveh* lady, always a *mikveh* lady, is my guess.

Provided my interest is genuine, she'll meet me close to where she lives in Santa Monica. We agree Venice. We agree a beach café. Makes sense to be near water. I describe myself to her, and what I'll be wearing. And she? 'I'll recognize you,' she says. And I'll recognize you, I think. Long print dress. Covered arms. Splayed feet. Snood. You don't have to know what a *mikveh* lady is to know what a *mikveh* lady looks like.

The nut-brown Mexican-slut cowboy boots are the first surprise. Then the bare, muscular, amber legs. After those, everything else follows as you'd expect. The strip of rubberized skirt. The heap-of-wheat belly. The round goblet navel. The apples, the pomegranates, the eyes like the fishpools in Heshbon.

'You Howard?' she asks. 'Hi' – no, 'Hiii' – 'I'm the *mikveh* lady.'

'Is that what you wear, is that what you *wore*, for the job?'

'This? No.'

She shakes her hair when she laughs. (*Thine head upon thee is like Carmel, and the hair of thine head like purple.*)

There is something else she is, *was*. A rabbi's wife.

'Orthodox?'

'Very.'

'You shaved your hair?'

'I wore a snood.'

'A Mexican snood?'

'Mexican?'

'Fashionable.'

'Very.'

(*Thy snood is as a cluster of camphire in the vineyards of En-gedi.*)

She is, she *was*, a returnee to the faith of her forefathers, and after a decade at it she is now a returnee to the easier ways she was born into. But she isn't ratting on where she's been. Any sign of irony from me and the fishpools of Heshbon immediately darken.

'I can't live like that any more,' she says. 'But I still believe in it.'

Among the ways of Orthodoxy she still believes in are the laws of purity and the stimulus they give to a marriage.

'Stimulus?'

'Sure. It's erotic for two people to suffer a forced separation for twelve days every month.'

'How is that erotic?' I can't extend the word as she does. My *erotic* has got a hard t and a clipped c in it. Her *erotic* is all soft ds and extended ahs.

She crosses one amber leg over another. Her cowboy boots creak like saddles.

'It's like, really, you know, like no one is taking anyone for granted. It stops things becoming automatic. And it's kinda like a honeymoon every month.'

'Are you saying that when God told Moses to tell the children of Israel to keep away from a menstruating woman, what He really had in mind was better sex?'

'Yeah. Why not?'

I don't know why not. I just know not.

'I think puritanism should accept its own logic,' I say. 'You can't claim the satisfactions of self-denial *and* indulgence.'

'Why not?'

I don't know why not. I just know not.

We are forced to pause when a black fire-eater on roller-skates stops to perform at our table. Then there's a muscle parade. After that, a man who juggles chain-saws and makes circumcision jokes absorbs our attention.

'So, anyway,' I say, during the nearest we are going to get to a lull in the beach-fun, 'you were going to tell me what a *mikveh* lady does, not why a *mikveh* is good for a marriage.'

'Well,' she says, 'they're connected . . .'

Any word of three or four syllables she drags out to five or six. She also has a slight upward inflection at the end of her sentences. Not the apologetic Australian interrogative curl, but a social and maybe even moral tentativeness. If you're not worthy, the sentence might not finish at all . . .

I drop a few concessionary nods. I accept that coitus after *mikveh* is the *ne plus ultra* of conjugal relations.

My reward is to learn of the twilight world of women's waters, whose volume must be a minimum of twenty-four cubic feet, whose accumulation must be by natural means – channelled rain, for example – and whose system of containment must be secure against cracks or seepage, else the woman's impure status remains unchanged and she is unfit to consort with her husband.

'I can see already,' I say, 'that there is a lot for a *mikveh* lady to keep her eye on.'

She puts up a hand. Wait.

In order to ensure that total immersion which alone changes a woman's status from impure to pure, the subject must be careful to remove any adhesive substances from her body, any plasters or powders, all make-up and cosmetics, any jewellery, ear-plugs, dentures, all traces of food from between the teeth, artificial finger-nails, dirt from under natural finger-nails, residues of dust and perspiration from all the hairy regions of the body, not excluding the nose and ears, and whatever oils or unguents or fixatives prevent the full separation of one hair from another. Once in the water, she must see to it that no hair floats on to the surface, and that she has assumed a relaxed position, with her arms held away from her body, and her limbs slightly parted.

'So you're the monitor,' I say. 'You're the one who shoves them back in if they leave a leg out.'

She smiles a dark Heshbon smile. I still haven't fully grasped what goes on in there. That sometimes, to take one instance, it's necessary for the *mikveh* lady to carry out an inspection. To go rooting for a strip of Elastoplast, a nose-plug, a false tooth.

'You'd check under their nails?'

'Sometimes.'

'Between their toes?'

'Sometimes.'

'Anywhere else?'

She nods. A purple affirmation, like lightning on Venice Beach.

'Not for residues of dust and perspiration ...?' I won't let myself finish, or her answer. I am wondering how much more disgusting this gets. 'I take it,' I say, 'that you are in no way responsible for ensuring that they have indeed put their menstruation behind them by five days. I take it that blood inspection does not fall within the terms of your contract?'

Funny I should mention that. No, that would not normally be her job, but there is something called *bedika*, the scrupulous examination of the vaginal tract with a cloth or a cotton-swathed finger, and there is something called *ketem*, or spotting, and when *ketem* or spotting is not spotted during a *bedika* or spot-hunt, but appears unexpectedly on undergarments or bedsheets, then we are into an irregularity situation, and it may be time to call in ...

'The *mikveh* lady?'

'No. The rabbi.'

'The rabbi?'

She has a way of holding herself in, compressing herself between her shoulders and rocking. A lot of her rides up and rides out when she does this. It's as if she means to half-spill herself; not as a treat to an onlooker, more as an act of disrespect towards herself. What is solemn in her punishing what is ribald.

A team of jugglers on skate boards offers to read our fortunes. Tarot cards, palms, whatever we'd like. She waves them away with a bare ochre arm.

'What happens,' she says, 'is this. If the wife is not certain about her condition, she can discuss it with her husband, show him the swab, and if they can't reach a decision together they send it to the rabbi for his ruling.'

'They send the swab?'

'The cloth. Whatever.'

'Which has been inside . . .?'

'That's the one.'

'For the rabbi to . . .?'

'Inspect. Yeah.'

'Are we still talking eroticism here?'

She thinks about making light. She thinks about saying, 'Kinda could be.' But her *halachic* training catches up with her. I reckon she's thirty. She said she was a *ba'al tshuva* when she was nineteen. She kicked over the traces, left her rabbi husband, fought him over the kids, no more than a year ago. That's a long time living and believing all this. On top of that she was a *mikveh* lady – she didn't just live it and believe it, she *officiated* at it. I can't expect her, amber limbs or no amber limbs, to see it as I see it. As unmitigated filth.

'I know a lot of people have trouble with this,' she says. 'But the whole concept of purity has no meaning unless there are rules . . .'

She doesn't go on. Her heart isn't in it. I order a couple more beers. We sit back in our chairs, watching the parade, admiring the day, enjoying the warmth, the smell of the sea, the hard glare of the light.

But I can't draw my mind from the thought that all over LA, all over America, Orthodox rabbis are holding up squares of white cloth or surgical cotton to this very same light, looking for questionable stains.

It's a reason for putting out the sun.

I finally make it to Fairfax, a traditional Jewish area of run-down shops and parched palm trees, tucked around the

240

back of Beverly Hills. I'm told this is a place where I'll be able to find books on family purity and associated matters. I have an urgent need for such literature. The last thing the *mikveh* lady told me, crossing one creaking boot over another, was that Orthodoxy prohibits oral sex in the male-to-female direction. The reason being that such intimacy of contact will surely cause the wife to be an object of repulsion to her husband. I want to check this. It is possible that she was having sport with me. Venice Beach is a place for play. But if she wasn't, if horror of the female is enshrined to this degree in my religion, I want to know it now so that I can become a tree worshipper or a Taoist.

I am not against one sex being horrified by the other; I just think it should be an individual decision.

Half the shops in Fairfax look as though they may have been haberdashers once, but can't remember what they sell now. An old black bra, bound like *tefillin* around the chest of a headless dummy, is the single exhibit in one window. Two doors along they have only a single bobbin of cotton for sale. In moth-grey.

The food stores, too, are mouldering. Many of them make their announcements in Arabic script. Dark, unfriendly men hover over their stock of bruised apples and tinned peaches. People beg in the streets. A Baltic bag-lady wheels her possessions in an old supermarket trolley. She has a cat with her, in a cardboard box.

It is a souk, in the middle of Los Angeles, a six-dollar taxi ride from Rodeo Drive.

Those shops which are alive are talkative. Notices everywhere. Freddy's Deli has a doubling-up-of-consonants problem. 'Please place your orders for hollyday's homemmade fodds in advance.' Comes, presumably, from being called Freddy. Others only confuse the confusion that already exists around this festival season. Some are closed, some are open. Some are closed earlier, some are open later. Some open on the Monday but not the Tuesday; some on the Tuesday and the Wednesday morning but not the Monday. Some can make you fodd for the hollyday's, some cannnnott. If you are able to work out who'll be operating as a business when, for the sale of what, then you're definitely Jewish.

On the wall overlooking a car-park, close to the SHALOM RETIREMENT MOTEL, is a mural celebrating Jewish life in LA. It's called the Fairfax Community Mural – dedicated September 8th, 1985, that is to say 22 Elul, 5745. It shows, *inter alia*, a version of Woody Allen playing baseball; a version of Mel Brooks throwing a discus; a version of Boy George being *bar-mitzvahed*.

Like most enterprises concerned exclusively with demonstrating the diversity of the Jewish contribution, it is counterproductive, and only makes it look as though Jews have done very few things, and those very badly. The catch is, of course, that we can't be portrayed doing what we're really good at – lawyering, pulling teeth, returning a version of the gentiles back to them on film – because that merely reinforces the very stereotype, as they say in Black Women's Studies, which the mural exists to correct.

The mural is on the side wall of Canters, a decaying cocktail deli that stays open twenty-four hours, that is frequently referred to in LA guides as one of the rudest establishments in the state and that is currently engaged in an ugly public fight with the unions over healthcare. Protesters picket the restaurant. The restaurant hits back with its own sign in the window. LOCAL 11 LOST $813,681 LAST YEAR, AND THEY DEMAND WE BUY THEIR HEALTH PLAN. WOULD YOU?

No, I say as I pass. No, I certainly would not.

I love the idea of the argument being aired this way. The old, excitable Jewish appeal to a fair-minded third party – God, if He's listening, but if not, you. Yes, you. You'll do. You in the street.

Eventually I find Solomon's, the oldest bookstore in LA. If you came in here asking for a bobbin of cotton, moth-grey, no one could accuse you of not using your eyes. There's no knowing what merchandise this shop specializes in, or even whether it's a shop at all. A few Chagall prints hang on the walls at odd angles. There are toys on the floor. A couple of jewellery cabinets that have got books in them. A number of bookshelves that have ornaments on them. There are objects here I cannot put a name to. *Tzitzits*-repair kits? *Yarmulke*-expanders? Second-hand bars of soap? Swab lockets?

This is not Crown Heights Judaica dereliction. In Crown Heights everything was new but carelessly displayed. There was no time for neatness in Crown Heights. And no rhyme or reason for it. *Moshiach* was coming. But here, no one is coming. Not even a customer.

Except that I'm here. And hard on my heels a trio of what I have heard Americans call scurves. A tattooed man, with a face like a Swiss Army knife, and a couple of loose, lethargic women in shoes that won't stay on their feet. One of the women is fingering a broken piece of jewellery at her neck. 'You gotta *mezuzah* that fits this?' she shouts at the shop.

A woman assistant, her equal in lethargy, shouts back, 'Sure. Sure. Come down here.'

They go down to where the jewellery *mezuzahs* for scurves and low-lifes are kept. (*And God said thou shalt put a mezuzah on the door-posts of thine house and upon thy gates and around thy floozies' throats.*)

A man who minds the shop, dark, Iranian looking, in a white shirt, white trousers, white skull-cap, puts his hand on the second floozy's back. She is wearing a thin Indian cotton top which adheres to her skin. You can see her pores through it. He wonders if she'd like a little *mezuzah* too.

'Nah,' she says. 'I've already got one.'

His hand lingers longer than his disappointment.

The women talk among themselves. 'That's a miniature Torah,' one says. 'Oh, it's so beautiful.'

Their male companion is leafing through a prayer-book which he has found in a basket of *mikveh* plugs. 'Don't you want a Torah, honey?'

'Nah. All my needs are met.'

The prayer-book is open on the counter when they leave. It's in Hebrew and English. I can't handle the Hebrew, but I spot a precept that at once restores all my faith in Jewish wisdom. 'Do not praise an author in the presence of another author,' it says, 'lest you will be the cause of some faultfinding.'

That, though, is the last wise word I read in Solomon's. I find the purity literature I came in for, and, although I can't lay my hands specifically on any law prohibiting a husband from putting his lips to what is most womanly in his wife, I do light upon a mad *mélange* of mysticism and mathematics which I take to be urging precisely such restraint.

How else to respond to this punch-line from M. Glazerson's *Revelations about Marriage*?

> The word 'modest' (*tzanua*, צנוע) can be analyzed into two parts, צנ and ע. The first part, צנ, forms the basis of the word, 'shield' (*tzinnah*, צנה), while the second part, the letter, ע (*ayin*), stands for the 'eye' (*ayin*). Modesty is a shield that guards the eye from gazing in the wrong direction.

Read the 'wrong direction' how you choose, I fear it spells tree-worship for me.

But first I buy the book. At the cash desk is a box of cassettes for Jewish listening. Jewish singers, Jewish entertainers, Jewish comedians. Jew Jew Jew. Something makes me ask the lethargic assistant whether she has any Leo Fuld.

'"Tell Me Where Can I Go"? No. Just sold it. Try Hatikvah Music across the road.'

'So it does exist? I haven't dreamt it?'

'"Tell Me Where Can I Go"'? Sure it exists. How else could I have sold it? Try Hatikvah.'

Which I do, and which is how I come to meet Simon, the proprietor. He is a little turkey-cock of a man, pugnacious, articulate, impassioned, wearing a short-sleeved island-hopper's shirt, open low, and with a lot of black hair showing for a small man, or maybe the regulation amount of black hair showing for a small man. He has the Leo Fuld. Sure. Sure. But is more interested in knowing what my accent is, where I'm from, what I'm doing here.

I tell him that I'm in movies and I'm thinking of making a mega-series of movies about Jewjewjews, and that if I do I'll be needing a lot of Jewjewjewish background music of the sort he appears to specialize in. He opens his shoulders and offers me his shop.

We fall into conversation. No – I fall, into *his* conversation. But willingly.

First, the area. Basically, the area is screwed. Because of (a) the Iranians and (b) the Israelis. He counts them off on his thumbs. Let's deal first with (a) the Iranians.

OK. The Iranians who have recently come to the USA in general, and to this part of Los Angeles in particular, came with money. Remember, please, that this is not the classic migrant pattern in America. People have had to claw their way up. Take Simon's own family. Poles. Did it the hard way. But the Iranians came as millionaires. They keep to themselves. They don't mix. They don't want to mix. They have shit taste. Afro-Mediterranean taste. They live in mansions of extreme ugliness. They have no manners. They drive white Mercedes. Show me the car, I'll tell you whether or not they are Iranian Jews.

I ask why the shops they run are such shit-heaps.

They don't care. They don't care what their shops look like. They have no pride in their shops. They just want to make money.

He shows me a stain on his carpet. 'I just had this shop fitted out,' he says. 'And I can assure you that ordinary Jews didn't make that mess.'

I show him how quick I am. 'Iranians did that?'

He fluffs more hair out of his shirt. 'Iranians. Right. They come in here with cigars. I say, "No smoking." They say, "I won't spill it," but . . .' He does an imitation that no Nazi could better of a pig-Jew Iranian deliberately dropping cigar-ash on his carpet and treading it in, screwing it in, with his heel. 'And they wanna bargain with me. Where they come from it's all bargain. But they don't even do that nicely. They just say, "I'll give you five dollar – take it or leave it – five dollar." I say, "Don't even try bargaining with me, don't even think about it, that's the price." They say, "Five dollar – that's all I give you." They're millionaires with mansions in Beverly Hills – I don't just mean houses, I mean mansions – and they're arguing with me over two bucks.'

Israeli music has been coming out of his speakers since I walked into his shop. Suddenly he turns up the volume. To keep out the Iranians.

Which brings him to (b) the Israelis. Whom he hates more passionately than he hates (a) the Iranians. He is full of stories of Israeli corruption, of famous Israeli men of office, public men, military heroes, archaeologists, who are on the take. 'Israel is the most corrupt country in the world,' he swears. 'I'll never give to an Israeli charity again. By the time it gets there, this one has taken a bit, that one has taken a bit, everyone's had a nibble. I was brought up, probably like you, to give to Israel. When I was a kid I went around with a collecting-tin for Israel. It's not the same Israel now. I know Israelis who'll never go back. Who hate what's happened to the country. Who laugh at the way Americans see Israel and idealize it. It's not what we think it is.'

I venture to suggest – what do I know? I've never been, but I still venture to suggest – that our idealization of the country is unfair to it; that all along we have wanted it to be what it could never be, what *no* country could ever be.

He shakes his head. Shakes the hair on his chest. Counts out the numbers of ways I am wrong on his fingers. 'I expect more of Jews,' he says.

'You shouldn't,' I say.

He is adamant. He's got Israeli crap coming out of his speaker system, but he's abstemious of soul. 'I expect more. The others are who they are. But we've had an exceptional experience. So we must behave exceptionally. We have to live by a higher standard. And when I see some of the Israelis that come in here . . .'

On top of everything else he wants me to know about Israelis, he wants me to know that in Fairfax they're running a protection racket.

He pauses to serve a large, wealthy, dark-skinned woman. If there were women who were sheikhs, she would be one.

'I want that,' she says, pointing to the stratosphere.

He knows what she means. She wants the music that is blaring into the street.

Amazing that anyone should want to own it. It's all fake folk spontaneity. A much more serious charge against Israeli culture, it seems to me, than anything Simon has complained of.

The woman resembles a large date, on high heels. When he gives her the tape of 'that' she eyes it suspiciously, as if she can't figure how it can be the one she wants when the one she wants is still playing.

'Is that that?'

'Yeah. That's it.'

'How much?'

I expect her to offer five dollar, but she doesn't. Instead, she says, 'And some dance music.'

Simon knows his business. He doesn't suggest Ted Heath. He has a tape of fifty Israeli songs, all for dancing to. It's called *Fifty Israeli Dance Tunes*.

She examines the tape. 'How many songs?' she asks.

'Fifty.'

'And this one?' She means *that* one.

'Twenty-four.'

She does a sum. Ripples her fingers, from one to ten, all gold-ringed. 'Do you have *Fiddler on the Roof*?

'That's not Israeli.'

'I know. I know. But do you have?'

'No.' It's a punitive no. There's principle involved in this.

She settles for the seventy-four songs she's got. Pays. And leaves.

I wait for his tirade. But I don't understand him yet. Or I don't understand how bad his customers can be. 'Nice Iranian,' he says. 'They're not all obnoxious.'

Before I go, he shows me a video the Lubavitchers have made and would like him to sell. It consists of unsteady hand-held shots of men in ringlets serving *kosher* hamburgers on Eastern Parkway, and plain women in long dresses and tipsy *shaytls* pushing prams. An unsteady commentary notes their modest beauty.

We agree it is not likely to be much of a commercial success as a video. 'They should pay me to give it away,' Simon says.

But the irony is that they should even want to sell their merchandise from a shop which many of them boycott.

'Why do they boycott you?' I ask. 'Do you stay open on *Shabbes*?'

'Of course not. They won't buy from me because (a) I don't wear a *yarmulke*, and (b) I transmit women's voices through my speakers.'

'They don't approve of women's voices?'

'Not singing in the streets, they don't. You should see some of those young Hasids go when I put a woman on. The young ones are the worst. They're more radical than their grandfathers. Sometimes, when I see them coming, I turn the volume up. They go mad. They put their hands over their ears and dash across the road. Which is dangerous when you've got Israelis and Iranians driving.'

For a second or two, Simon is able to conjure up the spectacle of a major Jewish pile-up, occasioned by Eastern European

Jewish ghetto fears and compounded by Afro-Mediterranean Jewish recklessness. The old and the new Jewish worlds colliding in a tangle of metal and fringes at Fairfax Junction, while a Jewish *chanteuse* belts out a folk-song that never was through the speakers of Hatikvah Music.

But my imagination is off in another direction. Call it gynaecologico-vocable. I am just beginning to grasp the degree to which a woman is unacceptable to Judaism. It doesn't matter what comes out of her – blood or music – the faith is in flight from it.

I surrender my last night in LA to Nagila Pizza on Pico. It caught my eye, although I never tried it, on my first morning here, so there's sentiment associated with my choice.

And practicality. Nagila Pizza is not a sedate, white-tablecloth affair where a single person is made to feel conspicuous, but a busy, self-service, food-to-go-or-throw-over-yourself-while-you're-here joint.

'Busy' turns out to be a euphemism. The word is turbulent. The cause, as I determine it, is fourfold.

First: it is Saturday night, *Shabbes* is over, people are relieved not to be having to cook, and are here, in their *yarmulkes*, with their families. Families are turbulent.

Second: there are American Jews here, Iranian Jews, Iraqi Jews, Israeli Jews, Armenian Jews, Russian Jews. This, like bestiality as defined in Leviticus, leads to confusion.

Third: there are two queues; one for salads, tuna-melt, hummus, eggplant baba ganush, felafel parmigiana, and something called baeked ziti; and the other for pizzas. The two queues meet in the middle where the cash till is. You don't always know whether you are at the front of one queue or at the back of the other. You don't know where to put your body if you want a felafel parmigiana *and* a pizza.

Fourth: no one, including the staff, understands the system. Do you sit when you have ordered, or do you stand? When do you pay? Where do you pay? (Don't say, At the till. You can't always see the till.) Whom do you pay? Do they call you by number? Do you have a number? (Some people have numbers.) Or do they shout out a description of your Goliath-size pizza when it's ready? (They do both.) Further, do you take your pizza in a box or on its steel tray? Where do you get a drink? How long do you have to wait after ordering your pizza and paying for it and hearing it described, before complaining that you haven't got it?

The customers have the air of people who come here every night – certainly every Saturday night – but they have the answers to none of these questions.

The men who make the pizzas are Israelis. Two of them might be twins. They cook in *yarmulkes* and hold long conversations with acquaintances who come behind the counter to argue with them while they're sprinkling the cheese. Children run in and out of the kitchen area. They climb the tables. Knock over chairs. Swing from the counter rails.

One family, obeying the Torah's injunction to multiply, comprises the two noble progenitors and fourteen children. I count them. The mother sits impassive, in long false red ringlets, the newest baby spread out lengthwise on her lap, his head hanging between her knees, his feet in her belly. She contemplates only him. The others punch and kick one another. They punch and kick their father. They pull his hair, his ear, his beard. They flick his neck. They put pizza down his shirt. He does nothing. Just goes on eating. Slice after slice. They cuff his *yarmulke*.

The staff sweep up around your feet as you eat. Not just crumbs. Whole plates of tuna-melt. Entire pizzas.

A young Jewish male in the felafel queue is carrying a book entitled *Jewish Theories of the Heart*.

Positioned in neither queue but stranded between both, a Mexican is reaching the end of his tether. Where is his pizza? He has paid, but he has no pizza. No number. No description.

'Do you wan' it cold?' the staff shout at him.

He falls quiet. Paces the restaurant. Hears other men's numbers called. Sees other men's pizzas arrive.

Children run into him. Staff sweep between his legs. The bins fill with what no one will give him. 'My pizza!' he cries. 'Where the hell's my pizza.'

Jews don't like swearing.

Especially when they're cooking for you.

'Give it him cold.'

'We're heating it for you.'

'Give it him cold.'

'Do you wan' it cold?'

'*Muy bonito,*' the Mexican exclaims ironically, when his Pepperoni at last arrives. He backs out of the restaurant, blowing on his steaming carton, and says it to the whole room. '*Muy bonito!*'

But he has no one's attention. A fight has broken out at the delta of the converging queues, where someone's Coke has gone into someone's hummus, and both have gone down the front of someone's dress. Nothing remarkable so far. The second of the someones, however – a man of fine bones, wearing beautifully cut linen trousers and open Italian sandals – is a deaf mute. I've been observing him signing to companions. Seeing his hummus fill up with Coke and then disappear from his tray entirely, he curses deeply but silently. Taking this to be a curse more deadly for not expressing itself in the usual fashion, his antagonist, who is Israeli, curses silently too. Mystified by the spectacle of the two men who are the cause of her distress not shouting, in a place where you shout as soon as sneeze, the woman who has Coke and hummus on her dress clasps her hands, looks to heaven, and utters not one sound.

Thus, for a matter of some thirty seconds, there is a single oasis of calm in Nagila Pizza, the more perplexing for having as its cause enough spilt food and drink to engender war.

As I am noting this in my diary, a woman who is standing behind me asks to use my pen. Since I am obviously using it myself I choose to believe she must be addressing someone else.

She speaks to a couple who have joined me at my table and who are fighting over the relative sizes of their pizza slices. 'Doesn't he speak English?'

'He didn't hear you.'

'Didn't he?'

'Don't think he heard you.'

I raise my head. 'I heard you,' I say. 'I didn't think you could be speaking to me.'

She is blonde Jewish. In a multicoloured jacket. But there is no multicolour in her eyes.

'I asked if I could borrow your pen.'

'When I've finished with it,' I say.

She glowers. She wants to write down the name of a clown who entertains at children's parties and whose card is pinned to a board near the door. She wants to give pleasure to her children. But she has to wait until I've finished writing about her.

The person who was reading *Jewish Theories of the Heart* in the queue, is now on to *How to Win Friends and Influence People* by Dale Carnegie. I can't understand why he isn't offering the blonde a pen.

Families come and go from my table. Waitresses mop up after them. I have no urge to leave. It's a challenge, seeing how long my nerves can go on taking it, and how much concentration I can muster against the din. At last I am joined by a young man in a rakish *yarmulke* and the sort of short-sleeved check shirt only ever worn by boys or men who let their mothers buy their clothes. He has a half-humorous expression which I like. I suck him into talk.

He is Arthur Goldgaber, of Brazilian extraction, a boy in his twenties, who is trying to become a journalist, a boy who badly needs a girlfriend, a boy with a letter-box mouth, a boy who tells me he was brought up reasonably Orthodoxly, not a fanatic, but Orthodox enough 'not to be able to believe his ears' when he hears non-observant Jews talking. How can you be a non-observant Jew? Truly, he cannot grasp the concept of non-observance on the part of someone calling himself Jewish. I tell him I cannot grasp the concept of observance on the part of someone calling himself human, and we go from there.

I feel that I know him from my youth. That I'm repeating a conversation I once had in 1957. He's a city boy, serious, educated, amused in a distant, melancholy sort of way, but never as amused as I want him to be. There's always a chance that something enlivening will come, though, from a person who wears his unhappiness on his sleeve.

We discuss the singles issue, since he is so very much a single. He confirms my sense that this is the beginning and the end of LA – finding a chum.

It's the freeways, he reckons. You spend too much time alone in your car. And there is too great a distance between suburbs. You get home and that's that. You're isolated and alone.

'One good thing about being Orthodox,' he confides, lowering his voice; 'you *walk* to synagogue. This morning, coming out of *shul*, I saw someone I liked, so I caught up with her and said "Hi!"'

(Good *Shabbes*. How're you doin'? Wanna sleep with me?) Is this the call of religion, then? Is this why LA is believing hard – so that you can walk up and say, Hi!

Something has to explain the burgeoning of Orthodoxy – all orthodoxies – in a town that was designed to be pleasure-bent. So why not this: that religion is the only alternative to spending the rest of your life alone in your car on the freeway. It's not God that's at the bottom of what's happening. It's the freeway.

I ask Arthur if he goes to Aish HaTorah, a few doors away, where acts of senseless beauty are commemorated and the sizzle of flesh and faith hits you whenever you pass. He doesn't recognize the description, but he goes there. Not for the flesh, he wants me to understand, though G–d knows, he wouldn't mind. But for the faith.

Then he asks me if I'd like to accompany him to a party. I say yes before I ask where it's at. It's at the University of Judaism. U J. Mulholland Drive.

'I know where it is,' I tell him.

On the way, on the heart-freezing freeway, he spills his soul to me.

He doesn't want just to be a journalist. He wants to be a writer. He keeps a journal. He's just had a very bad relationship. Wants to write about it. Wonders whether anybody would have the slightest interest in reading it. Has a brain affliction. Hereditary. Bipolarity. Recently went into mania. Couldn't remember anything about it. Haydn was bipolar. Wrote *Messiah* in six weeks. Couldn't remember anything about it.

I am too nervous, suddenly, to suggest that that perhaps was because he didn't write it.

I am in the front seat of a small and flimsy car, going too fast, on freeways that are not safe, on what still feels to me like the wrong side of the road, with a person whose brain forgets itself.

'How does this hereditary affliction affect your driving, Arthur?' I ask.

He laughs. Not unmaniacally. I wonder if we're going to U J after all. I thought I'd found him in Nagila Pizza, but what if he found me? I'm unable to concentrate on what he says. I'm navigating the freeway. Could it end like this, after the distance I've put between me and my upbringing, on the way to a Jewish dance?

We make it. Good to see the Judaica-kitsch souvenir-shop again. I pay Arthur's entrance fee. Six dollars. Six dollars times two equals twelve dollars. The people at the desk – she a student, he professorial – are short of change. When I give them twenty-two dollars for two, expecting a straight ten back, they are knocked out by my ingenuity.

'Wow!' says the girl.

The professor still hasn't cottoned on. Why am I giving him a twenty-dollar bill plus two single dollars when the whole thing only comes to twelve?

I ease him through it.

'Hey!' he says. 'Yeah!' In the end, he can only agree with her. 'Wow!'

We're supposed to be good at this sort of thing. We have a system called *Gematria* – interpreting the Bible through the numerical value of the Hebrew letters. Perhaps they would have understood me had I said I'd give him three *alephs* and a *gimel*.

But getting in looks as though it may turn out to be the most fun part of the evening. Arthur has not just taken me back in time, he has also worked some bipolar magic as to place. This is the Jewish Lads' Brigade, situated between Prestwich and Cheetham Hill, North Manchester. Thirty-five years ago. And everybody who was there then is here now. The same sad, hopeless boys looking for the girl they'll never find. Stumbling over their own feet, pretending to be gazing at the stars, pretending to like the music, pretending to be interested in the food, pretending to be here for the talk.

The music is too loud but you can still hear the apologies over it – pardons and excuses and compunctions going off like firecrackers, as these sad hopeless boys of my youth try to palm themselves off on exactly the wrong girls for them, the sophisticated, the hot, the supercilious, the otherwise engaged; while the ones they would really have luck with are sitting in corners, eyes down, leaden with mortification.

A few fake-feral Jews make as if they're dancing. They wear kibbutz-shorts and have their hair tied back. It fools no one. No one here is a dancer. I feel a surge of pride in their ineptitude. Dancing is a wonderful thing not to be able to do.

Arthur organizes for me to meet three good-time girls from my own country. We shout greetings over the music. They *do* want to dance. I am bored with myself on their behalf. If I were them I would not want to be meeting me. If I were me I would not want to be meeting them.

They poke me with their breasts. Rhythmically. In time to the Beatles. Not even the Beach Boys. We discuss Finchley and Solihull and green cards and Aish HaTorah.

They all go to Aish HaTorah. 'Don't get the wrong idea,' (poke) one of them says. 'It's not a meat-market.'

'Did I say it was a meat-market?'

'We go for the study.'

'I don't doubt it,' I say.

They are blind-drunk. They are standing so close to me, all three of them, that I can count back through what they've been drinking. I see how old I am in the gloss of their lipstick.

Although they're here for the study, their conversation drifts to Californian Jewish men. One of them complains that they're a bit *nebbishy*.

I can't get the word for the music. 'A bit . . .?'

'*Nebbishy*.' (Poke.)

'Rabbity?'

'*Nebbishy*.' (Poke.) 'Don't you know that word?'

'Oh, *nebbishy*!' No ones, in other words. *Klutzes, shmendricks, nudniks* – we have a rich vocabulary for them. 'But that's because you're spoiled,' I say. 'All those smart Jewish men you know in England.'

I lean into her breasts, reciprocally. What the hell, it's Saturday night.

She turns from me, in high drunken dudgeon. To show solidarity, the other two withdraw their breasts as well.

I walk out on to the balcony. A fog has descended, so I cannot pretend to look at the stars. Or the desert. Instead, I talk to a Latvian woman who teaches in downtown LA. Because of the loudness of the Beatles I catch only every third word she utters. But even thus truncated she's making more sense than the three English girls whole. She teaches small kids, many of them Russians. Her eyes shine when she tells me how bright the Jewish kids are. The old invidiousness – not just how bright, but how much bright*er*.

We discuss the Alan Dershowitz book that everybody's reading – *Chutzpah*. He's arguing for Jews to show their heads above the parapet. I say that's better than what the Orthodox are urging, which is a form of retreat, whichever way you look at it. She says she's for both. I say she can't be. I invent a theory on the spot, to go with the strobe lighting. To wit: the real aristocracy of the Jewish faith are its intellectuals and non-observant philosophers. They are the ones who lend glory and lustre to its name. The rest are a species of worker bee. They stoke the fires. They are indispensable, the *shul*-goers, the fringe-wearers, the *mikveh*-divers; just as, for the running of any metropolis, the postmen and the street cleaners are indispensable. They are even, if you like, the engine-room of faith. But navigation is done elsewhere and by others. The leaders, those who provide deliverance and direction, do not wear the work clothes of the proletariat.

It's possible she hears only every third word. Or she could just be in the mood for dancing. She leaves me to my theorizing, anyway.

I keep running into Arthur who, I notice, has discarded his *yarmulke*. But there's still the problem of the shirt. He has that what-I-wouldn't-give-for-a-beautiful-Jewish-girl-just-out-of-the-*mikveh* look on him. But, as usual, he's not looking where she's looking.

A devoutly serious young man called David Cohen, who knows better than to even think about dancing at a dance, demands to know who I am and what I am about. 'Right,' he says, once he has grasped it, 'right – then have you been to . . . have you read . . . have you seen . . . have you thought about . . .?'

No, no, no and no.

He starts to write me lists in the air. Names ricochet around us. Institutions. Harvard Hillel . . . David Cohen is a Harvard man. Harvard's where it's at. Harvard's where it's Jewishly at, that is. The combination of learning, civilization and a proper appreciation of the purpose of observance.

I gather he's observant himself. An intellectualized ritualist. The worst. He wears a small skull-cap which seems to have taken root in his scalp. He has an austere face. He could be here looking for a girl. But the first scent of an idea will always waylay him. He's on fire with me in seconds, smoking with suggestions. I try to get through to him that I'm not looking for authorities, that I don't want to interview eminent Jews and hear their views. Yes, he says, yes, he understands. But then sets about swapping one name for another, finding me more approachable ones, better company, Jews who are more surprising in their Jewishness.

Arthur joins us. They are acquainted in misery. They would both rather be somewhere else. David in Harvard, where it's at. Arthur anywhere it's not so lonely.

We're ready to go home. There's much toing and froing – lifts, friends, toilets, last-minute opportunities. Despair has now descended on all the boys in glasses and skull-caps. Another Saturday night and still no goddess from the *mikveh*. Some are so desperate that they're actually banging into girls, propositioning them on the steps, o'erleaping all the *halachic* niceties.

Arthur drives David Cohen and me back home. Bipolarity is about to strike Arthur. I can tell from his driving. It's become bi-lane driving – his brain cannot keep him between the line. He has become lugubrious. He would dearly like to talk about love and literature now, morbidity and the creative. But David is at work with names and contacts. He fills the car with them, until we are choked and have to wind down the windows.

258

Repulsion

I say my goodnights and thank yous outside my hotel. But we have to put ourselves through an address ceremony. David, looking more than ever thin-lipped and pinched in the nostrils, asks for my notebook. He starts writing in it. He won't give it back. His writing is fine and precise. Meticulous. Fastidious. Mad. He covers every inch of the page, then turns the book sideways and finds more room to squeeze more names in boxes. Every time I reach for my book – for it is late now and tomorrow I must pack – he pulls it back. 'I can't let you go without mentioning . . . Oh, and there's . . . And you can't go without meeting . . . you've got to see him . . .'

He is writing upside down in my book now. Finding minuscule spaces beneath words that don't have tails trailing. We have been here fifteen minutes. The hotel valet-parkers are getting irritated. Cars are not for writing in. Cars are for valet-parking. Just as I'm about to get my notebook back, Arthur says, 'Did you say you were going to Israel after this?'

That does it. 'Israel?' David is into my book again. 'You've got to see . . . meet . . . read . . .'

Finally we're through. Arthur shakes hands with me sadly. He can see what I can see. Many more Saturday nights like this one.

David Cohen is more intellectually rigorous. 'I like meeting interesting people,' he says. And then, just as Arthur is about to drive off, 'Could I have a list of your publications?'

But it's Arthur who has the last word. 'You know you're staying opposite the LA *mikveh*,' he says.

'You're joking?'

'I'm not.'

'He's not,' David confirms.

'Where is it?'

'Just there.' And they point to a low, discreet building, not unlike a lawyer's, a building with curves, gentle but not too suggestive undulations, and a long, narrow slit of a window, in dark glass, about two feet above Jewish eye-level. A building I've been idly looking at from my balcony for the last ten days.

259

I wave off my friends, making as though to go into my hotel, but once they're out of sight I essay the brief crossing of Pico Boulevard. I should have guessed. A sign on the Alpha Beta Supermarket next door to the *mikveh* says SPRINKLER CONNECTION. An arrow points in the appropriate direction. I see that a tiny pipe enters the *mikveh* wall from the street. And that the pipe has a tap on it.

The urge to tamper with it is very great. All those precise stipulations as to flow and volume. What would it take, how much of a twist would it need, to render unclean every Orthodox marriage in Los Angeles?

I bend before the tap . . .

Twelve

ON THE TRAIL OF TEARS

Few people go anywhere by train in the United States of America. But in Los Angeles they don't even know what a train is.

'We ain't got one,' the cab-driver tells me, when I ask for the railway station.

I show him my Amtrak timetable, which has a map of the country and the routes of the dozen or so trains that serve it.

'Maybe,' he says. 'But they don't come through here.'

We pull over. I look through the index of stations. Los Angeles, CA – Union Passenger Terminal, 800 N. Almeda St.

He shakes his head. 'Well, we'll try it,' he says.

When we get there, I wish we hadn't. This is downtown LA. The part nobody comes to at night. He drives the last ten minutes with his foot down hard on the accelerator. 'Hold on tight,' he warns me. We know from Tom Wolfe that there are parts of New York you don't want to stop your car in. In downtown LA you don't want to do less than seventy. We jump red lights. There is no one on the streets, except junkies holding their syringes to the moon, and hookers with lamplight on their throats, and Hispanics in white suits cleaning their fingernails with switch-blades.

Things don't improve when we get to the station itself. Things get worse.

There is only one train out of Union Passenger Terminal tonight, and that is the train to New Orleans, calling at Tucson – my train. Which means that everyone here, asleep on the slashed red benches, or murmuring in corners of the cavernous waiting hall, is travelling with me. Had you seen just *one* of these people standing in the queue for an aeroplane, you would not have boarded.

The train is late. By probably as much as two hours. There are only three *Sunset Limiteds*, travelling to New Orleans via Tucson, a week. They all start from Los Angeles. But this one is late.

A midnight cowboy, in a yellow bolero top and pink sunglasses, rages across the concourse, ripping at his midriff with his painted fingernails. He can't believe that he has to wait as much as two hours for this train. 'This is my first time on a train, and my last,' he tells anyone who cares to listen. A black braid of hair hangs out of his straw stetson. His face is pitted. A silver cross with a figure of Christ on it swings from his ear. I am careful not to catch his eye. Twist eye-beams in this place, and you get a disease.

A small snack-bar that serves hamburgers, chilli, and coffee in paper cups – except that they're out of hamburgers and chilli – agrees to stay open an extra half-hour. I wind myself around my luggage, stare into a drained coffee cup and make myself invisible.

I am going to Tucson, because that's where you get off to go to Tombstone. I am going to Tombstone because my researches have unearthed a Jewish cemetery where you would least expect one – in a jungle of catclaw cactus and underbrush at the low, drainage end of Boothill Graveyard. *The* Boothill, where Billy Clanton and the McLaury brothers, killed in the OK Corral shoot-out, are buried. The person responsible for restoring the Jewish cemetery was not a Jew but a full-blood Yaqui Indian – Judge C. Lawrence Huerta. I have a photograph of him, taken from *The New York Times* for February 29th, 1984. He is standing before a monument, bearing Stars of David and HoHoKam Indian sun-symbols. He is wearing bell-bottomed trousers, an Indian headband and, if I am not mistaken, a buffalo-skin *yarmulke*.

On the Trail of Tears

A Jewish cemetery in Boothill seems justification enough for an overnight train journey along the Mexican border. Or *seemed* justification enough, before I knew in what hellish company I would have to travel. But there is another reason for breathing in the air of Tucson. It was Wyatt Earp, together with his brothers Virgil and Morgan, and Doc Holliday, who put Clanton and the McLaurys into Boothill. When he went back home after the killings, it was to the soothing embraces of a nice Jewish girl from San Francisco – Josephine Sarah Marcus. A woman with whom he lived, and to whom he may even have been married, for fifty years. They are not parted now, but lie side by side in the Jewish Hills of Eternity Cemetery, Colma, California. A love story such as this, I cannot turn my back on, even though nice Jewish girls from good West Coast families are not supposed to run away with US Marshals.

But there was no Aish HaTorah in California in the 1880s.

It's almost two in the morning before we are allowed to board our train. We are led out to it in shifts, like the unforgiven on their way to their respective circles. First the murderers, then the rapists, then the pickpockets, then the gay cowboys, then the book-readers and travel-writers. I don't have a sleeping-car booked, but I get an upper-storey reclining seat and a pillow in a paper pillowcase. I have a double seat to myself; room to sleep, except I can't sleep. Forty minutes later, at Pomona, I am joined by a young alcoholized black wearing a Louis Farrakhan T-shirt which says, THE TIME AND WHAT MUST BE DONE.

I am keen to get into *I Married Wyatt Earp*, Josephine Sarah Marcus's recollections, but I can't be certain how the sight of the book will affect my neighbour. The love adventures of a white trigger-happy law-enforcement agent and the pampered child of the Jewish middle classes might not cut much ice with a follower of Farrakhan. He is too drunk also, in my estimation, to be trusted around the cover photograph of Josephine, with her head back and her jaw out and her neckline plunging and the

263

faintest outline of breasts pushing against her shirt. So I keep the volume in my luggage and pull out the Amtrak timetable instead. It is the right decision; even the timetable gets him angry. He asks me what time we get to Austin. He's got a grandmother in Austin. That's where he's going. I say the train doesn't call at Austin. He says he knows that, he has to change at San Antonio. I tell him what time the train gets to San Antonio. He says he knows that. I close my eyes. He begins to fart. I get up and walk about the train. I'm just not in the mood for talking politics.

There's an observation compartment on the train, where I spend a couple of hours looking out into the blackness. The cowboy in the yellow bolero top walks through every fifteen minutes, his bangles clinking. He is distraught. Finally, he asks me if I've seen the dining-car. 'I've been up and down here all night,' he says.

I show him where it is, then go to wash my mouth out in the bathroom. If you can catch something twisting eye-beams, how much more contagious must it be to exchange words. While I'm there I use the lavatory. It occurs to me that he might have used it before me. I recall his pitted skin, the state of his midriff, his syphilitic squint. I throw off all my clothes and bathe in the stainless-steel wash-basin.

There's something wrong with American trains. No one knows how they work. There are people lost everywhere. The guards and attendants are too officious. The dining-car steward wants you dead for daring to bother him for food in the middle of the night, even though it's been announced that he's open. You can't observe anything from the observation compartment. Jews are forced to travel next to Black Muslims.

I go back to my seat and snooze for an hour or so. When I open my eyes it is almost light. We must be very close to the Mexican border, for I see pueblos, mules, shacks painted in Mediterranean colours. Through the other window I see ranges that look like petrified surf. It feels a good hour to be in the

264

observation car, but when I get there all the seats are taken by people with the same idea. On my way back, I pass the cowboy. He has black circles round his eyes and has cut his lip. He looks as though the whole train has been over his face.

He should be so lucky.

At Phoenix, a huge black woman in a *shaytl* climbs aboard. She gives the attendants trouble with her luggage, then more trouble when they try to seat her. 'Is that a woman or a man? I ain't gonna sit with no man. I've had some experiences with men.'

They move her down the carriage, looking for spaces.

But it's still no good. 'Shit! I ain't gonna sit with *that* man. Shit! See – those men they play games with women. Oh, no. And you see you get me that brown suitcase. Anyway ... I'm not gonna sit with no man, that's for sure. Oh, dear. What a day!'

I wish I wasn't sitting with no man myself. What a day! – it's barely eight in the morning and we've all had enough of the day already.

I'm met off the train by Richard, who's an OK Corral and general shoot-out freak, and who I've arranged to drive me informatively to Tombstone. Almost the first words he says to me, after I've thanked him for being here, and apologized for my late arrival, are, 'You know, most people have got the wrong idea about Earp and the Corral. To begin with, the fight couldn't have started where they say, because the Corral is ninety feet from ...'

I haven't got the heart to say I'm not interested in gun-fights and want to go to Tombstone only for the Jewish cemetery. And anyway, after the train, which looks rather beautiful now I've left it, like a silver snake that's come down from the mountains, it makes a pleasant change to be with someone for whom guns are simply things you read about. I climb into his Ford, buckle up, and settle in for an hour of who really shot whom.

Boothill Graveyard is for tourists now. Which makes it less lonely for the dead.

I'm glad I've got Richard with me. Other visitors are limited to a bit of desultory amusement over the droller inscriptions – GEORGE JOHNSON: SHOT BY MISTAKE and HERE LIES LESTER MOORE, FOUR SLUGS FROM A .44, NO LES, NO MORE – but with Richard as my guide, striding out across the graves in a sort of romper suit for big men, I learn about Dutch Annie, the Tombstone Madam, who was followed to her resting place by the longest procession of mourners the town had ever seen; and Cochise, who died of stomach cancer, probably as a consequence of the grease-wood which Apaches used for brewing tea; and how stones had to be laid on every grave, to stop coyotes digging up the bodies, so shallowly were they buried in this unyielding ground.

'Over yonder,' Richard shows me, 'are the Dragoon mountains where Apaches would look for signs of dust and pick off stray adventurers from Tombstone.'

If I asked him what rifles they used, he would tell me. If I asked him their range, he would tell me. You have to be very careful in the company of some men, which questions you ask.

It's an intensely hot morning. So the cowboys who turn up in long white coats, some fifteen minutes after we do, must be dressing fetishistically. They go about in a group, all wearing stetsons the same colour as their coats, all in boots, all with open-necked shirts and silver crucifixes on their chests, and all videoing the same graves.

I wonder if they could be descendants of the Clantons and the McLaurys come to honour their forebears. Richard reckons not. Wrong builds. Wrong style of stetson. And the McLaurys were left-handed. Wore their holsters . . .

I persuade Richard to let me find my own way to the Jewish burial place, a short walk from where the gentile gunmen and dance-hall girls lie. The ground is stony, bleached grey by the

266

sun. A smell like creosote comes off the acacia shrubs. An adobe wall encloses a plot the size of a kitchen garden. In its centre is the memorial, a modest pyramid of local stone and ore, built rather too meticulously, in the style of those rustic fireplaces we all put into our country cottages in the Thatcher years. A metal box I recognize from *The New York Times* photograph sits on top, surmounted by an iron *menorah*, flickering like fire.

A plaque is Dedicated to the Jewish Pioneers and Their Indian Friends. This is the work of the Jewish Friendship Group of Green Valley, a community of retired Jews living in the Tucson area, chivvied into this particular enterprise, as I understand it, by Lawrence Huerta. So it's taken a bunch of Jewish old-timers and a Yaqui Indian to make a little bit of the Arizona desert Jewish again.

I sit on the bench, put there for contemplative purposes, and contemplate. I would enjoy silence, but there are electric wires running directly over the cemetery, and these hiss. There is also interruption from electric lawn-mowers being used in the gardens of nearby houses. I can't quite summon the pathos I would like, until I remember that I've read that the metal box with the Stars of David and Indian sun-symbols on its sides was once a safe, owned by Huerta. There is something touching about memorials that are home-made, and about the idea of giving objects in one's own possession up to death. After all, then, I manage to be upset. But they are Indian tears I shed, not Jewish.

'There's no hard and fast evidence,' Richard tells me, over ribs and beans in a ribs-and-beans joint in Tombstone, 'that Wyatt Earp actually shot Johnny Ringo.'

We are getting on fine, each pursuing his own thoughts and interests.

'Do you suppose there are any Jews living in Tombstone now?' I reply.

He is happy for us to go and find out. We try the offices of the *Tombstone Epitaph*, a few steps down the wild west film-set which is 1990s Tombstone. Our heels rattle the boardwalks. We make menacing shadows when we turn corners.

Janis is at the typewriter. 'Jews? Well, there's the cemetery.'

'Live ones.'

'Oh, live ones.' She's vivacious. A man's woman, the way they like them out west. 'Well, you could try Steven Goldstein, who owns the Long Horn.'

'Sounds Jewish,' I say to Richard.

'Long Horn?'

Life's too short to explain everything to Richard. I thank Janis.

'Just tell me,' she says as I am about to go; 'you'd know. Why do Jews know so much about making money?'

'It's the only thing they've ever been allowed to do, Janis.'

'Boy!' She does her saloon-bar laugh again. She is all the women Tombstone has ever loved – Crazy Horse Lil, Soap Suds Sal, Rowdy Kate Lowe, Lizette the Flying Nymph. 'Boy! They can sure coin it though, eh!'

Steven Goldstein isn't in when we ask for him at the Long Horn Restaurant. A waitress looks us up and down. She slips into a back room and returns with still more negative information. He both isn't in and isn't available.

The Long Horn is a personality restaurant. It has playful notices over every table. Such as, TODAY'S MENU ... 2 CHOICES - TAKE IT OR LEAVE IT. I am inexplicably relieved that Steve Goldstein is neither in nor available.

But – this just as we're leaving – his brother-in-law runs the Branding Iron a couple of doors down.

'Aha,' I say to Richard, 'a bullish theme.'

He looks at me strangely.

The Branding Iron is a T-shirt shop. I don't make the mistake of asking whether the brother-in-law is in or available. I spot him immediately – another Jew out of his habitat – hiding behind the clothes racks, on the look-out for tea-leaves and whatever other scoundrels you have to watch for in a Tombstone T-shirt shop.

I sympathetically trace every line on his face. I know small-business blues. The frustrations of seasonal trade. The usual shopping-associated psychoses exacerbated by the traumatic neurosis of tourism. So I am gentle with him. I don't want to be the occasion of further frights.

He starts when he hears the word 'Jewish'. It's always possible he came to Tombstone with his brother-in-law specifically to escape it. I express my surprise that there are any here. Any of *us* here.

'We're here to stay,' he says. 'There have always been Jews here, and there always will.'

'You sound defiant,' I say. 'Are there problems?'

'What kind of problems?'

'You know . . . The usual. Anti-whatnotism.'

I haven't made a very good job of not frightening him. He ducks behind a rail of Ninja Turtles. Checks to see that no one is pilfering or listening. 'There are people with attitudes in this town,' he says.

I remember Janis. 'Just attitudes?' I ask. 'Or do they take active forms?'

He gives me a sad, sideways look, which partly contains the question, What are you asking me about *goyim* for when you've got one with you? What he actually says is, 'One or two try to agitate. But that just makes us angry, and the more angry we get, the more determined we are to stick it out. The thing is' – and he whispers this so that even Richard, who is standing next to me, shouldn't hear it – 'to beat them economically.'

'And is that what you're doing?'

Some play of light in his eyes, some infinitesimal movement of his body which I infinitesimally duplicate with mine,

269

expresses the freemasonry of Hebraic exclusion which exists between us. 'What do you think?' he says.

Hollis Cook is dressed like a sheriff and built like three deputies. His official title is Park Manager, but his job doesn't seem to have all that much to do with parks. This may just be a way of describing an arts and environment and heritage portfolio in Arizona – parks rather than, as we have taken to calling it, fun.

It's Richard who has brought me to meet Hollis Cook in his office in the Tombstone Courthouse and Local Museum. And because I haven't fully grasped for myself why I'm here, I'm not able to think of an answer when Hollis Cook asks what he can do for me.

'Essentially,' I say, 'I suppose my interest is in Jews.'

'Jews? You tried the cemetery?'

It would only take him to call me 'boy' for this to be a scene from *In the Heat of the Night*. There is a Steigerish quality about Hollis Cook, a sardonic weight of presence that manages to feel at one and the same time sadistic and flirtatious. And I am, though only temporarily, Poitierish-touchy. This is not a town I ought to be hanging around in.

'Done the cemetery,' I say. 'With the help of my guide, here.'

I put it on Richard. Let him be the one to spend a night in the cells.

'And you know, of course, that Marshal Earp's wife, Josephine Sarah Marcus Earp, was Jewish?'

'I do indeed,' I say. 'A lovely looking woman to boot.'

'Ah, you think that?'

'I do,' I say. I do, don't I? 'Yes, I do.'

'Basing your knowledge on . . .?'

What does he mean? Is he toying with me?

'I can't claim anything so grand as "knowledge",' I say. 'But I've seen a photograph.'

'Ah, the photograph.'

Has he just hit me or kissed me?

'There's something I should know about the photograph?'

'If you're talking about the one on the cover of her book, yes.'

I am. The photograph I hid from the follower of Farrakhan on the train. Lest it inflame him. 'What should I know about it?' I ask.

'Only that it's not her.'

I raise a quizzical eyebrow. A week ago I never knew Josephine Sarah Marcus Earp existed; now I'm protective of her. Especially I'm protective of her in the presence of someone whose specialization is parks.

He gets up from his desk, puts on a white glove, goes to his filing-cabinet and withdraws an envelope in which is a bundle of white card tied with a ribbon. You expect wills to be bound like this, or sheets of music autographed by Haydn during his bipolarity period, when he thought he was Handel.

But this is a photograph of Josephine Sarah Marcus Earp, or the woman I thought was Josephine Sarah Marcus Earp. In fact it is the same photograph as the one reproduced on the cover of her book, except that where the latter showed the dimmest outline of breasts pushing against some sort of shirt or blouse, the breasts in this one are as good as naked, the merest diaphanous nothing coming between us and them.

Hollis Cook looks to see how I'm taking this. 'OK,' I say, 'they're the same. Only the one on the cover has been airbrushed for modesty's sake. Are you saying this can't be Mrs Earp because it's so fruity? She does admit she was an actress.'

He hands me a white glove. 'If you'd like to handle the photograph carefully you'll see this is a professional photograph with a copyright date embossed on it. 1914. And this isn't the only version I've got. A gentleman from Germantown, Wisconsin has sent me a similar one. Another has turned up in Mexico. And California. Now, if you look on the back here . . . be careful, your fingerprints will damage it . . . you'll see the stamp of the New York establishment that took the photograph. Our guess, given the frequency with which this photograph is now turning up, is that it shows a prostitute, probably a New York prostitute, possibly with pretensions either as a dancer or a model, and that this is now revealed for what it was – a pornographic photograph . . .'

'Hang on,' I say. 'I can see that Wyatt Earp might not like it, were he alive today, that pictures of his near-naked wife are popping up all over the west, but nothing you've shown me argues against its being her.'

We are nose to nose, now, Hollis Cook and I, glove to glove over Josephine Sarah Marcus Earp's uncovered bosom. Even Richard, who has shown no curiosity whatsoever so far today about any matter that is not gun-related, has joined us in our scrutiny.

'1914,' the Park Manager declares. '1914. If this is Sarah Marcus Earp, who was born in 1860, then she is fifty-four years old in this photograph, and I think we want her secret.'

'I see,' I say. 'You're sure of that?'

'There's the date.'

That something in Hollis Cook which felt at the same time sadistic and flirtatious now feels simply sadistic. He isn't giving me pain, but he is denying me pleasure.

'And we have no other image that offers to be of Mrs Earp?'

'Nope.'

'Whoever this beautiful woman is,' I press him, 'she still looks Jewish though, doesn't she?'

I have gone beyond the brief of an Arizona State Historic Park, Park Manager. 'I couldn't answer to that, I'm afraid,' he says.

We have not yet addressed the problem of a word printed in the bottom corner of the photograph. 'Do you think this might be her name?' I ask. 'Kaloma –'

'It could be her professional name.'

'Kaloma – it's got a Jewish ring to it.'

'. . . assuming she's . . . it is. You would know more about that than I.'

I force it on him. 'Kaloma.'

'It has a vaguely Middle Eastern sound, I admit that, but . . .'

'From Haifa. You think she could be a . . .'

'I don't know.'

'. . . an Israeli model? One of the very first?'

'But the fact is that Kaloma could also be the name of the studio.'

'Naturally,' I say. 'Of course. But if it did turn out she was an Israeli model . . .'

'I would vote for the studio, as opposed to the name of the girl.'

'None of this explains how the misattribution has come about,' I say. 'What if Kaloma is Wyatt Earp's daughter from Sarah?'

But there is to be no meeting, no harmony between us. I am to leave Tombstone empty-handed. 'They never had children,' he says.

I stay the night in Tucson. In the morning, I set about a simple task I should have attended to before I left Los Angeles. I look up the name C. Lawrence Huerta in the Tucson telephone directory. And find one.

Yes, he is the Judge Huerta who was, and indeed still is, associated with the Jewish Cemetery in Boothill. It might interest me to know that *Kaddish* has been said at the memorial every year since the restoration I read about in *The New York Times*. Every year but this one, that is. This year, the judge was not well enough to take part, and without him the thing somehow just didn't happen. But he hopes to get involved again next year to see it doesn't die off. The Green Valley senior citizens are very good people, but they need someone to stir them up, otherwise their interest may go off the boil.

He favours a deep, slow and exact delivery. The telephone seems not to inhibit him. As it never does inhibit men whose enthusiasms have become obsessive.

But will he meet me?

'Yes. We can speak. Whatever it is you wish. We can speak and we can meet. Wherever you wish to meet.'

We agree that he will collect me from my hotel in, let us say, forty minutes. He will take me to the museum he is putting together in his Eagle's Nest. No, it is not a Jewish museum. Nor is it Yaqui. It is HoHoKam. Before Columbus, the HoHoKam inhabited large tracts of southern Arizona. Mysteriously, the tribe disappeared. The name HoHoKam has been resurrected and officially incorporated because Judge Huerta wishes to do something that is for all tribes. And for all people. 'I want to extend a gesture of good will,' he concludes, and we are not off the phone yet, 'to the non-Indian from the Indian.'

'In forty minutes, then,' I say.

In fact, he is round in thirty. He knocks at my door at the same moment as the housemaid arrives with clean linen. I open it to both of them. She is standing to one side, by her trolley, gaping, because Judge Huerta is constructed on the same principle as the giraffe, if you can conceive of a giraffe in a stetson and long, grey plaits, and although this is Tucson and thousands of Indians live here, it would appear that they don't come knocking on the hotel rooms of English guests before ten in the morning. Not in this hotel, anyway.

He is older than he looks. In his late sixties. He has retired from the law, for all that he was doing well at it. There are not many Indian lawyers, particularly bilingual ones. But he is absorbed day and night now in his efforts for the HoHoKam, even though, if I have grasped it correctly, the HoHoKam exist primarily in his own mind.

We discuss these matters as he drives me out of town towards the mountains where he has his eyrie. As soon as we leave the freeway and hit the dirt we are on land owned by a Japanese businessman, Mr Fujinaka. Things are not rosy between Judge Huerta and Mr Fujinaka, because Lawrence wants to install water facilities in his museum, once a telecommunications building owned by Sprint, and Mr Fujinaka says – or at least Lawrence says he says – 'My thirty-two acres will depreciate if I have an Indian living and drawing water on the highest point of them.'

Our eyes meet quickly over this, Indian to Jew, Jew to Indian, for we have both depreciated a few acres in our time.

On a huge hill, cragged and steep, truth stands; and that does not exclude HoHoKam truth: he that would reach it about must, and about must go. The only difference between HoHoKam and Christian truth being the giant cacti. And the dust. And Lawrence's grave, grey pigtails.

Museum may not be the word for what he has brought me to. In the first place, the old Sprint shack is too inaccessible to encourage visitors. In the second, it is not Lawrence's idea merely to provide storage for antiquities. Remembrances and memorials are here in plenty – an extraordinary collection, laid out on trestle tables or nailed to the walls, of dolls, jewellery, skins, hemp, horseshoes, totems, rattles, rugs, pods, instruments, calendars – but it is as living, operational assets that Lawrence sees them.

'I would like to put all this in trust for anyone of good will who would like to become a member of the HoHoKam tribe,' he tells me. 'So that they may own a piece of the west, and so that they may reach an understanding of the Four Harmonies.'

I don't press him on the Four Harmonies. I know that I shall come to hear more of them in due course.

Whatever the word is for where we are, a gesture of beneficence, a wild hope that it may be possible to unite where there has been only difference, lies behind it. Among the items he has gathered, Lawrence shows me the smallpox rugs, the poisoned gifts that were given to the Indians by their white brothers, to keep them warm in the night and to kill them off by morning. An unthinkable vileness, in comparison to which a lynch party is a kindness. But nothing vengeful is intended by their exhibition. 'I don't want to dwell on that,' Lawrence says. 'Enough Indians dwell on that. I want to reach out. The Indian can be too keen to do what will please the non-Indian. He doesn't know what that is or how to do it. What we want is harmony.'

He is sixty-seven, but he makes me feel twice his age. This is the first time I have ever experienced sensations of tenderness, not to say fatherliness, for a judge.

For the sensations I experience when he opens the back doors and shows me what he has erected on the mountainside, I have no name. Masks. Scores of them. Masks made of plywood, with steel bolts for eyes and noses, and steel chains for mouths. Masks supported on tripods made of pipes and odd lengths of metal. He throws open the back doors of the disused telecommunications shed, and I see an entire mountain of masks and cacti.

'Lawrence, what are they?' I ask.

'Yeis. But not the whole Yei. These are just the faces. I had to remove them from their bodies and bring them up here because children were vandalizing them.'

'And you made all these?'

'Oh, yes. Sometimes with the help of young Indians.'

'So where are the bodies?'

'Oh, on the Trail of Tears in the sacred grounds. I will take you there now.'

We get back into the car and drive down the mountain and then around it. To get to the sacred grounds we have to drive up the path to Lawrence's house and park the car in Lawrence's garage. The sacred grounds are Lawrence's back garden.

And now I wonder how I could ever have been astounded by the masks belonging to the Yeis, for the Yeis themselves stand in an avenue that extends for hundreds of yards, are some sixteen feet high, and number in excess of fifty. They are totems, ethereal messengers, intermediaries between the spirit beings and the world of flesh. When the wind catches them they rattle and chime and bemoan the thanklessness of their task. Deprived of their masks their faces run with steel-chain tears, for it is no cheerful errand that they're on.

I learn that Lawrence has lavished a fortune on the twenty acres of desert which extend his garden into the mountain. Just as it was his energy that got the Boothill Jewish Cemetery restored, so it is his life's blood that is going into the resurrection of the HoHoKam. Every one of these Yeis he has constructed himself – as devotedly as any *objet trouvé* sculptor in SoHo or Cork Street – out of logs, broken bricks, metal tubing, rags, pegboard, bathroom tiles, gauze, wash-leathers, webbing, cable, glass beads, shards of pottery, bits of railway, bits of freeway, bits of everything.

He escorts me round the grounds. Shows me what else he has erected over the years. Avenues of remembrance, sweat-baths, pit houses, platforms of the dead, high in the hills. And most extraordinary of all, his own Seven Golden Cities of Cibola.

Do I know the story?

I do not.

Cortéz had heard that there were seven Indian cities made of gold. He went in pursuit of them and of course failed to find them. The laugh was on him. What can be more golden, the Indians say, than the land and its people. Crazed for mere metal, the Spaniards missed the true gold of the country. So the Seven Golden Cities are symbolic of man's materialism and blindness and unappeasable dissatisfaction.

In Lawrence Huerta's version they are a mountainside of sun-reflecting aluminium strips, former Tucson road-signs painted yellow and bolted into the earth. I stand at the foot of the mountain with him and count them. Each of the seven cities has its own cliff, and its own fortress of cacti. They glitter like delusions in the sun. We stand in silence as a solitary hawk hovers over the highest of them, waiting for any one of its lowly inhabitants to emerge.

There is the faintest change in the direction of the breeze. The Yeis begin to moan.

On the way back to his house, where I will meet his wife and have tea and cake, Lawrence talks to me about the Four Harmonies. Father Sky, Mother Earth, Fellow Man, Yourself. It's cosmos, ozone-layer, eco-speak, by and large. But I am softened up for simple wisdom by the beauty of the Seven Golden Cities of Cibola. And there is nothing wrong with Harmony with Yourself if you can manage it. As Lawrence says, 'I, Howard, consider this to be the most important Harmony of all.'

Grace Huerta is waiting for us. She is not Indian. She may have been golden-haired once. She too is quietly, gravely spoken. They both measure their words as if they know too well the danger that is in them. I suspect there is illness in the house, perhaps both of them are ill, and this also necessitates soft language.

There are dolls, made by Grace Huerta, on every shelf and surface. Not ethnic dolls, but seaside souvenir dolls. One is of Princess Di, radiant in a bridal gown. Funny what can be yoked together – Di and the Seven Golden Cities of Cibola.

We talk, almost in whispers. Lawrence remembers how it was his friendship for a Mr Israel Rubin that led to his interest in the Jewish Cemetery. On a visit to Tombstone, Israel Rubin learnt of the existence of the neglected graveyard. He took Lawrence with him to look for it. Jewish reverence for the dead touched Huerta's heart. He had known Israel Rubin since they were in Washington together many years before, working for the Office of Minority Business Enterprise. The Rubins welcomed Lawrence into their family. The Jewish connection has meant something to Lawrence ever since.

And to his wife. It is she who gets Lawrence's buffalo-skin *yarmulke* out of a drawer so that I can see it. It is she who finds me the list of objects that went into the vaulted memorial at Boothill – a *Kiddush* cup, a *menorah*, prayer-books, dirt from Jerusalem. And it is she who finds the phrase that sounds this hushed afternoon to its heart. She is describing some of the Jews of her acquaintance, and how they understand their Jewishness. They say, she says, 'Being Jewish is like a grace note in our lives, not the whole symphony.'

There is not much light in the house. The Yeis buckle in the sun, but indoors there is no such cruelty. We murmur among shadows. 'That's what Jewishness is for us too,' Grace says, 'a grace note.'

I think how many people who are not Jewish feel this way. And how rarely their tenderness is reciprocated. We recount the doings of our enemies endlessly, we Jews. But the affections we inspire slip past in the half-light.

How many of us will be sitting in a quiet, darkened house this afternoon, speaking of Buddhism or Islam as a grace note in our lives?

I know the reason . . . How could we? After all we have undergone, after all that's been done, after all that's been said, *why* should we . . .?

Yes, yes. But what if the mathematics work out the other way, and we can be shown to be indebted still, here and there, to some who have thought kindly of us?

Do we have any kindliness to show in return? Leave aside what may be owing – do we know what easing of our own hearts may follow the expression of affection for ways which are not our ways?

*　　*　　*

After tea, Lawrence takes me back out into the sacred grounds, sits me in shade, presents me with a bowl containing the elements of Indian concordance with what is self and what is not self, clasps my arm, and declares me a HoHoKam.

Not the expected outcome of my American journey, but who would not surprise himself if he could?

HoHoKam – it won't last and I won't remember to recite the Four Harmonies – but it sounds easier on the ear than Jew Jew Jew.

Thirteen

NOT ISRAEL PROPER

By the time I am returned harmonious from America, those Russian tanks that caterpillared towards confrontation in the summer, thereby keeping root-seeking Litvaks from their origins, have caterpillared back to their depots. According to people in the know, Lithuania is safe to visit. Not convenient, not pleasurable, but safe.

You cannot let safety determine everything. There are other considerations. In my estimation, Lithuania is now too cold to visit.

Israel, on the other hand . . .

I put it to my wife, who is Australo-Catholic, that we make an attack on the English winter we both fear by spending part of it in Israel on a quid pro quo basis – I give her sun in Eilat and Midnight Mass in Bethlehem, and she gives me the opportunity to find out what it's like for a Jew to return to the Promised Land with a prohibition on his arm.

It surprises me that she feels she needs to think about it.

But the louring London afternoons, shrinking to pin-points of sickly light, speak eloquently in my cause. By the end of the first week in December it is not difficult to get anyone to go with you anywhere.

Beyond beginning where it's hot, I make no preparations. Since everything in Israel is Jewish or has consequence for Jews, it doesn't matter what I do.

*   *   *

Sitting by the pool of the King Solomon's Palace Hotel, Eilat, among the bared breasts of matrons who should have a greater respect for the sanctity of the family, I am approached by Morris Singer from south Manchester. I don't know his name yet, but I do know he comes from south Manchester. There is no explaining this; it is just something you feel in your bones if you have been brought up in north Manchester.

He is wearing a towelling track-suit and French sunglasses. And he thinks he knows me.

'You from Wilmslow?'

'No.'

'Hale Barns?'

'No.'

'Got a business? A hairdresser's or something?'

'No.'

'I'm sure I know you. I'm sure I've sat in your chair. What do you do?'

'I'm a writer.'

'Then I don't know you.'

He has a high voice which doesn't get any lower when he joins me at ground level on the plastic deckchairs.

'My wife reads,' he says.

He is a surveyor, but wouldn't mind doing something else with his life. He's looking round for a hobby. This is his first time in Israel.

'How come?'

'How come I've come?'

'How come you haven't come sooner?'

'I'm not religious. I used to cry rather than go to *shul*. I still do.'

But the country got to him when his plane landed yesterday. I know it got to him. I was sitting in the row behind. I watched it get to him. It was getting to me at the same time.

'I felt choked,' he says. 'Men aren't allowed to cry . . .'

'Except when they don't want to go to *shul* . . .'

'No, but you know what I mean – you don't expect to cry. But I got this lump.'

Me too. Funny that. We neither of us expected it. We neither of us identified with Israel. We are both middle-aged and this is our first visit – that's how much we care. But we get off the plane at Ovda Airport gulping.

Ovda. It wasn't even Tel Aviv. Just a facility in the desert for getting you more quickly to Eilat which, as every Israeli will tell you, isn't Israel proper. Yet one bump on the tarmac in the middle of the Negev and we're gone.

Ros, too, got a lump in the throat. For *me*. What could Ovda Airport mean to an Australo-Catholic, you may ask. But as we came off the plane, she clasped my hand and whispered, 'Welcome home, Howard.' We could feel each other shiver. This is how deep the idea of return runs. This is how much of a foreigner she thinks I have been in England.

Things get frenetically aerobical around the King Solomon's Palace pool if you're still there by late morning. An entertainment platform, reached by a little arched bridge, extends into the pool. On this, a beetle of a girl with a Nefertiti profile and a voice more gravelly than the Negev is jumping up and down in black shorts and a red shirt with matching rolled-down red socks. She stretches out her bangled arms and ripples her skin until it looks as though it will slough off at her finger tips. She puts her hands on her hips and marches up and down on the spot, like a soldier in a pet, and thirty women and a handful of men stand around the pool and copy her. She gives a V for victory sign, she puts her hands where her womb is and makes a basket of them – she's Churchill and she's a chicken. And so are the thirty women and the handful of men.

So this is Jewishness with a body. The thing you come to Israel for.

At the Sheba Night-club, where they stamp your wrists with red ink so that you should feel you're eighteen again, I see Jews dancing in a way that makes a mockery of all the truisms I've formulated since I last had my wrists stamped. They can do it. They can do it with every bit as much ugly assurance and gracelessness as gentiles. They wear *goyische* leotards around the pool and go into *goyische* trances on the discothèque floor. I take back everything I've said. It applied only to what I've seen in the *galut* – in exile. Diaspora dancing – that's all I've been describing.

But that still leaves me with the problem of my diaspora fastidiousness. Every night the King Solomon's Palace entertainment staff put on their phosphorescent jazz-ballet costumes and do something which I take to be *A Chorus Line*. The same steps, the same tunes, are repeated in every hotel in Eilat. 'Why is it,' I ask my wife, 'that, secularized, the culture aspires to the trashiest form of musical entertainment of our times?'

She promises to put her mind to it.

A problem with Eilat: how do you tell the beach from the building sites?

It is partly the bitter smell of desert that encourages me to think of Eilat as Coober Pedy-on-Sea. But it is also the excitable impermanence, the weakness that people who live in dust bowls have for making more dust still. Hotels are being pulled down on every corner for no other reason than that more hotels should go up. Nobody seems to have heard the word 'extension' here. If a thing's not big enough you just hammer it back into powder.

Eilat is spectacularly set, with the Red Sea spilling out of its pockets; the russet hills of Jordan rising to the east; and, north, the Negev itself, climbing back to Israel proper in three serrated tiers, the middle tier lighter in colour, seeming to swim between the dun ranges below and the deep purple ones above. That, though, is all you get. The office and apartment blocks on the far edges of the town are nothing but up-ended cubes of concrete, the building bricks of fast development the world over, proclaiming impatience with the indulgences of aesthetics. Provision flats, basic amenities for a country in a hurry, careless of what other cultures have constructed hereabouts, defiant of the ways they have reached some accommodation with the landscape.

Closer to where the fun is, closer to the beach and the lagoon, the hotels that haven't been pulled down to be re-built as hotels are all parodies of parodies, Euro-oriental palaces and colossi, pastiches of luxury ziggurats and pyramids – the Middle East copying Europe copying the Middle East.

Israel is famous for its irrigation. This is the country that made the desert bloom. I have been here only a couple of days but already a dozen different people have talked to me about the delayed-timing sprinkler-system perfected by Israelis and the envy of a water-needy world. So you would expect Eilat to be sporadically flowery if not exactly verdurous. But the flower boxes are all dead. Concrete bunkers the size of domestic baths line the promenades, each an arrangement of sand, martyred weed and a length of rubber hosepipe. The municipal gardens are the same. Dead earth, strangled vegetation, and what looks like the murder weapon – the length of rubber hose. It's by means of the rubber hosepipe that the delayed sprinkler irrigation system works. But perhaps I have missed the point: perhaps what's meant to be on show is not verdure but the rubber hose itself.

Footfalls echo in the memory down the passage we did not take towards the door we never opened into the hose-garden.

A Jew lets T. S. Eliot echo in his memory only when he is feeling bad about his Jewishness, and I am feeling poorly about mine as I survey the building-site horticulture of Eilat. Back there in the diaspora it was all right to mock one's own incompetence around cultivation. We all knew why that was. Keep people off the land and they will forget what land looks like. But this is Israel. We are farmers again here. Aren't we?

I remind myself that this is Eilat. Not Israel proper. It will be different further north. But all is not quiet about my heart. It is not ineptitude I am complaining of. It is attitude. Combine the dead-flower bunkers with the up-ended cubes of concrete and there is something sullen about it all; as if no instinct for the decorative exists here, as if the place is angry with whatever doesn't further economic development. A thus far and no further policy seems to be at work, a brusque indifference to any of the Four HoHoKam Harmonies.

But this is Eilat. Not Israel proper.

Just to my left, however, as I look to sea, is Jordan. Jordan proper. That's if a Jew can allow himself to put the words Jordan and proper together.

I decide I would like to walk to the border. You can't cross. There is no crossing – no legal crossing – in either direction; but I fancy seeing the whites of my enemies' eyes. I may not have been to Israel before, I may be as surprised as Morris Singer by the lumps that the Ovda landing lodged in my throat, but I am seized by the most unreasoning patriotism for the country whenever there is a war, and I mean it when I say that the town of Aqaba houses my enemies.

The quickest way seems to be along the beach. Quickest but not quietest. There are any number of straw-hut, Pacific-island style restaurants on the sand, all of them with associated music systems. Some play records through giant Yamaha speakers tied to wilting palm trees. Others have live musicians on electronic keyboards, tormenting Aqaba with every song that has ever come last in the Eurovision Song Contest.

The closer you get to the border, the more hippies there are. On the last few hundred yards of Israeli beach, tents have been pitched. Washing-lines are thrown between trees even more miserable than those that have Yamaha speakers tied to them. Border-afflicted trees. Men with beards sit making fires. Women with scrubbed faces urge their naked children on to acts of healthy savagery and spontaneity. You can tell the country is running out here, that nothing has anywhere to go. Cars drive up, circle around where it's half-beach, half-road, and drive back the way they came. You want the border to be an event, but it won't be.

It isn't even a border. It's a rat-shit tumble of brick walls, mounds of earth, watch towers, corrugated huts, curls of barbed wire and radar. The sort of mess you throw together as children when your gang's the Israeli army and the others are the Arabs.

A jeep turns up, carrying bearded soldiers armed with sub-machine-guns. They look me over once, and then get on with throwing together more mess. Queer, if you're used to seeing British soldiers, how anarchical the army looks. No short back and sides. No Borstal subjugation. No crushed individuality. Beards are wild. Hair grows as long as you can get it to. Uniforms are designer-feral; the swagger is piratical-kitsch. You can see the swagger all over Eilat, the reservists affecting the air of men who have just woken up but are still ready for anything, the full-timers rolling along like sea-dogs with guns on one arm and girls on the other.

So is the difference that this is, as it were, a people's army? That here you fight palpably for your own survival, whereas the Borstal boys are press-ganged into a cause whose reasons are a mystery to them? Do you crop the heads only of men who are not fighting for themselves?

Preoccupied by these thoughts, I walk back from the dead border, without having met the stare of a single enemy Jordanian. On the outskirts of town I see another jeep, with three helmeted soldiers aboard, going around and round a roundabout. Round and round and round, just for the fun of it.

Morris Singer has taken to asking me, whenever he sees me, how my work is progressing. He scribbles in the air as I pass, the way you do when you are asking for the bill in a country whose language you have not mastered.

287

'Going all right, is it?'

He doesn't believe I am a writer. He is still convinced that I am a barber and that he has sat in my chair.

I catch sight of him sometimes, in the distance, pointing me out to other people from south Manchester and making a clipping action with his hand. When he sees that I've seen him he changes from scissors to a pen and writes an imaginary bill out in the air.

Because it's Saturday night and we will become morbid if we don't do something, we do something touristy. We take a bus from the Riviera and go to Kibbutz Elot, a few miles out of town, for an Israeli folklore evening.

We turn up in hundreds, are welcomed by extrovert kibbutzniks, are given a carnation each, and are seated at long tables in a sort of primary-school refectory. Apart from the wine on the tables, everything is suggestive of extended childhood. There are school stencils on the walls, depicting camels, palm trees, fish, melons.

A family I have observed doing sums all over Eilat sits next to us. It is the wife who works out what they can and cannot afford, hubby and the kids go along with her decisions quietly. She is petite, fair, with a boy's haircut and goldfish-bowl spectacles. She has a pen and paper by her on the table. A night out at Kibbutz Elot is not supposed to conceal any extras, but she is worried about the wine. She is not Jewish. Jews do not do this. Ros wonders if the husband might be. I tell her no, without bothering to scrutinize him. Jews do not marry women who do this. You go into debt, you start a business empire, you steal from your brother-in-law, you do whatever you have to do to afford a night out, but you never tot it up while it's happening.

They're here, like us, to soak up a bit of sun before heading for Jerusalem. Her best friend from school lives in Jerusalem.

She has married an Israeli engineer. I want to warn her not to do any calculations when she goes out with her friend and the engineer, but I dare not.

She asks me if I'm here on a pilgrimage. I'm about to say, 'Of course not,' but I catch my wife's eye. 'Maybe it will turn out that way,' I say.

She looks at me earnestly. She inclines her head, almost bows it. No irony, no scorn, no humour, nothing but reverence for someone who is here on what may turn out to be a pilgrimage.

I get a fleeting insight into a secret world. Forget spies, psychics, witches, paedophiles, bestialists – the truly hidden are those who never make jokes, are never disrespectful, and never go anywhere without computing the costs.

A difficult, balding Jewish woman from the terrestrial world sits on the other side of Ros. She wears a track-suit-for-going-out-in. Her face is strained, her mouth pulled downwards and sideways from reacting to imaginary slights. I see to it that I keep slighting her so that she shouldn't feel paranoid.

The cost-counting woman asks if I speak Hebrew. I shake my head. The paranoiac overhears. 'Me neither,' she says. 'Though if I'm not mistaken, we both ought to be able to speak Hebrew, huh?'

This is difficult-person-speak for, 'Are you a Jewish boy?' as well as for, 'So why, in that case, is your wife not?'

A moth to a flame, I flutter towards trouble. 'It's not even as though I have an excuse,' I say. 'We were taught it for I don't know how many years.'

'What, at school?'

'After school.'

'I had to travel too far,' she says, flicking at something that isn't there, some fantasy insect that is trying to crawl into her beaded track-suit. 'My mother didn't like me to go so far.'

'We all went by bus,' I say.

'Bus! Who saw a bus?'

289

As a punishment I decide to stop slighting her.

Folklore turns out to be more singing of the kind you get around the pool and on the beach and in the lounges of the hotels. Another Israeli barking to yet another Roland E–20 keyboard with Yamaha speakers. Eilat has not always been Eilat. It was Etzion Geber once, and then Berenice, and then Aila, and then Um Rashrash. The day will come when it will be known as Beth Yamaha.

But wait – this is to be Roland E–20 keyboard music with a difference after all. We have a master of ceremonies, a boy-man with a kiddy's haircut, wearing a pensioner's jacket and a little lurex performance tie. His voice is strong and confident, but he stands the way a child does when everyone is singing him happy birthday, awkwardly, with his feet together.

'He seems astonished,' Ros observes, 'to find himself in long trousers.'

'You used to say that,' I remark, 'about your accountant, your dentist, your optician and your solicitor.'

'That's because they were all Jewish.'

'Are you saying that *every* Jewish man looks astonished to find himself in long trousers?'

'No. N-no, not every one.'

She leaves it to me to work out who that excludes.

We are expected – no, we are *required* – to clap along with the singing. We are given tambourines. We are told to wave our hands in the air. And to put our arms around the people next to us. Ros gets the paranoiac. And I (oh, God!) get the woman who keeps the family accounts.

He may be uncertain in the jacket and trouser area, our impish MC, but the potency of the occasion is all on his side. He can discomfit us, should he want to, for not smiling, for not shouting 'Ole!' when he asks us to, for not entering into the Israeli spirit and joining in every *Lai-lai-lai* and every *Chiri-Chiri-Chiri-bum-bum-bum* and every *bim-bam-bong*.

There is a party of Finns here. I make spiritual connection with at least forty of them who feel as I do, that death would be preferable to *bim-bam-bong*. Their pale, wandering eyes meet mine. This is the first time I have ever felt bonded to one Finn, let alone a roomful. But the moment the singer looks their way, or one of the extrovert kibbutzniks approaches their table clapping, they know just as I do that they must join in, must laugh and clap and *bim-bam-bong*, otherwise worse may await them, even though there is no worse.

That's part one. Now comes the interval, during which food is served. Or rather, during which we serve ourselves. We run to the food. Only the Finns hold back.

It's the usual – hummus, shashlik, falafel. And good. Kibbutz-good.

Extrovert kibbutzniks go from table to table, checking that we're having an amazing time. 'Good?'

'Good. Good. Very good.'

'Good.'

But at our table, the paranoiac is having trouble with what's on her plate. If she hadn't served herself she would have sent it back. Above all, it's the beetroot that's puzzling her.

'What's this?' she asks us. As if it's our fault.

'Beetroot,' we tell her.

Beetroot! She's never been so insulted in her life.

'So what's this?'

'Aubergine.'

She shakes her head, and prods the plate with her fork. She turns to Ros. 'What's tahina made of?'

'Sesame seed.'

She fumes. *'Sesame seed!'*

We're all glad we're not on the end of her fork.

Once the tables are cleaned, a Finnish woman is given a special dispensation to sing 'Jerusalem the Golden' in Finnish. She is well-built, in the great tradition of Finnish sopranos. And vibrates thrillingly. When it's over she is presented with a box of dates and a tape of Israeli music. She is very touched. She flushes, bows, takes back the microphone. 'I have never been so . . . so . . . so . . .'

We were patient during the early verses of 'Jerusalem the Golden' in Finnish, we don't begrudge her a single date grown here in Kibbutz Elot, or a single *chiri-chiri-chiri-bum-bum-bum* waiting for her on the Israeli tape, but we cannot bear any more suspense. '. . . so HAPPY!' we shout as one.

Which frees us all to descend to a little auditorium where, once we are seated, a number of dance routines are to be performed, beginning with 'Preparation for a Yemenite Wedding'. This is the tragi-comic story of a man with twelve daughters and no sons – all to the good, as chance would have it, since there are twelve Yemenite women dancers and no Yemenite men.

There is much to admire in the troupe of Yemenite women, not least their fine, ancient profiles, and their capacity to ululate like Clytemnestra when her blood is up. This is not a skill I have encountered in Jewish women before. And it makes the hairs rise under my collar to be reminded that Jews were Africans before they were Europeans. But it is a little, elderly, bespectacled lady, looking more like a native of Brooklyn or north Manchester than the Yemen, who steals the show. She cannot have been with the troupe long for she recognizes none of the steps. The idea is to lose her at the back of the stage, but the more she is lost, the more she is visible. While the others gather for marriage, she retires to a remote corner of her own where she performs the world-famed Prestwich giving-with-one-hand-and-taking-with-the-other plate dance, thrusting a platter out and then withdrawing it, all the time rocking from one short leg to the other, and shaking her head from side to side to a rhythm neither European nor African. Were it not for the glee she is unable to conceal, you would take the movement of her head to denote unbearable grief.

Nothing, to my sense, can follow her. Least of all the Eilat Dance Company which specializes in choreographing Middle Eastern themes in the style of *A Chorus Line* or, at best, *Seven Brides For Seven Brothers*. The result, it must be said, goes down well with the audience. On the return of the Yemenite women for another wedding ceremony, serious talking breaks out among us. We want more *Chorus Line*. And we get it, with a bit of nostalgic Judaism thrown in to boot, when the Eilat Dance Company perform a Hasidic *Shabbat* Welcoming Dance – an event which poses a problem for a troupe of six men and six women, taking into account the ban on men and women dancing together which we know Hasids to impose. This is ingeniously circumvented by the ruse of having both sexes dance with their hands over their eyes.

So simple and yet so effective. It makes you wonder why the Hasids have not thought of it themselves.

To end, the dancers descend into the audience and bring us up by hand to do an Israeli hora.

'No, I won't be dancing,' I say, when it comes to my turn, and I say it so abruptly that the unfortunate who has invited me recoils as though I have leprosy.

Which, in a manner of speaking, when it comes to Israeli folk dancing, is exactly what I do have.

Speaking of culture:

I read that the Israel Philharmonic is going to play Wagner for the first time in Israel for fifty years. According to the *Jerusalem Post*, Knesset speaker Dov Shilansky has pleaded with the orchestra to drop its plan. 'I appeal in the name of all those who are in pain – and they are many – to have mercy.' But the orchestra is standing firm, having voted by thirty-nine to twelve, with nine abstentions, to whizz through some *Flying Dutchman* and *Tristan and Isolde* under Barenboim at the year's end.

I ring up the Philharmonic booking office to buy tickets, and am stalled. 'It's a question,' I am told.

'A question when or a question where?'

'There are many questions. There are problems. Nothing is certain. We will make announcements in the press when we know.'

'When you know if it's happening?'

'It's a question.'

The voice is suspicious and weary, like many Israeli voices over the phone. When I was small I was frightened to ask anything of the Jewish adults I knew. Jews, I thought, were an impatient people. Now I am in a country of impatient people. But I try one more inquiry.

'If there is a concert, will it be in Tel Aviv?'

'Of course in Tel Aviv. That's where the orchestra plays. But look out for announcements.'

I plan to do that.

I am all plans at the moment. I have to plan where to go when we leave Eilat. I have to plan which route to take, what size car to hire, how many days to hire it for.

A plump and unaccountably blushing woman at one of the offices of the Government Tourist Agency warns us off trying anything on our own. 'Oh, I wouldn't drive,' she says.

'Wouldn't drive where?'

'Oh, anywhere.'

There is a map on her wall. 'If we don't drive,' I say, following a road with my finger, 'can we get to Jerusalem via Hebron?'

'Hebron? I wouldn't go to Hebron.'

'Why not?'

'Nothing there.'

I smile. Nothing in Hebron? Isn't Abraham's wife buried in Hebron? Didn't Absalom live in Hebron? Wasn't Hebron David's royal residence before Jerusalem?

'And anyway,' she goes on, 'I wouldn't advise going to Jerusalem except as part of an organized tour group.'

'Is this about getting lost, getting bored or getting killed?' I ask. 'Are we talking Intifada now?'

She shrugs. The problem with the Intifada – or the success of the Intifada, depending which side you're on – is that Israel both has and has not to acknowledge it. 'You have to be careful in any country,' she reminds us.

But if we insist on driving, fine. She rings up car companies for us. Helps us to compare prices. Makes tentative bookings for us. Her last words, though, are as precautionary as her first.

Watch it. Go where you're shown. Obey the military. Skip Hebron.

Back at the King Solomon's bar, where Dean Martin and Frank Sinatra are coming out of the Yamaha speakers, I overhear a handsome devil of an Israeli entertaining an English couple by pricing everything on his body.

'Lacoste shirt – how much do you think? Sixteen dollars – not real. Feel, feel. See this watch – seven dollars. What do you think of these sandals . . .?'

When he leaves, I see his keys on the bar. I call him back. He flashes me his brilliant Middle Eastern teeth. 'It's only the keys for the aeroplane,' he says.

A glass ball spins on the ceiling. Overdressed kids run across the dance floor. Out of the corner of my eye I see that Morris Singer is at the far end of the room. If I look up he will write a bill for me in the air. I stare at the cut on my thumb, caused by a strip of magnetic tape that's worked loose in one of the hotel bath towels. Walk out of the King Solomon's Palace with a bath towel and bells start to ring all over the building.

Someone taps me on the shoulder. It is Morris Singer's wife, Linda, the one who reads. She asks if she can talk to me. She wants to know how I write, when I write, who I write for, what else I intend to do besides write, whether I ever dry up, whether I like Somerset Maugham . . .

She doesn't listen to any of my answers. She's too busy formulating the next question.

She's thinking they'll need to get out of Eilat for a day or two. Maybe go to Egypt. Cairo, the Pyramids, a Nile cruise. But that'll mean staying in an Egyptian hotel. What do I think? Will it be all right?

I tell her what I think. She doesn't listen.

She and Morris and the kids have got very quickly to the bottom of Eilat. 'We're intelligent people,' she tells me. 'If we stay we'll suffer brain death.'

I nod.

'What kind of words do you use?' she suddenly asks. 'Short simple words, or long old ones?'

'Very long, very old ones,' I rejoin, I riposte, I animadvert, I surrebut.

The trouble with trying to acquaint oneself with Israel by starting in Eilat is that everyone here is from Manchester. I am told that there are French weeks, Italian weeks, Dutch weeks. We have chosen a Manchester week.

So it's a nice change for us to run into a couple from Edgware in the piano bar. Though it runs ahead a little to call them a couple, since that's precisely what we talk about – whether they are or they aren't, whether they have a right to be or they haven't, whether they owe too much to the past and to other people even to enjoy being together.

They are both recently widowed. They have met up only lately and taken this holiday together in the face of disapproval from their children, mutterings from their friends and uncertainty, if they're going to be frank about it, in themselves. It's not just a question of whether they should be together, but of whether they even *want* to be together.

They are in their middle sixties. He may be older than that. She doted on her husband. He adored his wife. There is not a song that the gay Philippino pianist at the white grand gay piano plays that does not bring back some memory painful to one of them. Drinking champagne only makes it worse. But we have to drink champagne. It happens to be our wedding anniversary, and although we wouldn't have mentioned it had we known the sadness it would cause, we *have* mentioned it, and now we are in it together, the four of us, up to our necks in melancholy and bubbles and camp piano playing.

We have them out, drunkenly, the big issues of the heart – the issues that get bigger as the heart grows older. What is owing after fifty years? What is owing to the dead and what is owing to the living? How much does/should loneliness count? How far are you truly connected to another whose loss mirrors your own? Does that mirroring only make for difference in the end, and not for connectedness? What if it only serves to remind you of what was uniquely yours and cannot, *must* not be compared?

You take long views on your wedding anniversary. More than they might have been at any other time are they touching to us, the widow and the widower, hanging on to each other for dear life. Or is it dear death?

But when I am not being touched I am being irritated. We couldn't be more serious with one another. There are not more solemn matters to be discussed. Yet we have to have the Philippino pianist, than whom there is no one required to be more frivolous, running like a nursery tune through the tragic adagio of our late quartet.

'Look at him,' the widow breaks off her reminiscences of her husband to observe. 'I've seen pianists play while they're talking, but he can play while he's kissing. Isn't he amazing?'

The person kissing him thinks he's amazing too. It may be the champagne or the conversation, but I have trouble with this one – a gay Israeli kissing the gay Philippino. On the *mouth*.

The widower, too, can't get over the piano playing. 'What talent!' He is a businessman. He has made a small fortune in his life. He would give half of it to be able to do a quarter of what the Philippino can do.

The widow compares him favourably with every other hotel pianist she has heard in every hotel in Jewish-frequented Christendom.

'Do you see that boy taking photographs?' she asks me. 'Isn't he the spitting image of Sting?'

The widower releases Ros's hand, over which he's been weeping in memory of his beloved wife. He doesn't want to miss a likeness to Sting.

'Isn't that a Bee Gee?' the widow wonders, half-way through a story about her late husband's shoes. How many shoes he had.

I want badly to lose my temper. Regardless of what is owing to their grief, I want to swear at them. Perhaps it's *because* of what is owing to their grief that I want to swear at them. Never fucking heard of Sting, I want to say. Never fucking seen a Bee Gee. On principle. On a principle which you, at your age, but more importantly as Jews, should honour. What's the point of being a Jew if you're going to drool over the meanest idols of a hostile culture? This, truly, is apostasy. This is the very sin Yahweh feared when he warned against following strange gods. Baal with a guitar.

But he never stopped warning. Which must mean that he never once trusted us. And that is, when one comes to think of it, the story of the first five books of Moses – the books the Chief Rabbi believes to be divinely inscribed. Yahweh blowing his stack, and the Jews dancing and dancing around a likeness purloined from some other tribe.

Dancing and dancing to a Roland E–20 with Yamaha speakers.

I think about it all the next morning, as I sit overdressed and hung-over by the pool, watching my people in leotards or with their breasts bared, swaying to an inhuman beat.

(Do I mind the young, pretty ones doing it? I search my conscience. Yes. I mind even the young, pretty ones doing it.)

And I decide that what was operating in the widow and the widower was not the negation of the great Jewish love of culture and learning, and not its abjuration either, but its corruption. The widower raves over the professionally pansy Philippino pianist, and the widow knows the name of every baby entertainer in England, Spain, France, America and Israel, because Jews have been so demoralized, so efficiently excluded from European mainstream culture, that there is nowhere else for their instinctive love of genius to go. This is *faut de mieux* enthusiasm. They've mislaid Mahler (unless they live in Philadelphia) so they put their love of art into Manilow.

The more readily, given that the high culture which has spat them out is home to Richard Wagner, not played in Israel for half a century.

The aerobics are ending. The girl in the red socks puts her fingers inside the back of her shorts, pulls them free, and skips off. Ros wonders if we shouldn't take a walk before lunch. As long as I can go on musing over the intellectual gaudiness of my people, I say. That's fine by her. She doesn't want to talk. But outside one of the lagoon-side shops we stop to admire a window display of tennis shoes decorated with sequins and seed-pearls. And one thought leads to another.

'I consider that,' she says, 'to be a profoundly Jewish sight — allowing that everything I say about Jews has to do with what *you* tell me Jews are. Taking a pair of tennis shoes and bringing them inside. What a perversity of intention. Probably only Cicciolina and Jeff Koons are working with a comparable degree of perverse intention.'

'Only they don't have the excuse of being Jewish.'

299

I'm feeling suddenly sour again. Just as I was exonerating my suffering co-religionists from one vulgarity, we stand charged with another.

Except that it turns out Ros isn't charging anyone with anything.

'Seeing these here,' she says, 'in a place which is so brightly coloured, in a light that is so hard and clear, and thinking of those exotically perfumed Yemenite women we saw the other night, just serves to remind one that what one's really been looking at all along, and calling garish, is in fact a last recollection of the gilt and splendour that once belonged very specifically to this environment.'

'You mean everything's garish here?'

'No. Why put it like that? I'm saying that what looks garish in Manchester *isn't* when you see it in its natural habitat. Maybe this is the meaning of kitsch – that it's a memory of what was, in another place or time, vibrant and lustrous.'

'So we self-conscious European Jews, who travesty our own poor taste, have made a fundamental geographic error. We have forgotten where we come from and what made us, what climatic conditions shaped us and gave us our love of hot colours and bright lights . . .' This is getting exciting. Two exonerations in a single day. 'We are not, then, aberrant Europeans. We are not freakish Litvaks. We are normal, regular, displaced Middle Easterners . . .'

'Look around.'

I look around. The sky is no blue you ever see in northern Europe. The hills of Jordan are shocking pink. The Negev is three shades of purple. The sea is red.

'I think it's very upsetting to realize,' Ros says, 'that touches of colour have travelled through centuries. That filaments of gold that looked right here, have survived all the pogroms and everything else, and exist still in what people in Manchester put on their backs.'

Not Israel Proper

So now it's all explained – my love of aubergines and falafel and the West Australian Desert, and why I buy my wife earrings the colour of Cairo and would put her in diaphanous Casbah pantaloons if she would only agree to wear them. I am a Middle Easterner. Forget Poland and Russia and Lithuania and the ghetto and Yiddish. We are Bedouins. Tent- and oasis-dwellers, who like to festoon our pavilions with cloths that sparkle. And sit together, as a family, on camel rugs, and pop poppets.

It was worth coming to the sun to find out.

Fourteen

GONNA BE GREAT,
OR GONNA BE BLOODY

Out of Eilat. On a bus.

But not to please the plump, blushing woman at the Government Tourist Agency. We have a hire car booked; I even pay a deposit. But on the morning I am due to collect it, I read that there is to be a Peace Now march in Jerusalem the next day. No, not a march – a chain. Settlers have moved into the village of Silwan, emptied houses of their Palestinian occupants, pointed guns, and generally made Israel look foolish and brutal in the very middle of a much publicized peace conference. GIVE HANDS FOR PEACE says the notice in the *Jerusalem Post*. I can think of no better way of getting immediately into the thick of Israel proper. Which means there is no time for chugging through the Negev in a little Fiat. Pity about Hebron, but there's nothing there anyway. It's the bus for us. Straight to Jerusalem and step on it.

It's a hellish ride. There are twice as many passengers as seats. The driver has fought with his wife. To be as incensed as he is you have to have fought with both your wives. You get no help with your luggage. He sits at his wheel and watches you struggle. 'Ein Gedi this side, Jerusalem that.' Then he drives off with the luggage doors open and we have to hammer at the windows and yell at him to stop. We are dropping rucksacks in the very wilderness where Yahweh dropped manna.

Because there is no room to move on the bus, it is impossible to strike up acquaintances. I feel that I ought to talk to a soldier, but soldiers appear to take it as read that they are to be left to sleep on buses. Even the young ones go off as soon as they're seated, folding their guns to their chests like teddy bears.

A young man on the seat across the aisle to ours engages my attention. I have heard him speak briefly. He employs that queer, inauthentic middle-class English pronunciation favoured by north-London Jews who are both professional and Orthodox, in the world of the living and out of it. He wears a white business shirt, grey trousers, thick grey socks and a skull-cap. He keeps a light rucksack on his lap. When the bus pulls in at one of the few refreshment stops the incensed driver doesn't see why he should allow us, he goes on short loping walks, holding his shoulder to one side, like an injured bird.

For the first hour or so of the journey, he reads from a prayer-book. I watch his lips forming the Hebrew. He is not *davening* but he is agitated. Excited. Whether by what he is reading or by the experience of being in Israel, I cannot tell. But there is a touch of Holy Land pilgrim about him. And that doesn't disappear even when he puts the prayer-book away and pulls out a magazine called *Accountancy* from his rucksack.

It seems to me that his *yarmulke* should come off while he's reading *Accountancy*. Especially while he's reading RATNER'S GOSPEL FOR THE '90s. But that may just be the Jesus Christ coming out in me again, wanting to keep God and Mammon separate.

On the approach to the Dead Sea – a grand and fearsome descent into salt – he becomes more agitated than he has been all journey. His fingers have never been still; even when reading about Ratner his hands were shaking; but now he is close to convulsions. He goes red and then white. His shoulders spasm. He puts his hands in his mouth and bites. We fear that a fit is imminent, but he appears to recognize all the symptoms and to know how to forestall what's coming. He bites harder.

Later, when he is calmer, I notice that there are deep teeth marks, blood even, on his hands and fingers.

What I want to know is: did the sight of the Dead Sea have anything to do with this? Was he remembering Lot's wife?

We stop for a while at Ein Gedi and watch riotous Japanese tourists playing on the water, marvelling at the miracle of Dead Sea buoyancy. I would like to talk to the accountant but he is off on one of his loping walks, and won't meet my eyes. I wave to the Japanese instead. They are definitely not remembering Lot's wife.

I try for his attention during what is left of the bus ride, but I don't get it. Only when we are pushed by the driver into the frenzy of Jerusalem bus station does he say anything to me. Taxis? Taxis? Any idea where? But by this time I am not in a talking mood. I too just want to be driven away from here. Taxis? No idea, but I can find you policemen, prophets, touts, beggars, Bedouin, Druse, Armenians, soldiers, ambulances, ice-cream vendors, soothsayers, messiahs.

Two hours later, by which time I have worked out that if he didn't know where you get a taxi he must be on his first visit – though why I find his first visit more touching than I find my own, I cannot say – we see him leaving the Old City just as we are entering it. Ros recognizes the lope. And I see one of its uses. It enables him to sway out of your way, and put you out of his field of vision, at the very moment you pass. There is just time to notice that he is no longer shaking. A queer smile has taken over his face. The kind to which the religiously transported give the name serenity. A yellow light is coming off his skin. He has been in Jerusalem no more than two hours and already he is walking with the *Shekhina*.

The peace chain does not link up till two p.m. Which leaves the morning to go to the Wall.

An Arab boy grabs us as we're heading in what may or may not be the right direction. Not, according to him. 'Closed,' he says, gesturing to the alley we're following. And which hundreds of others are following also. But they are going to the mosque. 'For Arabs,' the boy tells us. 'For Arabs.'

Come with him and he'll show us what we want to see. The Wailing Wall? OK. Come with him, come with him into his shop, come now, OK, come later, follow him, the Wall's this way, through his father's shop.

So we get our first view of the Western Wall from high up, close to expensive apartments offering hot and cold running water and unparalleled Holy Views, in the company of a multilingual Arab Artful Dodger who, when we thank him and pay him and ask him to leave us now, haggles with us over shekels, pushes back on us the two we offer him because he sees a five in Ros's hand, so he'll do a deal with us, we give him five, he'll give us two, therefore he will only have cost us three . . .

But there's the Wall, and there's a believer backing from it, unable to show it the disrespect of turning from it, uncertain of his footing, but keeping going, a step, or rather a shuffle, at a time, the whole length of whatever you call the cleared courtyard – concourse, I suppose – where the non-prayerful can watch, and the police can polish their riot shields, and the reverent can wash their hands in a fountain before they touch the sacred stones.

Whoever would approach the Wall, must first cover his head. *His.* If you're a she, you go to the other end. At the Wall as in a synagogue, the sexes are divided.

Jew Jew Jew. Division division division. If they didn't have division, my people, would they wither and die?

About twenty young men, dressed in identical black belted raincoats, turn up in a gang and clear a space for themselves, twenty yards from the Wall. Hoodlums for Yahweh. They fall at once, but somehow not together, into hysterical *davening*. At one in separateness. In a harmony of dissonance. Each exciting the other, by very virtue of his individual performance, into greater excesses of solo ecstasy.

Half an hour ago, before the Arab boy plucked us out, we were following the Arabs to prayer, watching them flow down the steps of the Old City to the mosque, a sea of turbans, a movement as of a wave, calm but unified in purpose, numerous but not jealously divided.

Enough of that. I have made myself a promise. I will not be treating every Arab I meet as my enemy. But nor will I be marvelling over their natural grace, or their instinctual politeness, or the sinuous lines of their garments and their architecture. I am not T. E. Lawrence. I am not one more in a line of gay public-school Englishmen with a weakness for urchins and moustaches. I have not come to be thrashed.

Still, they sure know how to flow picturesquely to worship.

It perturbs me to see my people worshipping a wall. They press themselves against it, kiss the stones, sob into the cement. Some listen to the Wall, actually put their ears to it. Others dance before it, even dance *with* it. There are people having fits here. Losing themselves in the extremities of emotion, shaking, trembling, forgoing all earthly awareness.

I watch one old man, in a cloud of white beard, leaping at the Wall like a salmon. He slaps it, first with one hand, then another – smack! against the yellow stones. It is punitive but also plaintive, an act of hopeless frustration, as though he would punish the Wall if he could, if he thought it would do any good, if he could believe he would get any response out of it.

He holds his *Siddur* up to the wall, high above his head, to the Almighty, to admonish Him with it. He rattles the book of prayers and promises, *wields* it, you could almost say. A threat? A plea? His *davening* becomes rapid. He has no control of his body – or is it his body that has no control of him? He bends back and forth, *snaps* back and forth, with a suppleness that is hard to credit in a man his age. Then he raises his fists and shakes them at the Wall, at the Divine Presence the Wall represents. Both fists. Clenched hard. If they landed, they would hurt. After which he calms down. The fight, the spring, the preternatural vigour goes out of his body, and he advances on the stones with his lips and kisses them, gently, forgivingly, as if they are children who have misbehaved and whom he is now ready to indulge, or as if they are the feet of a tyrant he is now willing to revere.

He has had his fight with God, using the Wall as a go-between. How else do you reach the Jewish God? Now he is suing for peace. Pleading for understanding. All love.

Getting to God is a tricky business if you are Jewish. He hides Himself. A *noli me tangere* God. Which may be why the Wall is stuffed with notes and letters. Every crack in the Wall, every space between the slabs of stone, no matter how low down and, more surprisingly, no matter how high up, has paper in it. Paper of every size and colour, folded or crumpled into every shape. Paper aeroplanes for reaching the higher crannies of the Wall, twisted packets such as teams playing charades hand to one another, air-mail envelopes, filing cards, pages of foolscap, school essays, theses – and all for God's what? Intercession? Instruction? Delectation?

I would like to sneak some out, to read them; but the script appears always to be Hebrew (the only language God speaks?) and I am superstitious enough, even here, where all superstition should cease on the moment, to feel I must leave them alone. It would be like a postman stealing someone's pools coupons. I don't want to be the one who's ruined somebody's chance with Yahweh.

I am approached by a disreputably dressed, oriental-looking black coat. He wants me to put on *tefillin*. I politely refuse. I say something like, that will not be necessary. The fact that he doesn't press me harder should be a warning that the condition of my soul is not his first concern. He asks where I'm from. He's from Jerusalem – 'Here, here of course.' I try to engage him in talk about him but he isn't interested in him. He's interested in me. He wants to bless me and mine, say a little prayer for my little family. He asks my father's name, my mother's name, my wife's. For some reason, I give him my parents' Jewish names and then make one up for my wife. Without taking a second to think about it, I judaize Ros to Rachel.

He blesses her in Hebrew. Which she may or may not be grateful for. I may or may not tell her. Then he asks me for money. A few shekels. Not for him, he isn't interested in him, for charity.

Don't ask me why, but I refuse.

Never try to get money out of a man who's just changed his wife's name at the Wailing Wall.

It is time to be a link in a peace chain.

In photographs or on television, the village of Silwan looks rocky and remote, a far-flung tumble of breeze-block houses and boulders that can't be worth fighting over, but in reality it is no further from the centre of Jerusalem than Chelsea is from Westminster. You can see it plainly, even in an unseasonal heat-haze, from the walls of the Old City. Here is one of the reasons why the eviction of Palestinians from homes they are said to have sold to the settlers is causing such a stink. It is the first time that settlers have acted on a claim so close to Jerusalem.

There is confusion about the meeting point. Parking lot of Har Zion, it says in the *Jerusalem Post*. But Har Zion is Mount Zion, and Mount Zion has a parking lot at Zion Gate. Are these the same place?

The Zion Gate parking-lot attendant knows nothing of a peace chain. However, I am not the only one asking him. Gradually, a dozen or so of us more or less assemble. Modern, concerned, academic-looking Jews. The kind I have known all my life. Not the ecstatics at the Wall. Along with the modernity and the concern, though, goes uncertainty. Ecstatics don't have this problem; they know where they are meant to be. We scratch our heads for a while until a woman called Galia Golen and a man called Reuben – both recognized as organizers – arrive to march us down the hill. Silwan is just below us. We can see people gathering, police, soldiers.

I ask Reuben, who is American, about Peace Now. He stresses its loose organization; how its roots are in New Left associations, but it is free of party in the usual political sense. 'What happens in Peace Now,' he tells me, 'depends on who's in the room at the time.'

Cute, until you remember that Peace Now is the only organized conciliatory body in the country.

I get from Reuben a sense of like-minded people, liberals, humanitarians, given (like all liberals) to an excess of self-denigration. He's quick and humorous himself, a touch dashing, a bit of a cavalier of the mind. He is comfortable to talk to. Especially on a march.

'So how many people can we expect?' I ask.

He laughs. 'Between five hundred and fifty thousand.'

He actually expects around two or three thousand. Which is looking optimistic to me. If this *is* the march, we are now twenty-five strong.

He points out the disputed houses – there, there! to the left of the fluttering flag. And informs me that the valley we're looking into is the Hinnom Valley. 'Gai Ben Hinnom – Gehennom – you know?'

Gehenna I know. Hell. So that's where hell is. A few feet below us. There, there! to the left of the fluttering flag.

I suddenly recall Al Sharpton's 'I'm in hell, I'm in Israel' gag, and put a stopper on any slack liberalism of my own.

'They used to sacrifice babies there,' Reuben says. 'Which is not very Jewish.'

'It takes a long time to get civilized,' I remind him.

We haven't gone that far down the hill when someone says

that we're doing the wrong thing. It's only ushers and organizers who are meant to be in Silwan; the rest of us should be back where we started from, at Har Zion parking lot, if that really was Har Zion parking lot we started from.

So Reuben goes down, and we go back up. Which gives me the opportunity to talk to Galia Golen, a professor at the Hebrew University, and also an American. Her job, on this march, is to brief the press. 'In a sort of a sense that's me,' I tell her.

She is a neat, precise, intelligent woman. She has written a book about Soviet policy in the Middle East. As with Reuben, I feel I know her from some university common room. It's calming to be with people who are vaguely familiar, but I feel secretly disappointed at the same time. This is Jerusalem. That's Gehenna down there. Hell. Shouldn't I be engaging with someone or something a mite more outlandish?

She tells me, and assumes I will grasp the significance of this, that Peace Now has a permit for this march.

'Is that unusual?'

'Well, often when we apply for a permit to demonstrate, we get it, but only to demonstrate somewhere else.'

'But this time the permit clears you for Silwan?'

'Yes.'

'Why, do you reckon?'

'Because what's happening in Silwan has attracted so much notice. This is a demonstration the government can't stop and probably doesn't want to. They're fed up with the settlers for making an issue over Silwan. Especially now, with the Washington peace talks. It's brought the whole question of Jerusalem up again. They could have done without this one.'

'So you won't be expecting any trouble from the army, then?'

Even as we speak, a water cannon trundles past us.

'The army isn't really involved. This comes within the jurisdiction of Jerusalem City. It's police business.'

As a general rule, she goes on, the authorities hate it when a demo is joint Israeli/Palestinian. It agitates them. They lose their nerve. This is exactly what happened the last time Peace Now put a peace chain around Jerusalem. The police got flustered. Rubber bullets were fired. There were casualties.

'And this time?'

'We're not anticipating trouble.'

'Different climate?'

'I don't know about that. But this is a much more local demonstration. You can tell when a big confrontation is brewing. This isn't one. Not all our numbers are coming out. Maybe there'll be a few buses from Tel Aviv. But even regular people from here, who feel strongly about Silwan, have got other things to do today. It's Friday, after all.'

Friday. Got to get the shopping done. I've charged across the Negev to make it here on time. Missed out on Hebron. Missed out on a pootle around the Dead Sea. And meanwhile there are peaceniks living five minutes away who have to give it a skip because they need to get the shopping done.

It doesn't augur well for peace. And doesn't say much for the thinking classes of Jerusalem.

Who now number about forty. Banners are distributed. I won't carry one. I'm an observer, I explain, not a participant. A man with a loud-hailer directs us down the hill again. Silwan is looking beautiful in the afternoon sunshine. Bleached and sleepy. It is hard to distinguish dwellings from stone. The sounds of amplified Arabic prayers reach us from the valley.

I talk to Larry, an American with two false front teeth and a pony-tail. He is from Pittsburgh and isn't quite sure why he's here and why he's learning Hebrew, but he is. As we get closer to Silwan and the sound of sirens, he essays a pun around the idea of getting stoned. He's been in Israel before. Has relatives out here, Orthodox, living in settlements. Concerned only with breeding. 'All they do is sit around looking at babies,' he says.

Suddenly, on the say-so of a policeman, we are being marched back up the hill again. At first we imagine we are being re-routed, but in fact it takes a policeman to tell us that we have missed the main body of the demo which is waiting (aha!) at the real Har Zion parking lot.

Here there really are numbers. Hundreds. Thousands. Thousands of intellectuals. All the people whose names and addresses David Cohen wrote in my notebook on my last night in Los Angeles. I recognize the faces but can't make the right identifications. Which is Yehoshua? Which is Amos Oz?

Everyone knows everyone here. It's like day one of a conference. Everyone meeting again after the vacation.

They are well dressed. The men do not cover their heads. The women do not have convex bellies. After the Wall I go giddy, drunk on secularism.

For the third time we go down the hill to Silwan. But now we are a real march. Arabs slow their cars to raise their fists to us. 'That solidarity?' I ask Larry.

He shakes his head. 'If you were giving the sign,' he says, 'I'd know how to read it. But you can never tell with Arabs.'

Just as we're about to round the final bend, there is a scuffle involving an Orthodox family which is half-in and half-out of a rented car. The police push them in through one door, they squeeze out through another. A darkly handsome man in a white shirt, *yarmulke* and flying fringes calls out to us, calls especially to one of our number who insists on marching with two fingers in the air, 'Fuck you, Nazi!'

Larry wants to know how I feel being called a Nazi?

'It's novel,' I say.

Larry reckons the fringed man didn't say it with much feeling. I say I think he mustered feeling enough.

Nazis? The woman in front of me wears patterned librarian's tights and carries a shopping bag showing a map of the London Underground. We are so orderly we could be the ones who have skipped the demo in order to bring in the *Shabbes* provisions.

312

In a square at the bottom of the hill, police have penned in a gang of Kahane supporters. They taunt us with posters of their spiritual leader, Rabbi Meir Kahane, who was assassinated in New York last year, the founder of the Jewish Defence League, the advocate of Jewish violence. They wear black shirts.

Beside them, a group of settlers carry banners in Hebrew and Russian. There is only one in English, proclaiming WE SHALL CONTINUE TO SETTLE.

Hardly blood-curdling. Unless, I suppose, you happen to be one of the Palestinians living where they intend to continue settling.

Without leaving Jerusalem we are in Silwan. There are police everywhere, some on horses. (Jews on horses! I had promised myself I wouldn't do this – I wouldn't marvel at Jewish dustmen and Jewish bus-drivers. But Jews on horses! I can't get used to it.) A helicopter circles the village. Behind, on the ramparts of the Old City, soldiers stand with their rifles pointed, like figures in *Beau Geste*.

But the atmosphere is festive. Perhaps because they remember what happened last time, when they panicked, the police joke with the crowds. It's like a police open-day. We are allowed to pat the horses. If it could come any lower, we would be allowed to pat the helicopter. It's a day out in the park. Pretty girls holding roses stand in lines and pose for one another's cameras. Most of the marchers have brought cameras; they knew what I didn't, that this would be one big photo opportunity.

Palestinians join in. There is much self-conscious fraternizing going on. Palestinian boys take the arms of Israeli women in patterned tights, and they go dancing through the main street of Silwan. An impromptu choir of Palestinian girls sings national songs while an Israeli pretends to conduct them. When they're finished, he claps them wildly.

We're being such good friends.

Not all the Palestinian population of Silwan is mingling. Some stand on the roofs of their houses, or on their balconies, or in their gardens, or among the rubble between gardens. Some look mystified. Some wary. Some hold up Peace Now banners. But none looks entirely convinced.

It's a freakishly warm day. Shakily, precariously beautiful, in the way that warm days are which have been stolen from under the nose of winter. Silwan itself shares this unsteady beauty. I cannot decide whether it is picturesque-derelict, or just derelict. Are those boulders in the road, or piles of garbage? From the walls of the Old City, the whole of Jerusalem looks like this. It is a city littered with stones, an act of natural vandalism. But there are other vandals in Silwan. That *is* rubbish that has not been collected. And nature cannot be blamed for the jungle of television aerials, through which the Palestinians watch Israeli intellectuals having a nice time.

But I can see why a settler might fancy a place of his own, or a place belonging to someone else, in this part of town. The houses look comfortable, spacious little villas with courtyards, orange trees, vines, and wrought-iron window fittings and balustrades of the kind you get in bungalows built in the late fifties in Morecambe and Lytham St Annes.

Impossible to tell what year it is here. The Israelis have the air of Aldermaston marchers of a few decades ago. Their kids may wear Levis but in the sunny courtyards of their Lancashire villas, the Palestinian women stand robed as they have been for centuries. Only the helicopter sounds contemporary.

The mood of the peace chain lightens rather than deepens. More singing, more photographs, more mingling of police, Palestinians, Israelis. Eventually, the police become as hard to distinguish from the protesters as the cypresses are from the television masts, as the rocks are from the rubble. Everything is merged and melodious.

Except me. Birds build – but not I build. However I try, I cannot break into the cliquishness of the day. I search for eyes, in the usual way, but encounter only closed faces. So hard do I stare at one woman that she makes a moue at me – a feministical taunt meant to have me choke on my own predatory intentions. So where is the famous Israeli chattiness? Do you have to be Palestinian before these people will talk to you?

I overhear a voluble Israeli intellectual telling it his way to a dapper pair of French observers. He speaks of this day as a watershed, of the peace process being a watershed, the last real chance to preserve what Israel was supposed to be in the first place. 'It's a fascinating time,' he says. 'I prophesy that the coming months will be very telling, one way or another enormously significant. And if you ask me am I optimistic, then I must tell you that –' And I lose him in a complicated little fable about optimism that entails knowledge of indigenous wildlife.

The dapper Frenchmen, who of course possess such knowledge, laugh sagely. He leaves them. I follow him. Wait, while he asks about this person's family, and that person's research project, and then accost him. It is like an arrest. I actually feel his collar.

He isn't in the slightest bit flattered that I, a writer from London, have come all the way to Silwan and chosen *him* to speak for contemporary Israel. He won't stop to discuss anything with me, but if I keep walking alongside him he'll give me a bulletin, a press-release in short sentences.

'The people of Jerusalem. I won't talk about anybody else. The people of Jerusalem. Feel the integrity of their city has been put at risk. By settlers' actions.'

I try to keep up with him. 'You were saying something about a watershed . . .'

'In so far. As the settlers. Have made their move so close to the city. And at this time. When they have had their so-called. Legal right. To the property. For so long. Their action is yes. Significant.'

'And this march . . . ?'

'Just. The beginning.'

And that's it. He's off. And I don't even get a parable about the ostrich and the camel.

Just as we are dispersing, a car carrying one of the settler families who are the cause of today's demo crawls into the village. They have decided it is now safe, or allowably provocative, to return to the contested house. They sneak out of the car, two men in white shirts and *yarmulkes*, each with a wife paler than Jerusalem stone, and more pregnant than an Israeli intellectual's pauses. It is hard to tell whether their expressions denote sheepishness or defiance, but they don't wince when we jeer at them.

They carry walkie-talkies and other systems of communication. Like the village of Silwan itself, they bristle with aerials. Just when it seems the car has emptied, two younger men appear from it. They too are tasselled and crowned. Obeying all God's commandments. One shoulders a rifle. The other holds a playpen, folded. Bullets and babies.

In the square where the Kahane supporters had chanted, a group of young marchers sit on a wall. They are frustrated. They don't consider the demonstration to have been militant enough. They would have liked to be able to demonstrate outside the settlers' houses, but the organizers decided against being too confrontational.

'Confrontational? Who's doing the confronting here?'

One of them believes Peace Now has had it. 'The only time Peace Now had any effect was when it made that chain around Jerusalem and the police lost their cool. *That* got noticed.'

I walk back up the hill, as frustrated as they are. I can't now remember why it seemed so important I get here. I have that ashen, empty feeling that comes over you when you've descended into politics.

Outside Zion Gate I run into a couple of dusty, bearded American academics from Santa Barbara University, here on a joint project, which will issue in a book, on political factions in Jerusalem. Just what I need. More Americans and more politics. But at least they're talkative.

Professor Roger Friedland and Professor Richard Hecht, specializing in RELIGION AND POLITICS IN THE CITY: THE CASE OF JERUSALEM. Hi, Roger. Hi, Richard. Hi, Howard.

So tell me, you guys, what did you make of the demo?

'Pathetic,' Roger says.

Since we are close to the Dormition Monastery, and since they have a cafeteria on the premises, and since Richard has an appointment with a monk, we go there and drink coffee and chat.

The demo was pathetic because there weren't enough people there. And there wasn't enough seriousness. Just the same old crowd on a picnic. Not enough 'heavyweights' on either side. Not enough heavyweights? What about Oz? What about Yehoshua? Not enough *political* heavyweights.

On the other hand, they concede that it was a new, or at least a significant event for non-Palestinians to be walking through Silwan, which has been a no-go area since the Intifada began. So yes, it meant something that we were there, and that the Palestinians joined hands with us, but as heavyweight academics themselves, they judge the day to have lacked social and political *gravitas*.

'For some of us,' I say, 'it also lacked social and political *caritas*. Why would nobody talk to me?'

'This is a city under a microscope,' Richard explains. 'The people here are under constant surveillance. Whatever they say or do is watched. They're sick of answering questions. If they're Palestinians they want to be certain who's asking . . .'

'And if they're Israelis,' Roger puts in, 'they think, "Oh, no, not another ethnographer!"'

Roger softens towards the demo the longer we talk about it. He likes having seen Israelis and Palestinians linking arms, no matter how briefly and in what relatively small numbers. 'That's always been my dream – seeing columns of Palestinians and Israelis marching through Jerusalem together.'

Does he think the omens are good for such an eventuality?

'It's gonna be great, or it's gonna be bloody.'

We go out into the evening together. It's cold now, but the sky is clear. A silver moon hangs like a dagger over the Old City. We part on the ramparts, me for the American Colony Hotel, they for St Andrew's Scottish Hospice, which they highly recommend. 'Less than two hundred bucks a week and they speak Scottish. You'll even understand the accent.'

I watch them go, the new ethnographic pilgrims. They are frequently here, they told me. Grabbing a few days whenever they can. Drawn to the city – the spiritual magnetism facilitated by grants and fellowships. Imagining a time such as has never been in Jerusalem's history, when the religious factions will march in columns of accord. Curious, that peace in such a place can be imagined only through metaphors of war.

Fifteen

THE CURSE IS COME UPON US

War and peace.

Those are to be the subjects, then. See what happens to a happy-go-lucky Jew when he comes to Israel.

My attention has been grabbed by an announcement in the papers of a forum to be held at the Israel Center:

> In pursuit of peace: A Torah State in Israel. Real Peace can only come to Israel when Torah and *Mitzvot* are observed by all Jews. Do you agree or disagree? Come and share your opinions and those of others.

I don't know what the Israel Center is, and nobody I speak to can tell me what the Israel Center is, but I turn up to it anyway, as invited, at 8.30 on a Saturday night, with a view to sharing the opinions of others.

The building is on Straus Street, on the border between the fanatic, food-fearing ghetto of Mea She'arim and the fast-pizza and felafel squares of Jaffa Street. The people who pass are borderline too. But I can't gauge the cut of those arriving for the forum because so far no one is.

Fly-posters on the doors tell of what else the Israel Center has on offer. Nechama Greisman's Hasidic insights into Torah. Rabbi Chaim Eisen's PERSPECTIVE ON LIFE, THE WORLD AND ETHICS – AN IN-DEPTH STUDY. Rabbi Zev Leff's WITH ALL YOUR HEART: AN IN-DEPTH ANALYSIS OF THE AMIDA WITH INTER-PERSONAL APPLICATIONS. And on a lighter note, for not everything can be in-depth, THE FABULOUS ALTER

ROCKERS - LIVE! ('Enjoy a timeless potpourri of modern Hasidic melodies.')

A board announces the Israel Center's sponsors – UNION OF ORTHODOX JEWISH CONGREGATIONS OF AMERICA. I should have known from the spelling of Center. More Americans. But that, I am now beginning to realize, is what Jerusalem is – the fifty-first of the United States. The spiritual playground, just as Hawaii is the fleshly playground, of Americans with time on their hands.

It costs me seven shekels to get in. Four women and one man are already in the class-room where the discussion is to take place. All American. All Brooklyn except for one, a little woman in a white beret with tartan trimmings and a tartan rosette, who speaks out of the corner of her mouth like a Chicago mobster. She is complimenting the dress sense of a woman in a navy Totes rain-hat, a turquoise jacket, a black overcoat and pearls.

'I like your colours . . . Dramatic.'

'Layers,' the woman replies.

'I know. You have to learn to wear layers in Jerusalem. Like onions. This' – she points to her own scarf – 'is imitation silk. It keeps me warm. Typical Jerusalem. Layers.'

An unsettled young woman in a shapeless brown shift, flat running shoes and a cream woolly snood with glass beads on it, asks, 'Who's gonna disagree with this motion? You won't find anyone who's against the Torah today, I'm sure.'

Those who know her, ignore her.

She gets up to leave the room, as a couple more of the same drift in, then changes her mind. She has round shoulders, a curved spine. She speaks rapidly, through bad, prominent teeth. You would think she is not someone who should be let out on her own, but she is full of spluttering words. 'We're all for it. We must be. Who isn't for the Torah here?' As she speaks, she scratches herself between her legs. It crosses my mind that she may be pregnant.

The woman in the Totes rain-hat, whose colours have been admired, loses her temper with no one in particular. It might be the chair she's sitting on that's offended her. 'How can you go wrong?' she wants to know. 'How can you go wrong if you're all following Torah, how can you go wrong? Forget it! Follow the Torah and Moshiach will come. Look at democracy in America. Look how that works. You call that working? We don't have that here. Moshiach is coming – you just follow the Torah. There are no two arguments. You want Moshiach – you follow Torah!'

More people enter. Another fifteen or so. The men in hats or *yarmulkes*. A couple of *yeshiva* boys, with white faces and saintly smiles. A bear of a man in a zipped cardigan and with a brutally cropped beard, which may just be hennaed, takes the chair. This is Phil Chernofsky. He is experienced in ways of chairing. He possesses a procedural vocabulary and has the look of a man who will wait and listen in the name of evenhandedness and clarity, but whose patience is a short rope. Perhaps to introduce subliminally the idea of snapping, he plays with a rubber band. Sometimes, when a speaker goes on too long, Phil Chernofsky imprisons his hands in this band, or binds his thumbs together with it.

He begins by handing out a discussion document presented by a Mr Louis Fisch. This document contains many maps showing distances and boundaries, listing troop numbers of Arabs and Israelis before and after this or that conflict, showing partition lines, armistice lines, cease-fire lines. War and peace.

Phil Chernofsky, plucking at an elastic cat's-cradle, wants us to pay particular attention to a middle paragraph.

Prospects for Peace in the Middle East
The Torah gives us a simple formula for peace in Bechuko-sai, Leviticus XXVI.
   3. If you keep my commandments . . .
   5. . . . you shall dwell in your land safely.

6. And I will give you peace in your land, and you shall
lie down, and none shall make you afraid.
Followed by religious coercion – if you don't keep the commandments, you get the *Tochacha*.

The *Tochacha* – the reproach, the curse. What's waiting for us if
we're nice to Arabs.

Louis Fisch is with us in person. He is gaunt, white-bearded,
with a sad, small mouth. Wearily, as though he has been driven
to this pass against his own humanity, he takes us through his
solutions to the Arab problem – confiscation of their property,
expulsion, execution, compensation . . . *compensation?* No,
that's compensation for *Jews*, forced to flee Arab states.

Phil Chernofsky holds him there. It's discussion time. 'OK,'
he says, 'comments, questions, responses, feedback . . .'

It seems a tall order, but the Totes woman is possessed of all
four. The issue is simple. We aren't in a Torah state. How do we
become one? How do we get the secular population of Israel, the
non-Torah Jews, to observe? Simple – we *make* them observe.

I am grateful to her for one thing: she has given me a title. I
now know who I am – a non-Torah Jew.

A vast, indecipherable man with a Santa Claus beard, apparently agrees with her. School. *Tefillin*. Every morning. Why
not?

A strange pattern is taking shape. A progress from the language
of murder and hate to the minutiae of religious observance, and
back again. The key to peace, to dwelling unafraid in one's own
land, to getting rid of the Arabs, seems to lie in putting on
tefillin and not flying El-Al on *Shabbes*. Now it's executions,
now it's airlines. Now it's the PLO, now it's what Knesset
member Feldman has just said on television about women having
no right, *halachically*, to the vote.

The girl in the cream snood has a suggestion. 'Moshiach will
see to it,' she tells us.

The familiar, Jewish name for the redeemer doesn't do much

322

for his stature at the best of times. But on these lips he is made to sound like the village idiot – Moshiach the *draydl*-spinner, Moshiach who keeps the park benches clean in Stamford Hill. The gates of a straitened culture close around his *yeshiva*-boy name, enchaining him in paltry, local matters, denying him the blood and vengeance that belong to the last of all last things.

'I hope,' says Phil Chernofsky, 'that we are not going to embrace the theory one sometimes hears that we should fall into moral disrepute so that Moshiach *has* to come.'

Shades of Jacob Frank – serving God through the evil impulse. I don't myself see this gathering as a hotbed of Sabbatian heresy, but Phil Chernofsky snaps the rubber band against his fist, lest any of us be tempted.

It isn't long before the issue of whether we are or can be a Torah state meets the sister question of whether we should be secularly governed or rabbinically – by a Knesset or a Sanhedrin. And it is at this moment that a new and striking voice enters the debate. It belongs to a woman all in green, who has come in late with a woman all in black. They have an air of sharing views, though it is the woman in green, in my estimation, who decides which views they will share.

Let me describe her.

She is pale-faced, olive-pale. She wears spectacles. I don't mean she is in spectacles, I mean she *wears* them. All artificiality has been scoured off her skin, yet there is such a vanity of austerity about her, you cannot believe the effect has been achieved without artificial means. It takes make-up to un-make you to this degree. She would have you see her as a Hebrew nun, but there is more activity in her face than most monastic orders would allow – irony and knowingness and an elaborate play of condescension and wisdom. She is, and means to be, in other words, a formidable and frightening woman.

She is dressed, as I have said, all in green. She wears a green hat, fairly high-domed, which is at once dressy and sacerdotal. Beneath the hat she wears a scarf in the manner of a coif. Still more sacerdotal. A green suit to match the hat. The jacket full of pleats, so that the material falls from her arms when she waves them – and she waves them often – like the sleeves of a priestess's surplice.

When she doesn't wave her arms she points her finger. A very personal point – a teacher's point, in my guess, acquired in the process of instruction and command. She points her finger when she agrees, and she points her finger when she doesn't. But then she agrees only in order to disagree.

She assumes at once, despite arriving late, an air of moral and intellectual superiority to everything that is being said. She is not concerned that she may have missed something. She will not have missed anything she doesn't know already – that is the meaning of her assurance.

It is she who is responsible, essentially, for bringing the conversation round to Sanhedrin, the need for a parliament of rabbis. Her contention is that we do not live in anything like a Torah state, although we are a religio-nation, and that we do not adequately order our priorities or so frame the question as to get the right answer.

'We need a Sanhedrin. We don't have a Sanhedrin. We don't deserve a Sanhedrin, because we don't go about seeking a Sanhedrin in a way that will ever achieve one.'

She is not American. She is Israeli. She doesn't press this advantage overtly, but lets the fact of it play like music through her words. When she speaks, you hear it. Also when she speaks, she rolls a sweet between her fingers. Picks at the paper, exactly as Phil Chernofsky plucks at his elastic, twists it, extends it to the shape of a cracker, a Christmas cracker that contains funny hats and messages and that no one in this room but me has ever pulled. I am confident that she will unwrap the sweet eventually, and put it in her mouth while someone else is talking, so that her cheeks will bulge contemptuously with it. But not yet. She knows to save the sweet.

'I want a Jewish answer,' she says.

This means that no discussion of peace that does not have the Jew at its centre and derive from Torah is of any interest to her. She quotes from the Torah liberally, in Hebrew, chapter and verse. She even has a little Arabic, as when, to prove how feebly secular we Jews have let ourselves become, she imitates the Arab smiting us, any one of us, and crying to *his* God, '*Itbah Ha-Yehud!*' – Slaughter the Jews! She dramatizes this, actually rises from her chair in a cloud of green, lifts her hand – the one with the sweet in it – and plunges in the dagger. *Itbah Ha-Yehud!* And compares this proud, unhesitating deed with a Jew being forced to kill in self-defence and muttering his apologies afterwards.

Thus: two birds with one stone. We are reminded of the blood-curdling violence of our Arab brothers, what they cannot wait to do to each of us, *and* of our own dainty, irreligious cowardice.

'I'll tell you something else a Jewish answer means. It means valuing Torah above everything else. Above democracy. Above peace. Above caring what other people think about us. What do I care that I do things that are called racist?' Her voice is a falcon that swoops and rises, a high, breaking voice, with blood in it. 'What do I care that I do things that are *not* racist? Is this in Torah? My aim is not peace. Who says we need peace? Is peace a Torah priority? No. The aim is not so that we should know peace. The aim is to know the *truth*. Truth is above peace. Read the Torah. Open it.' She opens an imaginary one, beats the air with its pages, sends her voice on a wild curving flight, far beyond the reach of any little arrow we may send after it. 'Everything you need to know is in Torah. Who am I to guess Moshiach? Maybe he will come. I can't say. How can I say? But Torah says going to war can be a *mitzva*. There's a *mitzva* to go to war, to fight. The Torah tells us that victory is assured if you conduct the war full-heartedly. *Full-heartedly.* And if you don't, if you don't fight full-heartedly and Jewish blood is spilled, then that Jewish blood' – and here comes the finger – 'is on your head . . .'

She recalls with shame those who kept vigil the night Eichmann, that murderer, was executed. She drops the name Martin Buber. The Totes woman, the indecipherable man, the spluttering girl in the snood, seize on it with a contempt that is the equal of hers. *Martin Buber!* If it is possible to stone a name with voices, Martin Buber's name is stoned tonight. Martin Buber, who said that the death-sentence 'exasperates the soul of men . . . killing awakens killing'.

I think of Amos Oz's address to the Right in Israel, reminding them of their inability to produce artists or intellectuals. What I hear tonight is scorn for the act of intellection itself.

After Eichmann, the Green woman invokes Demjanjuk and other recent war-criminals. 'We are so demoralized, we are so emasculated, that we cannot even denounce them! And do you know why? We are afraid of seeing ourselves isolated as a people –'

Phil Chernofsky, reduced now to twanging the elastic only for his own behoof, tries an interjection. 'Let me refocus one more time –'

But there is no containing her. 'We are afraid of what will come of us if we are isolated. Well, I say this to you – you doing one more *mitzva* won't be a solution, me doing one more *mitzva* won't be a solution . . . We have to accept that *we will be, have been, must be*' – it's thrilling stuff; despite myself, I shiver – '*a chosen people.*'

Perhaps I was wrong. Perhaps this is a group that serves God through the evil impulse.

There are practicalities attendant on our acceptance of our isolated status. We can stop asking the Americans for money. And therefore the Americans can stop telling us what to do. So where will the money come from instead? Simple. Simple. 'We give so much to the Arabs, right . . .?' Right. Right. It's agreed. A fortune is being washed down the drain on the Arabs. So enough already. 'Simple. We have a solution. That's what.'

The indecipherable man with the Santa Claus beard is way behind. He is still wondering if the Arabs can simply be *persuaded* to leave Israel.

'*Alevai*,' says the Green woman. *Alevai* – it should only happen.

It's a common expression among Jews. Not Yiddish, but Aramaic. It has homely applications. *Alevai* they should settle down and have a family. Hearing it in the employ of diabolic political tactics, seeing the olive-pale sneer that sends it on its way, makes my blood boil. How much more of this will I be able to bear? Will I blow my cover? Although it's not my policy to interfere, and this isn't my country, and my safety isn't at risk every day, will I *have* to put an oar in, just for old-fashioned decency's sake?

But if the Arabs can't be persuaded to leave, *alevai*, what then? 'Look,' she says, 'I don't know what to do about the poor Arab. How can I know? But open the Torah and it will tell you. You want to know if the Arab has a vote? The Torah tells you. No. No vote. Taxes, yes. Vote, no.'

No one disagrees. It's in Torah. And God said to Moses – 'Taxes, yes. Vote, no.' No one disagrees. Not in this room. But this isn't the whole of Judaism. And the problem remains of how to get the rest of the Jewish people united in will to implement these Torah truths.

The woman in the cream snood knows. 'Moshiach will unite them.'

The Totes woman is not so sure. Coercion may be necessary.

The Green woman reminds us that a Jew is a Jew. Whether or not he lays *tefillin* or breaks the *Shabbat* or is familiar with Torah taxation law, he is still a Jew. 'And a Jew must care for every Jew.'

But this principle gets lost, somewhere along the line, when it comes to Jews who think money should be given to Arabs. Those Jews should not be loved by other Jews. *Those* Jews should be got rid of.

Phil Chernofsky cannot agree with this. 'You had me most of the way,' he tells her, 'but you've lost me now.'

And he tries to catechize her, take her through the stages of her argument so far. So, OK, is she saying she approves of capital punishment?

The black-bereted woman by her side answers for her. 'Yes.'

Does she agree with capital punishment for breaking the *Shabbat*?

The black-bereted woman implies yes, but with a suspended sentence.

The Green woman unwraps the sweet and pops it in her mouth . . .

And something snaps in my soul, and at last I break all my working rules – a felony for which the punishment is suffocation by snood – and cause silence and consternation to fall on the room by announcing myself as a non-Torah Jew from England (I know who I am now), who has turned up tonight to hear what fine examples might be set him by Torah Jews, and has found here in Israel – irony of ironies – nothing but blasphemy and sacrilege. For if the Torah is the thing of murderousness and inhumanity it has appeared to be tonight, then it is no Torah worth following – except, *except*, that I have read enough of it myself to know it is no such thing, and is only brutal and inhuman and, yes, ungodly, in your interpretation.

I have their attention. And they have mine. For the first time I get a good look at the Totes woman's crumpled, petulant face; and for the first time, now that she has turned to observe and to shout at me, can I count the hairs on the snood-girl's chin; and for the first time do I see a woman I had not noticed before, who wears a plastic rain-hood and tells me to go on, to go on, young man, reading the Torah, for its meaning will come clear to me in the end.

But the one looking hardest, of course, with a sweet puffing out her olive cheeks, is the Green finger-pointer, who would like to explain a fallacy to me . . . But, *but*, I have heard enough of her and tell her so, and berate her for dominating what was billed as an open forum, and describe to her the brutality of her mind, and warn her not to point at me, not to let the thought of pointing at me pass through her head, for I have been a teacher and a pedant myself, and I know the wrongness of spirit that leads one person to point a finger at another. Don't think about it, I say, and don't even bother to frame a sentence for I can foretell every sentence you will deliver. 'And tell me this,' I say, 'you who study Torah, the unmediated word of God, and find only violence of emotion in it – is it not a *mitzva* to feel humanity for another?'

'It is,' they say, all turned around to face me, a chorus of rain-hats.

'And is it not a *mitzva*,' I go on, 'to love and help those less fortunate than yourselves?'

'It is,' they say.

'And is it not a *mitzva*, is it not a cornerstone of our faith, to refrain from doing unto others what you would not . . .'

'. . . have done unto yourself? It is,' they say, 'it is. But it is also a *mitzva* to defend yourself. Torah says . . .'

But I have done with them and their accursed Torah, and tell them that if persuasion is their aim, they have failed miserably with me and will fail miserably with anyone not already of their faction. Naive of me. Persuasion is not their aim. You see it or you don't. And the more you don't, the more confirmed in their specialness and chosenness do they become.

Gehenna. I am convinced that I have spent the evening in an American-sponsored Israeli hell. Compared to this, the worshipping of Moloch, the sacrifice of children in the valley by Silwan, is nothing. Hell – Gehenna – is in Straus Street, where the new children of Israel worship the closure of their minds.

The meeting is over. My doing, I hope. Briefly, a fantasy of omnipotence has sport with me. I need never leave. I could stay here and become an adopted resident of Jerusalem as they all are, and close meetings.

They gather round me. But not to say I have shocked them into penitence. Oh no. They gather round – all except the Green woman and her black companion, who depart – in order to tell me how mistaken my understanding of Torah is. Someone even goes so far as to suggest that when the Torah exacts kindness to fellow beings from us, it only really means kindness to fellow Jews.

The girl in the cream snood bounds over, scratches between her legs, and tells me I haven't grasped the *halachic* implications of . . . I do not bother to listen. When humans lose their humanity, *Halachah* can go hang.

Phil Chernofsky is hurt because I've implied that they all think the same, whereas I should have seen from the way he was steering the discussion, refocusing it this way and that, that he had some hefty differences with some people. I accuse him, I accuse all of them, of being too close in their sympathies to the woman in green. Who is she, anyway?

Aha! She's a Kahane supporter. As far out there politically as they get.

'She did some teaching here,' Phil Chernofsky says. 'I didn't feel – you know – that it was proper for me to keep her in order.'

Like you could have if you'd wanted, eh, Phil?

A grey American in an anorak, who earlier had tried unsuccessfully to demur from some proposal to decapitate any Jew seen smiling at an Arab on *Shabbes*, hopes that I won't go back to London supposing that everyone who reads Torah thinks the thoughts I've heard here. I thank him. I can't afford to, I tell him.

A *yeshiva* boy introduces himself. Isaac. He wants to befriend me. He has a Bronx accent and an old beard on a young face. He'd like to put me right. See me around. Talk it through.

And the large indecipherable Santa Claus, whose name is Mordechai, won't let me go until we've had the big stuff out. Hitler, I think I hear him say. Arafat, I think I hear him say. Ultimate truth. His indecipherability is caused by speaking too fast, a slight lisp, and an over-eagerness to have the big stuff out. Do I believe in ultimate truth, he asks me.

I tell him I believe in several. (Actually, I believe in none, but I am too shaken up to remember what I believe.)

'Then you can't believe in ultimate truth,' he says, cipherable suddenly, because he thinks he's tricked me. 'Ultimate truth is ultimate. There can be only one.'

I tell him that you can believe in your own, but still respect the right of others to believe in theirs, blah blah.

'Right,' he says, 'so you respect a drug-dealer's ultimate truth?'

Do I have the strength for this? It's my own fault for trying to fob him off with a pluralism I don't subscribe to in my heart. In my heart I have never respected anyone's beliefs. I have just feared them.

Phil Chernofsky, meanwhile, is trying to get me to say what I'll do to defend myself when the Arabs come to push me into the sea.

'Hide behind the woman in green,' I say.

Isaac invites me to spend a weekend with the Lubavitch.

They are all crowded around me. I am a honey-pot.

'Right,' says Mordechai, 'do I have the right to live or not?'

'You personally?'

'Me personally.'

'You have a right. I'm not certain it's inalienable.'

'What! I have to let others take my life?'

'Your life is not the be-all and end-all,' I say.

'It is to me.'

'Theirs is to them.'

'But if they want to take mine . . .?'

Oh, then in that case, kill 'em, Mordechai, mow 'em down, drown 'em, boil 'em in oil. What, dare to do violence to Mordechai, to *Mordechai* . . .? I don't say that. Instead, I reply with a little Talmudical something I have committed to memory for just such an occasion. 'Belong ever to the persecuted rather than to the persecutors.'

Much of the Talmud is written in this spirit. Submissiveness was a quality valued in rabbis. It is at the heart of Talmudic Judaism that we should take it and not give it. But that is a spirit of the past. We tried that. After the Holocaust, what I have quoted is dynamite.

And they blow up. Now I am not just a honey-pot – I am a sackful of grain, tossed to the hungry.

Mordechai is flailing like a windmill. Phil Chernofsky invites me to come and talk to him in office hours. Isaac is tugging at my sleeve. The girl in the cream snood is scratching every part of herself.

I tell them I must go now. They ask me where I'm staying. I know the effect it will have. 'The American Colony.'

'Arabs own that!' Mordechai cries.

'Arab's own that!' the snood-girl wails.

'Arab's own that, you know,' says Isaac.

'Don't Arabs own that?' Phil Chernofsky muses.

That's why I'm staying there, I tell them. I describe the ball of violence that has been lodged in my chest all my adult life. Arab-directed violence. An unreasoning hate – there may be reason for it, but I have not done the reasoning – that releases its poisons whenever I hear the word Syria or see King Hussein of Jordan making up to the English on television or pass an entourage of women in black masks on the Edgware Road. Leave the Arabs themselves out of it; it isn't good for *me* to have this stuff leaking through my body. So I'm staying at the American Colony as a sort of act of moral convalescence. The thing you get close to is never half as bad as the thing you fear and despise from a distance. I have more Talmud for them – 'Groundless hatred is a sin that weighs as heavily as idolatry.'

'It's not groundless!' they all exclaim together.

'It is if you haven't grounded it,' I say.

What you feel is not violence, they tell me.

I know what I feel, I tell them.

'Would you stay at a hotel run by Hitler?' asks Mordechai.

That tips the balance. I am calm again. All I can think of now is what a good sitcom it would make, a hotel run by Hitler. The Adolfi.

Mordechai and Isaac follow me out into the street. Isaac still wants to be my friend. That's to say he still wants to put me right. Mordechai leans his bulk against me as we walk. It is a surprise to me to see normal people going about their business. Kids dressed up for a good time. Girls in high heels. Boys eating slices of pizza. There is a world then, outside Torah?

Mordechai has one more thing to say to me before I pull myself away. 'You won't like this,' he says, 'but we'll be destroying all the churches in Eretz Israel once the Arabs have gone.'

There is a ringing sound in my ears. 'Did I hear you say you'll be destroying *churches*?' I ask.

'We have to. They're not based on truth.'

I may be dreaming all this. There may be no Mordechai, no Israel Center, no Jerusalem. It's possible I'm having a bad night in London, after too much red wine. But even in a dream you have to keep your end up. I remind Mordechai, or the shade of Mordechai, that our people have seen their temples destroyed, their synagogues burned. Will we do to others what we can never forgive them for doing to us? Is this how we become a light unto nations? Have we been through the fires and learnt nothing? Do we possess, after all we have undergone, no imagination for equivalence?

He doesn't know what I'm talking about. There's no argument, no problem. 'Their truth is false.'

'They said our truth was false.'

'They were wrong. Theirs is.'

I don't even say goodnight.

Ros is waiting for me at the American Colony, but I cannot return yet. I know what will happen. I will regurgitate the evening in the hearing of Arabs.

It's still early. I have hung off the edge of the civilized world for a billion light years or two, yet back on Ben-Yehuda Street the cafés are working, couples are strolling, there is even a bookshop open, where I can buy yesterday's newspaper.

Over a sweet, creamy cappuccino, which is how they make them in Israel, I read about a couple of kids who went missing in Haifa for twenty-four hours. A little boy and his sister. The parents found a note on the floor, under a slipper. Dear Mummy and Daddy, we have gone to the mountains to establish a settlement in one of the *wadis*. Back at the weekend.

The *wadis* are searched and the settler-toddlers are found. Safe and well. There is no report of their having shot up any Arab villages.

'I don't know,' the mother says, 'where the kids get such a developed imagination – perhaps from books or television.'

A puzzle, and no mistake.

I take a taxi back to the hotel. The driver doesn't put his meter on. They seldom do. Official advice is to insist, but that means having a brawl every time you want to go anywhere. In the end, you settle for an easy life and let them enjoy their minuscule victory over whoever.

We drive through Mea She'arim, meaning 'Hundred Gates' – God's promise of increase and all that. A somersaulting Russian touch-me-not *shtetl* transported to Jerusalem. An act of the mind. A victory of will over geography. A phobia-drome. But at night, when you can't read the signs banning the human body, it looks picturesque. Yellow light escapes under the doors of tiny houses of prayer. In their post-*Shabbes* eighteenth-century Polish prince and peasant costumes, the *frummies* flit through the shadows like figures from Diaghilev.

The American Colony is just in East Jerusalem, about as far in this direction as an Israeli taxi-driver will take you. Go any further and the stones may start flying. But they all know the American Colony. It's where journalists and writers stay. A centre of rumour and gossip. A whispering place. If you want to take the political temperature of East Jerusalem, you come here. The staff are Palestinian. They can be charming to you over breakfast and refuse to look at you at lunch. This means that they don't like something the Israelis have just done in the occupied territories. If there's been an arrest in Ramallah at twelve, you'll know about it at twelve-fifteen by the expressions on the waiters' faces.

Tonight, the hotel is looking severely beautiful. It has been dressed for Christmas. The courtyard has an orange tree and a lemon tree, both in fruit. On warm days you eat out here. In the evenings, which are becoming sharp now, you take a quick turn around the goldfish pond, admire the fruit, and wonder why you never embraced a monastic life. For Christmas, four ghost-grey glimmering firs in terracotta pots have been brought out. There are pale lights in the trees, casting silvery reflections in the pond. If Mordechai ever gets his way, such courtyards will be no more. They are not Jewish.

Ros is in our room, intermittently writing her diary and watching American soaps on Jordanian television. She doesn't feel like a drink at the bar. The atmosphere, she says, is not good tonight. But I have been to Gehenna and back, and have an almighty thirst.

I see what she means about the atmosphere. George, everyone's favourite porter, who calls you 'My dear', sees me coming out of the lift and looks the other way. The bar-manager, who couldn't do enough for me yesterday, is hidden like an ostrich inside his black suit. At one of the low copper tables, a bearded Palestinian in a creaking leather jacket is making an arrangement which has to do with Christmas with a middle-aged English couple. He wants them to remember Tuesday. 'Tuesday, Jewsday – Tuesday, *Jews*day . . . you know?'

He laughs, throwing his head back charmingly, showing them the glistening underside of his beard. The English couple are not charmed. 'They're very good to us,' the man says. 'I won't hear a word against them.'

The Palestinian remembers himself. 'Good people,' he says. 'Very good people.'

Something else for him to resent.

Seeing me sitting friendless at the bar, a soldierly young man of the sort D. H. Lawrence wrote and E. M. Forster fantasized about, engages me in conversation. He is with a group, but swings away from them on his bar stool to give me his full radiance. It takes me a while to get a hold of his name, which I think is Philip, because I'm busy looking at his bristling moustache and wondering why it doesn't look real. Philip – I'm sure it's Philip – was once a journalist in Tunbridge Wells, but has given all that away – the lights, the excitement – and is now working for an economic think-tank on the West Bank. I am to understand that he has found his purpose in life. This helps me with what is wrong with his moustache. He is in too big a hurry to let you know he is on the side of right.

I ask him who sponsors the think-tank.

He goes vague. Could be the United Nations.

I ask him who else it could be.

He goes even vaguer. Maybe the EEC.

'Who pays your wages, Philip?'

He smiles. In Tunbridge Wells they probably call this smile winning. 'I don't exactly get *wages*. Just, you know, subsistence. I'm not supposed to be working, between ourselves. I'm here on a tourist visa. Money's not what it's about.'

What it's about is heart. Philip is staying in Hebron with his wife, who does get wages. She nurses for the Red Crescent. Heart is what it's about for both of them.

But Philip is employed by someone or other to work in a think-tank not a heart-tank; so what is he thinking about? Factories that the Israelis won't put any capital into, to help the local Palestinian population help itself; industry that does exist, but that people in the outside world haven't heard of. There is so much wasted skill and talent on the West Bank. And the Palestinians are such wonderful people. He takes it for granted that I know this for myself, since I am sitting at this bar, in this hotel; but he wants to add his testimony to others'. They are wonderful, intelligent, warm, friendly, shrewd, lovely, lovely people. They like Palestinians so much, Philip and his wife, they identify so completely with their cause, that they fear sometimes they may be growing anti-Semitic.

He means anti-Jewish. Palestinians are themselves Semitic. But I know better than to correct him. Where the heart rules, only republicans quibble over words.

In order to cure themselves of this creeping anti-you-know-what, they hop on a bus to Beersheba every now and then, and go and talk to newly-arrived migrants, Jews who have not yet been Israelified.

'What, you mean get to them before the country does?'

I take the measure of what I've said, only after I've said it. Could Philip and his wife be visiting migrant camps with a view to propagandizing against the state? Is that also what working for a think-tank on the West Bank entails?

He smiles at me. In Tunbridge Wells they probably call this smile boyish. 'We like to hear a dozen languages being spoken at once,' he says. 'It's nice listening to them.'

New Israelis are the only Israelis he does like listening to. As for the settlers, 'They're lunatics. You can't talk to them.'

'Have you tried?'

'No. Wouldn't want to. We have friends who have.'

And out it all rolls. Looting. Breaking windows. Shooting

pistols. Breaking their friends' heads with rifle butts. Army no better. Looting. Breaking windows. Shooting pistols . . .

'Aha,' I say. 'Mmhmm, yep, yep, ah well.'

Something causes him to ask my name. Not my Christian name. He has that. My surname. My not-Christian name.

After I tell him, he falls quiet. We take nuts and seeds from a bowl on the bar, and listen to each other chew.

At last, he says, 'What do *you* think of Israel – though I realize that might be an insensitive question, given your er . . . name.'

I leave out all the obvious things his discomfort means, and settle for just this: how could he have spoken to me for thirty minutes, on this subject, in this country, with my face as open before him as the plain of Jordan, and not have had a suspicion? What does that say about his powers of observation, his reliability as a witness of anything?

There is no obligation on me, as I see it, even to pretend to answer his question. Instead, I try him with a little moral conundrum. Is there such a thing as traveller's etiquette, does he think? Could one argue, I wonder, that while one may be as sanctimonious as one likes at home, being the guest of another country – especially a country in which one has just arrived on a three-month tourist visa – engages one in a contract at the very least to use one's eyes, suspend one's judgement and keep one's self-righteousness in one's rucksack?

Quite something, coming from me, after the line I pulled at the Israel Center earlier tonight. But I have rights that Philip doesn't. I don't come from Tunbridge Wells.

He doesn't see what I'm getting at, anyway. And is saved from having it re-formulated for him when his wife comes over to join us. She has an open-and-shut Irish face. She has spent too much time among like-minded people. She assumes, as she speaks, that there is only one attitude to everything, and that you share it with her.

They pack me around with baby-talk. It is like having my tummy tickled. They can't get over the warmth and friendliness of the Palestinian people. Travelling on a bus with them is just . . . well, just lovely. And they have this astonishing capacity to know what's going on, to communicate information at great speed across the West Bank. It's amazing but wherever they go, Philip and his wife, they are recognized by Palestinians. 'They just know we're here.'

Their eyes meet in a love tryst. They are getting off on the Palestinian people. It's a sort of extended honeymoon that they're on. 'We knew we would soon be tied down to children and a mortgage and things, and we felt: shouldn't we see something, do something, be of use?'

How many more are there in Israel, in this condition? Canoodling in PLO scarves? Eroticizing the oppressed? Being of use for a week or a month or a year, on a visitor's visa, for a pittance?

Philip's wife has an Irish Jewish friend here. Rachel. A musician. She doesn't believe what they tell her they have seen. Philip's wife's mother and Rachel's mother are friends in Ireland. So, for the sake of their mothers' friendship, Philip's wife doesn't disabuse Rachel 'too much'. I get a knowing, open-and-shut Irish look from her. Don't I too have people I white-lie to for humanity's sake? But – oh, well – let's leave poor Rachel in ignorance of the vileness of her countrymen. Ignorance is bliss. We know, though; oh, don't we know!

It has gone cold in the vicinity of my heart. We are past dealing with rights or wrongs, truths or untruths. I smell the enemies of my soul. Forget the Palestinians. With them we are just having a family quarrel. The enemies of my soul come from Tunbridge Wells. For a couple of mad minutes, thanks to Philip, I regret having fought with my people over the Torah. This is the effect the enemies of your soul have on you – they convict you of disloyalty, they turn you into Mordechai, they put a snood upon your head.

Sixteen

CLOAK AND DAGGER

One evening, after a blow-out afternoon tea amid the Assyrian and Solomonic extravagances of the King David Hotel, we step across the street to look around the YMCA, a non-denominational peace-haven in the very heart of strife, where you can rent a room, buy a coffee, learn a language, and enjoy spectacular views of Jerusalem, if you are able to find the roof.

The clientele is woolly and bearded. People sit around in berets, talking quietly, reading, smoking. The building itself is at pains to have a little something for everybody.

'Funny how much more soothing a Catholic/Moroccan/West Australian/Arthurian folly is than a Five-Star International Jebusite Hotel,' Ros observes.

As we can't find the roof, or justify a further afternoon tea, we decide to leave it for another day. We linger outside a while, in the cold, enjoying a palely illuminated colonnade. And it is here, in the shadows, that we are found, contacted, seized, accosted, picked-up, stumbled-on, bugged – who can say what we are? – by Mahmoud, resident of Bit Sfafa, the town that was divided by the 1948 armistice and united again after 1967, Mahmoud, the ideal historical child of the times.

None of which, needless to say, do we know at the moment he accosts us. Ros's diary reports a greeting in Hebrew. I don't remember that. Ros's diary plucks him more vividly out of the night than my memory can.

There he was. Eyes the colour of Jerusalem plums; an embroidery of

Bedouin black hair stitched too low on his forehead; skin spotted and pitted like a dish of aubergine salad. Garlic on the night wind. The moon a tart lemon crescent above.

Later, after I have had time and reason to look at him, I will see that his eyes are brown and have no bottoms to them. Later, after more meetings as accidental and fortuitous as this one, I will say to Ros that his eyes are pools which cannot be dredged. But tonight he is just someone on the make in the dark. And I am not convinced we should be talking to him. I don't know he's Palestinian. I suppose I unthinkingly take him to be Jewish. We are, after all, on King David Street. So it's not anything racial I'm feeling. Just ordinary, sensible caution.

But Ros's antennae are out, even if mine aren't.

'Do you not speak Hebrew? No Hebrew?' he asked in perfect English, as I stood tossed in mingled this and that, a collation of cold and hot dread.

Of course no Hebrew. No Arabic. No nothing. But who needs to make an effort here, where every urchin capable of throwing a stone is also capable of offering a guided tour in proper guided English to all the holy places within the Walled City of Jerusalem? The earthly poverty is great here. The earthly intellect is great too. All the humane skills, of charm, of humour, of opportunism, of courtliness, of corruption – ah! what a civilized place, what a civilized people the Palestinians in Jerusalem are. Will our latest encounter be rich in proofs of this?

He stood there, immobile. But I could see, or seemed to see, a shaking or a quivering both in the air around him and also just below the surface of his skin. He wanted something and straightaway my heart broke. We could never give him what he wanted. He wanted a resurrection. I'm sure of it. A new life.

But before the miracles, he asked the time, and when I told him it was twenty-five past five he told me he wanted to go to Australia. '. . . to Perth. I have a friend there. He is a painter. I am a painter, too . . .'

It is as abrupt as that. Time – Perth. Or is it Ros's voice – Perth? Can he be as good as that? Can he get her down to a specific Australian city on the strength of 'Twenty-five past five'?

It could, of course, just be that he really is hanging on for a visa, and really does have a painter friend in Perth, and really can't wait to be fishing and painting his days away in Perth himself. And when Ros says, 'But *I'm* from Perth,' he is marvellously astonished by the coincidence.

He has one for me too. He mutters it to me, something for my ears only, as we re-double our tracks and decide that a coffee in the YMCA would be just the thing after all. 'You know Blackpool?' he asks me. 'I lived there. My wife came from Blackpool. I have a child in Blackpool.'

Not dead right, but not bad. Blackpool's only fifty miles from Manchester. If you're measuring from Jerusalem, they might as well be the same place. And he got there, got the county, on the evidence of what? I don't think I've even given him the time.

We aren't in the same league, he and I. He's nestling in to us, narrowing us down to within a couple of streets of home, and I can't even tell whether he's a Jew or a Palestinian. I know pretty soon after I've asked him, though. Something goes off, goes rotten, in those Jerusalem-plum eyes of his. Ros's diary has it that he winces.

So it's that bad, is it, being thought a Jew when you're a Palestinian? Would it hurt me as much to be mistaken for an Arab? I don't think so. I thought I half became an Arab in Eilat. But there's more than one conclusion to be drawn from this. Either they're more thin-skinned than we are. Or we have a worse name.

He tells us the story of his village, how before the Six-Day War his father lived in Israel and his mother lived in Jordan. Having seen how he reacted to being thought a Jew, I don't make the mistake of suggesting that he should be grateful to the Israelis for reuniting his family.

Would we like to see his village? Meet his people? Of course we would. Let's fix a time, Ros says. I'll need to consult my diary, I say.

It's at this point that my recollection of things becomes confused. I hear my name called, look around, and see someone I know. Another coincidence. The sister of an Australian friend. And with her an American woman, an architect, a leftist, not a Jew, but has converted. Another of those who came, saw and was conquered. I swivel my chair and talk to them, while Mahmoud discusses with Ros the size of the fish he will catch in West Australia, and the length of the beaches he will swim from. *If* the Israelis give him his visa.

When I turn back, Mahmoud has gone and Ros is looking agitated. I ask her if she's all right. She isn't. Apparently Mahmoud suddenly grew alarmed, saw someone beckoning to him in the corridor outside the restaurant, made a silent question with his mouth – 'Me? You want me?' – rose, excused himself, and followed whoever was beckoning.

'His chest was heaving under his jacket,' Ros says. 'His blood was banging in the back of his neck.'

'Did you see who he went with?'

'No.'

'Did he say if he was coming back?'

'He asked me to wait.'

So we wait. And after half an hour or so he returns. His chest still heaving, just as Ros had described it. The blood still banging in his neck. He doesn't acknowledge me. It's Ros he needs to talk to.

'Rosalin, I must ask you, I *must* ask of you a favour.' ('OK,' Ros says in her diary. 'OK, here it comes.') 'Life here is hard. Every day, every minute of every day, trouble leaps up from under the earth. Everywhere I go. This is my land. My land. *My* land. When the police come, you will accompany me. You will say nothing. You will be a witness. You will see what they do to me. You will see how they treat us.'

'Mahmoud, what has happened?'

'My friend makes trouble for me. This is how we live.'

He sits down, then stands up, then sits down again. He is looking to see if anyone is looking for him.

I am out of this. Perth, painters, visas, wanted men, *my land my land my land* . . . What will it all come down to – a loan of a hundred shekels?

'Are you saying the police are coming for you here?' Ros asks.

'No. Maybe not. But they will make trouble for me.' He rises again. 'I have been asked to leave. I must leave.'

Ros is ready with her goodbyes, and her faith in Western Australia as a place where young men in leather jackets can talk in peace to people they have just picked up out of the shadows. 'Mahmoud, I hope you will soon be in Perth and that you will be happy there.'

'This is my land. I will leave it if I want to. I love to travel. I will leave it only if I want. I will come back, *when* I want.'

Is this for me? Am I meant to say, 'You will come and go as and when my people let you, buster,' so that he can then pull a gun on me?

He writes his telephone number on a piece of paper. 'Please ring me,' he says. 'Please ring me, tomorrow, and we will arrange for you to see my village. I must leave. Allow me to buy you your coffee. Promise you will ring.'

He shakes hands with us. Straightens his shoulders inside his leather jacket. And leaves.

And that, for the time being, is Mahmoud.

The entry in Ros's diary is cryptic. 'Mahmoud, why did you ask us the time?' it says.

Mahmoud, why did you ask us the time?

The politics suck you down like quicksands in this city. Or maybe I just can't keep away from the bar.

A woman called Drora Kass, big in peace, well connected, well placed, well-known here at the bar of the American Colony, talks to me drily about Israel's need to be loved. 'There's a national hankering for affection,' she says.

When the Israelis gave back Gaza they thought the Egyptians would love them. They saw the treaty as the beginning of a romance. But nothing happened. The Egyptians took it formally and coldly – OK, now relations are officially normalized, we will see how it goes. But we doubt whether our citizens will be dashing off for holidays in Tel Aviv.

This coldness and formality was a great blow to Israel, which needs a lot of loving. So there are some bruised and raw feelings in the country, and a reluctance, now, to trust promises of affection when they are forthcoming in other quarters.

'Once bitten,' I say, to show that I know the way of these things.

'Exactly,' she says. 'And the last thing the Israelis want is to appear to be acting on the rebound.'

I buy her a beer. I like the impression she gives of having sat at the bar of all the world's hot spots, exchanging the banter of war with all the world's journalists. She transports me to Cambodia and Angola and Sarajevo. She would probably argue that she transports me to Jerusalem.

I repeat to her some of the things my Australian friend's sister told me in the coffee-house of the YMCA, while Mahmoud was sweet-talking my wife. Isn't it true that for many bourgeois Palestinians the Israeli occupation has brought nothing but prosperity? I list the advantages to them, the examples of happy social commerce, as they were told to me.

Drora Kass, who has short, unsentimentally styled blonde hair and lazy, sceptical eyes, looks at me as though I'm an infant. I hear what's wrong with what I'm repeating even as I'm repeating it. She has the power to freeze your words in your throat.

'The Palestinians are pleased to have phones, if that's what you mean,' she says. 'But I know very few who are able to mingle freely with Israelis. Even where their movements are not restricted, they find they cannot make friends with Israelis, given the Intifada, given what's happening elsewhere in the community. They feel they owe a loyalty to those who are fighting, and cannot forget them sufficiently to relax even in the company of Israelis they like. Even someone like Faisal Husseini, who I've been talking to tonight, says that although he has lots of Israeli friends, he does not visit them frequently, is not able to have regular connections with them, in their homes.'

Faisal Husseini. *The* voice of Arab Jerusalem. On the principle of the Los Angeles gay synagogue's challa chain, I have only to touch Drora to be two links away from Yasser Arafat. That's how close you are to everything in the bar of the American Colony Hotel.

Another person who puts me right at the bar or at breakfast is a tall Spanish journalist with a liking for yellow pullovers, a big moustache, and a Scottish name – Adrian Mac Liman. He is sharp and watchful. Intolerant of naivety. And knows East Jerusalem well. In the early days of the Intifada, when most journalists were writing it off as a nine-day wonder, he was producing a serious study of it. We go to him when we are out of our depth, when something has happened on the streets that we can't understand, when the mood of the hotel swings so violently that we wonder whether it wouldn't be prudent to check out.

He knows what we mean about the mood-swings. He has been coming here for years. He has any number of Palestinian friends. He is trusted. But he too has been made to feel that he ought to leave.

So it isn't personal, I say. It isn't because I'm Jewish?

He smiles at me indulgently. As the evils of the world go, his smile says, being Jewish is not high on the list.

But Arabs still call, 'Jew, Jew, Jew,' after me, in the Old City. And Ros still insists on walking behind me in the streets of East Jerusalem, to protect my back.

I ask him about the desolation of the East Jerusalem streets. Were they always like this, post 1967, or is this the consequence of the Intifada?'

Intifada.

'So who is the Intifada really damaging?' I ask. 'If the consequence is the dereliction of Arab shops and Arab streets, isn't it a form of suicide?'

He's angry with me. Suicide? What do I mean, *suicide*?

I cannot say, Are they not merely shooting themselves in the foot, because of the levity of the phrase.

'By your own account they're making themselves poorer,' I say instead. I keep thinking of prisoners who foul their own cells, to punish those who don't have to live in them.

He narrows his eyes. 'So they earn $180 in four hours of being open, instead of $200 in eight,' he says.

I back off further discussion. I want to say, 'So the Intifada comes down to a nifty economic victory, does it?' But I don't want to say it to him. I like him. I am impressed by him. Intellectually, I am possibly frightened of him. But as with all those who speak of wrong here, there is something finally you must withhold. It's as if the things they tell you, the precise witness they bear, you know already. These things must be so, given the fact of war and occupation; they are bound to be, cannot fail to be, so what do I want with the precise delineation? Palestinians have remarkably good memories, Adrian Mac Liman remarks to me on one occasion; they remember exactly what he said to them four years ago. But how different is this from Philip of Tunbridge Wells marvelling over their charm? Are they all oppressed-persons collectors, in this hotel? Are they besotted with victims?

It may be my Jewish intransigence, but although I believe

everything Adrian and Drora say to me, I cannot feel any of it at my heart.

I feel something somewhere, though, when they mutter to me separately, as they pass me at breakfast, that the Palestinian delegation has returned from Washington and will be reporting to their people at a press conference in East Jerusalem later this very morning. The something somewhere that I feel is a wish in the pit of my stomach that they hadn't told me. Because now I know, I have no choice but to go. Yet even to just think of going is like breaking a taboo older than my tribe.

Before we take our lives into our hands in East Jerusalem, where a taxi was stoned last night, and a woman passenger slightly injured – if there is such a thing as a *slight* injury in Jerusalem – I stroll my favourite street, the pedestrianized Ben-Yehuda Street, home to buskers from all the Russias.

A brass band is playing this morning at one end of Ben-Yehuda. At the other, a wasted man sits like a bean-bag in a wheelchair, a recorder to his mouth. He has insufficient breath to play it. His hands shake. The sound he makes is more like the cry of an animal than music. A cardboard notice is pinned to his chair –

I AM COMPOSER
NOW I'M VERY ILL
AND SHORT WITH MONEY
PLEASE HELP ME SURVIVE
THANK YOU

A couple who look Ukrainian accompany one another on balalaika and electric keyboard. And a Russian bass stands at the corner of Mordechai Ben-Hillel Street, his brown leather briefcase open on a concrete post to collect coins, which he acknowledges with a deep old-fashioned bow, his nose red from the cold, his clothes poor, his repertoire operatic and heart-breaking.

The melancholy of migrant longing, of exile, of lost homes, fills the street.

I sit on a bench, in the cold, and watch the faces coming towards me – slightly *up* towards me, for Ben-Yehuda is on an incline – and for the first time I take the measure of what an extraordinary achievement it has been – the *ingathering* – what an enormous event, what an almighty risk, what a desirable outcome. For Jews. Of course for Jews.

Now that I am forcing myself to look, I cannot believe what a variety of faces I see, what a multitude of cultures have been brought together here, by the cruellest of accidents, by the most audacious of designs. And I am upset – helped, no doubt, by the bass and the balalaika – as I have not been upset before in Israel. This is my high spot, my emotional moment, not at the idolatrous Wall or among ancient stones, but amid the shops and shoppers. I could stay all day, watching the hatter at work, looking into the *yarmulke* shop, observing how generously people give to the buskers and beggars. And the faces keep coming, wave upon wave of them, Eastern European, North African, American, Dutch, Italian – the ingathering.

This is the place for them, for *us*, I don't for a minute doubt it, here in Ben-Yehuda Street. In this ingathered throng even the *frummies* look all right, look part of it, other pieces in a grand puzzle, rather than the whole thing itself, as they insist on in their ghettos. Which is the unforgivable wrongness of the Orthodox – to wish to shrink all this down to merely that.

I have arranged to meet Ros on Jaffa Street, where we'll pick up a taxi to take us to the press conference. But I cannot get up from my bench, even though the cold rises from the concrete and penetrates my coat. The Russian bass's nose is getting redder. He stands buttoned up in his anorak, like a schoolboy. It is partly this stance that makes him an object of my pity, but also the fact of his having no instrument to play. You are vulnerable when it's just you and your voice. Every now and then he pulls a green school exercise-book out of his briefcase to jog his memory of a song. He has competition. From the Army and Navy Surplus shop across the street comes the blare of pop music. It's Queen, as they would all know in Eilat. *Momma – I've just killed a man.*

On an impulse, I go over to him. I wait for him to finish a song. A dirge from the Volga. Before that it was *Boris Godunov*. Before that it was Tauber. If I don't get him now it'll be *Boris Godunov* again. He seems to alternate them.

He speaks a little English, yes. He's taught himself. I ask him if he'll talk to me. Yes. He is so self-effacing, he almost puts it as a question – Yes? He'll talk to me? I wonder if I can take him for a coffee. I realize he's working, but I'll pay him for his time. Not charity. I'm working too.

He waves away the money, but he cannot leave his concrete pillar. This is his pitch. The minute he quits it, someone else will take it. 'Many competitors for position,' he explains.

So we talk where he is, standing up, between songs, in the cold.

His name is David Chrishtain. He is from Leningrad. He came to Israel six months ago with his wife, a child of seven and a sick father. 'He has stroke – here.' He rubs the right side of his chest and flanks.

I ask him why he came.

'In Russia very, very bad anti-Semitism. More than anti-Semitism – Fascism. No order now. Many anti-Semitic groups. Not just Pamyat . . .'

And he counts them off on his cold fingers, the groups that have made him fear for his family's safety, for his daughter's future, the groups whose anti-Semitism was always there but concealed, suppressed by Communism.

'Now it is so bad,' he says, 'they are blaming Jewishes for the October Revolution.'

350

He was a teacher of mathematics and a singer with the Leningrad Philharmonic. 'I have no musical education, but a famous singer hear me and like my voice and train me. And so I get work. Sing in many choirs, concerts, at opera.'

'Professionally?'

'Yes, yes. In Russia I had much money.'

'And now?' As if it is not clear what now brings.

He looks at me confidentially. He touches my arm. He has an upsetting face – a kind, soulful man. 'Israel doesn't need singers,' he says. 'They pay for them to come from America.'

'And teaching is impossible here? Other work impossible?'

'There is nothing. Nothing here. I understand Israel is a little country. And many Russians are coming. I understand. But I have big disappointments. I thought in Israel Jewishes would be brothers. Would love other Jewishes. But it's not true. Some people are very nice. Very kind. But others laugh at me when I sing.'

'They laugh at you here? In Jerusalem? In Israel?'

'Yes, yes – here. They laugh and say, "Go to Russia."'

Would a Jew do that? Would a Jew say that? I have been here an hour. I have seen no one laugh. Maybe at night. Maybe when the kids come out.

Officially it's no better, he says. 'Very bureaucratic here. Many, many bureaucrats. I think Russia should learn bureaucracy from Israel. When I go to the offices, they say, "Why did you come? What did you come for?"'

'Will you stay?'

He doesn't know. 'Maybe I look Russia. Yes, maybe I look Russia again.'

'You'd go back?'

He shrugs. Yes, maybe he will consider going back. He was somebody, he was respectable in Russia. Whereas here – 'Here, I am nothing.'

I ask about his sick father. Doesn't he get good medical help in Israel?

'I hear Israeli doctors very good. But they're not. Perhaps scientists are good. But not good . . . care.' (He's pleased to find that word, 'care'.) 'They don't go home.'

I don't understand him. 'Don't go home?'

'They don't go to your home. I have to get ambulance for my father. The driver says, "It'll cost you ninety-three shekels. Do you have the ninety-three shekels, because if you don't, we can't take him."'

This isn't the Israeli friendship, the love between Jewishes that he'd been expecting. But then he'd been expecting too much.

He asks about England. 'Is there anti-Semitism there?'

I think of the stories I've heard about Philip Roth, unable to take the London pogroms of the mind any longer. 'No,' I say. 'Yes, but really no. Only of a subtle kind. Only if you want to join certain things or drink with certain people. Not in such a form that it interferes seriously with your life. Not like in Russia.'

'In Russia terrible,' he consoles himself with remembering. 'In Russia there is no law. No order. They can do what they want.'

'Then you're better off here,' I tell him.

I leave him to get on with earning his living. But I watch from a distance to see if anyone laughs. No one does. I see some discomfort, caused by the nakedness of his performance – just him, his buttoned-up anorak, his red nose and his voice. Otherwise, it's all kindness. Genuine appreciation of his fine, light bass voice. And tears. One woman weeps. A Russian woman. She stands by with her family, listening to Russian folk-songs, Russian opera, Russian operetta, and openly weeps.

She is at one corner of the junction between Ben-Yehuda and Ben-Hillel, I am at the other. And her tears, let alone David Chrishtain's voice, are unnerving me. It's too upsetting here. Too rich.

I head for Jaffa Street to find Ros, get a taxi, and mix it with my Palestinian brothers.

*   *   *

Except that no taxi will take us to the hotel where the press conference is being held. No fear. Too risky. I rant and rave a few times, but to no avail. Take us as near as you can then, I say at last. Which turns out to be the American Colony.

The address I was given was the National Palace Hotel, deep into on-your-own-head-be-it territory. But when we get there we discover they've changed venues. Now they're at the Palestinian National Theatre. We retrace our steps, feeling bad, feeling anxious – that stoning – but above all, speaking for myself at any rate, feeling guilty. Intellectual curiosity, I keep whispering to my conscience, is all that is bringing me here. But it wears the complexion of an apostasy, however I twist it.

Foolish. It's not as though I'm going to applaud. It's not as though I'm going to welcome them home. It's not as though I'm going to be persuaded by anything they say. I am just going to sit and watch – darkly.

And it is a dark event. A theatre, a stage, painted black. Black leather jackets. Row upon row of them. The Arabic press. Arabic television cameras. And a Christmas tree on the stage.

We arrive late, through a side door. We have to walk past the stage, in full view of the Arabic world and its spies, to find a seat. I try to look Arab, can't forgive myself, and try to look Jewish.

Of the six delegates, the impressive one is Hanan Ashrawi, the handsome, intelligent Palestinian spokeswoman and professor of literature. I begrudge her my admiration, as I've begrudged it whenever I've seen her on *Newsnight* and *Panorama*. She is too good at being the Palestinian we all like. But she speaks better English than I've heard since I've been in Israel. Ros says of her that she has a gift for making the fact of Palestinian defeat a moral strength, for turning a weak position into a strong, for transposing the systems and sequences of their oppression into actual no less than ethical power. And I'm not going to disagree with her in this room.

The other delegates are less persuasive, at least in English. More hangdog. More at the mercy of the habits and reflexes of self-pity. But I am grateful to one of them for an expression which alone justifies our having come here. 'We all know,' he says Arabically, 'that Mr Shamir has deep sleeves.'

In truth, for all the fuss my innards have been making, this is the only moment when I feel a long way from home.

Altogether more foreign is Mea She'arim, which we walk into after the press conference has broken up, crossing what was and still effectively is no man's land. We take what looks like the main street. Across it, hanging like bunting which has been left after a carnival, is a message of municipal welcome. PASSIG WITH IMMODES DRESS IS STRICTL FOPBIDDEN.

For all that she wears sleeves as deep as Mr Shamir's, Ros's simple presence, sans *shaytl*, sans snood, is enough to have every passing Hasid diving for cover. Huge men in little boys' haircuts and knickerbockers cover their eyes as we approach them.

It's worth marrying out for this experience alone.

Are we being watched?

Later that day we run into . . . But let Ros tell it. She hits it off with Palestinians.

Her diary is dated the following morning.

Last night we met Mahmoud again. This time in Jaffa Street and this time the air was heavy with the clash of civic disturbance.

He appeared – suddenly out of the night – calmer than before. Friendly and courteous, he stood with his back to the scores of armed and shielded riot police as they drove their armoured vehicles through a crowd of shoppers. A calm Mahmoud, idling by, fitfully full of inquiries about our escapades; unconcerned, even, perhaps, unaware of what rooted us to the spot, transfixed as we were by the struggle at the intersection.

And so, in fits and starts, I told him where we'd been and what we'd seen and who we'd met, and then he offered a kind of professional interest in our working methods.

'Yes, yes, I understand, a diary. Only notes, you say? Any photos, do you take photos of what you see and who you meet?'

Not thinking for a second he would find a single reason to be captivated by my story, I nevertheless told Mahmoud that once upon a time Howard and I had travelled together around Australia – 'My land, Mahmoud, my land, but Howard's travel book' – and we did not rely on a camera then and would not be using one now. What I did not tell Mahmoud was that someone in Alice Springs, showing the same curiosity, had gone on to forbid us to use a camera whenever we were on an Aboriginal reservation. I promised my diary I'd flesh this congruence out, later; but first I had to deal with a sudden narrowing in focus as Mahmoud brought our three-cornered conversation round to me.

'What is it that you said you do, my dear? What is it for the BBC? Is it justice? Are you getting justice for your ladies?'

I truly couldn't decide whether Mahmoud was a fool. Perhaps it was just that he couldn't camouflage a suspicion that I might be one. Then again, maybe justice is all that is on offer when you have no other resources.

He stood there, as though in a portrait of a Rennaissance Gent, right up against the edge of the frame. Behind him, all that he claimed, all that was ever to be his, stretched away into light and time. Armed might amongst the hurrying shoppers. Somewhere in that crowd, a Palestinian had raised his arm.

'Yes, Mahmoud, that's it precisely. My TV series will be about justice. Justice for all the forgotten, unrecognized and unrewarded women of British history.'

I had tired of the game, of him, of my own insincerities. It was time to slip away. I did not want to answer any more questions. Certain as I was that we three would meet again, and soon.

We were standing, our little group, at the head of a narrow

355

pedestrianized street, a place where three roads meet. Mahmoud was telling me that the women of his village were also looking for justice, and again he offered to take me there, this time to talk with Palestinian feminists. But something, some agitation, distracted me. I raised my gaze beyond Mahmoud's olive-black eyes just in time to see a Hasid, male, of medium age, height and volume, instantly become a pillar of salt. An Orthodox Jew, and no doubt a deeply religiously well-read man, he had been hurtling towards us. But no longer. For he had seen it, the evil eye, as it turned its stare upon him, in us – a diaspora Jew, a *shiksa* that looked like a German *shiksa* and Mahmoud. Oy! Too late? The salt shifted back to flesh. The flesh rocked hither and thither, the eyes in the head of the magic-ridden man truly popped in fear and horror. Flesh became salt once more. What to do, what to do? Retreat? Or leap for his life into the small space we three (toil and trouble, toil and trouble) had left in the road? Suddenly, instantly, quick as a flash, in the blinking of an evil eye, he leapt clear into the gap beside us, and, with head averted, he was gone.

Mahmoud had been watching me. He laughed. 'Rosalin, my dear, you are looking like a stranger in a strange land. That was a religious Jew you were staring at.'

Mahmoud laughed again. I laughed. Howard laughed. What, I wonder, did those three laughs have in common?

Mahmoud, you bend conversation to please me.

Maybe you are merely courteous.

Maybe you are looking for a deal still.

Mahmoud, are you laying a trap?

'The person you ought to meet,' Drora Kass tells me at the bar, 'is Ornan Yekutieli.'

'Who is he?' I am suspicious. *Ought* one to meet anybody?

'CRM – Civil Rights and Peace Movement. He was head of the committee to fight religious coercion for a while. Now he's a deputy mayor.'

'Oh, I don't hold with meeting officials,' I say.

Drora laughs. 'Ornan's not an *official*,' she says.

Ornan, Faisal, Yasser – I don't know about this chain of contacts.

'Is he Israeli or Palestinian?'

She gives me a dead eye. How could he be Palestinian? But he's the right sort of Israeli. She makes a gesture with her fingers, suggesting quality cloth. Ornan Yekutieli is a ninety-nine per cent mohair Israeli. A vicuña Jew.

So I go to his office to feel the texture of him for myself.

He is seriously late for our appointment. Nobody in the building seems certain which his office is. I can't find his secretary. I don't know if he's left any message for me. I sit and wait in the corridor.

And am rewarded for my patience at last by the arrival of a boyish figure in a cardigan, full of apologies. I follow him into his room. The phone rings. He lights up in conversation. He is small, dainty, full of nervous energy, with exceedingly white hands. He looks and moves like a champion chess player. His fingers flutter at his mouth and then pounce on a piece. Mate.

I am smitten, hypnotized, by his fingers. And by an air he has of mischievous delinquency. A boy's glasses, a boy's haircut, a boy's glee at getting into trouble. He may have a white mouse in his pocket. He is a native Hebrew speaker, but his English is good if broken. And Brooklyn.

He tells me about himself, over the noise of jackhammers in the street below, and the ringing of the phone. His father's family has been in Israel for over a hundred years. They came over from Iraq, of their own volition, on camels. His mother was a more recent arrival. She came from Vienna, on a girls' boat. So he's all kinds of Jew in one: Sephardic and Ashkenazi, ancient and modern, pioneer and refugee. He has worked with Abba Eban. He was Teddy Kollek's chief of staff and personal assistant. ('The best teacher in the world, Teddy Kollek, for love of Jerusalem.') And now he's assistant mayor of Jerusalem.

'This city is under a huge magnifying glass all the time,' he tells me. 'Three major religions are looking at one another every minute and waiting to be insulted. There is a real fear that World War Three *can* start here. It's not like Ireland. No one has ever believed that the Russians would be involved in Northern Ireland. Here, everybody's watching, everybody's interested, and there are so many issues . . .'

He loses the word. He is sitting on his desk now, rather than behind it, his fingers manipulating a toy sculpture made of magnets. Never before have I seen an executive playing with an executive toy.

We smile at each other as he searches for the word he wants among the magnets. 'I have this problem,' he says. 'My accent is misleading. It's better than my English.'

'Lucky you,' I say. 'I come from Manchester.'

He finds the word. *Concentrated.* 'The real issues of Israel are all concentrated here. Eighty or ninety per cent of demonstrations in Israel take place here. Everybody demonstrates in Jerusalem. You can suffer from it and flee, like a lot of people have done, or you can love it like I do.' The mischievous smile. 'After all, I was responsible for some of it. When it came to fighting against religious coercion, I fanned some of the flames.'

The phone rings again. He'll phone back. He tries to close the window on the jackhammers but the window is broken.

'Everything goes back,' he tells me, 'to Ben-Gurion's status quo letter. The mother of all sins is that he gave the most personal parts of our life to the ultra-Orthodox. If I want to get married I have to have a rabbi marry me. If I die . . . I had to go and look at them doing all that mumbo-jumbo over my father's grave. Which I don't believe and he didn't believe. In *Aramaic*! I tell you, you cannot treat the *Kaddish* with less respect than I treated it, believe me . . .'

He acts it out, the disrespect he showed to the great, solemn Aramaic prayer for the dead – 'blah, blah, blah . . .'

It shocks even me. Thrills me and shocks me all at once. And makes me feel ashamed – my own rebellions have been so tepid. But then he's an Israeli, and the whole point of Israel was that it would be a liberation from all that ... do I dare say it? ... mumbo-jumbo.

Come to Israel and you owe Orthodoxy nothing. Hang loose in the diaspora and there is always something niggling at your conscience.

But the liberation is by no means assured here. 'In the old days,' the deputy mayor tells me, 'we had our backs to the walls. But that's better than having our heads in the cement and the ultra-Orthodox dancing on our feet. If three rabbis say "Go out on the street", they can have forty thousand on the streets just like that. My actions are complicated by ... do you know what is *heshbon nefesh*? ... like mathematics of the soul, choices, moral decisions. When I call for a demonstration I have to have everybody decide at home, look in the mirrors, worry whether they can come or should come. I can't just call out forty thousand people like the rabbis.

'But when we fought to keep open clubs and restaurants on Saturday, and shops and cinemas, people opened their shirts, to show that we'd given them air. We'd loosened their ties.'

'Was it a tough fight?'

He glistens behind his glasses. 'Very tough. They burnt restaurants down. They frightened people out of their businesses. And they had a name for me ...'

He keeps me waiting. He wants me to ask. He knows I'll enjoy it. I ask. 'What was their name for you?'

'The Contaminator of Jerusalem.'

Enjoy it? I've never envied a man's name more. I used to think Attila the Hun was good. But the Contaminator of Jerusalem ...!

One of the compromises that was reached with the ultra-Orthodox was to close a restaurant for one *Shabbes*, so that the believers could feel they'd won, and then open it thereafter. But that's not the sort of deal he's interested in repeating. 'The Israel that we ought to have needs a Jerusalem that is modern, open, free, tolerant – that is a reflection of Israel. We want to be part of the modern world, not Iran, not some medieval walled city. That's what I tell them in Tel Aviv when I'm collecting money for my campaign. My grandfather was one of the seven families that built Tel Aviv. I tell them that the Jerusalem we're getting is not a Jerusalem that reflects them. We are not a light, we are becoming a darkness to all nations.'

Which brings us to what some call Eretz Israel, and others the occupation. I am not embarrassed to ask. When was I last not embarrassed to ask? When was I last not fearful of a question bringing the house down on me?

'The good of the Palestinians,' he says – and lo! it does not crucify him to say it – 'is for me a by-product of Zionism. In 1972 I was one of the few people to say we needed a Palestinian state – or rather, because nobody in 1972 dared say *Palestinian state*, we referred to the legitimate rights of Palestinians. People have been demonstrating against the occupation for fifteen years, and we haven't moved one inch. I was called to Silwan yesterday – you've been reading about Silwan? I went to meet one of the Palestinian families evicted by the settlers. They asked to see me. They have nowhere to go. You can't be emotional in this country. But when I touched the children's cheeks they were so cold, I nearly cried.'

So? Peace? When?

'Every intelligent person in the world has a peace plan for Jerusalem. They send a copy to Teddy Kollek, and give one to their mothers . . . However, you'll be amazed but I'm gonna say something optimistic.' He grins. Sits back in his chair. Plays with his executive toy. He is building a bridge with the magnets, unconsciously constructing an optimistic arch out of sticky silver arrows. I point out to him what he has done. Lights go on behind his spectacles, a wicked impulse seizes him, mirth spreads across his face like dawn. He raises his hand, meets my eye, dares me to dare him, and flattens the bridge.

The Israelis must have shot or arrested someone on the West Bank. The mood in the American Colony is foul.

I return from Yekutieli and find Ros writing in the bar, black as death. She signals to me to be careful, to watch what I say — not in a manner of speaking, but literally, to mind my back.

She nods in the direction of a barman I have not seen before. He's the one I have to watch.

'From Amman,' Ros whispers. 'Out of control. Starts on every Arab who comes in. What the Jews have done. What the Jews are doing. What the Jews will always do.'

I risk looking at him. He's darker than the others. A deep brown shining man, glistening with perspiration. 'He's a chocolatey bugger,' I say.

I mean to be appreciative. I like chocolate.

'Shh! He's very brittle. No milk, no fruit, no nuts, just bitter black chocolate.'

He's haranguing a Palestinian. I can't hear what he's saying. Ros is the one with the ears. She whispers his words to me, like a translator at the United Nations — also never much of a friend to Israel.

'It is finished. Maybe one year, maybe more. Who knows, maybe even five if we're lucky. But he who can read, can see it. It is over, over for us . . .'

'What is?'

'Shh! . . . the Jews, the Jews, they will come and they will never stop. They will settle where they want. The settlers *are* the government. They are the arm of the government. There will be no peace. Never. We are finished. They will come in their thousands of thousands and they will throw us out of our homes and they will fuck us and they will destroy us . . .'

'Fuck us? Does he actually mean fuck them or just fuck them up?'

'He's been ranting about rape all afternoon. How not one Arab woman will be safe.'

'That's bullshit,' I say, 'Jews don't rape.'

Ros throws me a woman's look.

'I mean it. It's not something we do. It's not subtle enough. We like to win by our wits. Even when the contest is sex.'

I should have said, especially when the contest is sex.

It is December 24th. Not a big day in modern Israel. Not a holy day. No meteor in the sky. Nobody drunk on the streets.

I, though, have my side of the bargain to keep. Let it never be said of a Jew that he would keep a Catholic from her cravings. But let Ros tell it her way, lest it be said of a Jew that he would hog all the mysteries.

Enough that we *invented* Christianity.

It had finally come to pass that I was on my way to Manger Square in Bethlehem on Christmas Eve to be present at the ultimate in Midnight Masses; and though I had long long ago last thought of such a pilgrimage, those long ago imaginings were sort of coming true even as they sort of weren't.

Gathered in the foyer of the American Colony Hotel, waiting for our bus passes and our security cards and our armed escort, we passed the time before we ploughed in convoy deep into the Intifada night, munching on gingerbread men from beneath Christmas trees dusted with icing-sugar and hung with apples and oranges and distant desert night silver stars.

Being a prohibition on a Jew's arm is not exactly a novel experience. I certainly didn't need to travel to find out what that feels like. Place yourself on any Jew's arm any place among Jews and that's what you become – a prohibition. But given I wanted a holiday, how could I stay behind in wintry London? In the end, it was images from my childhood of Christmas in Bethlehem that got me seated on the bus – once we'd all been counted and then counted again – and as we drove off the staff waved and called, 'Happy Christmas, my dears, happy Christmas, my dears.' It was beginning to feel a lot like Christmas.

Not very far down the road, we turned into a depot swarming with soldiers holding carnations in their other hands. We did as we were bid and left the bus to queue for a security check. Once through the machine without incident, we were each handed a carnation and a sticker in red and white, wishing us Season's Greetings from the Ministry of Tourism, Jerusalem Region. And then we boarded the bus, were head-counted, security-pass-checked, and with soldiers and machine-guns in place, we were once more on our way to Manger Square.

The night blackened. The villages we drove through were under curfew. Closed. Only army patrols out. Shops had transformed themselves into shuttered jails, having taken themselves into custody for the night. But we were informed that on this Christmas Eve the businesses on Manger Square would open by way of an experiment. Hamas, the Islamic Resistance Movement, had threatened reprisals against all Palestinians who broke the self-imposed business curfew, but this Christmas Eve was to see a quiet rebellion by local traders, and when we quit the bus and queued to enter the square through a security check-point and metal-detector, we found ourselves surrounded on all sides by bustling restaurants and gift-shops, atop all of which flapped army tents, searchlights and more machine-guns.

It was a cold night. We made for the inn, and finding plenty of room we settled down to felafel and white wine. I couldn't make up my mind whether I was in East Berlin or Melbourne. I decided East Berlin on the unlit streets, Melbourne inside the restaurant; but since I was certain Mahmoud was out there, in Manger Square, I felt it was time to face up to Palestine.

'OK,' I remember I said, 'let's walk out into it and say hello to Mahmoud.'

We walked out into the centre of the square and said hello to Mahmoud.

'Mahmoud,' I laughed, 'what took you so long? We've been here since 8.30. I was beginning to think we'd missed you.' And then, in a fit of bad faith, I laughed, 'I trust you are well paid to follow us?'

Ho, ho, ho. We all laughed in jolly Christmas spirit. Ho. Ho. Ho.

Mahmoud had a twist tonight between his horse-hair eyebrows. Behind him, twenty-five palmy Solomon Islanders carolled 'all is calm, all is bright' in the crisp night. But he wasn't in the mood to listen. There was something he needed to say.

'Rosalin, I want to tell you about myself. When I was young I was the PLO boss of my village. Finally I went to jail for three years. I was educated there. A good man, a professor, taught me how to think. He showed me what to read. Now I am no longer in the PLO, for me it is not the way. The way lies through education. Prison changed my life. Prison is a country, too, my dear. It is hard for us here. The Jews bayonet our babies and shoot them through the eyes. You must come to the village and see all things for yourself.'

As Mahmoud told of babies being shot in the eyes, his own began to water, mine narrowed and refused to ascertain what Howard was doing with his.

Now Mahmoud's mood became sentimentally playful, glazing the political point beneath. He bought me a PLO scarf. He wanted to place it on my head. I couldn't let him. I couldn't let him. I couldn't let him. Yes, I thought, jail has certainly changed his life, changed him, it seemed to me, into a lowly Mossad agent.

All I wanted now was to lose him.

Civilian desperadoes, wearing pistols high up on their hips, were pounding the square. Soon Christ would be born. Maybe it would be more like Christmas back in my room, with the Mass broadcast live on television.

We made our farewells – 'Until next time, Mahmoud' – and trudged off to the security-check and the bus. A sudden rage against, perhaps, myself made me accost a soldier. '*What* is this round my neck? *What* is it? *What* does it mean to you? *You* tell me its significance. *You* tell me why a Palestinian wants me to wear it,' I fumed.

The soldier, tall, fair and content, shrugged the smallest of shrugs and lied to me. 'That is nothing, just something the *Aravi* wear.' It sounded like 'Arabies'.

Later I discovered that only two years earlier it was an illegal act to wear just such a scarf in Israel.

Back in my room, with Howard snoring throughout, I watched Christ being born. In Bethlehem. On television. It was beginning to feel a lot like Christmas. There the altar and there the lace curtain and there the terrible exposure of the dark hole beneath the altar and there the baby doll in the wicker basket and there the scramble of priests on their knees, ripping and yanking the baby out of the blackness and there the priests kissing the doll and covering it with blankets and there the holding of it on high and then, suddenly sick of their sport, there the baby flung back into the black black hole.

Men.

Men and Mahmoud and Mossad and Moshiach and Ministers and Military Might and Midnight Mass.

Men.

It's still hard for a girl to get good Christmas, in Israel. Or anywhere else, for that matter.

And it's still hard for a boy to get good Wagner. When I ring the Israel Philharmonic to see how they are progressing with their problems they tell me they aren't. Bowing to immense public pressure – 'Why, in God's name, why?' – they have cancelled.

They have deep sleeves and long memories, the Israelis.

Seventeen

MESHUGGENERS

I have long known of the existence of a Stendhal Syndrome – that cluster of morbidities which boils down, at last, to finding art too beautiful to bear. But until I read the magazine section of the *Jerusalem Post*, I am unaware that a Jerusalem Syndrome has been diagnosed, the disorder being attributable, in this case, to religion rather than art, and manifesting itself not in fainting fits but the conviction that you are the son of God.

Professor Jordan M. Scher is responsible for the diagnosis, and after considerable difficulty tracking him down, I call on his practice, which is also his apartment, in a rising residential pyramid in Abu Tor, overlooking the Qidron Valley. Yet another of those natural quarries of bleached stone, whose beauty is so bare and God-forsaken that a permanent view of it must start to turn your mind.

I have to wander up several garden paths to find the Jerusalem House, and I have to bang and ring many times to gain admittance once I've found it. A moth-like person lets me in, then flits out of my vision. I am in a private lounge which doubles as a hospital ward. An emaciated figure is stretched out on a sofa-bed, receiving medication. Is his sleeve rolled up? Is he being given a syringe? Is he Arab or Israeli?

A flutter of hands shows me into Scher's office. Wicker desk. Wicker chairs. Books on psychiatry on the walls. Clay statuettes of unaccommodated man: a terracotta maquette of a woman crouching, a doubled-up African, millennia old in sensual knowledge. And from the music system, Mahler, very loud.

In one chair sits a Russian doctor, keeping his counsel. Professor Scher rises from his desk to greet me. A tall, rangy, craggy man, with undeterred grey hair and a mouth which, when he smiles, reminds me of Tony Curtis's. His head is large, lozenge shaped. He wears denims, blue jeans and a blue jacket, and a backwoodsman's shirt, open at the neck. He wears a big silver ring on each hand, and a gold bracelet round his wrist. It may well be a name bracelet. I look to see if it says Professor Jordan M. Scher MD, Ph.D., DABMH, DABPN, as it does on his notepaper, but my eyes aren't good enough. To match the gold bracelet, a gold chain adorns his throat.

I get the message. Professor Scher is a man you can relax with.

'I am a maverick,' he tells me.

It takes him a while to introduce me to the Russian doctor, who does not seem to be here for any reason. And even longer to turn down, and then turn off, the Mahler.

A Jewish boy with a scar across his right temple and eyes that he can barely open, comes in and out. He is wearing loose clothes – a yellow shirt, blue track-suit bottoms (a sort of pyjama?) – and on his third wander-through is given pills. Scher roots around for a few packets, says something to the Russian doctor, and dispenses. It's all cool. There's no hard and fast distinction between patient and doctor. I feel as if I've come to a very advanced experimental private school.

It doesn't take me long to work out that Jordan Scher is pleased to have me here. Not only does he not mind my notebook, he actually addresses it. He is in a battle with an ex-colleague over the very matter that has roused my interest – the Jerusalem Syndrome. He believes that this adversary has stolen his thunder rather – simultaneously failed to grasp for himself what the Jerusalem Syndrome is, *and* nicked Scher's ideas and gained publicity for himself with them. I am the opportunity for Scher to put a few things straight.

His adversary is Dr Yair Bar-El, director of Jerusalem's Kfar

Shaul Psychiatric Hospital. Acting on the advice of Dr Eli Witztum, a senior psychiatrist somewhere else, Bar-El rejected Scher's suggestion that a study of the Jerusalem Syndrome should be produced, arguing that no such thing exists. Blow me, if a couple of months later, Witztum doesn't turn up on the telly to talk about his and Dr Bar-El's version of the self-same syndrome. This they have the nerve to refer to as the 'true' Jerusalem Syndrome, which they see as a transient psychotic condition from which the fifty to two hundred people who suffer from it every year make a complete recovery.

'I told Bar-El,' Scher says, getting his mouth to curl wonderfully, 'that he had his head up his arse.'

'Right,' I say, 'I've got the politics. What's the syndrome?'

Scher does not accept the idea that it's a brand-new syndrome, or that it is to be understood as an example of reactive psychosis, a disorder which has no history but just crops up the first time the sufferer is in Jerusalem and then goes away again when he goes home. 'It's usually the case,' he says, 'that they've been very sick elsewhere for some period of time.'

This is the common way of it. A Jewish-American family sends its kid to Jerusalem in the hope that a period at *yeshiva* will help him get over his problems. He's over here precisely because there's already a psychotic disturbance. So the *yeshiva* takes him in, discovers he's too far gone, and puts him out on the street. There are Talmudic laws, they insist, that say some people are too sick to be allowed to learn religion. 'I say to the *yeshivot*, "Fine. Don't accept them. But once you have accepted them, don't just dump them on the streets." '

'Do they really do that?'

'They do. You see them on benches up and down Ben-Yehuda Street.' (That's what I've been doing – sitting on benches up and down Ben-Yehuda Street.) 'They're relatively benign characters most of the time. They rarely do harm. But they're very sick.'

'Don't their families come for them?'

'They do what the *yeshivot* do – they wash their hands of them. In the end they're just sent back. But why? Jerusalem's loaded with mentally ill people. Why send one back? Anybody should be allowed to stay if he's Jewish . . . and if he's crazy enough to want to stay.'

Scher is enjoying this. His eyes dance in his grey, lozenge face as he talks of the city being full of the crazed and the twitching and the deluded. I find his argument irresistible. Why pick on one poor *schmuck* just because he protests he is the Messiah too loudly?

I ask him about other religions. I take it it's not just the Jews who go to pieces here? No. The Christians go as well. 'The Christians have their own *mishegaas*,' he says. We talk about the Church of the Holy Sepulchre where people crawl on their bellies towards a hole into which they plunge a hand to touch the VERY ROCK WHERE . . . 'And it's all bullshit,' he says. 'Queen Helena just chose a spot. Whatever actually happened, happened outside the wall. But the experience can be too much for some. They've come from quiet suburban towns, and suddenly it's all here. If a problem already exists, if they feel empty or hopeless, they take on the personality of a great saint or leader.'

I think of Dorothea in *Middlemarch*. 'The weight of unintelligible Rome might lie easily on bright nymphs to whom it formed a background for the brilliant picnic of Anglo-foreign society; but Dorothea had no such defence against deep impressions . . . all this vast wreck of ambitious ideals, sensuous and spiritual, mixed confusedly with the signs of breathing forgetfulness and degradation, at first jarred her as with an electric shock . . .' And this is just recent little Rome. How would Dorothea have coped with Jerusalem, stripped to the bare rock by age and argument?

And Arabs?

'Yes, I believe Muslims have this condition too. But it comes out in different forms, depending on the political groups to which they're subjected. It can come out in the cry, *Itbah Ha-Yehud* – death to the Jews, slaughter them like animals.'

Itbah Ha-Yehud. I've heard that before. The Green woman. Is this all the Arabic Jews know in this city? Is this the only thought they fear Arabs have on their minds? Let's kill the Jews? Was that what Mahmoud thought every time he saw me?

It's possible.

On the subject of Arabs, Scher asks me if I have read Montesquieu's *Lettres Persanes*. He has a copy, as chance would have it, on his desk, beneath a large brass paperweight of a hand. He reads me an extract – page 215, Penguin edition – in which an Arab complains of the lethargy of his people, their energy for change and action sapped by their belief in Allah.

It's my impression that this is not just something he happens to be reading at the moment. This is his proof of the moral bankruptcy of the Arab nations, damned by one of their own. As if one couldn't do an equivalent job on the Jews with the help of almost any Jewish novelist one can think of.

Jordan Scher has been in Jerusalem for ten or twelve years. Before that he had a clinic in Chicago. Several hundred patients under his care. Then he decided to wander around a bit.

On a spiritual mission?

'No.' He laughs, rattling his jewellery. He can spot that I'm trying to lay a Jerusalem Syndrome on him. 'No. I suppose I came with a sort of spiritual inclination, but I'm not religious.'

He was director of the Jerusalem Drug-Abuse Centre for five years, then opened this clinic in his drawing-room.

'I started off with three Jerusalem Syndrome patients, two Messiahs and a Cabbalist.'

I refer again to his adversary, Dr Yair Bar-El – 'The name means Light-Son of God,' he tells me. 'Make what you like of that.'

Aside from once being his boss, Bar-El also faced him, acrimoniously I gather, across the court in the trial of Alan

Goodman in 1982. The Temple Mount shootings trial, no less. Bar-El was the prosecution psychiatrist. And Jordan Scher, of course, the shrink for the defence.

Alan Goodman was a thirty-eight-year-old American. He meant to liberate the Mount and become King of the Jews. He shot his way into the Dome of the Rock, killing a man, wounding others. A case of Jerusalem Syndrome if ever there was one. But – for political reasons, Scher is sure: because a Jew could not be seen to be let off the charge of shooting Arabs lightly – the three judges declared him to be responsible for his actions, that is to say, sane.

'He was a psychotic. No doubt about it. I argued his condition for eight solid hours. But he rots in Ramla to this day, sitting in his faeces. After leaving America he'd been wandering around Europe for ten years, looking for the perfect woman. But he was always beaten to her, he believed, by Arabs. So he came to Israel. Managed to get himself into the army, where his disturbance went unnoticed and he was given a machine-gun. And one night, after a bottle of something strong, he decided to liberate the Mount.

'As it happens, I went to the same school he did. A high school for very bright young men. While I was diagnosing him, after the shootings, I got him to draw a picture of himself. Then I got him to draw a picture of God. There was no difference. "They look pretty much the same," I said. "So you noticed too," he replied.'

We laugh over the impeccable logic of the loopy.

'I've a story to tell you,' Scher tells me. 'You'll like this. It's cute. Somewhere towards the end of my eighth hour of testimony, one of the three judges decided to take me on. "Let me clear this up," he says. "Dr Scher, do you think you're special?" He wanted to paint me as nutty as my client. "No, I'm a doctor." "So why are you here? You had a successful practice in America – what brought you to Jerusalem?" "I'm here because

I'm Jewish. Aren't Jews supposed to come to Israel?" Later, that judge left the bar. Went beserk. And threw himself off a mountain.'

A so-who's-the-nutter story.

Jordan Scher's lip curls. He plays with a ring. He is amused, victorious. Our eyes meet over all the madmen there are in Jerusalem. Not just the King of the Jews sitting in Ramla prison in his own faeces as a punishment for killing an Arab – the last word in Jerusalem Syndrome victims, declared sane by the authorities in this city of rabbis; but the authorities themselves, leaping from the tops of mountains; the head-bangers at the Wall; the haemophobics living on unleavened bread and cigarettes in Mea She'arim; the nuns on their bellies in the Church of the Holy Sepulchre, feeling through a hole for the place where, in ancient times, those feet . . .

At least with Stendhal Syndrome you just faint when the art gets too much for you: it's not a condition of the disorder that you *become* a painting. But once you start finding God in bricks and mortar there is no blessed relief you can look forward to in insensibility. This is what makes Jerusalem a sanatorium you are loath to leave – the patients are so animated.

Professor Jordan M. Scher rises from his desk, chinking. A rhinestone cowboy. All very well the denims and the Montesquieu and the primitive statuary, millennia old in sensual knowingness; but where's the poster saying You don't have to be mad to work here but it helps?

On our last night in Jerusalem we go to a Kahane demo.

A US court has just acquitted El Sayyid Nosair, an Egyptian boiler-tender, of the murder of Rabbi Meir Kahane in a Manhattan hotel in 1990. The *Jerusalem Post* calls the verdict 'stunning'. Veteran court observers, whoever they are, are said to be 'in shock'. Kahane's son, now leader of his father's militant Jewish

Defence League, has pronounced that 'the only punishment befitting the crime of this individual Nosair is death; therefore we vow that El Sayyid Nosair will not see a day without fear until his very last day . . . the day that justice and revenge will take hold of him. And then he will no longer be amongst the living.'

Euphemisms, euphemisms.

A Baruch Somebody-or-Other, speaking on behalf of Kahane's followers, has promised that 'if justice is not done, then a Jew will rise up who will do justice in this matter.'

But Alan Goodman is behind bars, sitting in his faeces.

In the meantime, while we wait for another one, the supporters of Kahane gather to make their feelings known in Kikkar Zion, a square at the foot of a bank near Ben-Yehuda Street, where I have enjoyed the ingathered Russian buskers.

The police are out in numbers. And not always in uniform, if I am right about some of the more conspicuous loungers who watch you very carefully when they think you're not watching them. The first Kahane members to arrive are the children, Kahane kids carrying leaflets and fly-posters and bundles of T-shirts which they offer for sale. Neither Ros nor I can think of anyone we would like to buy one for. It's a sign of our age: we just don't know people who like to wear a clenched fist in a Star of David on their chests.

I scrutinize the Kahane kids to see if they look different from non-Kahane kids. There seem to be no distinguishing features. They are just kids. And kids can be persuaded to believe anything. All that's remarkable is how many of them are fair-haired. Make what you like of that, as Jordan Scher would say.

We gather in a triangular corner of pavement, where there are benches for resting and spaces for idling. There are more police than onlookers, and more onlookers than demonstrators. Unless the plain-clothes policemen are in fact plain-clothes Kahanes.

Without warning, without apparent reason, something cold runs over me. One moment I am dry, the next I am running with icy sweat. I look around and realize I am being stared at – no, empierced, skewered – by my enemy, the Green woman from the Israel Center. Our eyes lock, like two mirrors in Iceland.

She is more of a nun tonight. She wears a scarf tied snood-like over her hair, and a long, grey clerical skirt, with a tiny split, forked like the Devil's tongue. Her face is white and angry. She circles me. Wide circles. Not little eddies, but whirlpools. I circle her. Her circle narrows. Mine widens. Soon our circles will intersect. She points me out to some of her Kach companions. I point her out to my wife. The two camps glare at each other. I have icicles, like acupuncture needles, in my spine.

People are trying out speakers. There are perfunctory collections. Kids hand out broadsheets. The police mingle more closely with us. I lose the Green woman in the crowd.

I circulate while Ros hangs back, watching out for my exposed shoulder-blades, as usual. A figure in rabbinical black, but somehow without rabbinical austerity, sits on one of the benches, writing. The incongruence is striking. I take him to be a reporter, though I cannot for the life of me imagine what his paper is. I sit next to him, starting at the far end of the bench and edging closer, hoping to steal a look at his copy. I make him self-conscious. He closes his pad – though not before I have glimpsed English – and says something to me in Hebrew, and then, quickly, in English, 'Are you visiting, too?'

I say yes.

He tells me he is writing a diary of his Jerusalem experiences for his wife, who is not with him. He has pale, gingery skin. Designer, rather than Hasidic, stubble. (Though the designer has been influenced by Hasids.) And a quick, nervous way of talking which I recognize, without any prompting, as originating from Manchester. In a trice I am in possession of his name – Chaim Ulman –his wife's name, his wife's father's name (a distinguished religious one, as it happens) and his occupation. 'Accountant.'

'I thought you were a journalist,' I tell him.

'Me? No. I'm ashamed of this.' He covers the closed notebook with his open hands. He changes the subject. It is a gift. He can move fast over surfaces, like a dragonfly. 'So where are you from?'

'Manchester, like you. Can't you tell?'

'What's your name?'

I tell him.

He frowns. Then, 'You're not the famous one? With the father who drives a taxi?'

'Did. He doesn't drive much any more.'

'So what are you doing here?'

'In Jerusalem?'

'At a Kahane demonstration. I thought you were a weak-kneed woolly liberal.'

'Me? No.' I remember what I was called in Silwan, the last time I saw people wearing fists and *Mogen Dovids* on their chests. 'I'm a Fascist.'

He looks me over. Under his black homburg he has a young face. The clothes are an old man's, but the eyes are a boy's. He doesn't believe me about being a Fascist. He shakes his head. 'I could have sworn you were a liberal. Anyway' – he pushes a Kahane newsletter at me – 'give me your autograph.'

'I can't sign that. Someone will think I'm endorsing it.'

'Write that you're not. Disclaim it. Anyway, what's wrong with it? I agree with them a bit. Not everything. But just sign. Go on. For my wife. But don't write anything indecent. She won't like it.'

I sign. In a space that is the furthest I can find from incriminating Kahane propaganda.

He holds the signature up to his face. 'Is that yours?'

'Of course it's mine. You just saw me write it.'

'I don't often meet famous people. Wait till I show my wife. Anyway, what do you write? I don't read *goyische* books.'

'I don't write *goyische* books.'

There is a noise in the crowd. Excitement. And cries, war chants – 'Kahane! Kahane! Kahane!' The syllables broken up, ka, ha, ner, as though the mute are learning to make sounds.

'The great man has arrived,' Chaim tells me.

I see a lean, dark boy, the son of Kahane, being led like a dignitary at a flower show up the steps to the forecourt of Hapoalim bank, which is serving as a stage. A man in a beret – the headgear of mad orators the world over – begins a peroration. I don't have the language but I can detect the cadences of immoderacy and unreason. You can squint-read the *Spectator* on the same principle.

'So what are you *potchkehing* around for?' Chaim asks me. 'What are you messing at?'

'I don't follow you.'

'What are you messing about writing books for? We've got a book. We've got the Torah. Isn't that enough? God gave us the Torah to keep Torah and do *mitzvot* – not to mess about.'

Despite the long black coat and the black hat, he's not a Hasid. More an undertaker. He wears a tie, knotted like a lawyer's under a stiff collar. A dead give-away. Hasids don't wear ties.

'And after Torah,' I say, 'there are to be no other books?'

'What for? Everything you need is in Torah.'

'If you believe it.'

'What do you mean *if* you believe it? How can you not believe it? God gave it.'

'How do you know?'

'Because He said so.'

'And what if you don't believe Him?'

He looks me up and down. He's restless. Impatient. But vaguely comic. As if he's doing this for fun, and thinks it's sporting of me to keep it up – this pretence of mine that I don't believe God's claim to be the sole author of the Torah.

'I suppose you go out with *shiksas*,' he says.

'All the time.'

'You don't!'

'And marry them.'

'You wouldn't!'

'I would. I do. I'm married to one now.'

'You're not!'

'I am. She's here somewhere.'

'In Jerusalem?'

'*Here.* At the Kahane demo.'

His next move is marvellous. Try as I might, I cannot render the smoothness of his transition. Like a fly on the surface of the water, one second he's here, the next he's there. And you don't see the journey.

'So you think the Palestinians should have Israel. You think we've no right to the country. Who would you say has the stronger claim?'

'I'm still on *shiksas*,' I say. 'In fact, I'm still on the Torah.'

But I interrupt myself – it's that sort of conversation, a Manchester conversation – to ask what the kook in the beret is saying. I take it Chaim knows Hebrew.

'A bit. But you're not interested. You're a woolly liberal who goes out with *shiksas*. What he's saying now is that Israel shouldn't be letting so many Russians in.'

'What! Isn't the whole point of Israel that it provides a home for every Jew? Right of Return.'

'Don't argue with me. I'm just an accountant. What he's saying is that we're not taking enough precautions to check that they're actually Jewish . . .'

'Oh no, we're not going to let a few non-Jews in by mistake, are we? Isn't that the Lubavitcher Rebbe's terror – that one day our children won't know whether they're marrying bona fide Jews or not?'

'I thought you wanted to know what this one's saying . . .'

'What's he saying?'

'He's attacking the Knesset for being weak. Now he's attacking the American legal system. Now he's attacking America . . .'

'And now – ?'

'Now he's saying it's an outrage that the lawyer who got the Egyptian off the charge of murdering Kahane is Jewish. What do you think?'

'I think it's wonderful when Jews win.'

'Then you should read the Torah.'

'I do read the Torah.'

'What for?'

'I like it.'

'How can you like it if you don't think God wrote it?'

'I like it precisely because God *didn't* write it. Things are more interesting when they're not divinely inspired.'

'Interesting? You find the Torah interesting?'

'Of course.'

'The Book of Numbers, interesting?'

He has changed sides, up-ended me completely. This is Talmudic.

'I didn't say it was *all* interesting.'

'None of it's interesting. It's only interesting if God wrote it.'

I stop him and get out my notebook. 'I want to be clear about this,' I say. 'You only find it interesting if . . .'

He stops me. 'If you're going to write this down, *I* want to get it right.' He clears his throat. Slows himself down. Scratches his head under his homburg. And says, 'If the Torah is a divinely inspired book, then I believe one can rationalize why it's unique. If it's a man-made book, then there's no reason to think it's better than any other.'

'You're happy with that? You're sure that's what you mean to say?'

'What do you mean, am I sure? Sure I'm sure.'

'Then I'm more holy than you,' I say. 'Because I start from the mediated word and find the truth when it blazes forth . . .'

'Don't argue with me,' he says. 'I'm just an accountant.'

As I rise from the bench and shake his hand, I notice that the Green woman has been standing behind me, watching me write in my notebook, and for all I know listening to every word I have said.

I mention this to Ros after the demo has broken up. We are taking a last walk up my favourite street.

'Put your head down, keep moving and say nothing,' is her reply.

'Was she following us?' I ask five minutes later, in the taxi.

'*She*? It was Mahmoud. I couldn't face seeing him again.'

'Was *he* following us?'

She thinks about it. 'Oh, probably not. Maybe he never was. Maybe we just kept wandering on to his patch. It's a small city. He probably just works the places most tourists with a political interest are likely to hang out.'

'You still think political?'

'Who can say? This is a hard country. He may just have been ordinarily opportunistic. But he was very frightened that first night. And if he has been turned, he must know Hamas will get him.'

We are not looking forward to leaving Jerusalem. Even though we've been frightened every day we have been here.

Let me have another go at that: because we've been frightened every day we have been here, we are not looking forward to leaving Jerusalem.

Eighteen

HOME FROM HOME

At a desk at the entrance to the breakfast-room of the Grand Beach Hotel, Tel Aviv, a young woman suffering from terminal tedium checks your keys against a room list so that no itinerant, no person staying at another hotel or sleeping on the beach in the howling gale, should sneak in to steal the baby-food which is on offer here in oval casseroles for Grand Beach Hotel guests only. Casseroles of cream, sour cream, sweet cream, curdled cream, cottage cheese, yoghurt dyed purple, yoghurt dyed canary yellow, casseroles of soft cheese cut into cubes, casseroles of what can only be chocolate semolina.

It is Saturday morning, and this is a *kosher* hotel, so no cooking has been done. Perhaps it will be better tomorrow. Perhaps tomorrow there will be green sausage and lilac herring.

The ceiling of the breakfast-room is lined with material resembling speaker covers on the dashboard of a motor car. On the wall at the far end of the room is a rudimentary Middle Eastern mosaic — domes and minarets and church towers: everything the Israelis do *not* build — for the delectation of Jewish guests from Mars. There seem to be Israelis here, spooning up their baby breakfasts, but where in Israel would they come from to stay in this hotel? And why?

Davening is going on in a small room to the side. The men are in it, breaking into occasional little patterns of melody of their own, but otherwise making sounds that could be the minutes of an office meeting speeded up. Still, they are doing it.

There is a *Shabbes* lift, waiting to whisk you clean out of

380

breakfast to your room without your having to press a button. How you then get into your *Shabbes* room I cannot guess.

Some of the waiters here are gay. One has a Kenneth Williams manner without the charm, the humour, the invention or the English. Mincing in Hebrew strikes me as unsavoury. He is in a mood, a *Shabbes* pet. He moves his little legs like compasses. He has a heavy, prophet's face, a flounce of grey hair, flung back, and difficulty stopping his lips betraying his disdain. He pushes the women guests around, enjoying moving them from the wrong tables to the right tables, although there is no meaning apparent to the straight world in this distinction.

An American couple in matching lavender T-shirts and gold medallions ask for coffee. 'Nescafé, do you have?' I've noticed this already in the coffee-shops in Tel Aviv. You are offered Nescafé.

The gay waiter encourages an elderly pair to sit at the table the lavender Nescafé-drinkers have taken. When they come back from the buffet with their bowls of mashed chocolate, they have nowhere to sit. Something like cheerfulness lights up the gay waiter's countenance. He trips back into the kitchens.

They are running out of tables. A man who lost his, while collecting his grated prunes, stands marooned in the middle of the room, a bowl of something runny in each hand, and nowhere to put them down. A queue has begun to form at the desk where you prove your identity. My waiter, Ivgenyi, tries not to see it. An expression of ineffable sadness clouds his pale eyes. In the queue, the face-pulling has begun – that terrible muscular garrulousness which my people can't resist and only Germaine Greer, among gentiles, can claim competence in. The exposure, at all costs, of one's emotions. One's exasperations made flesh. One's temper made manifest. Under no circumstances, a private domain of the feelings. Feel contemptuous – roll an eye. Feel wronged – drop a lip. Prayer is noisy and public in this country, and so is judgement.

A gay waiter who looks like Walter Matthau gets in the lift with me, carrying a tray of black *crème fraîche*. There are staff shortages in the hotel. 'Room service now!' he says. 'Now I do room service! I tell the boss – but last month no business, so this month no waiters.' He goes to slap the side of his head before remembering that he's carrying a tray.

Yesterday, on our numbed arrival, we sat in the lounge watching the rain come in, the doors bang, the heat escape into the street, the sand blow. A gale howled, screamed and yelped down the canyon which this building has helped to create. The sea itself was quiet; only between the hotels was there this maelstrom.

There are carpets on the walls of this hotel. Paintings, for sale since the Crusaders were here, hang crookedly or upside down. A Rules of the Tavern poster, printed on fake parchment, bought in Tintagel, enjoys prominence by the reception desk. The building feels as if it could easily blow down. The windows shake. Shiver. Leak. Drip. 'You can smell the concrete cancer,' Ros says.

Sometimes it just falls out this way: you take a part to represent the whole. Synecdoche of the soul. I chose the Grand Beach Hotel to stand for Tel Aviv.

I am purposeless in Tel Aviv. I want it to come at me. But it's Saturday. Not closed down exactly. Tel Aviv has not let the rabbis bully it. But closed down enough, for all the secular braggadocio.

If Jerusalem is the spirit of Israel, they say, Tel Aviv is the body. So where is the body?

For want of anything else to do, we take a taxi to Jaffa, the old sea port out of which Tel Aviv originally grew. Jaffa's been going a long time – 'perhaps the oldest port in the world', but now empty-hearted, according to my oafishly anti-Zionist, anti-

Israeli, anti-whatever-isn't-Palestinian, slavishly PC *Rough Guide to Israel and the Occupied Territories* – and has suffered more conquests than the Grand Beach Hotel has served cold breakfasts. When Ben-Gurion saw it he said it was worse than Plonsk. Now it has succumbed to tourists who like their Araby sentimental, and intellectuals from Tel Aviv who come to taste French-dressed sea wolf and grouper in sight of the sea that spawned them.

We do the same – why not? – in a restaurant that has paper cloths on the tables, and coloured crayons in a little glass, so that you can doodle while you're waiting. Crayolas, they are called: blue, green, brown, orange, purple – all the colours of the pap and squelch and junket we ate this morning. We sit, with no stomach for the Crayolas, watching the sea mounting the harbour wall, listening to sub-Abba popular music arranged for a people who have lost their culture. 'We don't know where we come from/We don't know who we are.'

Fish arrive, big enough to have eaten us when they were alive. We pick sullenly at the bones. What we really wanted was tabbouleh, chick-peas, pitta bread and Turkish coffee. We stare out of the window. Square in our vision is a jumble of rocks, a pile of stones, assembled without grace to buttress the harbour wall. And the issue is – as it has been since we arrived – what harmony, what elegance, what flair for the look of things, have my people brought back to this country from which they were once expelled? Because I fear, sitting before my glass of Crayolas in Jaffa, listening to the under-Abba, that they lose in every department, and that they have acted as vandals, building the wrong buildings, serving the wrong food, singing the wrong songs, thinking the wrong thoughts.

The crass *Rough Guide* would see the vandalism as a wanton, politically motivated destruction of Arab culture. This is to take the short view of the tragedy. When one learns that the boarded-up mosque on the main road between Jaffa and Tel Aviv might yet become a night-club, it is Israeli insensitivity to its *own* past that one laments.

While we are climbing back up to old Jaffa – Omar Khayyamed and Aladdinized now, for gewgaw hunters – Ros finds a camera. We decide to take it to the police station. I let her go in alone. Least I can do after failing to deliver a good Midnight Mass in Manger Square. I stand on the street outside, wishing there were some *frummies* to look at, when I hear panic break out in the station. *Bomba! Bomba! Bomba!*

When she comes out, some considerable time later, Ros tells me that the moment she produced the camera police officers began throwing themselves under tables and heading for exits.

'You're lucky,' I remark, 'that they didn't detonate you.'

'They nearly did. It was touch and go whether I spent the night in the cells.'

'You'd have had a more comfortable bed.'

'And a better breakfast ... I'm telling you, it was touch and go. They asked me my name a dozen times, and my address, and where I'm staying in Tel Aviv, and your name, and where I was born. It's just a tourist camera, I said. I found it underneath a lamp-post. And the next time I find one I'll leave it there. And no, I won't tell you how much money I've got in the bank *or* how old I am. Never again.'

'I suppose they're checking us out against the information Mahmoud gave them, this very minute,' I say.

But another thought has occurred to Ros. 'What if it *was* a bomb?' she suddenly wonders.

'Surely they checked while you were in there?'

'They did. They got me to point it at myself and take my own picture. But ... you never know. Now I'm terrified I've blown up the Old Jaffa police station. I won't be able to sleep tonight. Maybe I'll go back in the morning to see if they're OK.'

We don't say what we both know – that it'll be too late by then.

*   *   *

'Madam, the next time I come I do not give you service – I call the manager. All the time the same problem. Madam, I do not have time for this.'

Sol, the drinks waitress working the lobby of the Grand Beach, does not have time for anything. Her argument with the woman who does not want to pay for her brandy because she has already paid for a cup of tea, has been going on an hour. And she keeps another dozen such differences alive, without once forgetting who she's fighting over what. She goes from table to table, from trouble spot to trouble spot, her shoulders rolling like an American footballer's, telling each the problems she's having with the others. They should use her to negotiate with the Arabs. Not since Kissinger was last operative here, has such high-speed diplomacy been seen.

She is tall, slim, dark, not wearing much under a mustard pinafore. In between drink orders she slips into a small, screened kitchen area and lights up a fag. Whether she also takes a swig, we can't be sure. She doesn't so much walk across the lobby as shuffle. Because I have an eye for such details, I notice she is wearing a gold ankle-bracelet under her stockings. A nice touch with the red moccasins.

It goes with the job and the establishment that her mouth should turn down, 'but at least she has a clear brow', Ros observes. The first limpid thing either of us has found in Tel Aviv – Sol's temples.

We glow at her every time we order a drink, just so she shouldn't think we are demanding. As a consequence of which she gives us ten seconds of her time. 'I like very much my job in the lobby, but sometimes it is too much. And do you know how old I am? Don't compliment me. No . . . No . . . more. I am forty-two. True.'

She bows. The Cyd Charisse of Grand Beach.

I take a break from this, it being Saturday night, and leave Sol to Ros. I walk the boulevards, HaYarkon, Allenby, Dizengoff,

385

to see my people milling secularly in their own city; to enjoy the outdoor cafés, though it's a touch wet and blowy for sitting out; and to feel *safe*. For no one can hurt me here, can they? No one can threaten me or steal from me, for I will say, 'Hold it – I'm a Jewish boy, you're a Jewish boy,' and that'll be that. This may sound naive, but it's how I feel. There are no dangers on these streets. I have never felt frightened by a Jew in my life, and these are all Jews. Therefore . . .

And I *am* safe, and the crowds *do* secularly throng, and there's so little either to fear or to notice that I might as well be in Leeds.

The faces do not come at you as they do in Jerusalem, there's the difference; they don't come bearing their histories, their disparate misfortunes and adventures. They are just the faces of nice kids, coupled. Everyone seems to be coupled. You've got an arm, you put someone on it. I will take the good tidings back with me to England. I have seen the couples parade up and down Dizengoff and can report that the Jewish family is safe. Bored, but safe.

Only once do I think I want to live here. That is when I run into a theatre crowd coming out of a Hebrew play. At the foot of the iron fire-escape down which they make their exit, a man with a bicycle is waiting, selling bagels from the basket on his handlebars. Freshly baked, warm bagels. You do not get this when you come out of the National. Almost everyone buys. Only those in fur coats (women) and pony-tails (men) resist. Otherwise it's play, pavement, shekels, bagel, perambulation and home.

My solitary pang of envy for the life of Tel Aviv.

I turn off into a side street and walk at once into inexplicable shouting and groups of people staring. What it is, when I approach, or when it approaches me, is an old blind man yelling at his guide-dog, cursing it in Hebrew, absolutely at the end of his tether with it, and pulling it in the direction *he*, the blind man, wants to go.

Where else but in a Jewish country would you find the blind arguing the way with the sighted? If I go on walking I am confident I will come upon the deaf shouting at their ear-trumpets, and the lame trying to go in opposite directions to their wheelchairs.

The Israel Philharmonic has, after all, played Wagner!

They did it while we were not looking, behind closed doors, to an audience of six hundred let into the auditorium through a side entrance. The six hundred comprised 'friends' of musicians and officials. Barenboim did not wear his dinner suit. The performance was not a performance but a rehearsal.

'Why, in God's name, why?' I ask Ros as we sit reading the newspapers on our second morning at the Grand Beach Hotel.

She thinks I'm referring to the breakfast. Scrambled egg is the one cooked meal that has been added to the uncooked *Shabbes* selection, except that there is no egg where the egg should be, until a huge woman in a filthy white kitchen coat, through which you can see her giant black bikini briefs, comes out blowing bubble-gum, fills up the dish, stirs it around and sticks her finger in it.

The gay waiters, who work to their own calendar of moods, are gay this morning. But the guests are not. 'No food, no fish, no nothing,' I hear one complain, 'and even the nothing you take away before we've finished.'

I look to see who's copping the complaint. It's Sol, in her red moccasins. 'I only work here,' she snaps. It's barely ten a.m. and she is back at war already.

The Walter Matthau waiter takes an unused but much-fingered bread roll from a departed guest's side plate and tosses it over our heads clean into the fresh bread basket by the buffet. The other waiters clap him. He tugs his dyed fringe and skips off whistling into the kitchens.

While Ros is occupied filling out a formal letter of complaint at the Government Tourist Office in Sholem Aleichem Street – 'If the Grand Beach Hotel is four stars, what's a one-star like?' – I am falling in love with the name of the director of Belmar Tours Ltd, next door. The name, and I whisper it, is Bathseba Solowiejczyk. In itself an ingathering of the dispersed Jewish nation.

I am talking to Bathseba Solowiejczyk because the Government Tourist Office has suggested her as the person to consult in the matter of changing our hotel. It's a bit late for that. We have decided to change the city.

'As a person,' Bathseba Solowiejczyk says, 'I don't like it that you should be uncomfortable. And as a Zionist I don't like it that you should write badly of Tel Aviv or Israel.'

I explain to her that she has already half-saved Tel Aviv.

She goes with her name. Is the age and condition men of my generation admire. Not young, not thin, not diffident, not unpainted.

Her antecedents are Russian and Polish. The family trawled the world looking for somewhere to settle. Time in Belgium. Time in Cuba. And now Israel. She has been here for twenty-five years.

'Ah, you're so lucky,' I say. 'My lot have been stuck in Manchester for generations.'

She pulls a face. Shows the fullness of her lips, and the brightness, the burning blackness, of her eyes. '*You're* the lucky one,' she reminds me.

She leads me on, the way Bathsebas have always led men on, to the subject of inspiration. What a writer needs. The light in Jerusalem in the early evening. The talk in the bar of the American Colony, about my having stayed in which she is not without attitude.

'Tel Aviv is a good city if you're young,' she says. 'If you want to go out. And it's good for business . . . and I'm in business.'

I have no trouble with this.

We agree that if I'm to stay in Tel Aviv I should come to her and say, 'Bathseba, help me,' and she will.

'Like Israel,' she says as I leave.

She calls after me, a confident woman's voice, a voice of all the continents, a voice rich with the humour of business, its freedom from the pinched concerns of politics and intellectualism – 'And have good inspirations!'

The newspapers are full of *olim* stories. *Olim* are immigrants. Literally, those who have come 'up'. When you emigrate from Israel, you are said to have gone 'down'. So it's not unlike Oxford and Cambridge.

A study of recently arrived Ethiopian *olim* has shown that they suffer 'severe psychopathological symptoms such as anxiety, depression, psychosomatic illness, nightmares and insomnia'. The very same symptoms Ros described on her complaint form as attributable to a night in the Grand Beach Hotel. An inordinate number of suicides among the Ethiopian community is also reported. One of the reasons put forward for this is the dismay felt by many Ethiopians at the time it is taking the Jewish Agency to bring their families over from Addis Ababa. The hand of the rabbi is to be discerned here. Fear that asylum-seekers may not really be Jewish. *Nisht do gedacht!* The country will be swimming in gentile seed next.

Meanwhile a boatload of Russian *olim* has arrived seasick and complaining in Haifa. They are said to be 'tired, confused and angry'. One of the things they are angry with is the water. They didn't expect waves. Officials at Odessa were anti-Semitic. The sea was anti-Semitic. Luggage had spilled open on board. Absorption Centres were not ready for them. And this is day one.

I decide to spend my last morning in Tel Aviv talking to someone who is *olim*-wise, and find Leysa Shtane, employed in a sort of social-worker to *olim* capacity by RATZ, a small left-wing party with five seats in the Knesset.

She is from Estonia – a Balt, like me. Beautiful, if you forget Bathseba Solowiejczyk. Ballet-dancer beautiful, fine-boned, thin-skinned, with a shockingly fleshy mouth, given the overall spareness. She greets me quizzically, through large rose-tinted spectacles, in a room that reminds me of school. Two Russian women are sitting behind tables, arranged as though for an informal seminar, waiting to give advice to *olim* in distress. One is grand and slavic, with points to her cheek-bones, the other is much darker and more inward, Persian-looking. They are both dressed in the high indolent Russian manner, as if for a day on the cuticles at Nina's Nails on 43rd Street. But it is Leysa, in a striped jumper and jeans and running shoes, you would choose to fight for your rights.

There are no preliminaries, no pleasantries, the indignation boils over at once. 'It is usual for Jews in Soviet Union to be highly educated. We had some status. We had interesting jobs. And for Soviet Union it's another mentality. Jobs is everything, jobs was only thing in your life. Now, person comes here – he has emigration shock. He is renting a flat. It is a little bit shock too. Now all our money we are paying for flat. Usually *olim* don't know sense of agreement when they are signing . . . What kind of job they can find? Cleaning for woman. For man it is usually something connected with muscular force. For me, I was cleaning houses of rich people. I'm philologist and I'm cleaning houses of rich people. It didn't matter to me. It was interesting. An experience. I didn't feel it was the end. I'm young enough to believe I would be able to change it. It wasn't psychologically damaging. But for many it can be. Many people are in very high depression. Very many cases of suicide.'

She talks with her wrists. They are pale and very thin. Barely thicker than my thumbs. The two dressed-up Russian women watch her from behind their powder, as fascinated as I am. She is like some brilliant, talking bird.

'Many *olim* who were Zionists become anti-Semitists. They begin to hate Israel. Here they see Israelis not on same level. At home we were on same level, here they have connection with people they did not have connection with in Soviet Union. And they think this is a model of Israel. They are mixing with people they find dirty, who can't sit still on the bus, who scratch, who can't see beauty . . . common people not on their level. Market people who dismiss them, owners of flats, bureaucrats. In common mind we come from wild, wild country. They think we know nothing. These are the people they are getting their ideas of Israel from. Now, *olim* are living in Russian ghetto. All his books are in luggage which is waiting for more than year. So only reading newspaper. Russian *olim* are reading people. We have to read all the time. So we read papers, and it's all depressive.'

'Where are Russian *olim* going to meet Israelis they get on with and like?' I ask.

'Nowhere,' she snaps. Then remembers herself. 'I try to find these moments of connection. I am arranging Russian journalists to meet Israeli journalists, Russian philologists to meet Israeli philologists – at Beersheba University. Even if they don't get job they will get professional company. It is very important to feel equal among equals. And for me to show there is another Israel out there, not just the Israel they read about in paper, or meet in market, where they're abused. Give them an Israel that is equal to their aspiration and their imagining of the place. Otherwise they all become anti-Semitists.'

'So what about you?' I ask. 'Are you sorry you came?'

She shakes her head. 'It's a hard place . . . but it's only place where I'd never hear "Bloody Jew". I feel here very good emotionally. My economical situation is very bad, but emotionally I am very happy. From the first day I have felt myself like a person, like a human being. My son like it here. His teacher love him very much. He is only child with blue eyes in class. When he made something his teacher began to kiss him. That was enough for me – I am mother!'

A grave, grey Russian, carrying a music or a document case, arrives to talk to her. He waits on a little rickety school chair, lost, disconsolate, locked away in his thoughts, in his language.

Leysa Shtane moves closer to me, a dying swan, and lowers her voice. 'That one . . . The Israelis have made him a citizen of Nowhere. He is the father of a Jewish son. His wife is Jewish, he is not. But his wife stays in Soviet Union. Now the father is with his son in Tel Aviv but they won't let him stay because he is not Jewish. He cannot even get identity card, and without identity card he cannot travel. All he can do is go back to Soviet Union. But he does not want to leave son alone here because he is too young. While he is here, fighting to stay, he works. But he is not citizen of Israel and has no rights. He worked, the boss didn't pay, said, "Go away," and he cannot complain because he is not citizen. I'm sorry, but it's Fascistic. You have to be Jew to get an identity card?' Despite herself, her voice rises, shakes in her narrow chest. 'I'm sorry, it's Fascistic. I say to the authorities, "Man can change his wife every year – I'm sorry – but man can't change his son."

'And you know – this is very common. People who were most identified as Jews in Soviet Union, because of nose and father's name, here are not Jews. If their mothers are not Jews, they are not Jews. But in Soviet Union they were badly treated as Jews.'

The bane of her life, of the Russian *olim's* life, of my life, of everybody's life, are the Orthodox. He may not know it, this Russian gentile father of a Jewish son, lost in his thoughts in a school-room in Tel Aviv, but one of the authors of his misery is the Rebbe Menachem Schneerson, beavering away in Brooklyn to have barbed wire wound around the Law of Return, so that one of *them* should never slip through under the guise of one of *us*.

'The religious laws are easier on the wealthy,' she says. An argument poor Jews have been mounting since Moses. 'They have cars . . . But the *olim* is forced to stay at home on the days he has off, because no public transport. So, because of *Shabbat*, the *olim* is even more ghettoized.' Her face suddenly tightens. 'It is not so hard to become religious in Israel. Have you read Torah? It's a very cruel book. It's not difficult to understand why people believe it.'

The party she works for has been mounting a campaign against religious fanaticism. Some of the literature is lying around the room. Posters saying ENOUGH, showing buses, movement, freedom, obstructed by the black hat of the Orthodox. And there are more serious issues, not least the settlements. Leysa Shtane has been involved in bussing new immigrants around the settlements, so that they should see what the money that could be helping them is being wasted on instead.

'You know,' she says, reminding me that her time is limited, that the disconsolate gentile Russian is waiting to talk to her, 'problems of mixed marriage are very bad here. Proving a child Jewish, proving you are Jewish, is like going through Communist party again.'

'Too cruel,' I say, rising. 'Too cruel how things remain the same.'

She has a question for me before I go. More than a question – a catechism, a moral riddle, a mystery. She puts her whole body into sounding it. 'Tell me, how can a Jew – who has felt it with his skin' – she feels her own skin, runs her hands down her shoulders and her arms, shivers under her own touch – 'how can *he* forget how it feels to be treated intolerantly? A Jew – of all people!'

Nineteen

FROZEN BY THE CHOSEN

On the bus to Haifa I read a Haifa story.

A story of the Jewish heart and exclamation mark. A *haimisher* Haifa story.

It is the last-but-one day of the year. A man revisits a grove in Mount Carmel with his wife, the place where they first met. Then he leaves the car and shoots himself. His wife is called Michal. It turns out that her husband has left suicide notes. When she reads them she discovers he has requested that his organs be donated for transplant.

'He was always like that,' Michal says. 'A man who gave to others and not to himself!'

There are Germans in the Hotel Dvir in the heights of Haifa. Some sort of reunion is going on. Jews who knew one another in Germany before the unspeakable, the unthinkable, happened. Now they meet in Haifa every year, or maybe it's only every decade, to congratulate one another on survival. Many of them still employ their native tongue. The German speeches, the German toasts and jokes, ring oddly up here in Carmel. I stand on the balcony and look down to the magnificent sweep of bay and wonder if I'm on some sort of German Parnassus – Valhalla, if that's on a mountain.

There also happen to be two German guests – modern Germans, gentile Germans, international business Germans – having dinner here. One of them is so unhappy with the quality or mix of his tomato juice that he is close to weeping with rage. The other is sending a sequence of beers back. Too cold. *Zu kalt.* Still *zu kalt.* The waiter wonders whether there is a precise degree of cold the German requires: can he put a figure to it. The German puts a figure to it.

'These people are angry and insulted every second of their lives,' I say to Ros.

'Just like your people,' she says. 'No wonder you fought so bitterly with them.'

I am angry and insulted. 'We didn't fight,' I say. 'We loved them. They just didn't love us.'

'Maybe what's missing from both cultures,' Ros says, 'is the female influence. A moderating, ironic voice.'

Now I really am angry and insulted.

'*Scheisse!*' howls the German. His beer's too warm.

The weather in Israel has turned wild. Snow fell on Jerusalem the day after we left, bringing down power cables, closing roads and schools, forcing the Orthodox to protect their hats with polythene bags. Trees are down in the Upper Galilee. Army bases on the Golan Heights have been flooded. The Jordan Valley has seen its first snow for a quarter of a century.

The newspapers speak of worse to come. There's so intense an anticipation of natural disaster that meteorologists have been warning against an over-reaction – the weather will be 'severe but not unprecedented'. But how do you persuade a Jewish country that things are not going to be worse than they have ever been before? Preparations are on the scale of a major military operation. Now I know what it is to be in a country on a war footing. The navy in Haifa is reported to be battening its hatches. The air-force is taking special precautions to prevent flooding in the hangars housing the F–16s. Shoppers are panic-buying in the supermarkets.

Meanwhile, Haifa is wet and louring, though the air, to my London senses, is balmy.

I am in a pleasant, leafy part of town, in an area known as Hadar, half-way down the mountain. I have walked, preferring the thousands of steps, which sometimes seem to cut through people's private gardens, to the hairy zigzagging of the taxis. It's a wonderful, blowy day. Warm rain. Leaves turning to gluey Persian carpets beneath your feet. Your umbrella the shape of a Spanish inquisitor's cap. And the sea boiling below you.

Had I known Haifa was like this, I would have recommended it to Mahmoud. You want Perth? Go to Haifa. It's closer and almost as pretty. You can probably idle your life away as pleasantly in the one as in the other.

The only pity is that no Russian *olim* boat is expected. It would have been the ideal day to go and meet it. But no one knows when the next one's coming. Or *if* a next one's coming.

I am still in a sense on Russian business though. Leysa Shtane has passed me on to Yigal Amitai, a Russian journalist I am bound to like.

That's fine by me. I'll like him. And start liking him the moment he approaches me outside the Pevsner Apothecary where we've arranged to meet. He looks as though he's just risen from his typewriter. He has a mop of untidy hair, a big beard, and is wearing writing clothes, loose trousers, a work jumper that doesn't show the ink. His eyes are kind.

His flat is just across the road. He tells me we are in a suburb that was once exclusive. 'Still is,' I interrupt. Well, yes, but the wealthy have moved up the mountain, and now the area is home to many of the most recent wave of Russians making *aliyah*.

Yigal himself belongs to an earlier wave. He came in 1972, when he was sixteen. From Czernowitz, which is just a hop and a step from Kamenetz Podolsky. He was trained as an engineer, worked in educational theatre, worked for RATZ, and now works from home as a free-lance journalist.

Home is upsettingly homely, dense, hot, full of things, aromas, children playing Lego on the floor, Tamara. His wife, Tamara. I'm on a good run with names. Bathseba, Sol, Leysa, and now Tamara. I'm on a good run with vitality, too. Tamara has so much of it she is able to be in all the rooms of the apartment at once, and in the thick of all conversations. She may have tried once in her life to contain the animation in her face, but she doesn't try now. Her eyebrows arch, her lips part, she laughs, she interjects, she grimaces. She is older than Yigal. Not for a gentleman to say by how much, but by enough for me to like them the more for it. She has grey hair which she wears in two long braids, not unlike Lawrence Huerta, who made me the first of the English HoHoKams. These she plays with constantly, sometimes half-undoing one and then braiding it again. When you listen to her speak, you watch her plaits. Some people are radio only; Tamara is quadrophonic, full-colour, forty-inch television.

Because it is her husband I have come to see – I never knew of or even dreamt a Tamara before I saw her – she retires to the kitchen once we start talking. But she cannot stay there. The talk draws her out. She comes running back to add her view, then apologizes and withdraws, then comes running back again. I want her to stay. I want to hear what she has to say. No disrespect to Yigal, but I am a man and must always prefer talking to a woman. Besides, she not he is the Israeli. And I am short of Israelis to like.

Yigal tells me they are vegetarians. 'We eat biological food.' Hence the aroma. Beans on the hob. Herb tea in our cups. The apartment is bursting with knick-knacks, dolls, musical instruments, photographs (many of which are Zionist, pioneering in flavour) – objects of the heart, life histories – warmed by an Arab stove.

We talk generally, without direction, at first; about this and that, Haifa and its hopes that if there is peace with Syria it may

397

'open again and become an important junction as it was under the British'.

'What if Syria gives you the Egypt treatment,' I ask, 'and refuses to see why peace should make them suddenly love you and visit you?'

'You're talking about the "cold peace" with Egypt. Well, I have to tell you that a "cold peace" with Syria will do. Let me have it. I'll worry about warmth later.'

He has just been writing about the ironies of cooperation. The Israeli government accuses Peace Now of cooperating with Faisal Husseini and his people to undermine the security of Israel, whereas the truth is this – 'the real cooperation is between Gush Emunim, the settlers' movement, you know, and Hamas. It's a cooperation of extremism. A cooperation without agreement and without talk – but a cooperation for all that. They read each other.'

I hear the word read and I think the word write. I ask Yigal how long he's been a journalist.

'When this new wave of Russians came, I couldn't be on the side of what was happening. I wanted to write on matters of state and religion. When Russians came they made a kind of test of Israeli society. Systems go along quietly, then when something new comes, it shocks the system.'

So what's the particular shock the system's feeling at the moment? What questions has this most recent Russian *aliyah* jolted into life?

'The question of who is a Jew. It is ridiculous. The present situation is just ridiculous. Here you are not Jewish unless your mother was Jewish. If the prisoners of the Nazi camps would be in Israel today, sixty per cent of them would not be considered Jewish by Israeli civil law. Hitler was less particular. In Russia it is written in your passport "JEW" if your father was a Jew. And this man felt like a Jew. They said he was a Jew, his passport said he was a Jew, society saw him as a Jew – so he was a Jew. But he comes to Israel and suddenly he is not a Jew!'

Tamara pops her head around the door. 'They make what is natural to him unnatural,' she says. And goes away again.

'And it gets crazier,' Yigal continues. 'The wife of a Jew can come to Israel but her mother cannot. Her child can come, but he will not be a Jew when he does. If he wants to be a Jew he will have to be converted . . .'

'And you know what that means,' Tamara shouts from the kitchen.

'. . . circumcision. Sounds ridiculous, I know, but there are mass circumcisions going on here. You go to hospital and you line up.'

'You line up?'

'You line up.'

'And they do you in the line?'

'I don't know if they do you like that, but it's conveyor belt . . . You know, there are Russians dying here and being refused Jewish burial because they are not circumcised . . .'

Tamara cannot miss this. She flies in from the kitchen, a grey braid half-unwound. 'Unless,' she cries, 'and this is true, unless the families agree to circumcise the corpse.'

'We know a family, neighbours of ours,' Yigal says, 'who came here from Russia . . .'

'Who were *delighted* to come here,' Tamara says. 'They were proud Zionists –'

'But they had a son who died in a car crash in Germany. They arranged to have the body flown over to be buried here, but they were told he couldn't be buried here unless they gave consent for circumcision to be performed on the body . . .'

'Which they would not do,' Tamara tells me.

We stare at one another over these barbarisms – over herb tea, over the sound of the kids shouting about their Lego, here in a nice leafy suburb of Haifa, half-way up, half-way down Mount Carmel.

And we begin to talk about the Jewishification of Israel, the dire influence that religious Jews are having over life in a country which not so long ago did not mean by Israeli what Orthodox Jews mean by Jewish. Did not mean and did not mean to mean. 'I am much closer to a non-religious anyone than I am to a religious Jew,' Tamara says.

In relation to the Russians in particular, a vast hearts-and-minds struggle is going on. Yigal sees the new Russians as a bulwark against religious excesses; a wave of non-ideological intellectuals, hankering for western civilization. But the Orthodox, too, have their eyes on them.

'The trouble is that the Absorption Centres and such bodies are in the hands of the religious authorities,' Yigal says. 'They go to *ulpan* to learn Hebrew and they are met by rabbis who tell them that the reason Scuds fell here and not there was because the places where the religious lived were spared by God.'

'Certainly a powerful inducement,' I concede.

'And when they study Hebrew,' Tamara adds, 'they learn Jewish songs not Israeli songs. I never heard these songs. At school I learnt Israeli songs.'

She unwinds a plait. Both plaits. She is wearing black lipstick which is becoming patchy where her lips have come together in too violent an expression of secular passion.

'The Absorption Centres teach the very opposite of what was originally meant by Zionism,' Yigal says. 'Zionism did not mean being an observant Jew.'

'We were proud,' Tamara says – *were, were* – 'of being able to eat what we wanted, when we wanted. Of going where we wanted, when we wanted . . .'

I interrupt her. 'I take it they would argue,' I say, 'that to be as un-Jewish as that is not to be Jewish at all.'

She has arched a black-pencilled eyebrow at me more than once already. Now she arches them both. Jew Jew Jew, they say. A set to each eyebrow. Jew Jew Jew. Jew Jew Jew.

What she says with her mouth is barely less expressive.

'If I had to go to Africa I'd have to think I'm white – otherwise I never think about it. Same with being Jewish. I thought of Jews as being different from me in other countries. I didn't think I was like them. When they came to me and said their ancient "*shalom*", I didn't think they were part of me. Who won the Six-Day War?' She won't let me tell her. 'The Israelis. Not the Jews. I say to Jews, "Why are you proud of it? You're not Israeli."'

Yigal laughs. 'After the Yom Kippur War,' he says, 'which we didn't exactly win, then we said, "We the Jews". The less reason for national pride, the more Jewish we become.'

And now there is still less to be proud of. Yigal is scathing of those Russians – he calls them 'spiritual invalids' – who accept work in the occupied territories. 'On the economic side they say, "I'm not afraid, and anyway this is my chance to get job." On the moral side they say, "How can I judge what is happening – I've only been here a year?"'

Yigal is Russian; he has an immigrant's fear of Jewishness rampant. Tamara is Israeli; it is militant Orthodoxy's effect on the imaginative landscape of Israel that she regrets. 'There used to be names like Beth-el, taken from the Bible. They had poetry for me, these names. But now I hate them. They are the names of settlements.'

Funny how much more persuasive I find this sort of charge – diminution of language and all that – than the accusations of racism and the rest that fell trippingly at the bar of the American Colony. I say this to Tamara. I try to characterize all the Philips from Tunbridge Wells I met, come on expeditions of self-righteousness and spite.

There is a compliment to her in all this, but she doesn't care for it. 'Listen, Mr Jacobson,' she says, pointing a braid at me, 'if I weren't an Israeli, *I* wouldn't like Israel.'

I pay her the compliment whether she cares for it or not: seldom have I encountered a face less watchful or less concerned to register hurt or disagreement. Most faces are hungry. They want you to be careful, they want you to cede, they want you to be won. Tamara's just wants to get out of the kitchen and into the talk. Call it intellectual hedonism.

Just as I took the Grand Beach Hotel to stand for Tel Aviv, I toy with taking Tamara to stand for Israel.

Before I go, she tells me about her brother who has turned religious. Another one.

Suddenly?

On the surface suddenly, but . . . She makes a movement with her hands and plaits suggestive of lengthy inner turmoil.

They don't get on well now. How can they? Orthodoxy is a rejection of everything that isn't. That's what's so un-Jewish about it. It's a form of asceticism. The thing Christianity was invented to mop up.

'I must cover myself,' she says, showing me her naked wrists. 'And once Yigal noticed a spot on my blouse and flicked it off. "Modesty, modesty!" my brother had to remind us.'

'He won't come here,' Yigal says. 'Because there are dolls here – graven images. And Christian art.' Our eyes turn to a Piero della Francesca print on the wall. 'If he saw that he'd run out of the house . . .'

We all laugh. We are still laughing when we reach the front door. Tamara has already asked me about my wife, whether she is vegetarian, whether she is Jewish, whether she would like to visit them. Now, as I am leaving, she refers to her again. 'I am ashamed that your wife should hear such things,' she says.

And although I think I know what she means, I don't actually know what she means. What has been said that would be shaming if Ros hears but not if I hear? Israeli things? Neither of us is Israeli. Russian things? Neither of us – I'm a Litvak, remember – is Russian. It can only be Jewish things. It can only be things that Tamara is ashamed a gentile should hear.

Does that mean that she is more Jewish than she thinks is?

Intriguing.

402

Especially intriguing if I'm to take her as the part that represents the whole. Somewhere buried deep, are even the most secular and spiky Israelis still worried what the *goyim* think?

After a New Year's Eve never to remember in Haifa, with the rain coming down and coming in, and the sky ripped apart by lightning, and the US Navy on the streets, shaved as sharp as Scuds, looking for action, the poor bastards, and only *Bonanza* with Arabic subtitles to watch on Jordanian television, we make a fresh start the following day listening to carols sung in English on the radio in a flooded restaurant by the water in Acre – Akko to the Israelis – the Phoenician, Ptolemaic, Byzantine, Crusader city, fifteen miles around the bay from Haifa.

We're lucky to find anywhere open. It's been a violent night, and the sea hasn't finished yet. It froths over the rocks, like shaving foam, lathering the front steps of the waterfront cafés and bars. A handsome but heart-broken Arab sees us wandering in the spray and takes us in and prepares us wonderful Turkish coffee with freshly ground cardamom. The establishment is called Abu Christo and is owned by Israelis. The building is Ottoman. The nearby walls are Crusader. The waiter is Arab, the sea is the Mediterranean, the weather is Nature's and the voice on the radio is Julie Andrews's.

So, just which name do we give to the god of the storm in such a place?

The word is that relations between Israelis and Palestinians are good in and around Haifa. Many of the Arabs are Christian. They see themselves as Israelis, I've been told. Would want to be a part of any Israeli state, no matter what comes out of the peace negotiations. But on the streets of Akko, the Arab mood does not look so compliant and peaceable. It could be that no one had a good end to the old year. It is certainly the case that no one enjoys the first day of a new one. And the usual melancholy associated with this turn-round of time is compounded in Israel by the half-hearted response to a Christian-ized calendar system. Jewish New Year happened three-and-a-half months ago. I was in the Catskills at the time, throwing the crumbs of my sins into Kiamesha Lake. But whatever the reason for their grimness, grim the Palestinians are who pass us as we walk in the wet from new Akko to old Akko. Grim in their surveys of us, and grim, it would seem, in their hearts. Disfigured with distress, some of them. One has a mouth set in such a rictus of rage that his teeth show in a permanent grimace, actually protrude as a feature from his face.

In the old town, in the souks and the hidden squares, where we are encouraged to wander like tourists, we don't just feel we intrude, we do actually intrude; with mouths open and eyes wide – in admiration, of course, always in admiration – we brush by people's doors and windows. I stare into a woman's face and realize I am all but in her front room, where she is drying her hair. We interrupt families at breakfast. We collide with a couple in their pyjamas.

The food-markets are domestic. There is nothing here for us. But still we go gaping through. I watch the Arab traders, worn out and weary, no longer amused as coachloads of Germans photograph themselves in Palestinian scarves against a background of meat, Turkish sweets and the picturesqueness of somebody else's daily life. I don't see the Germans spend money. They just take photographs, borrow a child, borrow an adult, blind to the cold, dead, hapless stares of the people they're snapping.

In the souks of Jerusalem, where tourists are still seasonally stabbed, you take your chance in the vile routine of ingratiation and aggression, pimping and abuse. 'Jew, Jew, Jew,' they hurled after me, after I refused to meet the price of a Russian rag that had passingly taken Ros's fancy. That's the contract. Via Dolorosa or no Via Dolorosa, you quickly use up the charm of shopping there. Or you go back for the risk. Either way, you know the score. Here in old Akko, the terms of business, the Rules of the Tavern, have not been so clearly laid out, therefore the aggression is more muted. But in this very reticence the seeds of future troubles are being kept nice and warm.

As we are driving our little juggernaut of gasps and marvels through the narrow lanes, we meet, or are dragged into his crappy little shop by, Shlomo – 'the only Jew in the street'.

He's from Egypt, is wet-eyed, wears a torn astrakhan fez, and would very much appreciate it if we bought something. A Crusader's helmet. A pinky-greenish jade necklace. While we're seriously not thinking of buying anything, he busies himself with other customers who are seriously not thinking of buying anything either. He is master of all the European languages he is likely to need. In the ten minutes we're with him he shows himself fluent in French, Spanish, Italian, German and English. 'You should hear my Hebrew,' he says.

He asks us if we're from London. In that case, how well do we know Sotheby's? Can people buy at auctions and not pay at once? He's left some carpets at Sotheby's on his last visit to London, sold them, but not got all his money yet. Is that the way? We can't help him. Ah, well. He'll check it out himself when he's next over. He stays with his sister in Golders Green. Likes it in London, but finds the ice-cream too expensive.

He notices Ros noticing a picture of Schneerson, ripped out of a newspaper, pinned to his wall. 'A very blessed rabbi,' he says. 'A good man, who gives blessings. I like his face.'

Schneerson! In the souks of Akko! 'Why?' I ask. 'Why do you like his face?'

'He looks like a tiger.'

I ask if he has any trouble, being the only Jew in the street.

'No. I don't talk politics with Arabs. Just money and women. That doesn't get you into troubles. And everyone speaks it . . .' He pauses, a comedian: '. . . but money first.'

We leave him to his Crusader hats and languages.

But money first. Why, Shlomo? Why say it, even as a joke? It isn't funny. No one laughs. All it does is tighten the noose a little more. Round your own neck.

A custodian of the Al-Jazzar Mosque lets us in, although there are four or five Palestinians at prayer. It is an abandoned, not ecstatic, but self-abnegating ritual. They bow very low, many times. Almost flatten themselves. Almost fall. And privately, to their own rhythms and at their own speed. As at the Wailing Wall. There's no mistaking the family connections between the two faiths.

The emptiness of the mosque is good for the soul. A calming absence of furniture and idols. I think of the spaces the Jews pray in as spare, but this is picked to the bone. A carpet takes away the chill. In the middle of the chamber a bucket catches the drips. The worshippers are in their work clothes; they have interrupted their labours to pray a while.

There are snakes, though, in paradise. Not just us. Italians. Taking photographs. One moves in on the prayers. Drops to his knee. For one horrible moment it looks as though he's going to ask them to hold a salaam while he checks his shutter speed. He moves closer. His wife signals to him to withdraw. But a man with a good camera is hard to stop. Click. Click. Click. When the worshippers are finished, one of them turns on the Italian in fury. Only the absence of a common language prevents a common affray. But the Palestinian is beside himself with anger.

One more insult.

The condition of the old town itself is another. The skyline of domes and minarets and fortifications is famous. You buy postcards of it in Eilat. You search for it as you come round the bay from Haifa. It should be one of Israel's proudest possessions and resources. Yet it crumbles and leaks. One day it will just fall down. And people will wonder why the Palestinians are not looking cheerful.

Frozen by the Chosen

At the bus station, boys in Palestinian scarves stand around in circles spitting out sunflower seeds. I don't like the way they look at me. Or what they seem to be saying about my trench-coat. When they disperse there is a jagged circle of seeds where they have stood. Ros reckons you can tell what sort of conversation has taken place by the distribution of the husks.

So what sort of conversation was this?

Rancorous.

We are on the bus to Zefat, otherwise spelt Safad. There is no assurance that we'll get there. Zefat is high, already the country is wild, and snow is falling. I have my *Rough Guide to Everything That Isn't Israeli in Israel* open on my lap, and am arguing in my head with its titbits of complaint every time it points me out an Arab village; but the moment we reach Karmiel, a town that is all model new-Israeli, and I see a post-Holocaust statue (as I take it to be) in the town square – imploring figures, huddled masses, never again – I groan aloud. You can have too much of this. In truth you can have too much of it when you've not had very much at all. But I've had the great Holocaust museums of Jerusalem and Tel Aviv; to say nothing of the great Holocaust museums of the mind in London, Leeds, Llandudno, Long Island, Pico Boulevard.

It's not a question of needing never to forget. It's a question of liberating oneself from the museum. For that too is an incarceration.

So we get to Safad, or Sefad, or Zefat, or Zfat – pronounced fart with a sleepy sliding Z before it. Zz-fart is a holy spot, one of the four holy towns of Judaism, home for a while to Isaac Luria and the Cabbalists after their expulsion from Spain. Sparks of the divine being fell on Zz-fart, just as snow is falling on it now. And a sign reminding you of the town's mystic reputation greets you in the bus station the moment you get off the bus.

INNER DIMENSIONS OF JEWISH LIFE
THE ASCENT INSTITUTE OF ZEFAT
OFFERING HIKES AND TOURS
JEWISH SPIRITUAL
GROWTH SEMINARS
SHABBAT HOSPITALITY

'Oh yeah,' I say to Ros as we dismount, '*tefillin.*'

Since it's wet and cold, we decide we'll have coffee before looking around, or, preferably, for we are out of sorts, before going back. It has been a hairy ride – precipitous, icy, with fearful drops on either side of the mountain, none of which the driver seemed to notice. The thought of sliding down again when it is dark is not appealing. Besides, there doesn't seem to be much here we positively have to see. A holy city by Hebrew standards does not mean that there will be architecture to make your heart soar. Just a lot of books and a lot of scholars reading them, and photographs of Menachem Schneerson everywhere you look, and a few spiritual-growth seminars. Nothing in the way of spire or minaret to raise your thoughts to God.

This is the drawback of Judaism from a touristical point of view. Admirable as it is to worship through the intellect, it leaves you light on objects of physical beauty.

There are Orthodox Jews in, and running, the bus-station café. Wigs and children. The waitress asks if we want black coffee. When I say, 'One white,' she pretends not to understand. When I say, 'One with milk,' she pretends not to understand that. I say, 'Fine – two black,' and she laughs. So do her customers, a group of Jewish men who might have been photographed by Roman Vishniac, except that their hollow eyes denote disdain not despair. They talk in Hebrew between themselves, staff and customers, loudly, as it were *at* us, as it were *through* us, as if their words are stones.

The man running the joint, who wears a knitted *yarmulke* the

shape of a doily, pushes into me and passes a remark I don't
hear. I am looking at the food, where you are meant to look at
the food, but he believes I am in the way of something. What?
His life? His God?

I hold my ground. He pushes harder. I push back. For a
second or two I wonder whether this is going to end in our
wrestling on his floor. I make a rapid estimation of his bulk, to
decide if I can take him. I think I fancy my chances; but I
remember what the cop-taxi-driver told me in New York –
they're tougher than they look, these *frummies*.

Nothing comes of it. It's over in the twinkling of an eye,
almost before it began. No one else will have noticed it. It's
possible he won't have noticed it himself. But I am not keen to
stay. Ros, however, is. It's warm in here and cold out there. So
we agree that I'll brave the snow for a bit and she'll sit where
she is, drinking black coffee and writing her diary.

There seem to be bits of Zz-fart on all levels. I decide to climb,
following a sign to the Bible Museum, which is on the citadel, the
crown of the city, the eminence of the eminence. Since I'm here
among the mystics and have an umbrella of sorts, I'll get as close as
I can to Yahweh. Or rather – for I must remember where I am – to
En-Sof, the Infinite Being of the Cabbalists, who has withdrawn
into Himself to make way for the world He created.

On my way up, a young man calls to me from a veranda. I
shout back that I am unable to speak Hebrew. 'Lovely,' he says,
pointing to the falling snow. 'Lovely day.'

'It is,' I lie.

We beam at each other. Two exiled sparks of the Infinite.
Then he wishes me a happy holiday, because it is January 1st.
And I wish him a happy holiday, though it isn't one for him.
And I go on.

I don't try the Bible Museum. Apart from anything else, it is too
much of a business getting my umbrella down and then up again.
There is no one up here on the roof of the Hebrew world. You can

see why the metaphysics of exile, a cosmology of fragments and dispersal, found a congenial soil in this place. Zz-fart freezes you like ice, then scatters you like a snowflake.

Uplift and redemption, which are the next stage, I don't feel. You must need more than a single afternoon for that.

There is a Crusader tower at the summit. I skip it. I have had Crusader towers all morning. So I wind down, round and round as though I am descending Babel. And eventually I discover I am on a pedestrianized mall, hanging off a cliff face, from which the views must be stirring when you can see, but which is itself a bizarre thing to find suspended in a blizzard, all neat and paved, with *kosher* cake-shops and Felafel Baruch, and a brand new Chabad Lubavitch centre, with you-know-who pointing like a patriarch, 'like a tiger', from his posters, and *frummies* on the walkways with snow in their beards like Father Christmas, except that they don't know who that is.

A man passes, shouting. Apart from me he is the only person out who is not Orthodox; and he probably thinks I am because I have snow in my beard. I can't make out what he is shouting, apart from the single word 'Russia'. And since he is pointing to the sky and laughing or maybe crying, I take him to be saying that he has come all the way to Zz-fart only to find Russia, and that that either excites pleasure in him or its opposite.

And suddenly the street is full of black children – Ethiopians – astonished by the sight of falling snow. The most opposite thing to themselves, dropping from the sky.

One stops me and asks in a language I don't recognize what it is, this white stuff which is turning his fingers into cardboard.

I say, 'Snow, snow!'

He doesn't believe me. He is five years old, jewel-eyed, and distressed by the encounter. First something wet and white falls from the sky and takes the road away, then someone wet and white speaks gobbledegook to him.

Peculiar place, this Israel.

I roll him a snowball and offer it to him. He won't take it. He runs away.

And off I go again, skating the precipice, high up among the clouds, my feet slipping on man-made mall, my mind slithering among God-turned thoughts – the broken vessels, the holy sparks – encountering souls in uncouth garb muttering fragments I cannot make whole, and it is like a dream, an hour in the snow that will fade, that will just vanish from the memory like a fax, an hour that I will never be able to locate; and I am thinking about this and wondering how to make it stick, and whether I actually want it to stick, when I pass, on re-entering the bus station, a man with a Palestinian scarf around his neck and a pistol in his belt, clear for all to see, and then run slap into Ros, not in the café, not drinking coffee, but out in the cold, leaning against a stair-rail, frozen and furious . . .

'Your people,' is all she will tell me for the moment, all that she *can* tell me for the moment, 'have thrown me out into the snow on New Year's Day. They have done it again.'

But back on the bus, where we peer down the rifle barrels of reservists sleeping in the seats in front of us, she tells me what occurred in the café in words so blazing they defreeze the windows.

'What happened between you and him?' she begins by asking me.

'Between me and whom?'

'Between you and that fat creamy man/child . . .'

'The one who pushed me?'

'Why did he push you? What had you said?'

'Me? Nothing. He didn't like the look of me.'

'He didn't like the look of me, you mean. I was the one that got thrown out into the snow.'

'Are you telling me he actually kicked you out?'

'"Ve arr close-ed," was what he said. I had just opened my

diary. I had written one sentence. And he turned the lights out on me. Not all the lights. Just the ones in my section of the room. He turned the lights out so that I would be in the dark. I looked up. I raised my eyebrows. Big mistake. "Ve arr close-ed." I considered asking him to clarify the situation, wondering whether he would dare to spell it out as he was clearly dying to – "Ve arr close-ed to you, Christian bitch." Or something like. Other people in the café said something about it being New Year's Day – a special day for me – and to be kind to me (amazing what you can pick up when you have to in a language you don't understand). But he said it again. "Ve arr close-ed." I pulled my coat around me and walked out into the snow. No room at the inn, I thought, laughing hysterically to myself. And that's where I stayed, slowly freezing to death, waiting for you, while the lights in my section of the café went back on again, and busy busy – they're always so busy – religious Yahweh-fearing men ran in and out for their *kosher* baby-food. And now I probably have pneumonia and your people are to blame.'

'Are you saying he opened the café again as soon as you'd left?'

'Haven't you understood a word I've told you? I'm saying he never closed it. It was only closed for me.'

'You should have gone back in.'

'What, and spoiled a good story! Wasn't that why you brought me – so that I would get the *shiksa* treatment? Well I got it. What was the hell-hole called?'

'I don't know. The Bus-Station Café, I suppose.'

'Not the café, the town!'

'Zz-fart.'

'I hope you're not going to be nice about it.'

'Trust me,' I say.

But there's one thing I want to say on behalf of my people before we close it. I wait for the bus to find a smoother section of road, and for the nozzles of the reservists' rifles to be less agitated. Then I say, 'At least you weren't pregnant.'

I can't tell if she laughs or sneezes. But she says, 'Oh, you think that would have made a difference, do you?'

We both know what we think: that had she been pregnant they'd have kicked her out into the snow even sooner.

A night of dreams in Valhalla. I turn up at a hotel which is really a stately home, and receive a key from the desk clerk who is really a titled lady. The key is really a note. It says, 'Remuneration expected commensurate with the quality of accommodation.' When I turn the note in the door to my room I find three women sitting on a sofa, each of whom says, 'I understand you have your hands full, but you did say you'd take me around the galleries this afternoon.'

I wake, disgusted. I hate the unconscious when it goes literal-minded. So my own people threw my own wife out into the snow! So there's an issue of divided loyalties here! So there's a question of which is thicker: blood or water! Does that mean I have to dream about it?

The following morning I leave Ros shivering in bed under a dozen blankets and go off to nose around the *olim* transit camp I noticed yesterday on the outskirts of Akko. Transit, incidentally, can mean stays of up to five years.

There is snow on the hills around Haifa, and even on some of the roof-tops. This is the unprecedented bad weather we were promised we wouldn't get. Snow in Haifa? Never! Hail is reported to be on the way. Frogs, boils, slaying of the first-born, will follow. On the buses down from Carmel, people huddle in their overcoats. I have yet to see anything resembling exuberance in a public place in Israel, but even by the dour standards of the country, this is a wash-out of a morning. It takes six months of winter to flatten the English as comprehensively as the Israelis have been flattened in a single night.

I get to town and wait for the bus to Akko. It doesn't come. Perhaps this is the time to try a *sherut* – the shared taxi which, like a bus, plies a specific route. I've avoided them so far. If you want to run along a bus lane, it seems to me, you might as well take a bus. But buses there aren't, and *sheruts* there are. I let myself be touted for. Get in the back. And see the catch. The driver won't move until he's got more passengers.

Being a *sherut* driver isn't good for you. Mine acts and moves like a pimp. He has narrow, darting eyes, and a mean, narrow face. He has had to learn to look in several directions at once. He bites his fingers while he surveys the streets. No, that doesn't get it: what he bites are his hands. He puts a whole hand in his mouth and chews all four fingers and the thumb in one action.

He has two of us now. But he wants more. We have to wait until he's gnawed at himself for a further five minutes. Then finally he accepts that he will lose us if he doesn't get going. But now he has to slow down at every bus-stop between Haifa and Akko, honk his horn, and see if there's business. This is bad for his driving, bad for his knuckles and bad for the nation's morals. It is pimping *and* kerb-crawling all at once.

He drops me off near the *olim* site. The day is becoming filthier. I cannot see any entrance to the camp. I climb up a mud-soaked bank, by the side of a used-car lot, and see signs in Hebrew and Russian bearing a skull and crossbones. A warning to *olim* and their guests against crossing the railway line which runs between their camp and the road. I normally obey skulls and crossbones. But I see figures carrying umbrellas, straggling out of the mobile-homes and coming my way. The railway line is clearly regularly used. So I cross from my side.

In fact they live not in caravans but in prefabs. The building material looks like asbestos, but presumably isn't. The colour looks like off-white, but presumably is magnolia. Call them chalets and it doesn't sound so bad. I tick off their amenities. Sewerage. Electricity. Calor gas. Television. No phones, but a public phone in a prominent place. Macadamized roads. Buses. Taxis. Bikes. It's a life.

There is not much sign of public conviviality, but it is only ten o'clock in the morning and bucketing down with rain.

I am touched by the wooden packing crates which sit outside some of the magnolia chalets. They still carry their stencilled names and old addresses, and their destination – the world that's finished and the world that is to come. You can picture the excitement that accompanied that stencilling. Jerusalem, Tel Aviv, Haifa – ah, what names, what freedom! Who, when those stencils were put on, would have imagined a muddy field by a railway track on the outskirts of a crumbling Crusader town called Akko?

Many have taken their crates apart and used the wood to build lean-tos, shelters, porches, sheds, steps. One has carefully removed the plank with his name and destination on it, and hung it outside his chalet like the name-plate of a ranch. Elisabett Fridman has turned hers into a nifty porch. David P. Zavalunov has fixed it so that his stencilled Star of David swings in the wind. A patio table with plant pots on it says Odessa on one leg and Tel Aviv on another.

What is it about home-making that it should touch us when it's lowly and repel us when it's sumptuous?

A dentist must come to visit. I see a sign, hanging from one of the electricity pylons, saying BHUUAVE! – a word I take to be expressive of Russian pain – over a drawing of a tooth.

For a moment, the sun comes out. It is immediately warm, and at once people open their doors and start to move about. A borzoi gallops over to sniff me.

I stop whoever comes my way, ask if they speak English. They grunt or shake their heads. Some look anxious. Others are irritated. I cannot read much into this. I am snooping around their property. I am peering into their windows, transcribing the writing on their crates and on their furniture into my notebook.

So what am I up to? Do I *want* to find poor conditions? Why?

415

I've heard about their problems. I've spoken to buskers in Jerusalem. I've looked upon a man who can't get papers because he has a Jewish wife who won't join him but isn't Jewish himself although he has a Jewish son. Won't that do?

What if I do find that life isn't immediately paradisal for these *olim*? It's true that some of those I see out walking have the idle tread of the unemployed and the unexpectant, but it may – for some it *will* – change. And the site isn't too horrendous. There are palm trees here. In the water-logged fields beyond, sheep are grazing. You can see Haifa as you come out of your chalet. You can easily make out the towers of the Dan Panorama Hotel on Mount Carmel. And you can walk into Akko. It's even possible there's a way in that doesn't necessitate crossing the fatal railway line.

The English are only too happy to pay for holidays in places far worse than this. Asbestos-like boxes in muddy fields, few comforts? – why, I could advertise those in *Exchange and Mart* and get a hundred interested replies tomorrow.

So leave it alone, I tell myself. Stop bothering them.

I notice that Russian men spit a lot. They come out of their chalets, empty some rubbish, look around, spit, and go back inside. Maybe they spit because they see me. Maybe they think I'm secret police.

A battered van is delivering fruit and vegetables. It's only when customers start emerging from their prefabs that I realize the camp is divided, that one section has Ethiopians in it. I follow the progress of a woman wrapped in a white shawl, like a wraith. She wears yellow plastic thongs and is freezing. She buys a bag of tomatoes. She holds out an arm blacker than sackcloth, longer than exile, while the mobile greengrocer takes money from her palm. It is clear she has no idea how much the transaction is costing her.

The last time I saw a scene like this was in the general stores in downtown Areyonga in the Central Australian Desert.

But there is no other point of comparison. The *olim* are not

416

cast out into a rural slum. Now, as the sun breaks through for a further five minutes, many Ethiopians appear, some carrying their children on their backs in slings, African and Mothercare style.

In Jerusalem, where they shared hotels, Ethiopians and Russians fought and had to be separated. I don't know for certain what they fought over. Who was the more Jewish, presumably. It's impossible to tell how they're getting along here. But the Ethiopians keep to their side of the line, and the Russians to theirs.

'It's a very good *aliyah*, the ones from Ethiopia,' Tamara told me. 'But they have troubles. They are kept in hotels. Many kibbutzim don't want them, and the fanatically religious won't go near them because they're black.'

'They come with a great Jewish culture,' Yigal said, 'and they're expected to put *yarmulkes* on their heads. So what is Jewish culture? The religious say we should go back to Abraham. In that case we should be learning from the Bedouin.'

We mock the *goyim*, we Jews, for giving Jesus a blond wig and the looks of a Norwegian. But we are every bit as uncomfortable with the idea of a black Jew as they are.

I walk back as the rain begins to fall again. Back through the mud and across the tracks along which I see a woman ambling, skipping, gambolling under her Russian umbrella, as though relishing her one freedom, which is to break the rules.

Back through the mud, through the used-car lot, on to the highway. It is dispiriting, but I have no right to be dispirited on behalf of anyone but myself.

Later that afternoon we leave Haifa for Tiberias, on the Sea of Galilee. 'Why are we going there?' Ros asks. 'Because it's warmer,' I tell her. I don't mention that it was the one place in the country Jesus didn't have the stomach to visit.

417

Twenty

TLC

Christ might not have fancied it, but Christians do. This is serious Bible-tour country. Coaches circle the water whereon those feet ... Mormon-faced pilgrims pack into our hotel for a few hours' sleep before the next beatitude. They throw impromptu prayer-meetings in the lobby. On the way up to our room we share a lift with a brace. One says to another, 'Brother Bob didn't come down tonight.' They are carrying Bibles, serious Bibles with finger-indices for easy finding and confutation. They get off one floor below us. 'Have a good night,' they say, before the lift closes. We feel as though we've been blessed. Which is not always the way of it in an Israeli hotel lift.

They are talking night but it is still only early evening. I brave what Jesus wouldn't. Around the lake-front and the hotels you have to run the gauntlet of empty restaurants and take-aways desperate for your business. 'Felafel?' they shout at you as you pass, as though by saying the word they'll create the hunger. But the town proper is lively and working. Here, the schwarma and felafel bars are of the politically sound sort, indigenous, cheap, delicious. They put the felafel in the pitta and you spend the next hour spooning salads and chillies on top.

I am surprised by the number of Ethiopians on the streets. Wrapped up in white shawls and blankets against the cold, they slip through the descending darkness like black ghosts.

A family of them buys the wherewithal to stay warm in a kitchenware shop that spills out on to the pavement. They have sorted the pans out, but now they're after something else. There are language difficulties. They make shapes with their hands, long-fingered tubes in the air. Ah! The shopkeeper thinks he has it. He goes into a back room and comes out with a plastic vacuum flask. They clap. They look happy. If that's how an Ethiopian looks when he's happy.

First Akko, now Tiberias. Where do they think they are, these Ethiopian Jews? Have they heard of Tiberias? Do they know that Jesus gave it a miss? Have they heard of Jesus?

Tiberias is another of the holy cities of the Hebrews. There are graves here, of rabbis and scholars of renown. Most renowned of all, Maimonides. I'm not a great visitor of rabbis' tombs. But I intend to make an exception of Maimonides. It's too late now, though. I'll do him in the morning.

On the way back, I stroll around the central mosque which sits derelict and disregarded, allowed to fall into ruin, with no information about it anywhere, no markers, no signs, nothing. There is rubbish on the steps. Black plastic bags dumped in doorways. Human faeces. It is surrounded by cheap shops and empty restaurants, where boys in skull-caps sit waiting for customers and watching television.

I try to dismiss from my mind the insult to another faith. After all is said and done, politically and theologically every nation is a shit to every other nation. But what about the insult to oneself? It is *self*-wounding to destroy or ignore what is harmonious in favour of what is not. A country that refuses to build in a manner that befits it, out of a sort of spite towards those who did the befitting, will lose the love of its own citizens at last.

In the end there's no escaping the theology. Israel looks the way it does, not because it's been a nation at war and in a hurry, but because the theology has no instinct for what is beautiful to the outward eye. And so the mosque is unequalled and disregarded, and lies rotting in this graveyard of rabbis.

There's no getting back to the hotel without passing the pestiferons felafel vendors. 'You want felafel? Schwarma? Come into my restaurant! Come on, come in! Hey! Hey! You looking for food?'

If it's so quiet off-season in Tiberias, why don't they just close?

In the hotel lounge, where a hundred American Holy-Landers are sitting around in badges and pious expressions, a fat Israeli torch-singer in a grey sweater is getting ready to give us a good night. She has her little boy with her. To soften the glamour. She chokes into the microphone to test it. 'Echod,' she seems to be saying. 'Echod, echod, echodstein.' Modern Hebrew sounds like this – like a person coughing under water. But it shows how bad my Hebrew is. What she is actually doing is counting. One . . . two. *Ekhad . . . shtayim.*

The songs themselves have a whooping quality I have not encountered before. Not even in Eilat. One in particular promises to linger with me for life.

> Zoli into fari Oh Oh
> Yesterday a cookie
> Udi is it me
> Udi intifadi
> Oh – oh –
>
> Do you eveskora
> Oflinashi sorri
> Yventibarishishnu
> Solti intifardi
> Dod is a peach
> Ogli buy a googli
> Oh – oh –
> Zolti is it me

– she sings.

And I suddenly wonder if it's Russian and not Hebrew I'm hearing. After all, in her interval a balalaika plays *Hava Nagila*.

Who knows what gives here. Maybe it's Ethiopian. Maybe *Udi intifadi* is Abyssinian for vacuum flask.

*   *   *

A stone at the entrance to Maimonides' Tomb tells us that the entrance to the tomb is a gift to the city of Tiberias in memory of Alter and Sophie Peerless and Rabbi Louis and Rosa Feinberg, from their children. The names of Peerlesses as infinite as the sands of the sea – Melvins and Ronas, Sidneys and Miriams – follow. The architect is Arieh Rachamimov. He has had the idea of constructing a little aqueduct, made of grey sepulchral concrete, on either side of the avenue to the tomb. Water spouts from pillars, gathers in a round pond, and goes its way. The Sea of Galilee feeds the whole of Israel on a similar principle. But in this case we are to think of spiritual nourishment.

The tomb itself – and for this we are not indebted to the Peerlesses – is made of slats of marble and resembles a Swiss-roll sliced lengthways. It holds the centre of a small court, tranquil enough in the morning sun, and is shaded by palm trees, a fir tree and a cypress. It is not a soaring monument, but it is decorous, and given gravity by the dark stone walls that surround it, if not by the pillars with fluted chevrons of gold which rise above the walls. Pillars, presumably, which *are* part of the Peerless present.

I put on my *yarmulke*. I'm not sure why I've decided to indulge myself in reverence for Maimonides, dubbed the Rambam after the initials of his name, Rabbi Moses Ben-Maimon. Maybe it's because his work was once banned by the Orthodox, and because he admonished Jews to love the convert – 'A convert is a child of Abraham, and whoever maligns him commits a great sin' – and because he omitted the notion of chosenness from his Thirteen Articles of Faith.

A very dark young man, with eyes bluer than the night, prays quietly over the monument. He wears a silky black track-suit, and rocks a little, no, sways like the palm trees, from side to side. Unlike the Palestinians I watched at prayer in the mosque in Akko, his attention is fixed on printed words. They abandoned themselves physically, collapsed, dropped like camels; he is concentrating on the book. The book. The book.

Books are available at the entrance to the tomb. Scattered about, dog-eared, ripped, as usual, but still here, on a little table, for anyone who wants to read from one over the tomb of a rabbi who's been dead nearly a thousand years.

I just catch the young man singing – a soft lilt, not melodious, but not tuneless recitative either. The birds join him. It is hot suddenly. Above me, the town rises. There are small concrete estates, sand-coloured, on the hillside.

Because all the tablets are in Hebrew, I am shut off from knowing exactly what this place means to those who worship here, what it means specifically to the crooning young man in black. So I give in to dislocated sentiment, and spool back through the praying sites I've attended over the last month – the Wall, the sepulchre of Jesus lit by lights and guarded by a Greek, Golgotha, the tomb to millions in Yad-Vashem, the Holocaust memorial, the Al-Jazzar Mosque, and yet again it is brought home to me what folly it is, and what unrighteousness, to insist on *your* way above others'. I watch the boy swaying from foot to foot. Not once do I see his eyes leave the book or turn to the sepulchre. Not once.

Outside, sitting on a wall, enjoying the sun, are three young Ethiopians. One of them is wearing a lovely velvet *yarmulke*. They are smoking and smiling.

I watch them for a while, then saunter back into the Rambam's burial place in time to see the young man finishing his prayers. He closes his book. Puts his hands together. Inclines to the tomb. Kisses it. And leaves.

He cannot be more than seventeen. The Rambam is eight hundred and fifty-six.

What Jews love more than anything, more than art, more than music, more than words even: one another.

The Kibbutz Kfar Blum is named after Léon Blum – the French socialist, Dreyfusard, and for a while there, just before the capitulation of France to Hitler, prime minister. It was his contention that the ancient collective impulse of the Jews drove them inexorably towards revolution and socialism. So his is a good name to give to a kibbutz.

And I pick it to visit partly because of its dramatic position beneath Mount Hermon, with the Golan and Syria to the east of it, and Lebanon to the north and west of it; and partly because its praises were sung to me by a taxi-driver I met in Haifa, who while extolling the merits of kibbutzim in general – 'The best Israelis are kibbutzniks – the best soldiers, the best citizens, the best people: they are straight' – wished to put a word in specifically for Kibbutz Kfar Blum. His own daughter had lived there for several years. To show me how straight it had made her, he shaped an arrow-head with his hands, while he was driving. *That* straight.

It has other attractions. A Baltic connection. An Anglo-American connection. Accommodation. And it is not too far from Tiberias, where I leave Ros in bed with the pneumonia, or at least the heavy cold, meted out to her by the Jewish people for being Christian.

Almost the first sight I see when I come out of my cold little motel-type room on the kibbutz is a red marker on a tree saying CASUARINA EQUISETIFOLIA. This, then, is what a kibbutz is for: to give the lie to the idea of the Jew as a man ignorant of nature. Or, if that was a truth about the lost and lonely city Jews of the diaspora, to create a new truth. I've been here five minutes and already I am not the Jew I was. I feel straighter. In my excitement I forget to look at the tree.

It is bitter cold and darkening fast. The lights of Qiryat Shmona wink prettily. Mount Hermon has become a glacier again, but dusted with icing sugar, soft as floss. A dozen steps from the hotel complex and the silence is complete. Sometimes, I've been told, you can hear the guns from Lebanon, but right this moment no one's shooting.

Casuarina Equisetifolia should have been a clue – there are horticultural passions here. The grounds are beautifully laid out – hang on, let's not go mad: they are laid out. There are lawns. Trees planted for their picturesqueness. Farm sheds better ordered and more tempting to walk around than Eilat. Beauty is to do with how long you've been without it. I've been a month in Israel and the grounds of Kibbutz Kfar Blum are looking pulchritudinous.

I plunge into them. Kibbutzniks cycle past me. Young men speed in from the fields on mini-tractors. When the sound of their engines dies down I can hear nothing. It feels idyllic and misplaced, like a university campus at night.

Darkness has dropped dramatically. So has the temperature. It is only when the lights go on all around you in the distance, tracing the outlines of the mountains, that you realize what a vulnerable plain you are on, how comprehensively you are overlooked. So those will be military installations, calling you beguilingly from afar, more often than they will be villages.

Wherever a road leads, I follow. I am enjoying it, imagining the joys of communal life, college all over again, before coming to the conclusion that I am lost. I remain lost for an hour. I pass a hospital, or an old people's home, and see the young tending the old. If there is a chance of an idealization, I take it. Ah, the old. Ah, the young. Ah, the old *with* the young. I pass a school. A sculpture of a child scratching its genitals. Israeli art has yet to find itself. It will, I say, it will – as I get more and more lost by the second.

I ask someone the way back to the kibbutz hotel. He is an American kid. We don't even bother to try Hebrew. He puts me on the road. A direction confirmed by an aged man with a stick – ah, the old – whose English is at least broken.

It is too cold in my room to stay there even long enough to brush my teeth. The fan-heater blows out a Siberian gale. When you open the wardrobe a blast hits you between the eyes. In the bathroom you need to plug the sink with a towel.

That leaves only the coffee-shop. I sit writing in my notebook as parties of educational tourists turn up. First a group of blacks in woolly hats, then a bunch of American high-school kids in Levis. They are all given glasses of orange juice. You've got the Syrians pointing guns at you from one mountain range and Hamas trying to cut through fences on the other, and you get given a glass of orange juice. This is not a country that understands the virtue of a stiff drink. All of a sudden, I realize that that is what I have missed most for the last month – a goblet of blood-red wine. Over dinner, in the dining-room set aside for paying guests, I ask for a bottle of something very red, very strong and very dry. They have just the thing. A tumbler of something very pink, very weak and very sweet is put beside my plate of salted beef and strained potatoes.

'You like that, too? Isn't it great?' American voices.

I look up, my face a cold English question mark.

'The Carmel Sauvignon. We have a bottle with every meal.'

And this is how I meet the Posts – Max and Helen – a pair of affectionate, well-exercised New Yorkers, seventy going on seventeen, here on their umpteenth working-kibbutz-holiday. They know Kfar Blum well. They have old friends here. They like coming over whenever they can, you know, to lend a hand. They give me an insight into what Israel is for many American Jews – not just a charity but a sort of summer work-camp, a communal wash-up, a tent in the garden, a car-boot sale, a quilting-bee. If American Jews didn't have Israel they wouldn't look as well as they do.

Once we get over our differences regarding wine, we hit it off, the Posts and I. They introduce me to Saadia Gelb, one of the eminent elders of Kfar Blum, if such terminology sorts with the egalitarian concept of the kibbutz. Saadia Gelb is a Pole who was raised in Minneapolis and came to Kfar Blum in 1947, just in time for independence. He has written on kibbutz life generally and been a persuasive and important spokesman – a *macher*,

Max Post tells me – for this kibbutz in particular. Which is not a disqualification, any more than is his age, for the job he is doing at the moment – working at the hotel desk as a receptionist.

I've read and never been especially curious about the practical socialism of the kibbutz. Another experiment in social relations, another Utopia that's bound to end badly. But the august old-timers taking turns at running the hotel are having fun. There's a hint of disorder about, if not exactly of riot. They behave like parents left in charge of their kids' shop while the kids are away on vacation. Home alone.

Sure he'll talk to me. After his shift. Sooner, if he can just sort this problem with the laundry out.

He is a weather-beaten, shrewd, keen-eyed fighter of a man. The old style. Music hall and bolshevism. A dance, a joke, a pronouncement, a revolution. Full of charm and apparent easy-goingness, but as quick as a snake. His eyes smile, he flirts, he makes light, but the shortness of his temper, or the depth of his conviction, or both, are proved by his teeth, which have been ground into crenellations as jagged as the Golan Heights. You can trust a man who grinds his teeth.

He's an old Labour man, and he takes me through what's been happening in this country from an old Labour man's point of view.

'You are seeing Israel at its worst,' he tells me. But the deterioration hasn't happened overnight. It's been in process. The country is now at the peak of a transfer of power from left to right. In actuality, this transfer took place some time earlier. The effects are being felt now. And because they know their supremacy won't last, the minority groups of the right are grabbing what they can, while they can. If I want to know why Labour lost its influence, that's easy. Most of Israel's political leaders have been Ashkenazim. Now the Ashkenazim don't understand the mentality of the Middle East. This has been a time when the whole Middle Eastern region has been going through a cultural shock. Labour politicians did not adjust to this shock. Though whoever was in power would have borne the blame for it. As it was, a very skilful demagogue name of Menachem Begin focused all the disappointments.

We are sitting at my table in the dining-room, while I finish my dessert and have coffee. Saadia Gelb breaks off what he is saying to flirt with the waitresses. I say waitresses, but they may be professors of clinical psychology taking their turn at doing the washing up for all I know. Whoever they are they're more fun to play with than I am, waiting earnestly with my notebook at the ready like a fresher at a sociology lecture. I feel sorry for Saadia. He's seventy-eight. I wouldn't want to talk to me at that age.

But I have come to Kfar Blum to be impressed. I want to like something in Israel. I want to admire someone. And I've picked Saadia Gelb.

I ask about the settlers. Is there a sense in which they have stolen the kibbutzniks' thunder, as they like to say they have? Have they become the country's civilian front line?

'Settlers are the other side,' he says. 'We're the opposition. Their pioneering is genuine. It's the place of the pioneering, the point of the pioneering, the mysticism, the futurism, that is at fault. It's cultic. I think they're misguided. They think I'm misguided. Individually, I can't fault them. But I think they're harmful as a movement. I think they're dangerous. I want to weaken them.'

Can he go now?

Not yet. I'm still enjoying his roller-coaster teeth, and the reflection of my appreciation in the polished dome of his head. What about the *olim*? Where, as a Labour man, is he on the question of Russians in boxes?

'We've bungled both – the Russians and the Ethiopians – at the receiving end. We did well at the other end. When we were only 600,000 we could absorb two hundred per cent of our population. This government can't absorb twenty per cent. The Russian *aliyah* is going to be one of the positive aspects of this era – when I say they've bungled it I mean there's been too much suffering. A certain amount is necessary. Nothing we can do can totally eliminate the suffering. But we could have made it less. If our people had been in charge the entire picture would have been different . . .'

He interrupts himself to grab the prettiest of the waitresses. Not an unseemly grab. A grandfatherly encirclement of a narrow waist. The kind of thing you can get away with when you're seventy-eight.

'Do you know who this is?' he asks. But he doesn't wait for me to answer. 'Here is a product of Kfar Blum!'

She has a sticking plaster on her cheek. Otherwise you can't fault her. If you had to paint a kibbutz girl, she would look like this.

'You were born here?' I ask.

'Yes.'

'Been good for you?'

'Yes, I think. It's nice for a child to have grown up here. But now –' she pulls a face at Saadia – 'but now I'm ready to see the world . . .' She trips off with her tray of plates.

'. . . and leave me!' laments Saadia.

They find me someone else to talk to. Laura Kleinman. Born New Jersey. Been at Kfar Blum eight years. Devoted to it and the whole kibbutz ideology.

'The kibbutz is the only place in the world where there's functional representational democracy. We have an assembly every week. Everyone over eighteen who's a member of the kibbutz can go and vote at the assembly. Everyone gets paid according to age and family status. If something happens to you you're completely taken care of. If you're old and you can't wash your floor, the kibbutz will send someone to wash the floor for you. The kibbutz doesn't cater to lower cravings. People here are more concerned with ideas and principles than is usual elsewhere.'

She sees me smiling at her, at the rush of her words, at her conviction.

She smiles back. What can she do? 'I'm so proud of this kibbutz,' she says. 'It was unarable swampland . . .'

And she is off once again, draining the swamps.

It is not difficult to be taken with Laura Kleinman. She is diminutive, shy, with cheeks that easily go red, wavy hair parted in the middle, a toned-down Bette Midler profile and a sort of Irish-Jewish John McEnroe-ish curly mouth. A New Jersey battler. She starts soft and builds up and keeps a sentence going for as long as you can follow it. It's passion that drives her. Passion for Israel – 'After my first summer here I went back and read Golda Meir and Abba Eban and everything I could get my hands on about Israel, and I found it was a wonderful thing, people from all over the world starting from scratch, it was unparalleled . . .' Passion for the kibbutz. Passion for the original idealism of Zionism.

I did set her a challenge. Restore my faltering faith in my people, Laura. But I little expected her to take me at my word. What I like is that when I thank her, so that she can go – for she has friends waiting for her – she hesitates, lingers, feeling she should do more, bolster me further, shore up my crumbling foundations with just a couple more props. She can't bring herself to leave it at that. 'It's important,' she says. 'So many people find fault with Israel. And so many Israelis find fault with themselves. They run themselves down. They see how much better things could be. They don't make the best case for themselves. There are two kinds of Israelis. There are the braggarts, who tend to be Sephardic – excuse my bigotry. And those you have to tie down before they'll say something nice about themselves . . .' She hesitates . . . thinks about going . . . then starts again, 'It's so important . . .'

Her cheeks are red. Her brown eyes lit with intelligence. Not speculative so much as discursive. She knows how to tell the story. And she knows how to honour what she feels. She's one of those who will go away and berate herself for not being positive enough. For not adequately voicing her pride.

She won't have it that Israel is contemptuous of the monuments of other faiths. Rattles off Jordan's record in Jerusalem; how in 1947, when Jerusalem was an international city for a week, Jordan razed synagogues, turned Jewish houses into stables, used Hebrew gravestones to pave the roads. Whereas 'Jews fall over backwards to give Muslims the right to pray.' No, no, she won't have it. 'In the circumstances, considering we are at war, the treatment we mete out is not the worst. Arabs have votes, representation, they can come and go – they have a hard time at check-points, but, considering, considering . . . there are Arab parties, they can elect and be elected . . . there are Arab politicians in the Knesset . . .'

Then again, 'I get angry about the settlers' way of comparing what they do with us. Ha! They're going out after troops have conquered the place for them (albeit in defence). They go into territory that was occupied militarily, and take huge amounts of government money, and put tremendous pressure on the military, and do a tremendous amount of damage on all levels. They damage the country's moral fibre, they damage us financially and internationally – and they're tearing us apart from the inside and bringing us to the brink of civil war.'

As for the Orthodoxy that's creeping into the kibbutzim – 'Do you know that someone tried to make a to-do about our selling meat in the supermarket because it was close to the cheese? They wanted us to use a separate fridge.'

'What happened?'

'We voted it down!' She is triumphant. Whatever else, the kibbutz is still refusing to separate the milky from the meaty. I share her jubilation. It's not nothing, holding out against the Bible in this country.

*   *   *

TLC

At midnight the fan-heater in my room remembers how to blow out warm air. I decide to sleep with it on. I wake at four to discover it is blowing out cold again. Now I too have pneumonia. In the morning I see that my notebook has fallen on its back with its pages frozen open. I have to thaw it out under my shirt to prevent Laura Kleinman's sentences from snapping.

Surprise, surprise, it's a kibbutz life for me. Thirty-five years after other people discovered the allure of bracing communality under fire, I am warming to the idea. I go sneezing but cheerful into breakfast. 'Good morning,' I call, 'hi, *shalom*,' to the women of all ranks and ages working in the kitchen. How brisk they look, I think. How comely yet how modest in their white aprons, or are they tabards. I feel like William Cobbett riding into a Hampshire village, commending the industrious sobriety of the local matrons.

The Posts have already been twice around the perimeter fence. They have someone else they would like to introduce me to this morning. Judy Criden, wife of Bob who is the brother of Yosef who wrote the book with Saadia. If there is a Kfar Blum look, Judy has it. Short grey hair, spectacles, bantering manner, fit, willing and American.

'Pity you weren't up an hour ago,' she says. 'You missed the guided tour.'

The kids in Levis, the blacks in woolly hats – some of whom, I'm told, were polygamists from the Cameroons – have done the kibbutz and are off on another leg of their religious education.

I drop a hint. 'Pity there's no bright young person to take me around now.'

She rises. 'Why do they have to be young? What's important about being young?'

'By young –' I start, but she is on her feet.

'Provided you can come *now* – because I have to be an usher in the children's theatre in half an hour – I'll take you.'

So off we go, the young ones, Judy and Helen and Max and Me.

431

Judy is from Milwaukee. Is academically qualified – I never find out in what. But she teaches below her capacities at Kfar Blum.

('Between you and me,' Helen whispers, 'I think they take advantage of her.')

She came out eighteen years ago, after her first husband died. 'It's my home,' she says. 'You've no idea how good it is to know that you'll be looked after, if anything happens. There are people to take care of you here. And you don't have to worry about money.' She looks up at me quickly, as if she knows something about me. 'That's the best part – you can forget about money.'

She escorts us through the kitchens. Men with the profiles of philosophers are bent over mixers. She shows us the laundry, outside which string bags holding socks and smalls and marked with individual identifications hang drying, waiting for collection. I passed these last night on my walk, and, seeing them hanging phosphorescent in the darkness, had taken them to be agricultural in some way, containing chicken-feed or curdled cheese.

Fellow kibbutzniks greet her. Forgive my belated naivety, but there seems to be an atmosphere of uncommon neighbourliness about. Judy is worried about the health of the man who runs a little nursery. He shows us ice in his pail. 'I feel sorry for him,' she says, as we go on. 'He isn't well. I can tell he isn't himself.'

('See how lovely they are to one another,' Helen whispers to me.)

We pass a strange, transfixed woman, large, Baltic-looking, lost in her clothes, abandoned to her thoughts. She potters about her garden, absently. She doesn't look up.

'A survivor of the Holocaust,' Judy says. 'But she's been traumatized by it. We let her go her own way. That's what the kibbutz is for.'

A man approaches on a bicycle. He must be seventy-five. Helen recognizes him, hails him, kisses him twice on the forehead. 'There are 367 of us,' he says. 'You'll never get around to doing us all.'

It is Utopia. Erewhon. A New Jewish Atlantis. If I stay here they'll clean my floor, pay my bills and kiss me when I get to seventy-five.

'You know,' Judy says, 'a beautician comes to teach us about cosmetics. When you come out you look like a princess. I never took such care of myself as the kibbutz takes of me.'

('TLC,' Helen whispers to me. 'Tender Loving Care.')

Wouldn't you know it – despite all this there are problems. The usual problems. Youth problems. 'The modern world has found its way here,' Judy says. 'The kids want videos. They want to travel. If they do extra work they want to be given extra pay. They don't see that that's not the way of the kibbutz.'

'So they leave?'

'They're leaving, yes. But that's natural. They have to see if they can make it out there. They're not sure they're up to it. They have to try.'

Let them go, I want to say, let them go tour the world's Virgin Megastores. We can stay here and grow old together. Collect our smalls from the curdled-cheese bags, buy a tandem, do our nails. TLC. What else is there? Tender Loving Care.

Judy leaves us. It's time for her to be an usher at the children's theatre. But not before she lets us know what she thinks about a private *bar mitzvah* we get a glimpse of as we pass the synagogue. 'Huh!' she says. 'We didn't used to have those!'

Another innovation: first videos, now individual *bar mitzvahs*.

Not much TLC towards the new Orthodox, then. Catch me worrying. You can't Tenderly Lovingly Care for those who won't Tenderly Lovingly Care for you.

The buses delivering the children to the theatre from other kibbutzim have arrived. Helen and Max Post, still full of walk and talk, recognize one of the drivers.

'Hi!' Helen says. 'It's Mitzi, isn't it? You remember us? We were here last year doing volunteer work for the JNF. You used to drive us in from Qiryat Shmona.' And to me: 'Mitzi's a poet.'

'I would not call myself a poet,' Mitzi says, softly, self-effacingly, nudging a tyre with his foot.

But he looks more like a poet than a bus-driver. Delicately fashioned, black-and-silver bearded, eyes webbed around with gentle laughter lines, which could denote worry too – a muted sadness. His soft-spokenness is part of a strategy of intimacy: he is one of those men who insist that you must get close if you want to hear. But there's a touch of insouciant Israeli manliness about him as well; he wears sunglasses pushed back into his hair, his clothes are tight, despite the cold there is an expanse of hard chest on show. I am surprised to learn that he is fifty-three and a grandfather.

We stand by his bus, talking about literary societies. Up here! Literary societies! Why not? Mitzi goes to one every month. Over sixty people from neighbouring kibbutzim regularly attend. They prefer it if they can get the writer they are discussing to come in person, but if not then someone writes a paper. Last month they discussed Isaac Bashevis Singer.

Max and Helen Post glisten at us, almost as blindingly as Mount Hermon. They love it that they are the cause of a literary conversation between Jews and about Jews just a few miles from the murderous borders.

And I love it too, so that when Mitzi suggests that we go back with him for the afternoon to his kibbutz, Malkiya, I am almost as youthful in my enthusiasm for the idea as Helen and Max Post are.

We wait for the children to spill out of the Kfar Blum audittorium. They take their time. We keep thinking we can hear their applause but we are mistaken. We stamp our feet, rub our hands together. Mitzi polishes his bus, the cleanest in the line.

At last they come, Israel's future, shepherded by those

kibbutznik parents elected to protect it. Up here you are a general guard as well as a particular parent. They find their own buses. As the Malkiya kids climb aboard, Mitzi has a word or a touch for each of them. No eating allowed on his bus, though; he is bus-proud – even through the blizzards, his windows shine.

When one of his own arrives, she gets a special hug. His expression is as limpid as his windows. 'My grandchild!' he exclaims, smothering her in kisses. The creases around his eyes go into operation. When he is standing by himself, with no one to touch, I have noticed that his hands shake a little; but once they have a child in them they are firm, confident, loving.

I hang on to my reason. A busload of writhing hermaphroditic tadpoles in woolly tights has not previously figured with any prominence in my shrinking list of hopes and wants. But there can be no doubting that the affections across the generations are strong here; and I am curious about this because, although Israelis picture themselves as communicative and ebullient, I have not come across much in the way of extravagant warmth. People's eyes don't dance in Israel. It is hard to meet a stranger face to face in mutual enjoyment of an event, a joke. People stare, but that's another matter. There's not much talk in cafés. None on buses. Not having Hebrew of course contributes to the coldness; but I don't see anyone else talking either. It is a watchful, mistrusting country, without social pleasures.

So the warmth in Mitzi's eyes and arms arrests me.

It is good that he is an experienced driver. We are on a wild road, all twists and drops and ice. Soon, we are running alongside the Good Fence between Israel and Lebanon. Syria is over our shoulder, visible in the distance, but Lebanon is just here, close enough to reach out and steal a snowball from. We make out military outposts. 'Necessary,' Mitzi announces from the wheel. 'We have to have them.'

He is melancholy, regretful, musing about this, where Helen and Max – but especially Helen – are gung-ho.

I may have had to add to Kfar Blum to make it beautiful, but Malkiya is lovely without my help, a Swiss village in the snow, enjoying fairy-tale views of Israel and her enemies.

Over lunch in a panoramic-windowed serve-yourself University-of-the-Alps style refectory, we meet an impressively forthcoming wheeler-dealer named Natan Hacker. He is leonine, white-bearded, overweight, fast-talking, from Chicago, and looking for something from we internationals who have just dropped out of the heavens into his schemes. He shakes my hand and gives me his fax number. In a matter of minutes we know about the guest house he's refurbishing, the synagogue he's altering, the archaeological dig he's leading and the museum he's opening.

All this on behalf of the kibbutz?

Of course. Of course. He loves being on the kibbutz. He loves the ideal. 'The only successful form of capitalism,' he declares.

'I thought you were meant to be communistical,' I say. This could be why I've been dropped here. To be Natan Hacker's straight man.

He shakes his leonine head. He was a lawyer, still is a lawyer. 'Since when did a single kibbutz aim at selling an apple without making a profit?'

'So this is cooperative capitalism,' I say.

'You got it.'

I've got his fax number; now he gives me his card. One for the Posts too. He likes the idea of being up here on the Lebanese border dispensing cards.

But what's geography these days? 'With a computer,' he says, 'and I've got two, a man can run a company in the States from here. I'm running a law firm in Chicago. With my computer I can tap into the best law libraries there are. I'm short of nothing here. I'm no distance.'

He is the man of tomorrow. He sees the future. A fully computerized kibbutz.

Mitzi sits quietly while Natan Hacker – Natan the Hacker – gives us his *spiel*. He's not Mitzi's speed. And I feel bad, a bit treacherous, somehow shallow, buying into Natan in Mitzi's company.

We clear up after ourselves and follow Mitzi to his home, down a path through the snow (Lebanon across the wire), past an observation tower where Mitzi remembers sitting through the night with his machine-gun (not so necessary now that patrols drive around the perimeter fence), then up and then down again along a suburban Swiss street and into a pink-tiled chalet where you expect them to be serving Glühwein.

The house is hot with family. Children, children-in-law, grandchildren, nieces, nephews, a mother-in-law. The teeming generations.

The sons and the husbands of daughters are all strapping, variously dark, simmering, machine-men and mechanics, Jewish men who lie under trucks and buses. They are sitting in a phalanx on the sofa, watching *An Officer and a Gentleman* on video. We exchange greetings over the video, but the video stays on.

I meet Tami, Mitzi's wife, half-German, I think, and half-Czech – a woman of intense mien, with a lovely Eastern European mouth which I used to think of very specifically as Latvian, but now believe to be Litvak.

People come and go. More sons. The video runs. And everyone watches or part-watches. But the moment Debra Winger's brown little breasts appear and press themselves against Richard Gere's, the women miraculously fade away. Suddenly they are simply not there. They are at the sink, they are changing a baby, they are in the bathroom, they are sweeping snow from the path. Only the men stay where they were, stock-still on the couch like a battalion not wanting to give away its whereabouts, boring into the screen with their black eyes.

As soon as Debra Winger is respectable again, the women reappear. Without a word.

So this is how the decencies prevail in the world of sex, video and *halachah* – tacit transactions, discreet acts of personal

437

removal, not alluded to. The family is together again and you would not think for a moment that it had ever broken up.

It is a snowy languorous Saturday. We eat Swiss-roll and drink black coffee and feel a tiny bit *de trop*, the Posts and I, as Mitzi revels in being the paterfamilias, the engine and origin of all this life. The lines about his eyes are very busy. He is pleased now by this offspring, now by that. He hugs and fondles and kisses his grandchildren. Something like the stars from a sparkler fizz in his face. It is not adequate to say he beams. He irradiates. He is a *Shekhina*.

When I go to the bathroom I see that there are innumerable markings on the back of the door, registering the height, the progress upwards, of all the children.

But this is not the tumult of breeding you find in a Hasidic household. There is not that incessant, animal atmosphere. Tami and her daughters are women, not beasts of burden. The spirit of it all is affable and worldly. Another child is another companion, another playmate, rather than one more step in Israel's ascent, one more *mitzva* to hurry up *Moshiach*.

It's hot in Tami's and Mitzi's nest right enough, but it is secular heat. Not a *yarmulke* in sight. Not a photograph of a rabbi. Not a fringe. I think I see a *menorah* on a shelf, but it enjoys parity with artefacts from Africa, several volumes of modern Hebrew poetry and a book about Frederick McCubbin, the Australian painter.

To let a bit of heat out of the house, Mitzi takes those of us who aren't family for a walk around the fence. The sun is shining. Mount Hermon looks so clear, we feel we should be able to make out the faces of people skiing down it. The strips of the Arab farmers' fields – marked out by stones and making graceful curls down the hillsides, as sensuous as Arab script – show prettily through the snow, suggest a harder, more unyielding substance beneath the soft whiteness. Nobody is about on the other side of the fence. It's hard to imagine this part of Lebanon being farmed any more.

We assume that we are safe, that our safety is assured this afternoon, at any rate, by the soldiers we don't see. The towers are not manned. The barbed wire is not tested. And in this eerie suspension of life and danger we crunch along at the top of the world, at this meeting point of many worlds, and listen to Helen voicing the old diaspora intransigence – 'Since when did a conquering nation have to give back everything it took? If we hadn't taken this country can you imagine what sort of security we'd have had?' – and to Mitzi, who lives here, who doesn't just pop over for a few weeks' working holiday each year, not having any of this, not wanting any more fanaticism and stubbornness.

'So what would you give for peace, Mitzi?' Helen asks.

It's all rather absurdly matter of fact, considering where we're standing.

But Mitzi doesn't mind. A serious question deserves a serious answer. He stops in the snow. Ponders it through in his usual slow, quiet manner. If bullets were flying he would operate at the same speed.

'I would give back Gaza . . .'

Helen and Max have no trouble with this. Gaza you definitely give back.

'I would give back most of the West Bank, Bethlehem, Nablus . . .'

Now he's becoming a bit profligate for the Posts' taste. Helen is worried about the narrowness of the country, the meagre distances, security . . .

'What security do we have now?' Mitzi asks. 'If there is a chance it will work, we should take it. If there is the remotest hope of peace – and I have to say I am pessimistic and there may not be – but if we don't seek it . . .'

This isn't easy for Helen. Giving back, risking, seeking . . . I know how she feels. We all know how she feels. We all have a bit of soldier in us. I've fought to get that – you *made* me fight to get that – and now I'm to hand it back to you on my belly? We are standing at peace, in the sun, in one of the most contested corners of the earth. And right now it is ours. Yet we are talking of giving *back*?

Well, we're not talking of giving *this* back. Mitzi is pursuing reason not suicide. And holding on to the West Bank does not strike him as having reason on its side.

'It makes no sense,' he says, 'to keep Arabs within our fence who hate us. I think the Arabs should be outside the fence. Not because I agree with them. Not because I'm for them. I don't know whether I'm against them or for them. But for our sakes – for *us* – it's no good. It's no good economically, or militarily, or morally. It's not good for us, what we're doing. And if we want to enjoy the good will of the rest of the world, and it's a fact that we need that good will, then we have to make concessions. So what, if that makes us a small country. We're already a small country.'

Helen continues whispering in my ear – the marvels of Israel, the irony of the world's attitude to it, who else, where else – the usual stuff I know from Manchester and to which my gut throbs in unwilling sympathy. But it's Mitzi I want to hear, not Helen. Someone who was born here and must live with the problem, not a sentimental tourist. Sentimental touring I can do myself.

I dodge her and get back to him. The advantage of a man like Mitzi, who takes his time and weighs his words, is that you don't miss much if you're waylaid by Helen. He is stroking his beard, ruminating, working himself up to putting a proposition.

The proposition, when he finally puts it, is this. 'As a country we can be Jewish or we can be democratic, but we cannot be both. We can be Jewish and Arab and democratic, but that is a different thing.'

The quiet words drop like feathers in the snow, but they ring in my ears long afterwards, like church-bells. Funeral bells. Wedding bells. *We can be Jewish OR we can be democratic, but we cannot be both.*

By Jewish, of course, Mitzi means exclusively Jewish. Mea She'arim Jewish. *Moshiach* Jewish. Torah Jewish.

I look at him in the snow, a poet, a cosmopolitan figure, far from the *shtetl* atmosphere of the Jerusalem ghetto. Behind him, just over his shoulder, is Lebanon. If Lebanon is beautiful, I am not able to enumerate the ways. I take the scenery in abstractly. These are landscapes of the mind if any are.

And if this is the fruit of conquest I see, and he a conqueror – if this is the atmosphere of conquest I breathe – it all feels so tranquil on a January afternoon, at the very start of a new year, that I can after all believe in the idea of an ultimate accommodation. Up here among the kibbutzniks it's feasible – anything's feasible. It's only when I see in my mind's eye the *kipa*, the skullcap, the *yarmulke*, pinned in any of its countless ugly ways to heads stiff with obstinacy, that the impossibility of it all descends on me.

It finally rests, as the kibbutzniks know and have always known, on the age-old tussle between what is restless and critical in Judaism – what Léon Blum saw – and what is blindly obedient –the Judaism of the rabbis.

Friends of Israel should not lift another finger, should not donate another penny, unless they have assurances that their efforts do not in any way help religious movements, or the religious spirit, in this country.

Blessed are the unbelievers, for they shall inherit the Kingdom of God.

Twenty-one

GOING DOWN

Ironical that the one person who talks to me on an Israeli bus is an Australian with a silver stud in his ear. And more ironical still that I can't be bothered to talk back because my head remains full of Mitzi and all that appertains to him.

It's late evening. There is nothing to see from the windows but lights on the Golan. Occasionally we swoop around a bend and catch a reflection from the Sea of Galilee – the Kinneret – dead still and almost black. This is the last bus back to Tiberias from Qiryat Shmona. Mitzi got me on it just in time, after a giddying drive down from Malkiya. We had been talking. After my epiphany by the Good Fence we had gone back to his house, where another video was running, and had hammered a few family matters out. Self-reliance and communality. Love and the kibbutz. That sort of thing.

My fault. I had seen a chance, during a dull patch in the video, to tickle out some home truths, and I had taken it. 'This business about the young being on the move and the kibbutzim becoming age-heavy . . .' I had asked '. . . anything in that?'

Mitzi saw it as a testimony to what the kibbutzim had achieved that the young should be curious, restless, footloose. His own children are tireless travellers. They go everywhere. One is just back from Australia. Hence the paintings of McCubbin. And Tami and Mitzi go everywhere too. Next year, no, this year, it will be China. The whole point of the kibbutz: to open the mind.

But his daughter, nursing a baby of her own, was more vexed.

It did not seem to her that curiosity was the issue. Or that it was proof of something positive in the kibbutz philosophy that young people were moving about or even, as in her case, moving *out*. More to the point was worry about adequacy. The young weren't certain that the kibbutz adequately prepared them to live anywhere but on the kibbutz.

'People outside applaud our lack of competitiveness,' she said, 'but we inside do not applaud it.'

'You would like to be at one another's throats more?'

'We would like to see what we can do out there. Here, when I wanted to earn more money for travel and said I was willing to do more work, to do more overtime, I was told that that was not the kibbutz way. I think that's wrong.'

'So you left the kibbutz for that reason?'

'Yes.'

'For good?'

She laughed a sad laugh. A handsome woman with brown rings under her eyes. Not bags, just slightly discoloured pockets of care. 'I cannot say that. But it seems to me now that I won't come back. We have a business – a car business – and it's been hard, very hard, but what we have we have worked for and we know that it is ours.'

'So it was the socialism that got you down?'

Not only. There was also . . . She found this hard to put. But, well, being sent to the kibbutz school, to the kibbutz mother . . . It didn't . . . well, it didn't work for her. She missed something. She didn't doubt it made her independent – but did it also make her a less feeling, less affectionate person than she might have been, or would have liked to be?

'I hardly knew my brother there. It was hard to have special relations with brothers or sisters because we were all meant to be one family. And because everything was so public, I used to be ashamed of doing anything that would show up my parents. I have many bad memories of the system. Many. And the friends I

443

made there are not my special friends now. I can't explain it but I missed out on some warmth. I know from this one' – gesturing to the baby in her lap – 'some feelings . . . I don't know.'

Although there was no reproach, just a distant sadness, in her daughter's voice, Tami took the criticism hard. She wanted to modify what had been said. Thanks to the kibbutz, *she* had been able to spend more time with her children than most of the working mothers she knew outside the kibbutz. 'Whatever my daughter says to the contrary, the kibbutz freed me for motherhood.'

Her daughter didn't deny it. Wasn't looking for retrospective disagreement. 'I know, Mother,' and, 'I'm not arguing with that, Mother,' she was now reduced to saying. Having to pull her horns in, not thanking me for starting this. Her eyes tired. The marks below them turning just the faintest brown.

I watched Mitzi. He still blazed like a leopard over his brood, still moved about the room dispensing kisses. But he too was on the line now. And I could see the price the paterfamilias is bound to pay at last for staking it all on the family. He becomes too alive to it, has no escape from it, cannot transmute it, if only temporarily, in the way a man and woman can temporarily transmute their passion, dilute it, go blind to it, turn from it; for the family is unavoidable, always itself, inextinguishable, and so its disappointments are forever close to its successes. There is no barrier, no safety margin, between them. Therefore Mitzi's blaze of paternal pride was a vulnerability too, and I wondered whether what fizzed and crackled in his face right now felt like exultation to him, or sorrow.

'Whether or not it has worked for my daughter,' Tami said to me before I left, 'the kibbutz is and always has been a family to me. I've learnt about belonging here, and sharing here . . . and I haven't had to cook. As for money, well, you get little but you save it, you save it carefully, and next year, no, this year, we'll be in China.'

*　　*　　*

There had been so much panic in Jerusalem, on account of the amount of snow that had been falling, that the Mayor, Teddy Kollek, had been compelled to issue a statement calling for calm. 'Let's not treat this like the Yom Kippur War,' he had told his people.

Now that things are back to normal in the capital, the ultra-Orthodox are fire-bombing bus-shelters in Jaffa Street. The reason? The shelters carry obscene advertisements. The nature of the obscenity? Images of women. Images of unclothed women? Images of parts. Private parts? You could say that – lips, teeth, eyes . . .

'It makes me wish we were going back there,' Ros says.

I know what she means. We have been in an extreme place, the prey to extreme emotions, from the moment we arrived in Israel. This is the birthplace of extremity. We Jews are an extreme people – extreme in ourselves and the cause that extremity is in others. And given that, it seems wasteful not to be in the extreme eye of the extreme storm, the holy of holies, the extreme of extremities.

But we are on the way out now, not the way in. After a day trip to the Mount of the Beatitudes, which the bus-driver has difficulty stopping at because he has never heard of it, we leave Tiberias and the Galilee and head for Ovda Airport, where it all began, where we came in gulping, where Ros said, 'Welcome home, Howard.'

We decide to go by bus, so that we can enjoy a bit of country and rest assured that no one will talk to us. Stopping at Beersheba, on the fringes of the Negev, where Abraham struck camp and Jacob and Isaac were born. The *Rough Guide to Un-Israel* warns against expectation.

As always, nothing happens on the bus. In a country at war with terrorists I suppose one has to count that a good thing. It seems to be a day for reservists: girls wearing Alice bands, with teddies hanging off their bags, and rifles. They get on and off the

bus at remote places. Never talking, never smiling, never flirting
– not even with one another.

'This is a modest country,' I say to Ros, to pass the time.

'If you don't count the men who put their tongues out and
ululate when someone takes their fancy, then yes, it is,' she says.

I wasn't counting them.

The moment we get to Beersheba we wish we'd come sooner
or that we had more time for it now. It has a frontier feel.
Buildings are going up fast. There's a whiff of something dubious
about the place, such as you often find in last towns before the
wilderness, where men involved in the nuclear or espionage business come and go on mysterious but conspicuous errands. It's
good to have the acrid smell of desert in your throat again too,
the dry tickle at the back of the throat, small deposits of burnt
and no doubt radioactive sand that lodge where you swallow.

We drink Turkish coffee in a Bulgarian restaurant on a modest
felafel and schwarma mall. The restaurant is empty when we
order the coffee and full when it comes. A construction plant or
a secret underground bunker site must have knocked off. A
black blur of engineering worker blots out the light at the door,
then fills the restaurant. There are at least thirty of them, blue
eyes, skin darker than charcoal, hair as thick as cable trailing
from their throats and arms. We drink our coffee quickly and
leave. Some of them have begun to put their tongues out and
ululate.

There's an *olim* camp in town. Russian and Ethiopian. The
buildings going up everywhere will eventually be for them. In the
meantime they walk the streets in their pale blue summer suits
and voguish Muscovite leather boots with flirty heels, utterly
nonplussed. You can tell the ones who have just arrived by how
long they go on staring at the attenuated black women in white
sheets with babies strapped to their backs, and at the white-faced
bearded men with tassels hanging out of their trousers.

On a low wall outside a bank, a Russian woman has laid out

for sale five pairs of knitted woollen socks. They would keep you warm in Siberia. Just what you want in the desert.

Our hotel has french windows that open on to waste land. But they do not lock. Ros hears cries in the night. I hear dingoes. We sleep with our passports and valuables.

There is just time in the morning, before we catch our bus, to take in a couple of the sights. The British War Cemetery, where I see a memorial stone to W. A. Foy of the Royal Sussex Regiment – 'A good soldier of Jesus Christ'. And Abraham's Well. The latter makes me take back everything I've said about Israeli neglect of other faiths' monuments. It's more even-handed than that. They also neglect their own. This may not really be the place where Abraham made his covenant with Abimelech and called on the name of the LORD, the everlasting God, but since we're pretending, can't we pretend properly? Must there be old Coca-Cola signs strewn around, and a pair of step-ladders, and a broken wall clock advertising beer, and dead plants, and crappy spotlights, and a fan for blowing cold air?

The moment we get to the airport our spirits sink. In front of us in the queue is a London Jew wearing a gold chain round his neck and talking about Ratner. 'He's had it. He'll be gone by Monday. AGM meets in the morning, and that'll be it.'

Back to the trivialities of a country not at war, and we are not on the plane yet.

First the questions. Who packed your case? Where did you travel? Who did you meet? Who did you talk to?

So the last thought Ros and I have in Israel we have together, without communication, and it is about Mahmoud.

Twenty-two

THE LITVAK TOY-BOY

What I had found out about my Litvak great-grandparents was this:

He – Lazarus Black, Zayde to us – was born Lazar Schwartzbord, son of Yudel and Yache Schwartzbord, in Lazdai, then part of the Russian Empire, on August 14th, 1878. He met my great-grandmother in Serhai, twelve miles down the track, where he had gone to work in some capacity or other for her father. He married her, we are not quite sure when, came to England with her in 1899, by that time a father, and was naturalized in 1913. In the report supporting his application for British citizenship, it was noted that while he worked as a machinist, his front room was 'stocked with a large assortment of boots' which he sold in his spare time 'on the weekly-payment system'. (Except, say his surviving daughters, that no one ever paid him.)

She – known to us as Bobbe – was born Rachel Kregan (sometimes spelt Krigier or Krager or Krieger) in, it would seem, 1875. And in, it would also seem, Manchester not Serhai. The only available understanding of this being that her parents Abraham and Annie Kregan or Krigier or Krager or Krieger, who were either graziers or glaziers, came to England to have their children, who would then be eligible for English passports, and returned to Serhai when their family was complete.

In this way my great-grandmother, who spoke mainly Yiddish all her life, was both at home in Manchester and a stranger to it.

'But what interests me,' I confided to my Great-aunt Sylvia, daughter of Bobbe and Zayde, 'is that your mother appears to have been three years older than your father, to have married him when he was in his teens, and therefore to have taken herself, in modern parlance, a toy-boy.'

My Aunt Sylvia has a sense of humour. She opened her eyes very wide. 'Don't you dare write that,' she said.

'I don't see how I can resist,' I told her. 'It casts such a warm light on our past. And makes such a good title for a chapter.'

'You wouldn't!'

Maybe I misread her, but it seemed to me she was so, as it were, inversely taken with the idea, that I had no choice but to honour it.

Later on, when I was in New York, I made contact with one of Bobbe's nieces, Pauline Kaplan, who was herself born in Serhai, ninety-three years ago. She was too ill for me to see in the flesh, but I talked to her over the telephone, on a promise to her son that I would not fatigue her. Fat chance of that. Ninety-three going on ninety-four she may have been, but she spoke to me at length and with perfect lucidity of what she remembered.

How she came to America from Serhai when she was thirteen. How her father had died three years before that, on his way back from America where he had unsuccessfully attempted to establish a new life for his wife and children. How musical they – we – had all been: her father on the fiddle, his brother a cornet-player, her grandfather (my great-great-grandfather) on the bass. How they played in a klezmer band in Serhai, at weddings and *bar mitzvahs* and the like. How her grandfather had gone to Manchester – ah! – and then returned. And was a glazier – 'Not a grazier, then?' 'No, a *glazier*' – and baked bagels and sold things on the markets. 'He did all that?' 'It was a small town. You had many occupations.' How anxious life was for the Jews in Serhai. 'Each night that passed over peacefully we thanked God.' How we had a goat and a horse. And how the town – the Jewish town – was finally wiped off the map by the Nazis – 'Not one person left to say anything.'

Lazdai the same. Not one person left to say anything.

This isn't quite true. Avraham Tory's book on the Kovno Ghetto – *Surviving the Holocaust* – mentions how Rivka Gershtein and Ze'ev Michnovsky hid in a peasant cowshed and watched, on the day the entire remaining Jewish population of Lazdai was rounded up and shot. November 3rd, 1941. Sixteen hundred Jews in a single day. The *Einsatzgruppen* superintending, Lithuanian civilians offering willing support. And only Rivka and Ze'ev making it out.

So they did well by us, Bobbe and Zayde, putting a thousand miles between them and Lazdai and Serhai in 1899. They did us a good turn, whatever their relative ages.

And there, it could be argued, is where it should be left. Why go back? What am I doing turning such a felicitous one-way journey into a round trip? It's not as though it was so wonderful for us in the east that I must return in homage. A sheep and a goat and a bagel business! True, we were *Mitnageddim*, we Lithuanian Jews – opponents of whatever was not of the intellect. But what the historian Graetz said of the Polish and German Jews must have applied equally to us, that devotion to the Talmud had accustomed us to 'all that was artificial, distorted, super-cunningly wrought'. We were poor and we were subtle. A combination that always makes for morbidity. And isn't it a morbidity to be going back?

It's not as though I'm African, either. I don't have to trace my source. I know where it all started. I've *been* where it all started. Abraham's Well and the King Solomon's Palace Hotel, Eilat. I'm a Bedouin, a lover of bright colours, not a peasant from the lightless forests of Lithuania.

All this, of course, is rhetorical. There can be no question of my not going. I've had the family – the Litvak side of the family – digging out documents for months. And I've told the Chief

Rabbi I'm going. What will I say if I meet him on radio again – I thought better of it, Your Reverence, from the moment I found my Jewish roots in a Red Sea souvenir-shop selling spangled tennis shoes for indoor wear? And give him the opportunity to roll me a second time?

After all, it is not the Jewish past that is the cause of my reluctance, but the Sovietized present. The Russians may have pulled their tanks out but everything else is bound to remain, the red tape, the deprivations, the dispiritedness. Quite simply, I cannot present a single picture of Lithuania to my inward eye that doesn't fill me with despondency.

Vengeance is the best justification for my journey I can command. They gave a warm welcome to the Nazis, my gentile Lithuanian brothers. They rolled their sleeves up when it came time to dig holes in forests to bury Jews. Good, if things have been unpleasant for them since. Good, if things are unpleasant for them now.

I wait until February, when the capitalist airlines begin flights to Lithuania, and at last, on a miserable Saturday morning, very early, I leave for Vilnius. But my reluctance has become more than an attitude of mind; it sits in my gut like rotting fruit.

The SAS desk is unlike itself. Not a phlegmatic Swede in sight. There has been a world-wide breakdown of their computer system. The fear under whose shadow all booking clerks now live has been realized – 'Today we will have to do everything *manually.*'

At any other time I would have enjoyed this. A Luddite to my bones, I feel energized and even queerly vindicated whenever mechanical things go wrong. As if it's them or me. But after five days and nights failing to get a single phone-call through to a single Lithuanian hotel – those that are not unlisted are unobtainable; those that are not unobtainable are engaged; those that are not engaged don't answer – I am a different person. I have seen a world without machines, and it doesn't work.

The plane is called Alf Viking. It is carrying passengers unaccustomed to flying. They fight with one another for space in the overhead lockers. They say, 'Excuse me, that's my *fur coat* you're crushing.' I don't know whether this marks them out as Balts, but they have white faces or broken-veined complexions that remind me of my grandmother's. I am entering a world where there is no etiquette of the air or of the telephone. The rotting fruit in my gut, which is my reluctance, is now exploding fruit.

A young and initially affable Sikh from Essex sits next to me. He's married to a Jewish girl who is a born-again Christian. I say I don't see how that can be. He arches an eyebrow. I say I don't see how she can be born again as Christian when she was born the first time as a Jew. He accuses me of nit-picking. I arch an eyebrow. He asks me about Israel. I try to calm things down between us by voicing one of two mild criticisms of that country. The wet breakfasts. The excessive smoking indulged in by the Hasids. He loses his temper and reminds me of the thousands of years of my people's suffering.

Out-manoeuvred by a Sikh, not speaking the language, not having anywhere to stay, not wanting to stay, I land at Vilnius, capital of Lithuania. No Ros, this time, to take me by the arm and whisper 'Welcome home, Howard.'

Is it home? Is it home to anybody? In 1915 the Germans pushed the Russians out of Vilnius. In 1919 the Poles pushed out the Germans. A week later the Bolsheviks pushed out the Poles. Then the Poles pushed out the Bolsheviks. Then the Bolsheviks pushed out the Poles. Then the Lithuanians, remembering whose capital this was supposed to be, pushed out the Bolsheviks. Six weeks later the Poles were back. And that just takes us to 1922.

As things stand at present, the Lithuanians have pushed out the Russians. But do the Lithuanians know who they are any more?

Home! Through the windows of the aircraft everything looks

452

dead. The terminal building seems to be lit by a single forty-watt bulb. Airports rarely raise the spirits, especially in the winter dark, but usually you can make out the glow of the humming city on your descent. Not through my window, not through anybody's window, does anything hum or glow.

There is a chance that I will be met by David and Simon Rozas, two English-speaking Jewish boys whose names have been given me by the 35s – the London branch of the Women's Campaign for Soviet Jewry. The 35s did well by me with Lynn Singer on Long Island. But Lithuania is not Long Island. I have managed to reach the Rozas boys on the telephone, though not the last few times I tried. They have said that they will meet me, but they sound casual, matter-of-fact, as if it's no big deal whether I'm left like a waif in an airport without facilities or not.

'You will recognize me because I will be carrying a copy of *Time* magazine,' David said.

My family have been out of Lithuania for a century. After that sort of time away you can't be expected to know what's a Lithuanian joke and what isn't.

The moment I emerge from customs I see a tall, fair, frizzy-headed boy with sharp features carrying a copy of *Time* magazine. I do no more than glance his way before he has my suitcase off me. Another pair of hands is pulling at my briefcase. This is how it must feel to be kidnapped. My luggage is in the boot of a Lada held together with Elastoplast, and I am in the back seat, still holding my passport, almost before a word has been spoken.

'I hope you're sure you've got the right person,' I say, as we skid out of the deserted airport.

'I hope you're sure you're in the right vehicle,' David says. 'We're K G B.'

He's twenty at most. His brother Simon, who's driving, is younger than that. David tells the jokes, Simon tells me where we are. Which means, for the moment, that David has more to do, for we are not anywhere. The forty-watt bulb which illuminated the terminal is the last bright light I am going to see. Snow lies upon the city like a shroud. There are no sights and there are no sounds. A Saturday in Vilnius.

Serves them right.

I tell the boys that I have not been able to fix up a hotel, but that I've been recommended the Lietuva. They can't be bothered to take me there. It would be too difficult at this time, David says.

'Difficult or not, it has to be done,' I say. 'And anyway, I welcome difficulty – that's what I've come to write about.'

'He means too difficult for us,' Simon says.

Their English is better than most Englishmen's English. They have Yiddish, if I want to try them in that. And Russian. And Lithuanian. Oh, and Simon has Hebrew.

'You will stay at our apartment,' says David.

Simon wants to know whether you say apartment or flat.

'Either,' I say, 'but I can't possibly.'

'What you mean you *can't*? You mean you don't want? Can is about capacity, isn't it?'

'And don't you say possibly,' Simon chimes in, 'when you are saying what you *may* do? But we say you may do, so you can possibly.'

I see how it's going to be. Suddenly I understand what it might have been like to be a Hasid hereabouts a couple of hundred years ago, why you might have felt that you needed to take a break from the pedantry and try cartwheels as a means of reaching God.

They laugh at each other's efforts. And they laugh again when I ask them if they live with their family. Of course they live with their family. No person their age can afford a place. Things are so bad they can't imagine a time when they ever will be able to afford a place. Their parents would like a bigger apartment but there is no question of it. Not for years.

'But it's all right,' David says.

'You get on with your parents?'

'Of course. I can't imagine not getting on with them. I can't imagine how it is, not to like to live with them.'

'You will see for yourself,' Simon says.

I say again that it is out of the question that I should dump myself on them. But they have the car and we don't seem to be going near any hotels.

'My mother will be insulted,' David says, 'if you don't stay with us.'

Funny about the word mother. No matter how old you get, it always suggests someone older than you. In my mind's eye I see Mrs Rozas. A plump little babushka with hairs on her chin, chasing hens around her backyard like my great-grandmother. Will she pinch my cheeks and give me a zloty?

Had I thought longer about the ages of David and Simon, I would have been better prepared for the young woman in her forties who greets me in the Rozas apartment. And had I looked harder at Simon's melting dark good-looks, I would have been better prepared for her beauty. So I don't get my cheeks pinched and I don't get a zloty. But I do get a few shy, glancing smiles shot my way while I tuck into the feast she has prepared – a feast by any standards, but in a country where they fight for a lettuce, a banquet – and I do send a few shy, glancing smiles back, as I compliment her cranberry juice and hear how she waded thigh-high through a swamp to pick the berries for it with her bare hands.

Not having sufficient Yiddish, or any Lithuanian or Russian, I can only smile my congratulations on his good fortune to Mr Rozas.

Simon pulls out albums of photographs before we've finished eating. David pushes food at me. I say no, enough. He accuses me of being polite. Of being English. Of having spent too much time at Buckingham Palace.

'OK,' I say. 'No more potato kugel, thank you, means more potato kugel, please.'

455

When I say, yes, please, I would love more cake and berries, he inquires whether that means no, thank you, no more cake and berries.

He is quick, agitated, a fencer. Simon is more imploring. Molten-eyed, yielding, a receiver of pain. They've sorted it out. The wounder and the wounded. At least in public.

They ask me about writing. About royalties. Sums, however modest at home, that cannot be mentioned here. Already Simon has seen the price of a map of the Baltic States I have brought with me. 'Five pounds?' He does some rapid calculations. 'That's my scholarship for a month.'

They want to know the price of books in England ... the price of one of mine, say. I mumble a sum.

'Fifteen pounds! For a novel! Do many people buy?'

'No,' I am able to assure them. 'Not many.'

They are gloomy about things here. The sick joke is that they're all thinking back to the 'good old Brezhnev days'. Yes, yes, there had to be a change, but the deterioration in material living standards is hard to take. They could travel once. They did travel once. They drove to Germany. David has been to Italy. And to Israel. Now, the bad news is that Aeroflot will be charging hard currency and they won't be able to afford to fly. Not for years. Not for the foreseeable future.

Meanwhile, they have a happy home life, at least. They are gallant, both of them, towards their mother. The way Jewish boys are supposed to be. It is as a kind of tribute to his mother that David tells me, as we're looking through photographs, that he wants and expects to marry a Jewish girl. He remembers his grandmother saying that he should.

I turn to his mother, to Taube – 'Do you want it?'

She waits for David to translate. 'No,' she says, laughing. 'No – I don't care.'

But she knows the compliment her son pays her. And, after all, deserves it. She is dark, gleaming, with a firm nose and heavy eyes and a strong jaw. In some of her old photographs she resembles Anne Bancroft, in a fur hat, gambolling in the snow. In another photograph that isn't there, but exists in my mind, in black and white, she is Anna Magnani wading bare-thighed through a swamp to pick cranberries.

She has a contralto voice, a rich laugh that would have been even richer, you can tell from these photographs of her with her friends, in the days when there was more to laugh about. Funny how familiar so many of the faces are in these albums. Their snaps and our snaps, stills from different episodes of the same drama. The principals are distinct, but the minor players have strolled through their lives and through mine. World-loving Jews, not Orthodox, not ritualistic, not spiritual, but Jewish in every gesture, Jewish in every thought – that was enough, wasn't it?

We put the photographs away. Too much past. So what about now? How does it feel to be independent?

As far as independence means freedom from the Soviet system, fine. But they are lying low and waiting. They do not forget how cooperative with the Nazis the Lithuanians could not wait to be. They don't feel threatened. But all in all the country is more dangerous than it was.

'I used to be able to go through the streets safely at two in the morning,' David says. 'But now, if Simon stays out till twelve, my mother is frightened.'

That's not a specifically Jewish fear, but they've had those too. When the TV tower was surrounded and there were rumours of coming civic unrest, they fell prey to old, old alarms.

David suddenly laughs and turns to his mother. 'Do you remember what you said?'

She does. She said, 'Do we have an axe?'

They feel they should have gone to Israel. All of them. Together. Now it might be too late. There is a right time for such a move.

And they fear it has gone. Many of their friends who went to Israel write to warn them against coming. No jobs. No housing. No prospects. They may be better off where they are. They are in work, at least. They have an apartment, at least.

Simon still leans to it. David to America. He is a physicist. ('An exceptional one,' Simon whispers to me.) It has to be America. But he needs a scholarship. Both boys are writing letters to foreign universities. The family is watching and waiting. There are postcards of faraway places pinned to David and Simon's walls and doors. In their heads they are living overseas.

They won't hear any more hotel talk from me. 'You have explained English manners to us,' David says. 'When you say please take me to a hotel, that means thank you I would like to stay here.'

'And when I say please let me stay here?'

'Then we say, that will be our pleasure.'

And so I pass my first night back in the Lithuania that the Schwartzbords fled almost a hundred years ago, in the spare room of a small apartment in a Communist tower block, the guest of a working, witty, lustrous Litvak family I can half-believe in as my family.

What Jews love more than anything, more than jokes, more than potato kugel, more than Taube Rozas's cranberries picked bare-handed from a swamp: one another.

I wake to the sound of television, the Winter Olympics on the Eurosport Channel, and then, on NBC, coming into Vilnius by satellite, news of an Israeli raid on Hizbollah. Simon and David are shouting. Whooping. I get up to see what the excitement is about. When it is confirmed that a leader of Hizbollah has been killed, they slap each other's open palms, like street-smart blacks closing a deal. Then they go into a routine, imitating Arab leaders, Arafat to a T – explaining to the western press how for him Jews are cousins.

No finessing, then, in Vilnius. No agonizing over the rights of Jews to be as blood-thirsty as the next chap.

They are closer to Israel – this is how I understand it. They are closer to Israel in the sense that they need it, as a bolt-hole, more than an English Jew does, and they need the affiliation more too. You have to realize that Lithuanian is coming more and more to mean *ethnic* Lithuanian, Simon told me. 'And we are not that,' said David.

So they're still on the edge here. And not much has changed since my Great-great-aunt-and-a-half Pauline Kaplan thanked God every night that the day had gone peacefully.

I wouldn't mind slapping palms with them, across the decades, but I'm liberal and squeamish. Where I come from you don't whoop when an enemy's been killed. Not even if you're on the very spot where your enemy whooped over you.

I am determined to move in to the Lietuva, the big Intourist hotel in the centre of town. Charmless but handy, I've been told. David and Simon caution me against it. It's a den of pimps, thieves, dealers, rip-off artists, they warn me. Men of eastern Russian appearance who will engage me in conversation, slip drugs in my tea, rob me and then ransack my room.

'Good for a writer,' I say.

'Except that you won't remember anything of what happened to write about it,' David says.

But I am insistent. They ring me a taxi and, to my astonishment, a taxi comes. They will not, however, let me go on my own. I won't be the first foreigner to get into a taxi and end up in the forest *sans* clothes and *sans* credit cards. Not like the good old Brezhnev days.

It's hard to say which is the worse for wear, the taxi or the taxi-driver. At night, the taxi doubles as a dog's home. There are long white hairs, as thick as cable, on my seat. I cannot put my mind to what the driver doubles as. His eyes water. One is closed up altogether. This is the one he drives with. He wears green tartan trousers with button flies. All the buttons are undone.

The fare comes to about a farthing. Simon reckons we've been ripped off.

This is my first view of the city in the daylight. Snow has fallen again overnight. A light covering. The usual contemptuous socialist architecture dominates the skyline – ugly for one, ugly for all. Like Lambeth. There is a regulation Communist telecommunications tower, in this case, of course, a recent monument to national resistance. But the river is handsome, not broad but snakey and accessible. Church spires have begun to cluster prettily. And the light is peculiarly lovely: soft, crisper than London light without being southern European hard, more as if it has pale orange crystals dissolved in it, a yellowish, weightless sort of light. Lithuania is known as the Land of Amber. That may be the colour of the light – amber.

The Hotel Lietuva is set in a concrete complex that resembles Piccadilly Plaza in Manchester. But is not quite as desolate. This complex has a planetarium, and women with brooms who sweep away the snow. Men with eyes wetter than our taxi-driver's sit plotting in the lobby. They are discussing how best to slip something into my drink. David and Simon shepherd me through the formalities and bodyguard me up to my room. It has a grubby brown carpet, so badly worn that it moves under you as you walk. There are fairgrounds where you pay to walk on floors that do this. There is a one-inch mattress set on a hardboard plinth, an old groaning fridge, and a television on which you can watch the Winter Olympics via Sky. So what else do I need?

I make an arrangement to see David and Simon later in the day. They will act as my guides. It will be with them that I do Lazdai and Serhai. In their car. No, they won't hear a word against it – in their car. All we need is to find the petrol. But that is for another day. Now I will settle in. They are loath to leave me. They have a way of buzzing around me which sometimes I find winning and sometimes I don't. I assure them I'll be safe. I am more than their combined ages. 'Yes, but you're a writer,' says David.

I give them time to be clear of the hotel, then I make my way down to the lobby where the trouble is. Something not Jewish for five minutes.

I need to change dollars into roubles. One of the advantages of the Lietuva is that it has an exchange bureau. There are only two or three of them in the whole of the city. And this one speaks English. Writes English, too. A hand-written sign is stuck to the grille. It says SORRY WE DO NOT HAVE ROUBLES.

A woman is sitting behind the counter with nothing to do. She is dreaming of warm countries. I ask her if there will be any roubles later. Ever. At once she becomes busy. She points to the sign.

I saunter back past reception. A beautiful young woman in a fox-fur coat is entertaining a circle of men. It is like a scene from *Zuleika Dobson*. She has just been to a bank where they told her, 'We have no roubles.'

Everyone is laughing. 'In a bank!' she explodes.

She doesn't seem to think it will ruin her day, so I decide not to let it ruin mine. I go back for my coat and walk into more EEC mirth. A party of Germans who have just checked in are taking possession of their rooms. One after another they fall into the passage, clutching their stomachs, howling with laughter. You would think that only an indecency could be the cause of such ribaldry. But it isn't indecency, it's decor. They roll around in their green coats. One hammers his head on the wall. A woman, all in black leather, an otter woman, roars hoarsely, rousingly, and leans into the men. They take turns to look through one another's doors and fall about some more. The maid, meanwhile, lolls against her trolley. She wears short socks. She isn't amused, but she isn't angry either. She is accustomed to the way Germans behave when they check into a hotel.

I rub my eyes. I won't say it, I won't think it, I won't ask it – whether there was laughter in Lazdai on November 3rd, 1941.

Roubleless, I go out into the aery light. More rheumy-eyed men, idle, drunk, looking for something whose name they have forgotten, cluster under the concrete pillars that hold up the hotel. One is trying to sell a book. I need David and Simon. Too many peoples have pushed one another in and out of this city. I need a guide to the human sights, someone to say, 'That one's a Pole and that one's a Russian and that one's a Lithuanian. He came with the Grand Duke Vytautas, he came with Stalin, he'll go when the ethnic Lithuanians start to push him.'

I'd like to be sure which is which so that I know whom to say serves you right to.

I cross the Nerys by a bridge on which heavy black statues depict sinewy socialist youth – girls holding sheaves of corn, boys looking to a rosy future. I'm surprised they haven't gone the way of statues of Lenin.

It is bitterly cold. In England you wouldn't come out on such a day unless you had to. In Israel the army would be mobilized. But the streets are full. Away from the hotel, people move briskly, appear law-abiding, are shoe-string smart. You soon discern a local look, somewhat Nordic: contracted, slightly blinded expressions on the men, razor-blade cheek-bones on the women. When they are slim and do not allow their faces to become too square, the women can be beautiful – eyes narrow, almost at a slant; small nose, a little too turned-up; a full pouting lip. If they look at you, if you catch the amber light in their narrowed eyes, they have no choice but to flirt passingly. They are not in love, it's just the way their faces tend. Noses turn up a little more. Eyes narrow a little more. Lips purse a little more.

If they are furred-up as though it's 1950, and wearing clicking boots as well, it may be you that's in love.

How both sexes manage to look as presentable as they do, given what's for sale in the shops, is one of those dreary consumer mysteries that absorb you, against all your better intentions, the moment you set foot anywhere that is or has been Communist. I've resolved not to play News at Ten reporter and go nosing along queues and into unstocked shops. But the sheer picturesqueness of non-commerce, the aesthetic fascination of a commodity-void, sucks you down every time. You wouldn't pause to look into Harrods' windows; but an entire store with only six dirty plaited plastic belts on show – how do you tear yourself away from that? People eating ice-cream, even in the snow, are nothing much; but I see them buying ice-cream without the ice-cream, just the cones, which they grip tenaciously at the bottom as they walk along, lest in their gourmandizing they spill thin air.

I would like coffee but am unable to distinguish a café. Probably just as well as I have no local currency. I return to the hotel. The sign is still up in the exchange bureau. No roubles. And no teller with nothing to tell to be told off by either.

I ask a motherly receptionist what chance the bureau will open again today. Little. I ask where the coffee-bar is. Down. I ask if they'll take hard currency. No. Will I be able to charge to my room? No. So how do I get coffee? With roubles. And where do I get roubles? The exchange bureau.

I show her the hole in my bucket.

'Maybe I can change for you,' she suggests. How much do I want to change?

Forty dollars, I say. I don't want to flash it around. For forty dollars I can buy the hotel.

And how many roubles I want?

Oh, oh. I can't get into this. I say I've heard that the rate is about a hundred, a hundred and ten roubles to a dollar.

She says she can change me, personally, at rate of eighty.

I say I'll change ten dollars.

She sends me round the corner of the counter. Discretion. I watch her fishing in her handbag. Out come eight hundred roubles. In go my ten dollars.

So: I'm mugged in my hotel, just as everyone says I will be. Only it's not the Tartar pimps and Kazakhstani tea-druggers that get me; it's the receptionist in the navy suit and peacock brooch and spectacles identical to my mother's.

I'm not complaining. Someone needs to be enterprising round here. But I know the boys will be annoyed when they come to collect me later. The exchange rate is a sensitive business in this country. They have already told me what rate I must not be talked below. Do I lie to them or come clean?

It carries responsibilities, being ripped off to the tune of a few pence in a place where a few pence is all they earn a week.

In the time he's been away, David has had his hair cut. Now he looks skinned as well as startled. With more head showing, there is more pressure on him to be clever. And with some serious old-city touring to be done, there's more pressure on Simon to be informative. For the second time in two days I am kidnapped. One on each side, a hand under each elbow, they all but frog-march me out into the snow.

And it's all very pretty, with Italianate churches and Russian Orthodox churches and cobbled alleys and grand boulevards, called Prospects (something the country doesn't have: serves them right), and palaces and theatres and a hill with a castle on the top, and absolutely nowhere to sit with a beer or a drugged tea to enjoy it.

Before the Second World War there were very nearly one hundred thousand Jews living in Vilnius – a third of the city's population. After the Nazis made their easeful entry, most of those one hundred thousand Jews were rounded up and walled, ten to a room, within a ghetto that still partly stands, a once elegant neighbourhood of classical façades and professional, secular, aspirations. We pause outside the Judenrat, where the Jews were processed and selected and notified of each day's new ignominy. A plaque, in Lithuanian and Hebrew, marks the building which is now the headquarters for the restoration of the old city. And here, the boys deliver themselves of some icy contemporary realisms.

A few years ago, in the early days of the independence movement, there was much talk of the wrongs done to Lithuanian Jews by the Nazis and, especially, by the Russians. What I have to grasp is that while the Russians were here, no special mention was permitted of what the Jews had suffered under Nazism. There had been only one victim of the Nazis, and that was the Soviet Citizen. This plaque, commemorating a specifically Jewish fate, in Hebrew, would once have been unthinkable. So the need to right the wrongs of the Jews helped give impetus to the drive for independence. Now they have achieved their aim, Lithuanians are happy to revert to the old reading of history. As witness President Lambergis's inaugural decision, since fudged, to grant a pardon to Lithuanian Nazi war-criminals on the grounds that they were heroes in the struggle against Bolshevism.

'As always,' Simon says, 'the Jew is taken up or dropped, according to the political uses to which he can be put at the time.'

David is the physicist and joker, but he defers to his younger brother in matters of history, philosophy, architecture, theology, topography and human rights. It is hard to remember, sometimes, that Simon is only eighteen. I marvel that an eighteen-year-old brain has had time to see so much information, let alone digest it, but then I recall that this is Lithuania, where Jews have prided themselves for centuries on their scholarship. More particularly it is Vilnius, home to Elija Ben-Solomon, surnamed the Gaon, scourge of the Hasids. It is possible that the Gaon was even more precocious than Simon Rozas, having delivered a Talmudic discourse at the great synagogue of Vilnius when he was seven, having mastered the literature of the *Halachah* at eight, having gone into the Cabbala when he was nine, and having turned his talents to astronomy when he was ten.

There is a street named after him in the old ghetto, a quaint cobbled tumbledown of narrow lanes and passages, where you are encouraged by pleasing decay to think of confinement as charming. Gaon Street. Nobody knows which his house was, or whether he lived in this part of town at all, but I choose a building which is shuttered and think of him, sitting behind drawn blinds, so as not to be distracted by events, reading by candlelight, with his feet in a bowl of cold water to keep him awake, preparing treatises on algebra and anatomy, collating the Babylonian and Palestinian Talmuds, fulminating against the ecstasies of the Hasids, whose defence of their incoherence was that they 'roamed remote worlds in their thoughts'.

But there is another call on my loyalty here too. Stikliai Street. Glazier Street. In which is Vilnius's most famous private restaurant – Stikliai: The Glazier. My great-great-grandfather's occupation. The trade in which Zayde had been employed as some sort of apprentice. Odd, I had thought, a Jewish glazier. But not odd at all. It was something we were good at. Putting in windows. And never looking out of them.

Twenty-three

A PLAY ON A CEMETERY

A bad night in the Lietuva. Whores in the bars. A drugged, mugged and beaten lamb chop for supper. You'd think he'd want to keep his name secret, but the Chief of Production signs the menu. Gamybos Vldejas – unless that means Chief of Production.

The bed is a rack of pain. The heating rattles, overheats, and poisons the air. You can open the window to counteract this, but then you have rattle, poison, overheating and a single stream of freezing air directed at the bed. I call the desk at midnight and ask for help.

'We'll send you up more blankets,' the girl says.

'No. That's not the problem. The heating's on.'

'On!' She's astonished. Obviously I have the only room with a heater that works. I'm getting everybody else's heat.

'Then turn it off,' she says.

'It doesn't turn off.'

'I'll see,' she says. 'I'll find someone.'

I wait half an hour, then the maid who sits in the corridor with her legs up, watching the Winter Olympics on guests' televisions, arrives looking sleepy. She has an engineer with her, smelling of alcohol. They speak no English. He puts his hand by the heater, feels the currents of sticky, oily hot air, and looks at me. Do I want it hotter than *this*?

Too hot, I say. *Zu heiss*. I make to mop my brow, like a man lost in a desert.

Ah! He understands. He is pleased. We are the first men on

the planet and we have communicated. Language will be born in another thousand years. He moves furniture, gets on his back, taps, bangs, screws.

No good. It gets no colder. He shrugs.

What about the noise? I put my hands to my ears.

Ah! He moves the furniture again. Gets on his back, taps, bangs, screws.

It becomes quieter. He smiles. I smile. She smiles.

He leaves a smell of vodka behind him, which I have to throw open the window to dispel. As though fired from a space-gun, an enfilade of cold air blasts the room. I think about ringing the desk and asking for more blankets. Or another engineer. In the end I close the windows. When I wake in the morning I am boiling, my eyes are running. I wonder why I am smelling of alcohol when I didn't drink. The banknotes which I secreted about my person while I slept, for fear the Tartars would get in and rob me, are wet with my perspiration, or with their own.

But it's a fine morning outside. The sun is coming up spectacularly in a turbulence of cloud and fractured amber and smoke which billows from the factories in the middle of town. When I look out of the window I see floats of ice drifting down the Nerys. An old woman is sweeping the entire plaza with a besom. There is a dusting of snow on the dome of the planetarium, and on the spires of the baroque churches.

I descend to a breakfast of weak tea and potato pancakes. The tea is made palatable by the Lemsips I've brought against the illnesses I'm bound to suffer. Medicine apart, the tea and the lemon and the aspro go well together.

The exchange bureau is due to open at nine. I get there at quarter to. There is already a queue. A woman wearing no make-up – which is in itself an aggressive act in Lithuania – arrives behind the counter carrying an old plastic bag. She takes various things out of it, including a cardigan which she puts on. She goes to the safe. In the queue, we all strain to see if the safe contains anything. She brings something out – a small handful – and deposits it in a tin box on her desk. Then she roots around for a pen. Some paper. A calculator. She takes some sheets of carbon – used carbon – selects one, and begins to tear it into strips. Very precise, very meticulous, strips. The queue gets longer.

More paperwork. More pen sorting. More carbon tearing. It's now a little after nine. She puts on a light. We stir. Then – a masterstroke! – she makes a phone call. A personal phone call. Long and chatty. Lithuanian for 'You didn't . . . you never did!'

Our excitement subsides. There are businessmen here from all over the world except England, entrepreneurs ready to raise Lithuania from its depression, but they must wait in line while a woman in a cardigan finishes her conversation with her friend.

She opens her window at ten past. A German is at the head of the queue. He could be the managing director of Mercedes, come to open a plant in Vilnius. He proffers thirty marks. She will only change twenty. We all immediately embark on subtle psycho-financial adjustments. If you ask for too much, she will punish you with little. If you ask for too little, she'll think you've no confidence and reduce you still further. We are searching for the golden mean. I had meant to try seventy American dollars; I decide to try thirty. An Italian in front of me hands over thirty-five. She will only change ten. I attempt the same, but get only five. My ploy of giving her twenties – too big for her to have loose change for – backfires. One of them she rejects because it's got writing on it. The other she can negotiate downwards because the schmuck in front of me gave her all fives.

An inscription in the visitors' book at the Jewish Museum on Pamenkalnio takes my eye. It reads,

This is my first visit to Lithuania. 50 years later since the World War II. I believe that the new age has come and it will light so many things that has been hidden.

July 19 – 1991
  Keisuke Fujino
  Tokyo

I decide that a young person wrote that.

The Jewish Museum is also young. It is a scissors and paste job, mainly photographs, cheaply and, to my sense, eloquently mounted. Local photographs. It is a museum devoted not to the long history of Jews in Lithuania but to their destruction. Something like two hundred and forty thousand Jews lived in Lithuania before the war; something like two hundred and twenty thousand were exterminated. This modest museum, housed in a wooden building that feels like a barn or a dairy, is their memorial. Rachile Kostanian tends it like a flame.

She talks to me in her office, at the rear of the museum, while the phone goes and people come in and out with biscuits and a grave white-haired woman sits writing in a corner. 'That is Mrs Margolis,' Rachile Kostanian tells me. 'She was in the ghetto. She is writing her memories.' The grave white-haired woman nods.

Rachile Kostanian lives memories. She seems to have no protection against the past. So it is impossible to tell what age she is. Her skin is extremely fine. If you looked at her hard enough you would start to see through her. She is hypnotically distressed. Her eyes swim in sadness. You would register her beauty more, were you able to register her nervous system less. She plays with a piece of jewellery at her throat the whole time we speak. I notice that she has small feet, in red shoes.

She is short-tempered with me to begin with. I make the mistake of telling her that I have been around the ghetto with David and Simon Rozas. She knows them, of course. This is a tiny community now. They know one another. Yes, very clever boys. But *boys*. 'What can they know?'

More than I do, I say.

She opens her hands, her shoulders, her eyes. She doesn't mean know in that sense. She means *know*. Know as in suffer. 'Very many people here are coming and talking. People who know not deep ... who know only of surface. This kind of research is not correct, excuse me please.'

I attempt to smile away the idea of 'research'. Every Jew is a witness to Jewish life, I say.

'Jewish life?' Now it's her turn to do some smiling away. 'Is there Jewish life?'

The morbidity runs as deep as that. We are to talk only of Jewish death.

I ask about the museum, how long it has been open, why, given the history of Jewish civilization here, there seems to be so little left to show other than photographs of dejection and defeat.

She sighs. Plucks at the chain around her neck. Every question is a road back to the same place.

A Jewish Museum was opened after the war, in 1945. In the ghetto. To preserve a memory of what had been, and what had happened. But under Sovietization a different story had to be told. Historical inscriptions in the ghetto were painted out. 'No one took photo. The beautiful synagogue, which had been damaged during the war, was exploded. It would have been possible to rebuild. The foundations were there, but the Soviet government decided it was not safe. They wanted to wipe out the memory. Now there is kindergarten in this place. In 1949 the museum was closed ...'

Mrs Margolis looks up from her work. 'June 10th,' she says. 'June 10th, 1949.'

Rachile Kostanian lets me swim in her brown eyes. We say nothing until the last echo of Mrs Margolis's stark recollection has died away.

'Jewish school was closed. Jewish papers. Any word that had expression of Jewish – Jewish theatre and so on – was wiped out. They tried to wipe out even the bloody memory, not just the culture. All the memorials say, Here are victims of Fascism. No mention of Jews. Even in the big memorial at Ponary, where sixty thousand bodies were found, even there you can see that from 1941 to 1944 Soviet people were killed by Fascists. Only two years ago we managed to put up plaque in Yiddish and Hebrew telling that victims were Jewish ... The Jewish history, all was silenced and wiped out.'

She clasps her hands as she speaks, compresses her lips. Her feet look tiny in their red shoes.

'Now, Emanuel Zingeris – you know him? he is politician – has idea to recreate a Jewish museum. Today we have about thirty Jewish institutions. We are very glad. In spite of it, I have to say to you, it is a play on a cemetery. All our activities resemble those of half-life corpses. My eyes are full of tears saying so. It's tragedy of our people everywhere, Israel as well.

'I've read a Russian philosopher who said it is tragedy from God, and Jews will have to carry it. Even if they have their own state they will be isolated. I'm very, very pessimistic. At first, I was hopeful. But now, evidence of anti-Semitism is deep. A week ago – you can take photo – a window over our poster was broke. They spilt white paint over it. They say in papers, which are free, *which are free from Stalin now*, you Jews brought Communism, you Jews took part in destroying the Lithuanian nation – and *that* is why some Lithuanians took revenge during war.'

She sees me writing in my notebook, and pauses. I wonder if she is going to become angry with me again.

'At the highest level,' she says, as if she has to remind herself that there are other considerations besides feeling, other people to take into account besides the dead, 'I must underline, they are not interested in anti-Semitism. I am giving you my personal opinion. I want you to know it. I want you to underline that it is *my subjective opinion.*'

I underline it, but I don't get it. Is she saying that at the highest level they don't encourage anti-Semitism, or at the highest level they can't be bothered to address it as a problem? All I can tell is that there is a problem of power-play in the air, and I decide she might be running scared of Zingeris, the local Jewish deputy who is famous for being here, there and everywhere, and for liking to be the one to make the pronouncements when there are pronouncements to be made.

Her dues paid to politics and realism, she returns to the inner world of hopelessness in which she is more at home. 'I get more pessimistic every day,' she says. 'I'm not talking about revival of Jewish life. We must have some, but it is some kind of play, because we know in our hearts we are denied to live here, although the Grand Duke Vytautas gave privileges to Jews in 1383 or 1388. We Jews' – she sighs, she palpitates, like a hunted hind – 'we Jews are condemned to live only day at a time. Our first duty is to build up a memorial for the vanished world – try – *try* – to tell this was history, to show the culture, the immense impact that Jews had on culture and daily life. And the other part is to tell the truth about the Holocaust. I think that the task of Jew who remains is to rebuild a memorial in the form of museum – I think – in memory of our parents and our grandparents, in memory of our families which perished here . . .'

She holds on to her voice, her tears. At this moment she doesn't look dressed, she looks *wrapped* in her clothes.

She hands me over to Mrs Margolis, who is going to show me around the exhibition, and later in the week will escort me through the ghetto. The ghetto she was immured in, and doesn't forget.

'You can listen to someone else,' Rachile says, 'and not my sick heart.'

I'm surprised how much I begin to miss her sick heart the moment she withdraws it. Being shown around my old country by a couple of clever Jewish kids whom I can think of as alternative versions of me – me if we'd stayed – has a lot to be said for it. Already I've made connections of the heart – of the living, not the sick heart – I never anticipated. But I need some of Rachile Kostanian's determined morbidity. At my age you have to keep company with people who have mastered all the arts of bitterness. It may be a harsh light Rachile sheds on the country, on herself, on the whole business of being Jewish anywhere after everything that's happened. But what do I expect – a rosy glow? It's controversial, right enough – she means it to be controversial – to assert that the first duty of a Lithuanian Jew is to look backwards, to commemorate the past, to dance on the grave of his ancestors. She strikes the cheeks not just of forgetfulness, but of optimism, vitality, the callous energy without which there can be no present let alone future life. And I enjoy the stinging sensation.

She measures her effect. When I see her next – ten minutes later – she is dressed to go out, in a shaggy fur coat and, I either think or invent, a beret. She has that Lilli Palmer (born Lillie Marie Peiser) broken European look. She does it brilliantly.

Mrs Margolis is another matter. She does not wear dainty red shoes. She is looking at being elderly. Perhaps with relief. She is grey, severe, not at all Slavic. We have agreed to communicate in French and whatever Yiddish I can muster and whatever English she can. I have already been around the exhibition on my own. It was touching then. Now it is harrowing.

That document demanding one hundred thousand roubles from a Jewish doctor – a hundred thousand roubles from every Jew – was once in her possession. That Jewish doctor was her father.

We go through the day-by-day horrors of the German occupation. The edicts saying that Jews were not allowed to buy from

Christian shops, that Jews were not permitted to walk on the pavements, but only on the roads – *'comme chevaux'*. The food shortages, the Jew who was killed for secreting a pound of pears.

Then we come to photographs of resistance workers. She points out her husband. *Echappé? Oui. Pas tué? Non. Mais, il est mort maintenant.* He looks – he looked – like a calmer Mahler. And then, below him, a photograph of her. Beautiful, pensive, fine-boned.

It starts to get harder for her. Her voice stays steady but her eyes are watering. She isn't crying. Her eyes are not red. But they fill. They hold moisture. They are doing too much work. 'It's hard for me,' she says, 'I'm seeing many things and people here.'

She lived in the ghetto for two years. Then fled to join the partisans in the Rudinko Forest. A map on the wall shows the direction the escapees followed. Some to freedom, some to death.

I apologize to her for being instrumental in her present distress. She shakes her head. *'C'est mon travail.'*

She is employed here. Among the family documents and photographs. Her work. Her travail.

A cold, clear morning. Simon and David are taking me by train to Kaunas, once the provisional capital of Lithuania. If you want to see Lithuania, I've been told, see Kaunas. Unlike Vilnius, which is chock-full of Russians and Poles, Kaunas is for Lithuanians.

Serves them right.

Simon comes running out of a taxi to collect me. He is always running. He has the run of a person who prefers to think. 'We are a little late,' he says, de-misting the front doors of the hotel with his breath, 'maybe three minutes, I think.'

The railway station has the look of a transit camp. People are bundled-up, carrying boxes tied with string. There are no amenities to speak of here. Just rudimentary toilets, hard benches and a kiosk which doesn't sell drinks but hair-grips, a ball of brown wool, a single pair of spidery-patterned tights, two or three notepads with illustrations of girls in Odessa swimsuits on the covers. A crowd is gathered round the kiosk.

David runs into two university friends. They are shy to meet me, and incline their heads when we shake hands. One smiles quietly to himself. He has Baltic grey eyes and wears a black pork-pie hat. The other boy is bareheaded and has a nose red from the cold. They don't venture any English, but when I speak to David and Simon I can tell they understand. They are dressed poorly – cheap anoraks in dead colours, plastic shoes that fasten with Velcro but do a better job of keeping out the snow than my suede ones. They make me feel meretricious. And ignorant. They know languages. They possess facts and are hungry for more. They want information from me about my country, which I am not able to give. Their deprived youth, set against their curiosity, shames me. When I get home I will put myself on a reading programme.

'The train will be either very hot or freezing,' David warns me. It's freezing. We have to stamp our feet to keep them warm. Although it's not crowded, and not going for half an hour, the old women in woollen head-scarves fight to get aboard. They shove the backsides of those in front; they kick out at those behind. I look at them coldly. They are of the age, all of them, to have done . . . things.

The journey is a hundred kilometres, but we will be on the train two hours. A sound-system crackles. The boys die with laughter whenever they can make out a word. They translate for me – 'Roughly,' they say –

'Travel can be a pleasant experience of mind and body – and we aim to make it so. But you, too, dear passengers, can contribute. Please help everyone to enjoy the pleasures of travel by not smoking, not drinking, and not making writing on the walls.'

At Kaunas you dismount from the train in the street itself. I like this. It feels western – I mean wild western. David and his friends are in Kaunas on university business; Simon and I take a taxi to the IXth Fort, one of a number of forts built by the Russians at the beginning of the First World War and subsequently used by the Nazis to hold Communists, Russian sympathizers, Jews, whoever needed to be held. 'But most Jews,' Simon says, 'were simply killed outside and disposed of on the spot.'

A massive concrete monument dominates the scene. It comprises three towering sections, each leaning away from the others, as though the rafters of the universe itself are coming down. Faces emerge from the slats of grey and unadorned concrete, and great hands, suggestive of confusion, strength and weakness. I can't decide whether it avoids Holocaust kitsch, but it undeniably makes an impression by its bulk alone, in this cold, dead landscape, ten kilometres or so from the centre of town. If nothing else, it compounds the desolation.

We examine a number of plaques set in the ground. Competing plaques. The original, Communist, commemoration mentions 80,000 killed and leaves it at that. A Jewish stone, added two years ago, elaborates. 'This is the place where the Nazis and their assistants killed more than 30,000 Jews from Lithuania and other European countries.'

Their assistants. Here's the rub. Here's the reason for reticence. Those assistants were Lithuanians.

A peroxide blonde, my age, lets us into the fort. She wears boots and a slinky skirt. Just a hint of petticoat. Her lips are painted in the shape of a bow. One of her stockings has been repaired. Her hips roll. Simon seems never to have seen a woman like her. For the first twenty years of my life I never saw a woman who looked any other way. Before she leaves us to the cells, she puts her head on one side, touches her cheek and shows us a gold tooth.

It's the usual chamber of horrors. Made remarkable for me by a photograph of a monument to the slaughtered at Lazdai. This is the first photograph of Lazdai, of any kind, that I have seen. There are about twenty names listed on the monument. They are just legible in the photograph. Simon goes through them. Not a single Jewish name. Just the gloss, at the bottom, IR KITI – that is, AND OTHERS.

If there were any Schwartzbords among them, this is how they are remembered . . . IR KITI.

Back in Kaunas itself, we take ourselves along to a pretty powder-blue synagogue that has the builders in. Money has been made available for renovation. And private benefactors have also coughed up in order to have the central-heating named after them. It's hard to get in past the scaffolding, but an old boy with a Jewish face I know from all over Europe, only this time surmounted by a Russian hat, sees that we're Jewish and lets us through.

He could be the caretaker, the *shammes*, or he might just be someone who likes to be here. Synagogues often have old men in them, who just like to be there. He loves the building and invites our admiration. We look up at the ceiling, painted blue, with Stars of David for ceiling roses. The Ark is a fine piece of carving, over a hundred years old. The Nazis wanted to take it away as an example of *Kunstwerk*, he tells Simon who tells me. Hard to see the Nazis wanting an Ark of the Covenant, however, no matter how nicely executed. On either side of the Ark is a *Yahrzeit* calendar, listing all the towns and villages in Lithuania where Jews were murdered by the Nazis, together with the dates of the principal executions, so that candles can be lit on the appropriate anniversaries. We find Lazdai and Serhai, and I write down the dates I should light candles, though of course I never will.

Another Jewish old man who has been here all along, *shmoozing* the workmen in a loud, squeaky voice, comes over to us. There is a Yiddish word for the way he walks – he *crichs*. Every joint is set solid. He too wears a fur hat, but this one is more like a droshky-driver's, with ear-muffs. He lets me know that a donation won't go amiss. I say I will make one before I go. He shouts a bit more, rubs his fingers together. Not for him, not for him, for the *shul*. I go over to the metal box and put some dollars in. When I return, he shakes my hand, says *shalom*, shakes my hand again, makes a blessing over me, and kisses me. I enjoy it. Kissed in Kaunas. By a *criching* caretaker.

I ask Simon to ask him if the synagogue is currently in use. In use! They have Hebrew school here. They give Bible lessons. Every week they read a portion of the law – a chapter from the Pentateuch. They're well advanced into Genesis. 'This week,' he says, 'we sold Joseph already.'

We leave laughing, blessings all round. Outside of the gay *shul* on Pico Boulevard, this may be the first synagogue I haven't been afraid of. Do *shuls* have to be reduced to nothing, then, before I can feel at home in them? Must Jews be poor before I can love them?

We promenade a while, pleasantly, for the town is airy and spacious. Easier to negotiate than Vilnius, more cheerful. More intellectual, too, Simon tells me. Fewer Russians and Poles here, he means. Kaunas was the capital when independence was declared for two and a half minutes in 1918, and it has the air of a regional principality, a once-capital.

Something makes Simon ask me about Stratford-on-Avon, and I realize that that's the sort of town we are in. Stratford-on-Avon, without Shakespeare or shops.

David is waiting for us at the Metropolis, the Café Royale of Kaunas, once a temple to luxury, with grand windows, a vestibule, red drapes, waiters in dinner-suits. We are the only people here for lunch. The tables are set with odd crockery and bent cutlery. When I go to the gentleman's toilet I find a smiling woman in it. When I go back I find it fouled. Chicken soup with no taste of chicken is served in mugs. After that comes stale bread and something-or-other-Kiev which sprays out boiling oil when you cut into it. The waiter serves us water tinted with juice. He pours, as he's been taught in waiting school, with one hand behind his back. It's these little touches that make all the difference.

The Rozas boys are in a less skittish mood today. It occurs to me that they may be having trouble getting petrol to take me to Lazdai and Serhai. But as they don't mention it, I don't. I wish I had some news of a successful Israeli raid to cheer them up with. Since we still have a few hours before our train back, we go to the Kaunas Art Gallery where there is a permanent exhibition of the works of M. K. Čiurlionis, 'outstanding Lithuanian painter and composer'.

I read on the wall that,

> Impeded by the multi-faceted nature of his own genius, the larger part of his creative energy Čiurlionis directed towards painting.

Do they mean *impeded*, I wonder. Aren't they after something more like impelled? Importuned? Impacted?

All the while I am pondering this, Čiurlionis's music plays.

Imploded?

The other speciality of the Kaunas Gallery is the Rasputin-eyed portrait. Deifications of playwrights and poets with flowing hair and streaming beards and fixed, mad stares. The eternal art of far-flung minorities who have never enjoyed stable governance long enough to acquire scepticism. When you are this far away and so frequently put upon, you turn every instance of individual instability into heroism. After the portraits, the sculptures.

Bronze and wood thinkers, philosophers, with craggy faces, fine noses, deep-set eyes, jutting brows, posed with their hands under their chins or wreathed around their brains. Deep reflective souls who are nevertheless manly, martial in the mind.

Impostured?

This, then, is the local fancy; this is how Lithuanians imagine themselves – as hypnotically intelligent martyrs of the spirit, soul-soldiers of the people. In which case the Kregans and the Schwartzbords were always going to be in trouble here. Where there is no national sense of the ridiculous, there is no safety for the visitor.

Almost as if they have read my mind, David and Simon march me across the road and through a little park to the Devil Museum. A curiosity of Kaunas, the Devil Museum houses on three floors an extensive collection of diabola – masks, puppets, charms, pipes, ashtrays, walking-sticks, vases, hat-stands, nutcrackers: objects made of every material and for every use (if the encouragement of superstition can be counted a use), but always featuring a Satan or a Mephistopheles or some comparable demon of the Lithuanian woods. A hypnotically intelligent painter friend of our friend Ciurlionis assembled these items just for fun, just for the devil of it, before passing them on to the state.

What is remarkable about the collection, to my eye, is how Jewish, right down to the Moses horns, most of the exhibits look. No, not look – *are*.

'No question about it,' I say to David and Simon, who are too young and too close to their own culture to have said it this way to themselves, 'when a Lithuanian imagines a devil he sees a Jew.'

They are resistant. Do I think so? Mmm. Mmm. But later on, as we are making our way back to the train, Simon tells me of a cute country custom, revived of late now that there's no Communism to keep the lid on it, of dressing up at Shrovetide in masks of witches and devils and saying, 'Now we are going Jew.'

'Going what?'

'Going Jew.'

'But it's not considered anti-Semitic,' David says.

'They put on a bent-nosed mask of a devil and say they are going Jew but it's not considered anti-Semitic! What is it considered? Zionist?'

'It's a way of speaking,' Simon explains. 'Like when my mother puts on her jumper inside-out, her friends at work say, "Did you sleep with a Jew last night?"'

I stop them in the street. They're smart but they're too young. They don't grasp the import of what they're telling me. 'This is fascinating and terrible,' I say. 'The devil stuff isn't exactly new to me – Christian theology has always needed the idea of Jewish evil. But if an ordinary unthinking Lithuanian associates an inside-out garment with a Jew, then it's time you got out of here. It means they'll never think of you as anything but the inverse of what's natural. Back-to-front. The wrong way round . . .'

And I become so agitated by all the meanings of this 'way of speaking', I get so exaggerated in my gestures and so hot and hellish in my denunciations, that if Čiurlionis's chum were passing he would have me for an exhibit in his collection and not think twice about it.

On the train back to Vilnius a passenger is so drunk that he falls to the floor and stays there. To get out at your station you simply step over him.

I count the advantages of deprivation as they affect train travel. No lap-tops. No Walkmen. No leather briefcases clicking open and shut. No reps doing their reports. None of that pornography of the heart we call the woman's novel.

Nothing to look at but the dead forgotten fields of Lithuania. How come there's no fruit here and no butter and no anything, I ask the boys, given how agrarian the country still is. Collectivization. Like the Russians, like everyone who has been Sovietized, the Lithuanians have lost the trick of farming. All they know now is how to mope around cities. What bliss! It used to be said of the Jews within the Pale of Settlement that they had no aptitude for agriculture and were only good for trade and commerce. Hardly surprising, said the Jews, since we've been forbidden the land for centuries. Every now and then an edict ordered or allowed them back. See! said their enemies when they botched it. We cannot pick it up again overnight, the Jews protested. Parasites! said their enemies. Now – what bliss! – the earthloving Russian and Lithuanian peasant prowls the town, while the Jew farms his heart out in a kibbutz.

Serve them right.

Tempting fate though it may be to say it, the hotel is not living up to its seedy reputation. No pimp has yet accosted me. No person from Porkhov has eyed-off my wallet. Invitations to change money under the counter are rare, and those that do come, come from me.

I try staring at the wet-eyed Tartars. I hang around the fringes of disreputable groups. Nothing. Soon I will be winking and throwing dollars in the air.

What does regularly disappear from the hotel is any bar or restaurant you were at the day before. Sometimes you go back and find it shuttered; at others you go back and find it gone completely. No chairs, no tables, no sign that it was ever there. It is Shangri-La here, every evening.

Sitting in a cocktail lounge which has astonished everyone by its unannounced opening, including the staff, who don't know how to make a cocktail, I watch a German businessman becoming intimate with a washed-out but painted-up Lithuanian escort. Listening to him learning local words and pronouncing them in an erotic manner, I realize what it is above all things I am not liking here – the preponderance of white northern races. There are too many Germans, Russians, Swedes, Finns. Nothing dark.

Nothing lustrous. Except, of course, Taube Rozas. Otherwise everyone is pale, bad-skinned, polar.

This, of course, is what Hitler longed for. A blindingly white anaemic world.

Would he have liked it, I wonder, had he got it? Once they have emptied their lives, or the world, of the thing they have argued with, are people pleased with their work? Do they settle back happy into a monochrome retirement? Or does it dawn on them too late that without your opposite you are nothing?

Mrs Margolis is waiting for me in the Jewish Museum. She looks older today, perhaps because she is wrapped up so well against the cold. I have walked from the hotel, hardly more than a mile away, but in that distance I have frozen over. I probably should not have lingered by the Nerys, but it looks beautiful today, if that is not a perverse thing to say about a river that has become pock-marked with ice-floats. It must be the ice-floats themselves that are beautiful, expanding as you watch, as though they are frozen flowers opening.

I am not looking forward to my tour around the ghetto with Mrs Margolis. It is going to be hard without a common language. It is going to be upsetting. And it is going to keep me pegged within a Holocaust context which I had hoped to overleap. My interests – my special interests – pre-date the Holocaust. But there is no getting beyond it. It did not just destroy lives and artefacts and fabric, it lies like an obstacle in the mind. It has changed time itself. There is no access, now, to a time *before* that event. You see everything in the light of what happened, happens, always did happen, always will happen.

For me this is a problem of perception. For Mrs Margolis it is the labyrinth in which she lives her life.

As we walk in the direction of the ghetto I ask her if she likes the city, if she feels it to be her home, despite everything.

My 'despite', my *'malgré tout'*, is naive. Of course she loves it here, not despite but *because* . . . *'à cause de* . . .'

She has so many memories . . . every building, every street, reminds her of her youth, of her friends, of her family. There the street she played in, there the school she went to, there her father's house.

She says things about her father that I cannot catch. And because they are things near her heart (I catch that much), I feel I cannot bend lower, lean into her, ask her to repeat them. Why should her poor heart have to beat even faster because of my poor French?

I talk to her about her good French. How come? Because in her youth every educated young Lithuanian spoke French – it was the language of sophistication, ideas, literature, philosophy. I suddenly see Mrs Margolis as another Anna Karenina, brilliant in a ballgown, negotiating these very streets, whose elegance is still visible, in a coach or an early Lada, on her way to meet her friends at *Les Huguenots*, not one word of which will cause a flutter in their vocabularies.

No sign of a French-speaking Vilnius now. All gone, the lustre and the life. All gone, the quarrels and divergences.

Mrs Margolis has other languages. Russian, Lithuanian, Hebrew, Yiddish, English (if she really has to) and Polish. Polish, too, was a language that denoted sophistication. It distinguished you from the Russians.

Now we are before the ghetto. She stretches out her arms to show me its boundaries, not as lines on a map but as streets, passageways, doorways, beyond which she was not allowed to pass. We turn into narrowing lanes, backyards, small houses, some of them almost unchanged in fifty years. The old maddening ghetto contradictions start to seize me – finding picturesque, missing, mourning the destruction of, a thing that should never have been here in the first place.

She shows me a lane she used to walk down with her fiancé, a balcony she used to stand under. We stand under it together. From here she would look out – that way, that way – and see the only tree that was visible from the ghetto. Because in the ghetto itself – *'pas des arbres'*.

I follow with my eye the length of a thin, cobbled lane. In the days of the ghetto it was gated. And through that gate Mrs Margolis made her escape one night, using a copy of a stolen key. Out through the gate, into the night, into the forests, leaving behind a family she never saw again.

She walks briskly, a short grey woman with no laughter lines on her face, living deep inside herself. Over here, she stood and watched people being led to the burial pits at Ponary. Over there was the great Jewish library, twenty thousand volumes or more, all destroyed. And there the hospital, where her father worked.

Every now and then it's too much for her. I see something wintry, not a tear but an icy pearl, in her eye. Do I touch her? Do I say something comforting? Do I know how?

It's so cold that I now have a handkerchief held semi-permanently to my nose. She may well think I'm the one in need of comforting.

As we stand outside the Judenrat she becomes distracted. She appears to be looking for someone. It turns out that she has a rendezvous with a Lithuanian TV crew. They want to film her taking a person round the ghetto. I'm the person. I'm the proof of the renewed curiosity in things Jewish in Vilnius. We wait, stamping our feet. At last an expressionless man with a video camera on his shoulder comes round a corner. Behind him is the producer, an exaggeratedly westernized woman in a deep-blue shaggy fur coat and an excess of personality. The pelts of her coat swing as she walks. She would like to interview me, hear what I think of Vilnius, what I'm here for, what I'm up to. If she had better English she would be calling me lovey and pet.

When I was in the Jewish Museum, signing the visitors' book, I was painstaking in my determination to avoid the usual post-

Holocaust responses to Holocaust material – 'deeply moving', 'never again', 'bearing invaluable witness'; but the moment Lithuanian television points its cameras my way, I find myself saying how deeply moving it is for me to be here, what invaluable witness Mrs Margolis bears, and how we must use all our powers to ensure that never again . . .

I will be kinder in the future to emotional inscribers in visitors' books.

The cameras follow us around. I'm getting less and less of what Mrs Margolis is saying. The temperature has dropped to something like sixteen or seventeen under, which is too cold for my French. But we settle into a quiet intimacy where she can say whatever's on her mind, whatever her old haunts make her say, and I can listen, not understanding verbally, but in the other, sentimental, way, just understanding.

She is as grave a person as I have ever walked with. It is not easy to go on thinking of her as Anna Karenina at the opera. I fall to wondering whether her experience is the sole explanation of her cast of mind, or whether she was always going to be a sombre woman. But it's an idle query. It forgets what the Holocaust has done to time. Her experience was always going to be her experience.

Twenty-four

GOING JEW

Lazdai is a hundred miles from Vilnius, going west. When you get there you have reached the Polish border. Many a time in the past, when you got to Lazdai you were already in Poland. My great-grandfather's naturalization papers describe his place of birth as being in the province of Suwalk, Russ-Poland. But the certificate of postage for the last parcel he is known to have sent from Manchester to Lazdai, in August 1939, is clearly marked Lietuva – Lithuania.

Nobody in the family remembers who the recipient of that parcel – Sora Hita Cvikler – was. And we don't put our mind to what happened to that person subsequently.

David and Simon's father drives. This is at Taube's request. She is worried about the boys driving to the borders of Poland on icy roads, even though it was her husband who was responsible for the injury to the Lada which still keeps it in Elastoplast. Apparently he went into a skid on a country road and hit a sign.

'Bad luck,' I say.

'Good luck,' says David. 'If he hadn't hit the sign he would have fallen down a ravine.'

I take this to be an exaggeration. I see no ravines. I see no signs either, come to that. Nor any other traffic.

But that may have something to do with its being Independence Day. People are at home, or parading in squares, or in church.

We stop a short way out of Vilnius at Trakai, another town with past pretensions to principality. It is built around a lake, in

488

the middle of which stands a grand-ducal castle, and at the perimeters of which stand pleasant wooden weekend houses, reminiscent of Cambridge boat-sheds. But the most intriguing architectural feature of Trakai – intriguing theologically if not aesthetically – are the three-windowed dwellings of the Karaites, those break-away Protestants of Judaism who prospered under the Khazars, spread through the Crimea, and trickled into Lithuania with Tartar blood in their veins when the Grand Duke Witold took a few hundred of them captive in the fourteenth century and settled them in Trakai.

There is still a Karaite synagogue – a *Gnesser* – in Trakai, and still Karaites who worship in it. But they don't think of themselves as Jews any more, for all that their original argument with the rabbis was about who could claim to be the more authentically Jewish. Rabbinism believed in an oral Torah which supplemented the written one. The Karaites hearkened only to the direct word of God. They go on hearkening, but un-Jewishly. Which has got them out of a scrape or two in the last few hundred years.

The lake is frozen over. On our approach to it, I see a queer sight: men apparently on sleighs in the middle of the ice, immobile, wondering why they're not moving. I could tell them. They're not on a slope. But as we get closer I see that they are actually sitting on crates, fishing. The need for fish must be great to take such risks and suffer such discomfort. From the bridge leading to the castle they look even stranger – prehistoric sea creatures, as shapeless as Caliban, come up through the ice and not knowing what to do next.

We look around the castle. In every room, a woman wearing ankle socks sits without expression, on a low chair, as though she is guarding a toilet. I am unable to look at objects in glass cases. I fear it will be dark before I get to follow the road my great-grandfather took from Lazdai to Serhai.

It is darksome already, a drear, misty day, begrudging of

light. Don't believe dictionaries when they tell you *darkling* is a poeticism. Darkling is what days are in February in the Baltic states.

We drive on, watching the needle on the petrol gauge. Run out and you have to walk to Moscow with your gallon tin. We pass few towns, nothing but lakes, forests, timber houses. A world of wood, waiting to be carved into devils.

Lazdai has the air of a town that was evacuated fifty years ago and to which no one has ever wanted to return. There has been an Independence Day parade in the square. The Lithuanian flag hangs dispiritedly from concrete posts. The entire square is concrete. Bleak. Blasted. A few elderly women in scarves, a few elderly men in fur hats, straggle home from the parade. The only people left in the square are youths, doing business. Some pull wallets out of their back pockets. Some carry wads of roubles in their fists. They eye us without interest or malice. If you were mugged here you wouldn't take it personally.

This is not an emotional home-coming. I never expected it to be. Whatever there is of emotion around all this I'm saving for Serhai. Lazdai is just a name; whereas Serhai has been described to me by someone who remembers it. Serhai was where we had our klezmer band and our bagel ovens and our goat. It was Serhai where we thanked God every night for every day that had gone by without incident. It was in Serhai, I have recently discovered, that the Gaon spent a year tutoring a student.

Since we're here, though, we agree that I ought to set eyes on something Jewish. That won't be a person. No Jewish persons have lived in Lazdai for some time now. But I wonder if there's a synagogue standing, or a cemetery, or even a *mikveh*. We go over to a police car and ask. All the police in Lithuania now have new uniforms. Green, with a grey triangle on the back — the easier for criminals to aim at, goes the joke. A policeman with fat hands and an incurious demeanour surveys me while Simon talks to him. I can tell that Simon is overdoing it. Giving the cop the whole history of my relations with Lithuania. Trying to touch his heart while all we want is a direction.

At last the policeman points. To what? Well, they're not quite sure – a ruin or something. We take off. The town peters out immediately. Only put the cankered-concrete square behind you and you're on a country road. White fields stretch out beyond the wooden houses. Dogs bark. Logs burn. I see a woman reeling up a bucket from her well. She isn't a peasant. She is a townswoman. But she gets her water from a hole in her garden.

We pass a house in which the poetess Salomeja Neris once resided. A plaque commemorates the fact. Salomeja Neris fell in love with her professor when she was a student. The professor already had a wife. The university gave him an ultimatum – Salomeja or career. He chose career. And so a poetess was born.

If I have the story right, she chose Lazdai as a sort of erotic exile. A good choice. Looking for happiness rather than a rhyme, my great-grandfather chose Serhai and Manchester. As it turned out, an even better choice.

We find no synagogue, no cemetery, no ruins of a *mikveh*. David and Simon, and indeed David and Simon's father, have now taken to running into people's houses to ask for directions, no two of which are remotely similar. Some say that there's an enormous Hebrew edifice, still intact, a couple of blocks away; others insist that the best we'll find is a single gravestone in a field at the other end of town.

I stand outside someone's gate while the Rozas men go about their inquiries within. I watch two men approaching. One is respectable, well-dressed, wearing an elegant fur hat. The other looks poor and has a red face. They are linking arms, the respectable man keeping the red-faced drunk from falling into the gutter. They separate just opposite me, on the other side of the road. As they come apart, I see that it is the red-faced man who has been doing the supporting, and that it is the well-heeled burgher who can barely stand. He staggers towards me, making for this very gate. At the same moment, his wife comes out with Simon, David and their Dad. She is pointing in still yet another direction and seems unpleased to see her husband. He is just as unpleased to see us. Were he steady enough he would fix us with his stare. What happens next is my fault. I decide to get a good long look at him, to judge how old he is, to estimate how old he would have been in 1941, to see if he holds the key to Lazdai. My scrutiny is very personal. I want to look into the sort of face Zayde would have looked into. But he takes it amiss. He staggers a bit. Raises a futile arm, and yells. Bawls us out on Independence Day. It's a fierce denunciation. Florid, fluent, foul. In his rage he recovers the capacity to stay upright.

'What's he saying?' I ask David.

'He's saying, "What are you doing here? Why are you standing outside my house?"'

You don't have to speak Lithuanian to know he's saying rather more than that. But David is Jewish, and Jews don't like to repeat obscenities. My great-grandfather would have been the same.

We walk back the way we came. For some considerable time we can hear the householder cursing at his wife. 'Pray tell me who were those gentlemen and what were you discoursing with them in my absence . . .'

What is interesting is that while no Jewish remains are to be found where anyone says they're to be found, not a person we ask will own up and say he doesn't know. Perhaps in Lazdai they don't wish to admit ignorance of such matters.

There is agreement, though, about the place of the Holocaust memorial. It is a little out of town, signposted, on the very spot where, a little more than fifty years ago, the Christians of Lazdai settled their argument with the Jews of Lazdai, once and for all, and in a single afternoon.

Despite the signposting, we get lost. Simon jumps out of the car and runs into a house. That way – across the field. We get

Going Jew

lost again. Simon again runs into a house. The tracks get muddier. We see another sign. I make out two words – ZYDUMASINIU ZUDYNIU. I remember a Zydy Street in the old ghetto. Zyd, Yid ... No offence meant, David told me at the time. Zyd does not carry opprobrium. Good to know, given where we're going.

The car bogs down in mud. We decide to leave it where it is and head for the memorial. Up a squelching bank, through a clump of trees, and there it is – a paddock, a small field that would do nicely for a child's gymkhana, with a wooden fence around and a picket gate. The fence marks the area within which the shooting was confined and the bodies buried. It doesn't look big enough to have housed sixteen hundred corpses.

'After the war,' Simon tells me, 'Lithuanians would come and dig in such places to get the gold from the teeth of dead Jews.'

This is not the memorial of which I saw a photograph in the IXth Fort, referring to IR KITI. This is a new memorial, put up two years ago by Jews themselves. It is not well tended. Hardly surprising, given that there are no Jews hereabouts to tend it. A couple of baskets that once held flowers lie on the ground. Something dead is still in them. A scarf, saying it is from the Jewish Cultural Society of Lithuania, is tied to one of the baskets. 'For our brothers and sisters,' Simon reads, 'who were tortured to death.'

The memorial itself is a metal plaque set into a boulder. A length of lilac ribbon – presumably from the flowers – falls across it. An upturned pickled-onion jar stands nearby. Now that they have been reclaimed, these places will fall back into neglect. They cannot be kept up. No one will keep them up.

When we get back to the car it has sunk further in the mud. The wheels spin, as we push, flicking us with dirt. The Lada is so light – most of it being Elastoplast – we could have lifted it on to dry land. Except that there is no dry land. Before we leave Lazdai we go for petrol. The pumps are rusted and empty. They

493

don't look as though they've seen petrol this century. Despite that, men wait about in their cars, form discussion groups outside their cars, fall into shady conjunctions like the Tartars at the Lietuva Hotel, because there is a rumour, a rumour of a rumour, that petrol might come.

Their lives, I think to myself, are as neglected as the memorial. They too were reclaimed for five minutes when they became the heroes of the free world, and now they cannot be kept up. No one will keep them up.

We wait for as long as it takes to eat a sandwich. No more. Simon puts petrol in the Lada from a Pepsi-Cola bottle which they'd filled from God knows what source the day before.

Then we're off. To Serhai.

It's no distance. My great-grandfather could easily have walked it. Probably did walk it. I imagine him the only way I can remember him, in his oddfellows waistcoat with a watch attached to a silver fob-chain, and it's thus attired that he walks the lanes again for me – a Litvak toy-boy of seventy, mad with love for the glazier's daughter. We overtake a horse and cart. And then another. I would never have conceived such a thing had I not come here and seen the geography of the place with my own eyes, but now it seems obvious – I am the offspring of a rural idyll.

David interrupts my reverie. 'Do you have oaks in England?' he suddenly asks.

'Oaks? In England? We invented oaks. We *are* oaks.'

He asks because he wonders whether I have noticed there are none here.

'None on the road from Lazdai to Serhai?'

None in Lithuania. All the forests we pass used to be oak forests. But the oak was an object of heathen worship, and when Lithuania at last became Christian the oaks were chopped down.

Just what the ancient Hebrews would have done. I could find him the very section in the Talmud where it says that a tree worshipped as part of idolatrous rites must be burned and entirely destroyed. And not only that tree but the tree next to it if it has served the first tree in any beautifying or beneficial capacity.

Chop. Chop. The only way a new belief can prosper. Or an old one defend itself. 'Do we have an axe?' Taube Rozas had asked, on the night she thought the Lithuanians might be in the mood for patriotism again.

Serhai is more agrarian than Lazdai. More a *shtetl*. An elaborately carved cross – not made of oak – reminds you, as you enter, of who lives here now. The smell of burning wood is even sweeter than it was in Lazdai. As is the smell of chickens.

We park opposite the church. David removes the wing-mirror from the car. His father removes the windscreen-wiper. The little Lada is subject to many rituals. Although you would think no one could possibly want to pinch it, they like to park it where they can see it outside their apartment. It has an anti-theft device which must be twice the value of what it's anti-thieving. You'd steal the device and leave the car. And when they bring it into a foreign place like Serhai, they remove all its pinchable protrusions.

Life used not to be so in Lithuania, they tell me. Jews may have been slaughtered in paddocks and their graves plundered for gold fillings, but at least your car mirror was safe.

I breathe the air. A chicken runs across the road to look at me. A cock crows. Everyone seems to be a bit of a small farmer here. Everyone seems to have land. Do I feel anything? I look around. Between the wooden houses you can see ploughed fields, gentle valleys, water, smallholdings, modest raids on the earth. People are inside their houses. You can taste their warmth. It *almost* gets me, it's *almost* something I remember, from somewhere, but it isn't quite, it isn't truly, it isn't in *fact*.

Across from the white brick church is a supermarket with nothing for sale, and what they call a Service Centre – a place where you go to get your clothes mended and your hair cut and your shoes repaired. The logo is a figure – taken from folk literature, I believe – with a scissors through its back. Needles in the eyes would be your equivalent if you had a haberdasher's shop. Simon tells me that the Jews would have been the town's craftsmen in my great-great-grandfather's time. I know it. We fitted windows ourselves. They wouldn't let us farm, so we baked bagels and played fiddles. A hundred years ago you would have called in to any one of these wooden houses to get your shoes repaired. Now you take them to the dead building with the figure of a man with a scissors in his heart.

Down from the church is a bookshop, closed for Independence Day. I look through the window and see a few dreary-looking children's books, cheaply published, cheaply illustrated, cheaply bound. An abacus is on the counter. It bears the same relation to the stock as the Rozas' anti-theft device bears to the Lada – you would rather have it than what it serves. Hard to see why you would need an abacus anyway. If someone bought every volume in the shop you could do the arithmetic on your fingers.

But the laugh is on us, not the Lithuanians, when it comes to books. We have tons on sale and can't find anyone to buy them. In Vilnius I have seen a shop sell out within an hour of its new stock arriving. And I am pleased that Serhai has its own bookshop whether or not there are books in it. In a way its very emptiness is a proof of its discernment. I see it, suddenly, as an example to Waterstone's and Dillons – if it's been a bad year for fiction, leave the shelves empty.

We trudge aimlessly to the edges of the town, watching out for dogs, dodging the chickens. I want *shtetl* ambience, and I get it. But I hanker after something specific, something indubitably Jewish that the Kregans would have seen, that I can share with them. It needn't be much, just a sign, just a token.

'What we could do with,' Simon says, recalling our failure in Lazdai, 'is a teacher. If we could only find a teacher. They always know where things are.'

But it's Independence Day and schools are closed.

Mr Rozas stops a man and asks him something. David bangs his head. 'It's a miracle!' he cries. 'It's a miracle! What did my brother just say? – "It's a pity we can't find a teacher." Now my father stops someone and he's a teacher!'

I know David isn't kidding me. The man couldn't be anything but a teacher. He has a beaked, eager nose, wears a grey beret and spectacles, and shouts while he directs us, as though he is addressing thirty people who aren't listening. Although we are taller than him, he looks down at us. Like all school-teachers who have been doing the job any length of time, he moves in a universe of dwarfs.

There is no synagogue. No Jewish public building. Before the war there were a thousand Jews living here. Now there is none. All that's left is a cemetery. He can show us where that is.

I didn't expect anything else, though it's a shame about the synagogue. It contained an interesting item. Napoleon's coat. The French army camped in Serhai in 1812. It being a rushed time, the Emperor left without his coat. This was in the days before a Service Centre, remember. The Jews did all the tailoring. They found the coat, took out their chalk and scissors, and sewed it into a curtain for the Holy Ark.

> Imperious Caesar, dead and turned to clay
> Wraps up the Book from which the Hebrews pray.

The school-teacher walks us back up the hill, past the church. Turns us left and points the way to the Jewish cemetery. Through the field, across the Christian cemetery, and we'll find it. His final, shouted instructions have all the dogs barking.

The Christian cemetery is one of those you would be glad to lie in, were you Christian. Is almost worth converting for. It is on several levels, rising and falling, the undulations suggesting hope and change and variety, undimmed by death. It is virtually forested, so you can enjoy shade, quiet, no end to benign protection.

It is forested no less with wrought-iron crosses than with trees. Many feature an elaborate star-burst, in the centre of which are little lead Jesuses in postures so settled you take them to be comfortable – ankles crossed, heads fallen on one shoulder as though grabbing an after-dinner nap. The favourite alternative to the star-burst is etched stone or marble; the advantages of these being the scope they offer for more crowded compositions – coy virgins, their heads averted, more in shame or delicacy than grief; hypnotically intelligent soul-soldier Jesuses in complicated landscapes, vistas of the world to come, bathed in the beams of eternal promise which pour down from eternal skies.

And then there are the etched portraits of the dead, sometimes competing with actual cameo photographs set into the stone. Look here upon this picture, and on this. Invidious comparisons, even unto death.

But what is most striking is how well-cared-for the place is. Fresh flowers on graves twenty or thirty years old. Signs everywhere of recent attention. Even today, people have been here, paying their respects. You can tell that because some have left their gardening tools, as though they mean to return a little later.

My companions go ahead of me while I mope between the stones. They're following the school-teacher's directions. Across the Christian cemetery, keep going, and we'll see it. But where? The Christian cemetery ends in ploughed and muddy fields. David strikes off in one direction, his father in another. Simon, who is the runner, runs in a third.

I stand on a low stone wall, look back over the wrought-iron star-bursts and the little lead snoozing Jesuses, look out over the bare icy fields at nothing, and try to imagine. The scene won't yield. I can't make myself have any feelings about where I am. Perhaps if I'd never lived in an English *shtetl*, if I had come here before the years I spent in Cornwall, immediately from Manchester, say, perhaps then the shock of the nullity of nature would have been greater. But I already know the dead ground chill, the muddy ruts and trenches holding grimy scraps of leftover snow almost into the next summer, furrows that should take your thoughts somewhere, but never do, only leave them cold in the earth.

The brothers call to each other. Simon runs – run, Simon, run – towards a farmhouse. Nothing. There is no one in the farmhouse. The door is open but no one's home. At church. All at church.

We go through the school-teacher's instructions, lesson by lesson. We've done everything he said. There is no Jewish cemetery. But we go on trekking through mud. David is on an eminence, a small mound, scouring the earth's circumference. His father has come to a halt with me. We stand in the squelching mud and sink in, an inch at a time, together.

But Simon is still running and, suddenly, he's calling us. Come quickly. Follow him. He's found it.

We wind down, following the external wall of the Christian cemetery, to where the cultivated land gives out to overgrown but winter-dead grass, to what looks like waste land, and there, sticking up at odd angles, twisted, chipped, faded, broken, mis-shaped, discoloured and utterly utterly ignored, are the gravestones.

There is no form left to the ground they seem to grow from. You do not know if you are standing on a grave or not. There is just the long-dead grass and weeds and matted stalks and deep piles of snow, kept from melting by the wall of the other cemetery, and by the gravestones themselves, some of which lean so acutely that they make a shelter, a ghetto, for the snow.

We fall very quiet. The excitement of finding what we thought we never would find yields to the disgrace of this treatment of hallowed earth, its cruel contrast with the affectionate, hysterically commemorative Christian burial ground we have just walked through.

It is hard to read the writing on the stones. Most are faded. Or overgrown with moss and lichen. Where there is Hebrew to be discerned, Simon copies it out in my notebook. These are not ancient graves. We find some dating from the 1930s. The lucky ones.

Simon is on one knee for some time, trying to make a faithful copy of what he reads. It feels a solemn act. We are distressed for one another. I register the ignominy for them, as Lithuanian Jews of now. And they for me, standing in a burial place of my ancestors. Simon does not find a name that is known to me, but the people buried here would have been known to Bobbe and Zayde, and it cannot be that I am not treading on the graves of relatives of theirs, however remotely they are relatives of mine.

While Simon changes knees, David charges about, distracted, looking to see what else he can find. His father stands quietly, staring out at the pylons and the power station and the wooden cross, just visible, on the roof of the white church. And I wander between the stones, touching the odd one, and yes, I admit it, feeling that it is something, not nothing, that a Jew descended from this community has come back and for an hour or two on a wintry afternoon entertained a thought for those who lie here.

I'll admit more. I may not have been able to make Serhai itself throb for me, but I am upset in a way I never expected to be by the modesty of these memorials – mere aggregation, most of them: nothing more than a door-step – and by the power of the old simple Hebrew script. Anonymous yet uniting. And it becomes necessary for me to separate from my companions for a little while, scramble through the snow and the undergrowth, so that I can say something to the stones, in private. Not much. Just a bit of a mutter to the effect that I am here, and that it is ironic that it should be me of all people, the least familial, the least loyal, the least nostalgic of Jews, who has come. But that that's part of it, even makes it better, for anyone can be remembered by the easily moved, but to be remembered by me, whoever they are, well, that's less to be expected, enough to make the least friendless of men trust that one day someone may happen by and spare a passing thought.

My presence is the proof, if anything ever can be, that no one should count himself forgotten and unvisited for ever.

We hang around in the cold until the light has almost gone, and then we idle back, skirting the Christian cemetery, not prepared to face the contrast again, through the mud and the snow. We get back to the car just in time to see the people of Serhai coming out of church, the women in their scarves, respectable, devout, God-fearing.

AFTERWORD

Not long before he died, my father reminded me of an anecdote which he hoped would go in this book. He knew that I'd loved it when he first told it me, a couple of years earlier. We both felt it was the final word on the subject, containing all we knew of the absurdities and the pleasures of being Jewish.

My father was a magician in his spare time, a member of the Magic Circle, and a children's entertainer. One day he received a request to do a party for an Orthodox Jewish family. They had one stipulation: no rabbits. Intrigued by this, and wanting to know where he stood – *halachically*, so to speak – when it came to rabbits and the Orthodox in the future, he consulted a rabbi.

The rabbi asked for time to deliberate on this. To consult sources – the Torah, the Talmud, the opinions of the sages. He didn't feel it was a matter he could pronounce on just like that.

A week later, he contacted my father. 'Mr Jacobson –' he said, 'Max – I have given your question the most serious thought. I have looked at it this way and I have looked at it that way. I have read and re-read everything the great scholars of the past have written on the subject. I have taken account of *Mishna* and *Gemara*. The laws relating to animals and the laws relating to magic. And the ruling I have reached is this: Listen, if they don't want rabbits . . . don't give them rabbits.'